MOST
SECRET

THE SECRET HISTORY
OF WORLD WAR II
SPIES, CODE BREAKERS & COVERT OPERATIONS

NEIL KAGAN   STEPHEN G. HYSLOP
FOREWORD BY KENNETH W. RENDELL

NATIONAL GEOGRAPHIC

WASHINGTON, D.C.

BOARD OF ADVISERS

HARRIS J. ANDREWS

Harris J. Andrews, historian and consultant, specializes in American and world military history and material culture. He is a historian and artifact consultant for the National Museum of the United States Army Project, spanning four centuries of American military life and history. He was a consultant and contributing writer for National Geographic's *Eyewitness to World War II* (2012), *Eyewitness to the Civil War* (2006), and *Atlas of the Civil War* (2009). He long served as a writer, editor, and consultant on military maps, arms, and equipment for Time-Life Books, contributing to its landmark series *World War II* and to numerous volumes on the Civil War.

KENNETH W. RENDELL

Kenneth W. Rendell is the founder and executive director of the Museum of World War II, Boston, which houses the world's most comprehensive collection of original artifacts and documents relating to the causes, events, and consequences of World War II. He began the collection in 1959 when no similar private or public collections were being formed. He opened the present building as a private museum in 2000, and opened it to the public in 2013 as a nonprofit museum, with unique exhibits and archives that tell the human story of the war, on home fronts and battlefronts. He is the author of *With Weapons and Wits: Propaganda and Psychological Warfare in World War II* (1990), *World War II: Saving the Reality* (2009), *Politics, War, and Personality: Fifty Iconic World War II Documents That Changed the World* (2013), *The Power of Anti-Semitism, 1919–1939: The March to the Holocaust* (2016), and two reference works on historical documents, *Forging History: The Detection of Fake Letters and Documents* (1994) and *History Comes to Life* (1995).

LEE RICHARDS

Lee Richards is a military historian, researcher, author, and occasional broadcaster who specializes in the history of psychological warfare and propaganda. He is the founder and director of the psywar.org website and was previously editor of *The Falling Leaf*, the PsyWar Society quarterly journal. His book *The Black Art* (2010) documents the use of clandestine propaganda produced by the British Political Warfare Executive in World War II. He is also the author of *Whispers of War: Underground Propaganda Rumour-Mongering in the Second World War* (2010), and he has contributed to several television programs broadcast by the BBC and the History Channel.

ANN TODD

Ann Todd holds a doctorate in history from the University of Texas, and has served as a historian for the National Museum of the Marine Corps and conducted extensive oral history interviews of World War II veterans. She is the author of *OSS Operation Black Mail: One Woman's Covert War Against the Imperial Japanese Army* (forthcoming from the Naval Institute Press), *Komsomol Participation in the Soviet First Five-Year Plan* (1987), and articles on Office of Strategic Services (OSS) activities in the national parks during World War II and on recent battles at Fallujah and Al-Najaf in Iraq. She served in the U.S. Coast Guard and is presently researching Marine and Coast Guard operations conducted with the OSS in the China-Burma-India Theater.

CONTENTS

PAGE 1 A red "X" marks the back cover of an Allied document labeled "Most Secret," detailing plans for the D-Day invasion of occupied France. PAGE 2 The hollowed-out pages of a book hide a small revolver used by a Dutch resistance fighter. PAGES 4–5 People take cover in front of a hotel in Paris, where German forces clashed with French partisans fighting to liberate the city in August 1944. OPPOSITE U.S. Army military police tie the hands of German spy Gunther Billings, about to be executed by firing squad in 1944 for conducting espionage behind Allied lines disguised as an American soldier.

UNCOVERING THE WAR'S SECRETS

World War II was truly a secret war. Military operations shrouded in secrecy altered the conflict time and again, despite efforts on all sides to discover through intelligence or theft what the enemy was up to. The Germans surprised France and Britain when they advanced in May 1940 through the Ardennes in Belgium—and staggered Stalin in June 1941 by invading Russia after the Soviet dictator dismissed secret reports that the invasion was imminent (see pages 57–59). Japan's surprise attack on Pearl Harbor stunned the United States, even though American commanders knew from deciphered Japanese cables that war might soon erupt somewhere in the Pacific (pages 68–86). Hitler was taken in by Allied deceptions and caught off guard when the D-Day invasion occurred on the coast of Normandy. And Allied forces who believed the war was almost over were shocked when Hitler struck back in the Battle of the Bulge.

Military technology was top secret throughout the conflict, including the Allies' radar, Germany's rocket technology, America's Norden bombsight, and the fateful weapon that ended the war, the atomic bomb (pages 329–337). Military communications were often top secret. Breaking the code of the German Enigma machine decided the Battle of the Atlantic and short-

BABY CARRIAGE This innocent-looking baby carriage was used to hide weapons and equipment for armed resistance in occupied France.

ened the war in Europe. Breaking Japanese codes helped the U.S. Navy achieve victory at Midway and turned the tide in the Pacific. Secrecy prevailed even on the home front as people were warned in various posters that "Loose Lips Sink Ships," "The Enemy is Listening," and "Careless Talk Costs Lives."

Uncovering the secret history of World War II has long been an important part of my work as founder and executive director of the Museum of World War II, Boston, which has the world's largest and most comprehensive collection of World War II artifacts, including 7,500 on exhibit and over 500,000 artifacts and documents in its archives. The museum displays everything that made up the mosaic of life during the conflict, and emphasizes that the war was personal and complex. Included are artifacts from every country caught up in the struggle, from home fronts as well as battlefronts. Many of them appear in this book, which features more than 240 secret weapons, documents, and devices from the museum's collection, including the baby carriage shown here, used to conceal a radio and sabotage materials. Those artifacts testify to the urge for secrecy and the anxiety that gripped people who had to watch their every word and were constantly on guard against spies, secret police, or surprise attack. Perhaps their worst fear of all was not knowing

CONCEALED WEAPON At far left, a member of a Dutch resistance group hides a rocket launcher in the bottom of a baby carriage similar to the one below. A woman then places a baby in the carriage (near left) before wheeling the concealed weapon to its destination.

FALSE BOTTOM This close-up of the baby carriage pictured opposite, on exhibit at the Museum of World War II, Boston, shows its secret compartment, concealing sabotage gear and a radio.

FUGITIVES A wanted poster issued in 1941 by German authorities in occupied Belgium and printed in three languages—German (far left), French (center), and Dutch—offers a reward of 10,000 reichsmarks for information leading to the capture of two Belgian resistance fighters involved in assassination attempts, Henri Talboom and Robert Lelong, pictured to the right of Talboom. Lelong killed himself when he was about to be captured, but Talboom escaped to Switzerland.

what they didn't know. The shock of the assault on Pearl Harbor instilled in Americans fear of other surprise attacks. Paper currency in Hawaii was overprinted with "Hawaii" so that it could be voided in the event of a possible Japanese invasion. California braced for air raids. Fear gripped the country—the fear of not knowing the enemy's secrets.

The museum's collections were gathered over the past 57 years. For decades, I was asked why I was collecting this material. Growing up, I witnessed the transition from the trauma of war to the celebration of America's victory and the glory it reflected on the country. People wanted to forget the reality and leave the war behind. In the 1950s, no one was systematically collecting artifacts from the war. There were no World War II museums in the United States, and those in Europe were interested mainly in producing exhibits relating to their own countries. There were only a few research libraries in the U.S. actively pursuing material in wartime archives that documented the

conflict. It was the most momentous event of modern times, and a large part of its history was being lost.

Some time ago, the question of "Why?" changed to "How?" The collection evolved in ways I could not have imagined, because no one had ever set out to collect everything related to an event as recent, as complex, or as vast as World War II. When I began collecting, there were no specialized dealers or auctions, and it was decades before the Internet was invented. Estate auctions frequently included souvenirs that soldiers had brought back, and occasionally an estate would be sold that had very important material. Douglas MacArthur's chief of staff for public relations—an important position under the publicity-conscious MacArthur—had kept all of his World War II files. They were thrown haphazardly into boxes and sold by the box lot on Cape Cod.

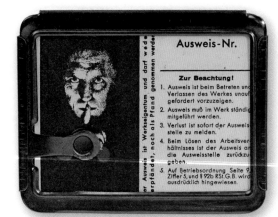

SILENCER An ominous figure warns workers to keep their lips sealed on the back of this ID badge, issued to employees in a wartime German factory with printed instructions to wear it "at all times."

Meeting veterans at reunions led me to acquire many important artifacts for the museum. Those vets hadn't thought of selling their valuable mementos, nor had they thought of donating them. I found that I had to offer something unexpected, something that would make a difference in their lives. A new car could make that difference—over the years, the offer ranged from a Porsche sports car to a Subaru station wagon. One of the most important uniforms in the museum's collection was acquired by paying off the veteran's mortgage. Flea markets in farmers' fields in Britain and France were good early sources for European artifacts and also great challenges. Everything had to be paid for in cash, and I became adept at figuring out how to move and ship impossibly large items in the days before services like FedEx were widely available.

CODE BREAKERS AND SPIES

The revelation that the British had broken Germany's supposedly impregnable Enigma code—and that throughout the war the Allies' most closely guarded secret was that they were reading German military communications—was a worldwide sensation.

The unveiling of that secret in the 1970s led to reevaluations of battles and commanders such as British general Bernard Montgomery, whose great victory at El Alamein in 1942 was made possible in part by Ultra, the code name for decrypted Enigma messages and the secret intelligence reports drawn from them (pages 220–229).

It wasn't long before people in Germany realized that the strange-looking typewriter-like machine they had was the newly sensational Enigma. Some surviving Enigma machines were put up at auctions, and seven different types were acquired for the museum. The one shown here illustrates why they are so rare. Most were destroyed by retreating German forces. This one was blasted by a hand grenade but survived. It's an artifact that dramatically tells its own story. Germany went to extreme measures to prevent the capture of Enigmas. U-boats in danger of being boarded were deliberately sunk to prevent those machines from being seized by the Allies, who managed to salvage one of them despite such precautions (pages 217–221). At the end of the war, Britain offered a large bounty for every surviving Enigma machine turned in, and nearly all seized by the British and Americans were destroyed for security reasons.

Spying and sabotage are what people most associate with secret warfare. Artifacts such as hidden cameras and concealed weapons evoke the hair-raising adventures of James Bond but

ENIGMA
This salvaged Enigma machine used by German armed forces had a panel with basic operating instructions.

also serve as reminders that espionage could have deadly consequences. Covert weapons and other spy gadgets from World War II are rare. There weren't many secret agents to begin with. Few saved their miniature cameras after the war when they had better ones, and they had no need for their old weapons or dangerous explosive devices. The museum's virtually complete collection of espionage and sabotage devices, many of which appear in this book (pages 174–191), was obtained from a commando who saw action late in the war before serving with British intelligence. He not only saved all the devices he personally came into contact with, but also sought out those he didn't have.

SECRET PLANS AND DECEPTIONS

Allied plans to invade occupied Europe were among the war's most closely guarded secrets. If the Germans knew in advance, they could reinforce their coastal defenses and push the invaders back into the sea. An invasion by sea was already

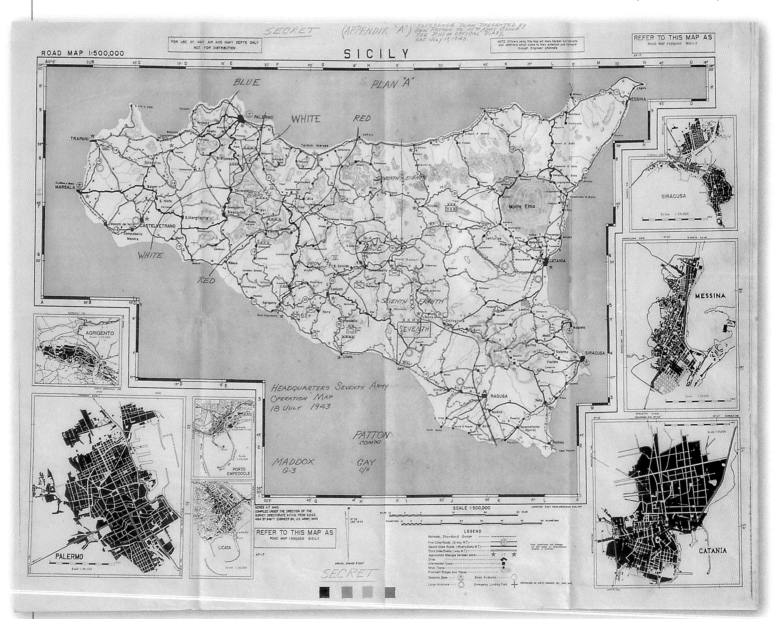

CHARTING A HECTIC CAMPAIGN General Patton made good use of this secret map while preparing for the invasion of Sicily in July 1943. After landing on the south coast, his forces advanced northwestward to Palermo, then hurried eastward to Messina, arriving there before British troops in what Patton called a "horse race."

fraught with potential disaster, and disaster was guaranteed if the plans were discovered. After the conquest of North Africa in 1943, it was obvious that the Allies would next advance northward across the Mediterranean. There were several possible targets, but Sicily was by far the most likely. The Germans had to be kept guessing, or they would reinforce the Italian divisions on Sicily with several German divisions, dooming the invasion forces. Operation Mincemeat (pages 253–259) was devised to make the Germans believe that the Allies might instead invade Greece or the island of Sardinia. Meanwhile, maps or documents relating to the invasion of Sicily were restricted to those officers with "need to know" status. George Patton, the commander of the American forces destined for Sicily, had a map of that island (opposite) on the wall at his headquarters. The word "SECRET"

was handwritten in red letters in the map's margins along with Patton's annotations.

Security was even tighter for the forthcoming invasion of France. As shown below, initial plans for D-Day were drawn up in England long in advance and circulated to a select few under the heading "Most Secret," the British equivalent of "Top Secret." Churchill's famous comment that truth is so precious that it must be protected by a bodyguard of lies inspired Operation Bodyguard, which included misleading the Germans into thinking that the Normandy landings were merely a diversion by conjuring up a massive, make-believe invasion force, supposedly led by George Patton, that would cross the English Channel after D-Day and storm ashore near Calais (pages 268–279).

The Allies conducted another deception in

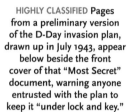

HIGHLY CLASSIFIED Pages from a preliminary version of the D-Day invasion plan, drawn up in July 1943, appear below beside the front cover of that "Most Secret" document, warning anyone entrusted with the plan to keep it "under lock and key."

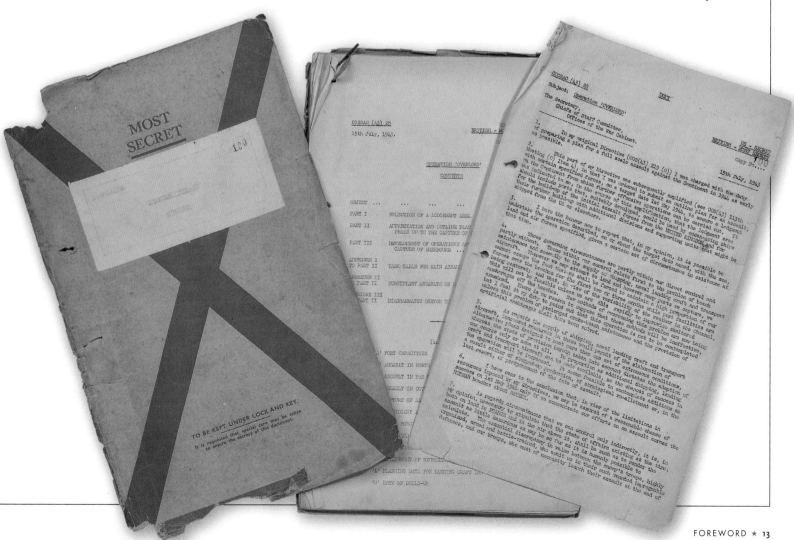

the early hours of June 6, 1944. Shortly before American and British paratroopers began to land in Normandy on D-Day, dummy paratroopers were dropped from aircraft (page 282). Made of burlap and straw and armed with fireworks that simulated gunfire, they made a convincing show in the dark, and misled German commanders into moving troops away from the real landing zones. What those fake paratroopers really looked like was only guessed at until I arrived at a flea market in France and an Englishman spread out some dummies with white parachutes on a tarp. He told me he had found a crate of 12 in a storage shed at an airfield in southern England—the only survivors of the simulated D-Day landings. I bought them all, kept two, and gave 10 to other museums.

OBJECT LESSONS FROM THE WAR

Otto Skorzeny was Adolph Hitler's favorite commando, saboteur, and spy. The enamel-and-gold cigarette case and the solid-gold death's head SS ring pictured below were gifts from Hitler to Skorzeny

for rescuing the Italian dictator Benito Mussolini, who had been overthrown after the invasion of Sicily and was being held secretly at an Italian mountaintop ski resort. Skorzeny and his commandos landed there in a glider, and he then flew Mussolini to safety in a tiny plane that barely lifted off.

During the Battle of the Bulge, launched by Hitler in December 1944 to repulse Allied forces approaching Germany from the west, Hitler assigned Skorzeny to lead German commandos dressed as American soldiers behind enemy lines, where they caused confusion and fear among American troops. Although the covert operation had little impact on the battle, which ended with the Germans pushed back to their original lines, it made Skorzeny notorious. Intelligence officers who had failed to anticipate the German attack mistakenly concluded that he remained somewhere behind American lines on a mission to assassinate General Eisenhower and other top commanders. The wanted poster shown here was hastily produced and widely circulated. Thousands of copies were likely printed, but this is the only one I have found. Skorzeny survived the war and escaped conviction in war crimes trials. After his death, I acquired from his estate those tokens of Hitler's appreciation for his favorite commando.

The Skorzeny scare was mild

REWARDED AND REVILED Shown at left atop Hitler's stationery are gifts the Führer presented to commando leader Otto Skorzeny for rescuing Mussolini—an SS death's head ring and a cigarette case crafted in a Nazi concentration camp. After leading a covert operation behind Allied lines in late 1944, Skorzeny became a wanted man (above).

TRUE TO HIS COUNTRY
Japanese Americans Tom and Ruth Kasai are shown here in a family album along with his U.S. Army dog tag and medals Tom received, including the Purple Heart, awarded after he was wounded in action in France. The telegram at top left, stating that he had been wounded, reached Ruth at an internment camp in Arizona, where she and others of Japanese ancestry were confined while he served his country.

compared with the fear of Japanese spies and saboteurs on America's West Coast after Pearl Harbor was attacked and a Japanese submarine surfaced off California in early 1942 and shelled a fuel depot. Those fears prompted the roundup and internment of Japanese Americans, including Ruth Kasai of Los Angeles, pictured above with her husband Tom. Despite the fact that he had joined the U.S. Army, she was sent to an internment camp in Arizona. His dog tags bear her address there, as does, ironically, the telegram advising her that he had been wounded fighting in France. On the East Coast, there were very real fears of German submarines—which sank freighters offshore and landed would-be saboteurs in New York and Florida—and of German spies, more than 30 of whom were rounded up by the FBI (pages 51–55). It was thought that Germany might even launch bombing raids on

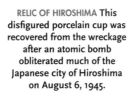

RELIC OF HIROSHIMA This disfigured porcelain cup was recovered from the wreckage after an atomic bomb obliterated much of the Japanese city of Hiroshima on August 6, 1945.

the U.S. from aircraft carriers, as the Japanese did off Oahu, but Americans were spared the ordeal of strategic bombing, which ravaged Germany and devastated Japan.

For many decades, I never encountered any artifact related to the atomic bombing of Hiroshima. My French agent brought the first piece to me—the teacup below, showing the effects of the bomb, whose searing heat melted and marred its glazed surface. It had been picked up by a French scientist who was in Hiroshima at the end of the war, and it was accompanied by a French certificate stating that it was no longer radioactive. That was as important to me as the teacup. I didn't want to be the last victim of the war.

KENNETH W. RENDELL
Founder and Executive Director
The Museum of World War II, Boston

SETTING EUROPE ABLAZE

FIREFIGHT A German arm
unit assaults concealed R
sharpshooters near Smo
in July 1941. Adolf Hitler'
invasion of the Soviet Un
caught Joseph Stalin off g
despite warnings he rece
from spies.

A WAR OF NERVES

No reporter working in Tokyo as war loomed in the late 1930s had better connections than German journalist Richard Sorge. His confidants and informants included Hotsumi Ozaki, an adviser to Japan's prime minister, and Col. Eugen Ott, a military attaché who became Germany's ambassador to Japan in April 1938. Ott shared German intelligence with Sorge, who in turn helped Ott keep Nazi leaders apprised of Japanese war plans. Adolf Hitler had annexed Austria in March 1938 and would soon expand his Greater German Reich by targeting Czechoslovakia and Poland. His aggressive agenda in Europe, which he fully intended to dominate, meant that he would eventually have to do battle with one or more of the great powers that opposed Germany in the First World War, including France, Great Britain, Russia (reconstituted now as the Soviet Union), and the United States. Hitler and his foreign minister, Joachim von Ribbentrop, viewed imperial Japan—which had invaded China in 1937 and posed a potential threat to French, British, Russian, and American possessions in Asia and the Pacific—as a promising ally if Germany became involved in another global conflict.

Ott's appointment as ambassador in Tokyo made him one of the Reich's most important foreign envoys. He owed his promotion in part to Sorge, whose briefings on Japanese

SOVIET AGENT Richard Sorge, portrayed opposite, carried the Japanese press pass below while serving openly as a reporter for the German newspaper *Frankfurter Zeitung* and operating secretly as a Soviet spy. His coded reports to Moscow warned of German efforts to draw Japan into the Axis alliance and Hitler's intention to abandon his nonaggression pact with Stalin and invade Russia.

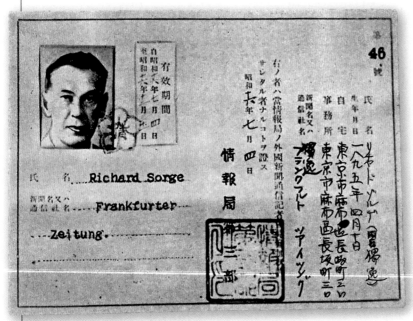

NAME: RICHARD SORGE

OCCUPATION: RUSSIAN SPY

ASSIGNMENT: JAPAN AND GERMANY

intentions and war readiness were so highly regarded by Ott and his superiors in Berlin that Ribbentrop sent Sorge a letter on his 43rd birthday in October 1938, thanking him for his "outstanding contribution." Sorge made his greatest contributions not to Berlin, however, but to Moscow, where he had been recruited a decade earlier by the Soviet military intelligence agency later known as the GRU. While reporting on Japan for German newspapers, Sorge secretly ran a Soviet spy ring that reported to Moscow by radio and courier. Ott did not suspect Sorge, a decorated German war veteran who bore the scars of a severe wound he suffered fighting Russians on the Eastern Front in 1917. Rash and boisterous, Sorge was a registered Nazi but often criticized the party's leaders and engaged in wild drinking bouts and reckless affairs, including a fling with Ott's estranged wife that the future ambassador overlooked in the interest of preserving his rewarding partnership with Sorge. An acquaintance later concluded that Sorge's loose talk and carousing were "a calculated part of his masquerade. He created the impression of being a playboy, a wastrel, the very antithesis of a keen and dangerous spy."

In fact, Sorge was one of the most dangerous agents ever to work undercover against Hitler's Reich. Born and bred for espionage, he had family ties both to the Germans he betrayed and to the Soviets he served. His Russian mother had given birth to him in the Russian province of Azerbaijan, where his German father worked as an industrial engineer in the Baku oil fields. The family moved to Berlin when Sorge was two years old, and he was raised as a loyal German, who eagerly went off to fight in 1914 but emerged from World War I disgusted with the crumbling imperial regime of Kaiser Wilhelm II, who abdicated in 1918 amid revolutionary turmoil. Sorge sided with the insurgent communists, whom Hitler later blamed for Germany's defeat, although their failed uprising occurred when the war was already lost. After enlisting as a Soviet spy, Sorge severed ties with the German

GO-BETWEEN American journalist Agnes Smedley became involved with Sorge in the early 1930s and introduced him to Hotsumi Ozaki.

CO-CONSPIRATOR A Japanese correspondent and official, Hotsumi Ozaki became a key member of Sorge's Soviet spy ring.

UNWITTING AIDE Col. Eugen Ott was unaware that secrets he shared with Sorge at the German embassy in Tokyo were passed to Moscow.

Communist Party. In 1934, a year after Hitler took power, he joined the Nazis, whose ranks were growing so rapidly that background checks for new party members were sometimes cursory. His ties to Moscow went undetected.

Sorge occupied a strategically vital position for the Russians in Tokyo. Soviet dictator Joseph Stalin had two potential enemies to reckon with—Nazi Germany to the west and imperial Japan to the east. Sorge was well placed to uncover the plans of both nations through his close contacts with German ambassador Ott and Japanese adviser Ozaki, a covert communist sympathizer who hoped to deflect Japanese aggression away from the Soviets toward British, French, and American possessions around the Pacific. Sorge also recruited a resourceful spy named Odai Yoshinobu, who served with Japanese occupation forces in Manchuria, which bordered the Soviet Union. In mid-1939, fighting erupted along that border, and Odai provided Sorge with detailed reports on Japanese troop strength and movements that helped Soviet commanders prevail there.

Westerners preoccupied with the threat of war in Europe paid little attention to that brief Asian border war, but it had far-reaching consequences. Although Hitler and Ribbentrop would soon draw Japan into a defensive alliance with Germany and Italy, the Japanese grew wary of joining their Axis partners in an all-out assault on the Soviet Union, whose destruction was Hitler's ultimate objective. Even before the Manchurian border war shifted in favor of the Russians in the summer of 1939, Hitler concluded that he had other axes to grind before taking on Stalin and his Red Army. British and French leaders had yielded to him at Munich in late 1938 and abandoned Czechoslovakia, but they now vowed to fight if he invaded Poland. He could not risk war with those Western powers unless he was sure the Soviets would remain passive. To that end, Ribbentrop met confidentially in Moscow with Stalin and his foreign minister, Vyacheslav Molotov, and concluded a stunning nonaggression pact between Germany and the Soviet Union on August 23, 1939. Many ardent communists were shocked by Stalin's deal with the hated Nazis, but seasoned agents like Sorge who often posed as friends to their ideological foes recognized the agreement for what it was—a ploy that allowed two antagonistic regimes to focus their aggression elsewhere before reckoning with each other. Sorge's Russian motherland and his German fatherland had seemingly patched up their glaring differences, but that was no reason for him to stop spying on the Reich. He would be quick to alert Moscow when Hitler wearied of the accord and prepared to shatter it. In the covert war waged by spies, saboteurs, and secret police, those like Sorge who remained wary of friends and foes alike and recognized that no oath was too sacred to be violated were among the masters of their profession.

Hołd pruski w Moskwie

STALIN. – Pakt my tobie, Ribbentropie podpisali. Ty w rączkę nas pocaluj, pakt bierz, a co my zrobimy dalej, to jeszcze podumajem.

GERMAN AND RUSSIAN SPHERES OF INFLUENCE 1939–1940

Germany
German Sphere of Influence
Soviet Union
Soviet Sphere of Influence

FINLAND

North Sea

ESTONIA

LATVIA

LITHUANIA

Moscow

SOVIET UNION (RUSSIA)

Berlin

GERMANY

POLAND

Molotov–Ribbentrop Line August 1939

SLOVAKIA

HUNGARY

Bessarabia

ROMANIA

0 mi   400
0 km   400
1939 boundaries are shown.

CYNICAL PACT At top, German foreign minister Joachim von Ribbentrop kisses Stalin's hand while Russian foreign minister Vyacheslav Molotov gloats in a Polish cartoon mocking the August 1939 nonaggression pact. Modified in September, the deal left eastern Poland, the Baltic states, Finland, and Bessarabia at Stalin's mercy in the Soviet sphere (see map above), while Hitler seized the rest of Poland and made obedient allies of Romania and Slovakia, as well as Hungary, which was not covered by the pact.

UNHOLY ALLIANCE

The nonaggression pact between the Germans and Soviets was bad news for Poland, but few people there or in other countries who sympathized with their plight realized just how ominous and sinister the agreement was. On its surface, it assured that Hitler would face no Russian resistance when he attacked Poland—an invasion that began on September 1, just nine days after the accord was reached. But a secret protocol to the pact exposed Poland and other countries to Soviet aggression as well by dividing Eastern Europe between Hitler and Stalin. The line drawn between the German and Russian "spheres of influence" left eastern Poland as well as the Baltic states of Lithuania, Latvia, and Estonia at Stalin's mercy. He and Hitler would enforce that secret protocol not just with regular troops but with security forces that waged war on civilians by seeking out supposed enemies of the state—a definition that Nazi and Soviet authorities applied to entire racial or ethnic groups—and executing or imprisoning them. In Poland and neighboring countries, far more people would fall victim to two dreaded security forces, Hitler's SS and Stalin's NKVD, than would perish in conventional fighting.

The SS originated as Hitler's Schutzstaffel (protection squad) but evolved into much more than the Führer's elite bodyguard. Under the direction of Heinrich Himmler, who shared Hitler's belief in Aryan supremacy and his virulent contempt for Jews and others defined as non-Aryans, SS recruits pledged "obedience unto death" and prided themselves on carrying out fearful orders without flinching. Some fought as soldiers in frontline units of the Waffen-SS. Others served as secret police, interrogators, or torturers in Germany and German-occupied territories, or ran concentration camps and death camps that claimed millions of lives before World War II ended.

In expanding the authority of the SS—which oversaw all German police forces—and tightening its grip on the Reich, Himmler was greatly assisted by Reinhard Heydrich, who established an SS intelligence and security service known as

TOP NAZIS Appearing in Vienna, Austria, a country annexed by Hitler in 1936, SS chief Heinrich Himmler (left) stays one step ahead of the ambitious Reinhard Heydrich, whom he chose to direct the SS intelligence and security service designated the SD (Sicherheitsdienst).

the Sicherheitsdienst (SD). Unlike Himmler, who worshipped Hitler, the cold, calculating Heydrich considered himself equal if not superior to those above him in the Nazi hierarchy and bowed to them only because it served his interests to do so. When his first child was born in 1933, he asked two powerful Nazis to serve as the boy's godfathers—Himmler and Ernst Röhm, chief of the Sturmabteilung (SA), whose brown-shirted storm troopers battled communists and other political foes in the streets. A year later, however, Heydrich helped contrive a case against Röhm, accusing him of plotting against Hitler, who used that as a pretext for a "blood purge" in which the SS did away with Röhm and other SA officers. The storm troopers never recovered from that blow. SS men in black replaced those unruly Brownshirts as Hitler's trusted enforcers and carried out murderous tasks at home and abroad with greater discretion and efficiency than the SA had shown. Himmler took pride in the sinister reputation of his corps. "I know that there are millions in Germany who sicken at the sight of the black uniforms of our SS," he wrote. "We understand that well, and we do not expect to be loved by too many."

As the invasion of Poland approached in 1939, Heydrich took charge of a secret operation code-named Tannenberg for a great German victory on the Eastern Front during World War I. It began as a deception, staged on the evening of August 31 to create the false impression that Polish commandos started the war by carrying out assaults on the German side of the border. Tensions ran high along that border, which provided some basis for claiming that Polish incursions ignited the conflict. To render those phony attacks more convincing, several concentration camp inmates and a Polish sympathizer in Germany were killed, dressed in Polish uniforms, and deposited at three sites near the border, including a radio station at Gleiwitz, where SS agents broke in and tried to broadcast an angry message in Polish. That plan went awry, but the bodies of victims—referred to by their SS executioners as "canned goods"—were offered as evidence

"I know that there are millions in Germany who sicken at the sight of the black uniforms of our SS. We understand that well, and we do not expect to be loved by too many."

HEINRICH HIMMLER

BELT-BUCKLE GUN Himmler reportedly ordered several of these curious weapons, concealing four small retractable gun barrels (left) beneath a belt buckle adorned with the Nazi emblem (above). The guns were likely used for show by Nazi leaders rather than in actual combat.

NIGHT OF THE LONG KNIVES

The bruising, brown-shirted storm troopers of the SA (Sturm-abteilung) who helped Hitler achieve power by battling political opponents in the streets became a liability for him once he took firm control of Germany in 1934. They numbered nearly three million men, and their combative leader, Ernst Röhm (inset), envisioned them as a revolutionary Nazi army that would supplant the regular armed forces, limited to 100,000 men under the Treaty of Versailles imposed on Germany in 1919, which Hitler had not yet repudiated. Röhm was feared and loathed by army commanders, whose support Hitler needed to strengthen and expand his Reich, a task that required well-trained soldiers rather than unruly street fighters. He owed much to Röhm, however, and hesitated to target him until Röhm's SS rivals, Heinrich Himmler and Reinhard Heydrich, contrived evidence that he was plotting a coup. Hermann Göring, in charge of the secret police force known as the Gestapo before the SS absorbed it, also conspired against Röhm. Hitler may have suspected that the case against the SA chief was flimsy, but it gave him grounds for eliminating the leadership of the troublesome storm troopers.

Hitler set the purge in motion by summoning Röhm and his top lieutenants to a meeting on June 30, 1934, at a hotel in Bavaria, where they were seized by SS forces. Most were shot to death within hours. Röhm hoped for clemency from the man he called "mein Führer," but he was assassinated at Hitler's order the following day by Theodor Eicke, commandant at Dachau, the first Nazi concentration camp. Meanwhile, SS executioners were targeting public figures who had no connection to the storm troopers but had opposed Hitler in the past or might do so in the future. Among those killed were Kurt von Schleicher—a general turned politician who preceded Hitler as chancellor—and his wife. More than 80 people were identified as victims of the Blood Purge, and the actual death toll may have been much higher.

OLD FIGHTER Ernst Röhm, standing before storm troopers he led, was one of the founding figures of the Nazi Party, known as "Old Fighters," and Hitler eliminated him reluctantly.

Army chiefs had been informed of the purge in advance and were pleased with the outcome, which strengthened ties between the armed forces and Hitler, to whom German officers subsequently swore an oath of loyalty. He used the trumped-up charges against Röhm to portray what he called the "Night of the Long Knives" (a phrase borrowed from a Nazi song) as a righteous action in defense of the Reich. "If anyone reproaches me and asks why I did not resort to the regular courts of justice," he declared, "then all I can say is this: In this hour I was responsible for the fate of the German people, and thereby I became the supreme judge of the German people! . . . Everyone must know for all future time that if he raises his hand to strike the State, then certain death is his lot!"

In fact, few presumed enemies of the Nazi Party or the new Nazi state had ever been dealt with in "regular courts of justice." Many had been attacked by storm troopers and left for dead in streets or back alleys. Such flagrant intimidation would continue sporadically in Nazi Germany, but it would be surpassed by a more secretive and insidious form of terror, administered by the SS, many of whose victims would be hauled off in the dark and never seen again in public. The "Night of the Long Knives" was a stern test for the SS, which proved that it would stop at nothing to advance Hitler's menacing agenda—and would do so more discreetly than the boisterous Brownshirts did. Years later, Himmler would recall that night as the occasion when SS men earned their reputation for utter ruthlessness and unquestioning loyalty. "Every one of us shuddered," he recalled of those killings; "nevertheless each of us understood clearly that he would do it the next time if ordered and if necessary." Himmler added that murdering their fellow Nazis hardened them for a much larger and grimmer task in years to come—the attempted "annihilation of the Jewish people." ☢

to support Hitler's claim that Polish aggression provoked the invasion on September 1. Few outside the Reich were fooled, but Hitler and Propaganda Minister Joseph Goebbels controlled domestic news reports and may have convinced some Germans that Polish forces instigated the war.

The staged attacks on August 31 were merely a prelude to the main act of Operation Tannenberg—a murderous campaign by the SS to eliminate the Polish elite as called for by Hitler, who stated that "only a nation whose upper levels are destroyed can be pushed into the ranks of slavery." Hitler's objective was to destroy Poland as a state and exterminate, enslave, or banish its non-Aryan inhabitants—including Slavs as well as Jews—to provide *lebensraum* (living space) for German settlers. The first step in that massive assault on the populace was to eliminate Poles in positions of power or influence who might encourage resistance. Liquidating those civilians was a job for the SS, which organized task forces called *einsatzgruppen,* each consisting of several hundred armed men who rounded up their victims and shot them to death, often in places where the carnage would not be readily observed. Those task forces included some German police under SS direction and were authorized to call on German soldiers to help them when required. Army commanders later refused to involve regular troops in such atrocities, but some officers and military police cooperated with the SS as it conducted mass murder on a larger scale in years to come. Heydrich's plan called for the execution of 61,000 prominent Poles, including priests, professors, aristocrats, and officials. "Of the Polish upper classes in the occupied territories," he boasted in late September 1939, "only a maximum of three percent is still present."

The operation was not as thorough or systematic as he claimed. Some men in his task forces had killed before, but they were novices when it came to committing murder en masse. They were not always careful about who they slaughtered or how they accomplished it, gunning down up to 900 people at a time in conspicuous massacres whose victims were not all members of the upper classes. Heydrich himself was imprecise in defining the operation, which targeted many Jews who were not among the Polish elite. "We want to save the little people," he said, "but the aristocracy, priests, and Jews must be killed." Hitler, however, had not yet settled on the Final Solution—the secret plan to murder all Jews in occupied territory—and most of those living in Poland were spared temporarily and herded into Jewish ghettos.

The SS would greatly increase its capacity for quietly eliminating people as the war progressed. But the true masters of surreptitious terror when the conflict began were Soviet agents of the NKVD, which Stalin had used since 1934 to execute or commit to dreadful labor camps called gulags millions of his own people. Many Russians were seized in the middle of the night and were never seen or heard of again by their neighbors. During the Great Terror that Stalin orchestrated in 1937–38 in an effort to eradicate opposition to his brutal regime, a team of 12 executioners at a prison outside Moscow—one of dozens of

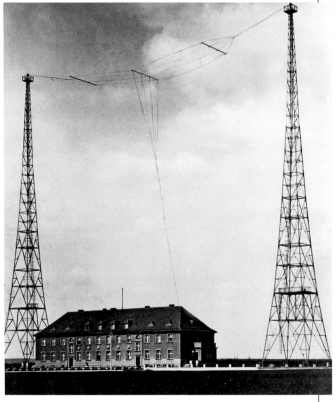

PHONY PRETEXT An attack on a German radio station at Gleiwitz (top), staged by the SS on August 31, 1939, was falsely attributed to Polish irregular troops in a Berlin newspaper (above) to provide a pretext for the German invasion of Poland on September 1.

ATROCITIES IN POLAND The SS officers at right, pictured in the Polish city of Bydgoszcz, commanded paramilitary units of the *Volksdeutscher Selbstschutz,* a self-defense force of ethnic Germans in Poland who took part in Operation Tannenberg, the murderous SS campaign to wipe out the Polish elite after the German invasion. Among those targeted were the priest below, who stands amid the bodies of other victims with a gun pointed at him, and the teachers at bottom, who are about to be executed.

NKVD killing centers—shot to death 20,761 people. Victims were often beaten before they were killed and induced to confess to political offenses they did not commit and to accuse other innocent people of crimes against the state. All ethnic Poles in the Soviet Union, whose ancestral homeland had long been at odds with Russia, were considered suspect, and more than 80,000 were executed before the Great Terror ended. Stalin wiped the slate clean by ordering many of the officers who oversaw the bloodbath put to death, including NKVD chief Nikolai Yezhov, who was replaced by Lavrenty Beria. When Joachim von Ribbentrop returned to Moscow in September 1939 to resolve border issues left unsettled by the nonaggression pact in August, Stalin introduced Beria to Ribbentrop as "our Himmler."

On September 17, Soviet troops invaded eastern Poland. By then, Polish defenses were crumbling under the weight of the German onslaught. The Russians met with little resistance and detained more than 100,000 Polish prisoners of war. Most of the enlisted men were eventually released, but some 15,000 officers were confined in camps run by the NKVD. After annexing eastern Poland in November, Soviet authorities ordered many civilians with close ties to the Polish government, including policemen, civil servants, and military veterans, deported to gulags along with their family members. On a single night in February 1940, NKVD agents evicted nearly 140,000 people from their homes and packed them into freight cars. One girl, whose family was deported because her father had defended Poland against a Soviet invasion in 1920, remembered the ominous sound of the door to their cattle car being slammed shut and bolted. "We knew then that we had been locked in," she recalled, "and we were in slavery." Around 5,000 of the deportees died in transit of exposure, hunger, or disease, and many more perished subsequently in dismal Siberian gulags.

In March 1940, Beria proposed doing away with all of the Polish officers being held in NKVD camps. Those prisoners, he wrote, "were just waiting to be released in order to enter actively into the battle against Soviet power." Beria's plan was readily approved by Stalin, who like Hitler was eager to eliminate all Poles in prominent positions who might resist his regime. Many of the Polish officers in the camps were reservists who had served in peacetime as officials, lawyers, or doctors. They and 6,000 other Poles in NKVD custody were condemned to death and sent to be executed at several sites, including a prison in Kalinin, not far from Moscow. Dmitry Tokarev, the NKVD officer in charge there, was alarmed when he was asked to kill 300 officers a day. That was "too much," he said. "The night was too short and we had to work only at night." Nighttime operations were less likely to attract attention, and Tokarev kept things quiet by lining the execution chambers at Kalinin in velvet to muffle the gunshots. He found that his agents could handle 250 executions a night, using standard NKVD procedure, which called for two men to hold the victim by either arm while a third shot him in the back of the head. One seasoned killer at Kalinin wore a leather cap, apron, and gloves to avoid becoming covered in gore as he worked.

(continued on page 30)

"We want to save the little people, but the aristocracy, priests, and Jews must be killed."
SD CHIEF REINHARD HEYDRICH

UNCOVERED **The exhumed remains of people murdered in Poland testify to the ferocity of Operation Tannenberg, which claimed nearly 50,000 lives.**

THE KATYN MASSACRE COVER-UP

In April 1940, more than 4,000 Polish officers held in Russia as prisoners of war were shot to death and buried in a mass grave in the forest at Katyn, near Smolensk. It was one of several massacres carried out secretly that month by security forces of the NKVD under orders drawn up by their chief, Lavrenty Beria, and signed by Stalin. Like Hitler, Stalin wanted to eliminate Polish leaders who might inspire resistance to the armed occupation of their country, divided into German and Soviet zones. More than 15,000 Polish officers and 6,000 civilians were executed by the NKVD in actions known collectively as the Katyn massacres because the killings there were the first to be uncovered. In April 1943, nearly two years after Hitler turned against Stalin and invaded Russia, the Germans exhumed the bodies of Polish victims at Katyn and found evidence implicating the Russians. Propaganda Minister Joseph Goebbels inflated the death toll by claiming that 10,000 Poles had been executed there, and Soviet authorities responded by blaming the massacre on the Germans.

Privately, British officials agreed with the Polish government-in-exile in London that Russian

INNER CIRCLE Stalin pores over papers as his daughter Svetlana sits in the lap of Lavrenty Beria, the security chief who set the Katyn massacres in motion.

efforts to deny responsibility for the slaughter at Katyn were suspect. Owen O'Malley, British emissary to the Polish government, wrote a confidential report in which he condemned the Russians but concluded that "the urgent need for cordial relations" with the Soviets left their British and American allies with little choice but "to cover up a massacre." Winston Churchill sent a copy of the report to President Roosevelt with a note describing it as a "grim, well written story, but perhaps a little too well written," an apparent reference to O'Malley's admission that the Allies were whitewashing an atrocity. To ensure secrecy, Churchill asked Roosevelt to return the report "when you have finished with it as we are not circulating it officially in any way."

Roosevelt was no more inclined than Churchill was to accuse the Soviets and never mentioned the report. Russian claims that Nazis were responsible for the killings at Katyn appeared plausible at the time. Not until 1990, as the Soviet Union unraveled, did President Mikhail Gorbachev reveal that the massacres at Katyn and elsewhere had been approved in Moscow at the highest level. ✪

Les mŕtvych v **Katyne**

DEATH SENTENCE Signed by Stalin and other Soviet leaders, this order issued on March 5, 1940, resulted in the slaughter of over 20,000 Polish prisoners of war. Each prisoner's file was reviewed in cursory fashion by a troika, a group of three judges, who sentenced to death nearly all those in custody.

DAMNING EVIDENCE The clothed skeleton of a Polish POW (above) was uncovered in a mass grave at Katyn (left) by Germans who publicized the Russian atrocity in broadcasts and posters (top).

LOST IN RUSSIA These portraits commemorate a small number of the thousands of Polish officers executed by the NKVD in April 1940. Many of them were reservists who left their jobs and families to defend their country shortly before being captured by the invading Soviets.

The executions were less discreet at another Soviet killing center, Katyn, where Polish officers were trucked into the forest and gunned down. "I could hear the shooting and screaming of men's voices," one farmer who lived nearby recalled. "In my area it was no secret that Poles were being shot by the NKVD." When the Germans later turned against the Soviets and invaded their territory, they uncovered thousands of bodies at Katyn and publicized the atrocity in an effort to embarrass the Western democracies that were then allied with Stalin's totalitarian regime. Before the Germans and Soviets became enemies, however, they were partners in massive crimes against the Polish populace. Between September 1939 and June 1941, when their nonaggression pact collapsed, the two regimes killed more than 100,000 Polish civilians—a higher death toll than suffered by soldiers in combat on all sides there—and sent more than a million Poles to gulags, prisons, or concentration camps. Much of that was carried out covertly by security forces and went largely unnoticed by the outside world.

AGENCIES AT WAR

Like the SS, the NKVD conducted espionage at home and abroad, engaging in operations that sometimes overlapped with the military intelligence functions of the GRU. The often heated rivalry between the NKVD and the GRU was mirrored by sharp competition between Reinhard Heydrich's SD and the Abwehr, the German military intelligence agency led by Adm. Wilhelm Canaris. An archconservative who was close to Heydrich and supportive of Hitler before the war, Canaris grew increasingly alarmed by Nazi aggression and atrocities, which he feared would expose the German military and the nation as a whole to shame and ruin. He secretly joined a small circle of like-minded officers and officials who plotted against Hitler to little effect until conspirators came close to assassinating him late in the war. Meanwhile, Canaris clashed openly with Heydrich and Himmler, who undermined the Abwehr whenever possible and kept a careful record of its intelligence failures. Canaris faced a tougher task than Heydrich, whose SD operations were confined largely to the Reich and its occupied countries, with occasional forays into neutral territory. The Abwehr's theater extended to hostile nations that were never occupied by German troops and dangerous for German spies to penetrate, including Great Britain—which joined France in declaring war soon after Germany invaded Poland—and the United States, which aided the British militarily before taking up arms against the Axis in December 1941.

Soon after the war began, while Abwehr spies infiltrated England at great risk, the SD targeted two British agents operating for MI6 in neutral Holland. Responsible for foreign intelligence operations, MI6 was founded in the early 20th century as the Secret Intelligence Service (SIS), a title that clung to the agency long after it was redesignated as one of several MI branches of the British Directorate of Military Intelligence, including MI5,

TERROR TACTICS Nazi Germany waged war overtly with terrifying strikes by warplanes like the Stuka dive-bomber (above)—and covertly with undercover operations by the Abwehr, in charge of military intelligence, and by rival SS agencies such as the SD and Gestapo.

IAN FLEMING'S INTELLIGENCE

Ian Fleming was a 30-year-old London stockbroker and occasional journalist when he embarked on a mission that launched his career as a British agent and future spy novelist. In early 1939, Fleming accompanied a trade delegation to Moscow as a correspondent for *The Times* of London while confidentially assessing Russian strength in a report he submitted to the British Foreign Office (below, right). He acknowledged that he had no Russian "secrets" to share and that his conclusions were based on published sources, supplemented by his observations as a reporter. But such "open source" intelligence from journalists, diplomats, and others operating legally in foreign countries could be as informative as reports from spies who risked execution if caught. Fleming offered a balanced assessment of Russia's wartime potential, noting that Stalin's murderous purges had stripped the Red Army of "tens of thousands of competent officers" but that authorities were seeking to rebuild morale by promoting young "men of ability" to fill the void left when leaders were liquidated. He did not foresee the forthcoming Hitler-Stalin pact, but he concluded astutely that Russia had more to gain in the long run by siding with Britain against Nazi Germany. "Russia would be an exceedingly treacherous ally," he warned. "She would not hesitate to stab us in the back the moment it suited her . . . Russian co-operation with the Allies would be of great strategic value, but such co-operation should only be accepted as a last resort and with grave misgivings."

Not long after his mission to Moscow, Fleming became personal assistant to Adm. John Godfrey, Director of Naval Intelligence. By 1941, Lieutenant Commander Fleming (inset) was in charge of Operation Goldeneye, which would take effect if Germany drew Spain into the Axis or invaded that country and seized Gibraltar, threatening the Royal Navy's access to the Mediterranean. Fleming entered Spain with a courier's passport (below, left) and arranged to maintain radio contact with spies there and sabotage radar installations and other targets if Gibraltar fell. Spain remained neutral and his plans were scrapped, but he took pride in his first secret operation and later named the Jamaican estate where he began writing his James Bond novels Goldeneye. ○

CODE NAME: 17F

SPIED FOR: GREAT BRITAIN

SPIED AGAINST: RUSSIA, SPAIN

responsible for domestic counterespionage operations. The Royal Navy and other military services also had intelligence agencies, but MI6 was Britain's preeminent spy service. Its prestige was acknowledged and enhanced by author Ian Fleming, an accomplished British naval intelligence officer during World War II who later designated his famous fictional spy, James Bond, as Agent 007 in Her Majesty's Secret Service—a fancy title for the Secret Intelligence Service or MI6. Like the Abwehr, however, MI6 faced a daunting task when Britain and Germany became enemies in September 1939 and heightened their defenses against espionage.

The perils of spying in or near enemy territory in wartime were soon demonstrated to Maj. Richard Henry Stevens—who worked undercover for MI6 as a British passport control officer in the Dutch capital of The Hague—and his colleague Capt. Sigismund Payne

ASSASSIN'S TARGET Hitler addresses Nazis on November 8, 1939, at the beer hall in Munich where he had first tried to seize power in 1923. Soon after he left the hall, a bomb meant for him went off, killing nine people.

Best, who posed as a British businessman there. In October 1939, they were contacted by a German refugee in Holland who offered to put them in touch with high-ranking opponents of Hitler in the Wehrmacht ("armed forces"). Best and Stevens then met secretly with a German officer who identified himself as Captain Schämmel and invited them to confer with Gen. Gustav von Wietersheim, who was known to have quarreled with Hitler over his plan to invade Czechoslovakia earlier that year. The meeting would take place at the Dutch town of Venlo, on the border with Germany. Wietersheim and his confederates were prepared to take forceful steps against Hitler, Schämmel promised, if Britain and France would in turn grant Germany a peace that was "just and honorable." To engage in such talks with an enemy commander in wartime, Best and Stevens required permission at the highest level. Stewart Menzies, chief of MI6, sought approval from Prime Minister Neville Chamberlain, who had tried in vain to appease Hitler and now hoped that high-ranking Germans would turn against their Führer and make peace before bombs fell on London. Chamberlain endorsed talks with Wietersheim, as did his War Cabinet, despite objections from Winston Churchill, an ardent foe of appeasement who was then First Lord of the Admiralty.

After Wietersheim twice failed to appear for a meeting with them in Venlo, Best and Stevens returned there on November 9, 1939, accompanied by a Dutch intelligence officer, Lt. Dirk Klop, who went armed for the occasion. When they reached their destination, Best noticed that German border guards had raised the gate at their frontier. Schämmel was standing on the veranda of a café in Venlo and waved as if to signal that the general was awaiting them inside. As they stepped from their vehicle, a large car crossed the border from Germany and bore down on them. "It seemed to be packed to overflowing with rough-looking men," Best recalled. "Two were perched on top of the hood and were firing over our heads from submachine guns; others were standing up in the car and on the running board, all shouting and

SHIFTING BLAME SS officer Walter Schellenberg (near right) led the covert operation that captured two British agents in Holland who were then blamed for planning the Munich beer hall bombing—S. Payne Best (pictured at far right on the front page of a German newspaper) and Richard Henry Stevens (pictured beside Best). In truth, the man who planted the bomb, George Elser (pictured to the left of Stevens and Best) was solely responsible for the blast, which shattered the hall (below).

"And now,
set Europe ablaze!"

WINSTON CHURCHILL'S DIRECTIVE
TO THE NEWLY FORMED SOE
(SPECIAL OPERATIONS EXECUTIVE)

waving pistols." Klop traded shots with them and was mortally wounded, leaving the British agents stranded. "Our number is up, Best," Stevens said. Their assailants forced them into the car and sped back across the border. "The black and white barrier closed behind us," Best observed. "We were in Nazi Germany."

He and Stevens were in the hands of SD agents led by Alfred Naujocks, who had conducted the covert raid on the Gleiwitz radio station on August 31 and was working for Walter Schellenberg, a master of deception who served as counterintelligence chief of the SD and posed as Capt. Schämmel. Schellenberg had used the promised meeting with Wietersheim—who was not plotting against Hitler and not involved in this SD operation—as bait to lure the two spies, hoping to coax them into revealing details about their agency's contacts with genuine German dissidents. He received orders to kidnap Best and Stevens from Himmler just hours after a failed attempt on Hitler's life in Munich on November 8 by Johann Georg Elser, a communist sympathizer. Elser acted alone, but Hitler blamed the British. Mug shots of the captured Best and Stevens—both of whom survived the war in German custody after being relentlessly interrogated—appeared alongside that of Elser in the German press.

The Venlo Incident was a severe embarrassment for MI6 and a bitter setback for its efforts to penetrate the Reich and exploit high-level German opposition to Hitler. The fiasco did not endear the agency to Churchill, who succeeded Chamberlain as prime minister in May 1940 when German troops invaded France and the Low Countries. Two months later, convinced that espionage and intelligence gathering were not sufficient to undermine the Reich, Churchill formed the Special Operations Executive (SOE) to sabotage enemy assets, support resistance movements, and subvert German authority in the occupied countries. It was a risky business, and many SOE agents fell into enemy hands. But by 1941, the agency was mounting operations that caused trouble for the Germans, notably the Shetland Bus, a maritime operation conducted in the North Sea by daring fishing-boat captains who eluded enemy patrols and introduced agents, weapons, and explosives to occupied Norway to promote resistance there.

Churchill's plan to "set Europe ablaze" through covert action by the SOE worried British military commanders—

CONTESTED CONQUEST Hitler stands before the Eiffel Tower in late June 1940 after his forces conquered France, prompting determined efforts by SOE agents to infiltrate the country and promote sabotage and subversion by French resisters.

who felt that their own services were better qualified to conduct special operations—and appalled Menzies and his officers, who feared that SOE "amateurs" would wreak havoc abroad and trigger crackdowns by German security forces, placing MI6 agents and their informants at risk. While Menzies' time-honored SIS wrangled with the upstart SOE, a third agency, MI5, quietly conducted one of the most elaborate and successful counterintelligence operations ever conceived by rounding up nearly all the Abwehr agents who landed on British soil during the war and playing many of them back against their German spymasters.

DOUBLE CROSS

In September 1940, the Abwehr launched Operation Lena, a hurried effort to infiltrate spies and saboteurs into Britain in advance of an anticipated German invasion of England. Contrary to Hitler's expectations, the British had remained defiant after France fell to the Wehrmacht in June. Admiral Canaris was ordered to resuscitate covert operations in Britain—thwarted at the start of the war when enemy aliens were required to register there and hundreds of suspects were interned or placed under surveillance. German commanders wanted spies on the ground to determine the effectiveness of the air war being waged by their Luftwaffe and report on British defenses against invasion. Many of the Abwehr's new recruits came from occupied countries. If questioned by the British, they could claim to be refugees from lands under German domination, but that alibi was unlikely to hold up under close scrutiny. Hastily trained in sending coded radio messages and the use of weapons and often less than proficient in English, they were thrust into one of the war's most hostile environments for enemy agents—an island nation whose citizens were alert to threats from abroad and on the lookout for intruders.

Before dawn on September 3, a German trawler in the Strait of Dover released two dinghies—each manned by a pair of spies—several miles off the English coast. Karl Meier, born in Germany and raised in Holland, paddled ashore with another German agent, José Rudolf Waldberg. Unable to converse in English, Waldberg laid low while the more fluent Meier hiked into the village of Lydd, entered a pub before 10 in the morning, and ordered a drink, unaware that British bartenders were not allowed to serve alcohol at that early hour. Having aroused suspicion, he was soon being questioned by police, who dismissed his claim that he was a Dutch refugee. Without too much coaxing, he admitted to being a spy and informed on Waldberg, who was caught in possession of a wireless radio transmitter. The two other agents who came ashore that morning—Dutchmen who had taken on their hazardous duty to avoid prison terms—were seized in short order along with their transmitter.

All four detainees were sent to Camp 020, an MI5 interrogation center in London commanded by Lt. Col. Robin Stephens, who disdained torture and instead used (continued on page 38)

CAPTURED SPY At top, German agent Karel Richter, arrested soon after he landed by parachute in England in May 1941, points out where he hid his parachute, which was then retrieved from a hedgerow (center) and carried off as evidence (bottom). Richter refused to serve as a double agent against Germany and was sentenced to death.

THE SOE: MASTERS IN THE ART OF DECEPTION

The SOE established top secret shops and laboratories in England where scientists and technicians, known to British soldiers as boffins, produced weapons, disguises, and other devices for secret agents, many of them crafted with an eye for the stealth and concealment that lay at the heart of spycraft. Boffins at one SOE station near Welwyn in Hertfordshire designed the Welrod pistol (below) and other silent weapons, while arms makers at nearby Aston House developed a deadly arsenal of clandestine devices for sabotage and assassination as well as conventional weapons for commandos. The agency's Camouflage Section, housed in a former inn called the Thatched Barn, devised ways of concealing equipment for agents, including guns, explosives, and radios. At another SOE facility, expert forgers reproduced German documents to help spies and saboteurs infiltrate occupied territory. The SOE's *Descriptive Catalogue of Special Devices and Supplies*, published as a training manual, described hundreds of weapons and techniques designed for the Allies' secret war against the Third Reich. ✪

WELL-DISGUISED This page from an SOE instruction manual describes various ways of disguising agents, ranging from simple but effective makeup techniques to prosthetic devices and plastic surgery.

MUFFLED GUN The Welrod was designed for a single task—silent assassination. The short-range, single-shot pistol contained a silencer and a magazine in its short grip.

SPOOFING HITLER SOE forgers recruited from British prisons demonstrated their skill by producing this fake German passport for Adolf Hitler, marked with the red "J" to signal that he was Jewish. It bears a stamp indicating that he had immigrated to Palestine.

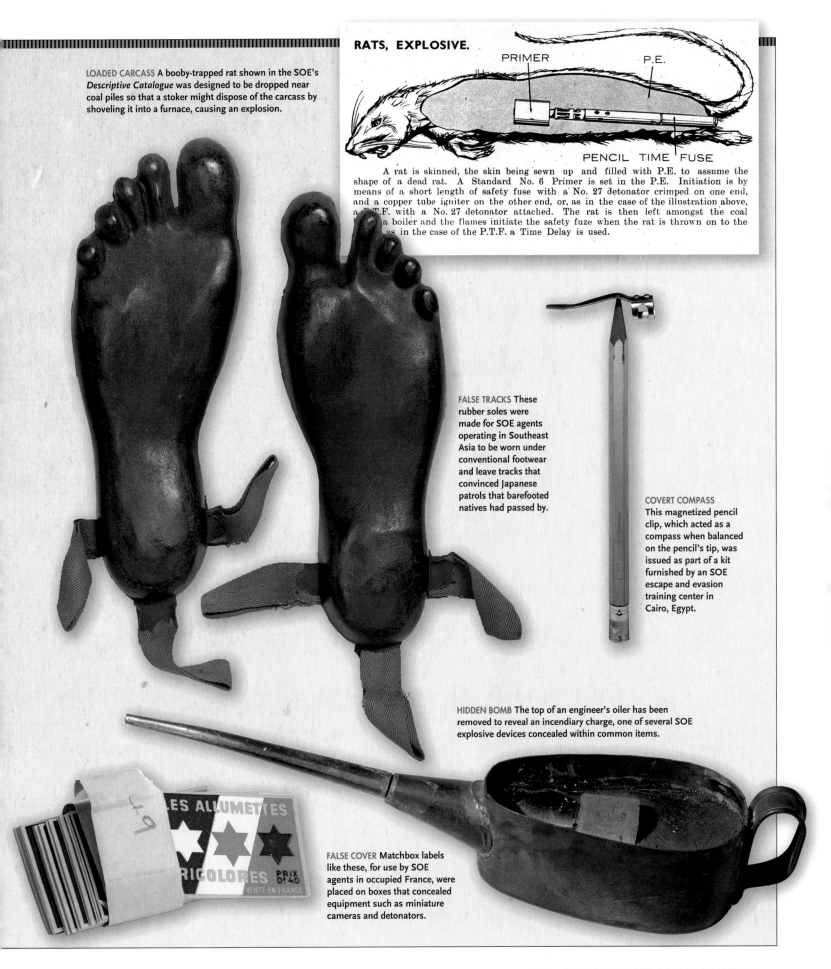

LOADED CARCASS A booby-trapped rat shown in the SOE's *Descriptive Catalogue* was designed to be dropped near coal piles so that a stoker might dispose of the carcass by shoveling it into a furnace, causing an explosion.

RATS, EXPLOSIVE.

PRIMER   P.E.

PENCIL TIME FUSE

A rat is skinned, the skin being sewn up and filled with P.E. to assume the shape of a dead rat. A Standard No. 6 Primer is set in the P.E. Initiation is by means of a short length of safety fuse with a No. 27 detonator crimped on one end, and a copper tube igniter on the other end, or, as in the case of the illustration above, a P.T.F. with a No. 27 detonator attached. The rat is then left amongst the coal ████ a boiler and the flames initiate the safety fuze when the rat is thrown on to the ██ as in the case of the P.T.F. a Time Delay is used.

FALSE TRACKS These rubber soles were made for SOE agents operating in Southeast Asia to be worn under conventional footwear and leave tracks that convinced Japanese patrols that barefooted natives had passed by.

COVERT COMPASS This magnetized pencil clip, which acted as a compass when balanced on the pencil's tip, was issued as part of a kit furnished by an SOE escape and evasion training center in Cairo, Egypt.

HIDDEN BOMB The top of an engineer's oiler has been removed to reveal an incendiary charge, one of several SOE explosive devices concealed within common items.

FALSE COVER Matchbox labels like these, for use by SOE agents in occupied France, were placed on boxes that concealed equipment such as miniature cameras and detonators.

LES ALLUMETTES
RICOLORES PRIX 0f40
VENTE EN FRANCE

psychological pressure to make agents talk. Prisoners stood as if on trial before him and his fellow inquisitors, and were reminded that the penalty for espionage was death. Those who came clean and confessed might be offered a chair and a cigarette—the first step in the delicate process of "turning" an agent and using him to deceive his German controllers. That was not an option for the four men who came ashore in early September, however, because Waldberg had radioed Germany that police were on to them. Abwehr officers might suspect them as double agents if they remained active. Under pressure from Prime Minister Churchill, who wanted the public to know that German spies were being apprehended and punished, MI5 handed them over for trial. Waldberg, Meier, and one of the two Dutchmen were convicted and executed, and the other was sent to prison after testifying that he was forced to spy.

MI5 soon had more prospects for their Double Cross system as German agents continued to land in Britain by boat or by parachute. In the early hours of September 6, a Swedish-born spy named Gösta Caroli—trained by the Abwehr along with Wulf Schmidt, a Danish recruit he befriended—jumped from a converted German bomber with heavy radio equipment strapped to his chest and was knocked senseless when he hit the ground. Local defense volunteers scooped him up that morning while he was still groggy, and he was soon being grilled at Camp 020. Caroli was initially hostile, but he eventually disclosed that he was not acting alone and that a fellow spy was due to join him. Interrogators exploited the bond between the two agents by offering to spare both men if Caroli cooperated and gave a description of his friend, which MI5 then shared with police and defense volunteers. Schmidt parachuted down north of London on September 20, twisted his ankle on landing, and was seized within hours. He stuck to his story that he was a refugee who had arrived by boat from Denmark until told that Caroli had informed on him to spare his life. He eventually revealed all to his persistent interrogators and joined Caroli, who received the code name Summer, as a double agent under the code name Tate, transmitting reports scripted by MI5 to the Abwehr.

Summer and Tate were not the first spies to be played back against their German masters during the war. MI5's Double Cross operation began in 1939 when the agency took charge of a slippery spy from Wales named Arthur Owens, an electrical engineer and salesman who had gathered intelligence for MI6 on business trips to Germany in the mid-1930s before offering his services to an Abwehr officer in Hamburg, Maj. Nikolaus Ritter. Owens claimed to be a dedicated Welsh nationalist opposed to British rule, but he was not above accepting cash and other favors from Ritter, who hosted him lavishly when he visited Hamburg, picking up his tab at nightclubs and providing the unhappily married spy with female companionship. Back in London, his MI6 case officer grew suspicious and had Owens tailed. Fearing exposure, he confessed to dealing with the Abwehr but claimed he was only doing so to extract German secrets for the British. As proof of his loyalty, he divulged that Ritter was sending him a radio

EXPOSED British authorities took this x-ray of a timer and detonator hidden in a tin of talcum powder, which Arthur Owens of Wales (opposite) received while posing as a German agent. Owens was supposed to conduct espionage and sabotage in Britain but came under the control of counterintelligence officers at MI5, who played him back against the Germans.

SHIFTY AGENT Arthur Owens, portrayed above, was enlisted as a German spy before World War II began by the Abwehr, which supplied him with a radio set like the one at left, designed in Germany for espionage and consisting of a battery, receiver, and transmitter concealed in a briefcase. Arrested by the British in 1939 and confined at Wandsworth Prison (top), Owens became a double agent for MI5, which gave him the code name Snow and had him radio misinformation to his Abwehr case officer, Nikolaus Ritter. MI5 later concluded that he could not be trusted when he met with Ritter abroad and returned him to prison.

transmitter, concealed in a suitcase checked at London's Victoria Station, where Owens retrieved it. Despite his apparent cooperation, he remained suspect and was jailed shortly before the war began after his wife accused him of trying to recruit their son as a German agent. He might have languished in prison for the duration had not MI5 taken over his case and used him as a pawn in their opening gambit against the Abwehr.

Soon after Britain declared war on Germany, Owens began sending coded messages to Hamburg with the radio he received. By all appearances, he was serving the Abwehr faithfully, but MI5 was drafting his reports, which combined accurate details whose disclosure did no harm to the British war effort with false leads designed to distract and deceive the enemy. Code-named Snow, Owens was fully under MI5's control on home ground, but he continued to venture abroad now and then to meet with Ritter, who remained convinced that Owens was his man. Mercenary and mercurial, Snow may have offered Ritter more genuine intelligence during those meetings than the British meant for him to divulge. They never entirely trusted him, but his services to the crown—which included betraying several of Ritter's agents to MI5 and revealing codes that helped cryptanalysts decipher Abwehr communications—were too valuable for them to dispense with him until he lost his nerve in 1941 and was sent back to prison.

By then, MI5 had a stable of more than a dozen double agents, each with its own handler. They were watched over as a group by Maj. Thomas Argyll "Tar" Robertson, who after serving as controller for the shifty Snow found other difficult cases he supervised straightforward by comparison. Wulf Schmidt was a feisty Dane who traded blows with an officer who violated the rule against physical intimidation at Camp 020, but Robertson soon befriended Tate, hosted him at home, and helped transform him into one of MI5's most reliable operatives.

Unlike Tate, some spies and saboteurs sent by the Abwehr surrendered voluntarily as soon as they reached Britain, including two Norwegians who attracted the attention of police a few hours after they landed in 1941 and readily admitted they were German agents. Code-named Mutt and Jeff because one was short and stocky and the other tall and thin, they were an odd couple in more ways than one. Mutt was English on his mother's side, eager to betray the Germans, and highly cooperative. Jeff was moody and suspect, having served the Nazis in Norway as a censor. Doubts as to his reliability increased when he slipped away from his handler and spent the night with a woman who had not been vetted or furnished by the agency—a requirement for those double agents who preferred not to remain celibate. Before long he was dismissed by MI5 and interned. Mutt and Jeff remained a team only in the minds of their distant German overseers, who were reassured when MI5 staged an explosion at a food storage depot on Guy Fawkes Day—an occasion for bonfires and fireworks—and credited the two Norwegian agents with the deed.

The main objective of Abwehr espionage shifted in 1941 from gathering intelligence that would support an invasion of Britain—a plan Hitler abandoned when the Luftwaffe failed to achieve the air supremacy required to shield an invasion fleet—to gauging the impact of relentless U-boat attacks designed to throttle the British into submission by cutting off transatlantic shipments of food, munitions, and ultimately troops when the U.S. entered the war. Questions submitted by the Abwehr to MI5's double agents revealed

SPYMASTERS Key figures in MI5's spectacularly successful Double Cross system were John Masterman (above), chairman of the Twenty (XX) Committee that determined what information would be fed to the Germans, and Maj. Thomas "Tar" Robertson (top), who supervised the double agents and their handlers. "It was always in the back of our minds," wrote Masterman, "that at some time in the distant future a great day would come when our agents would be used for a grand and final deception of the enemy."

REGISTRATION CERTIFICATE No. 1022652
ISSUED AT *Piccadilly Place W.1*
ON *5th February 1941*
NAME (Surname first in Roman Capitals) *POPOV Douchan*
ALIAS *Dusan*

Left Thumb Print
(if unable to sign name
in English Characters).

Signature, *Douchan M. Popov*
of Holder:

Nationality *Jugo Slavian*
Born on *10/7/12* in *Lelet Serbia*
Previous Nationality (if any) *Serbian*
Profession or Occupation *Representative*
Single or Married *Single*
Address of Residence *Cumberland Hotel W.1.*
Arrival in United Kingdom on *22/5/1928*
Address of last Residence outside U.K. *98, Boulevard Sevastopol*
Government Service
Passport or other papers as to Nationality and Identity. *Jugo Slav St. No 4832 Issued Belgium 16/11/40*

MASTER SPY Dusko Popov of Yugoslavia—pictured at left on his alien registration card, which foreigners in Britain had to carry—was one of MI5's most accomplished double agents. His letters to Maria Elera (below), a young Brazilian living in Lisbon, Portugal, who became one of his many girlfriends, contained deceptive reports that she passed along to his Abwehr case handler.

that strategic shift, and could not be ignored or answered with entirely false reports without arousing suspicion.

The Twenty Committee, so called for the Roman numerals XX, signifying Double Cross, decided who should continue functioning as double agents and what accurate information they would be allowed to reveal to the Germans to maintain their credibility. Represented on the committee were MI5 and MI6—whose cooperation was essential because counterintelligence operations conducted abroad were under their supervision—as well as the War Office, the armed forces, and home defense forces. John Masterman of MI5, who taught history at Oxford and wrote crime novels on the side, chaired the weekly meetings. A former cricket champion, he later likened running double agents to "running a club cricket side. Older players lose their form and are gradually replaced by newcomers." Some promising newcomers, including recently inducted double agents and the handlers assigned to guide them, required much practice "before they were really fit to play in a match," he added. "The prime difficulty was that we never knew when this decisive match would take place, and our best batsmen and the ones we had most carefully trained might be past their best or even deceased before the date of the final game."

MI5's initial efforts to deceive the Abwehr were training exercises for what Masterman called that "decisive match," which would come when the British were no longer on the defensive and were prepared to attack not just in North Africa, where they began battling Axis troops in late 1940, but also in occupied Europe, where deception would be crucial to prevent German forces from concentrating against and repelling an Allied invasion. As MI5's counterespionage chief, Guy Liddell, pointed out, the ultimate purpose of the small tricks double agents and their handlers played on the Germans in the war's early innings was "to mislead the enemy on a big scale at the appropriate moment."

Two double agents in particular would figure prominently in MI5's deception efforts when that crucial moment arrived. Unlike spies who were captured and turned after landing in Britain, Dusko Popov of Yugoslavia and Juan Pujol García of Spain (known by his father's surname of Pujol) enlisted as Abwehr agents with the intention of crossing over

DOUBLE AGENT MATHILDE CARRÉ

After leaving her husband and suffering a miscarriage, 32-year-old Mathilde Carré of France nearly leaped to her death from a bridge before resolving instead to "fling myself into the war." She tried nursing wounded French soldiers but found a more secretive and satisfying way of serving her country in late 1940 when she met Roman Garby-Czerniawski, a Polish officer who had fled to Paris and planned to set up a spy ring that would monitor German occupation forces in France and report to the British through exiled Polish officials in London. He spoke French haltingly and enlisted agents through Carré, to whom he gave the code name La Chatte (female cat) for the quiet,

stealthy way she moved. Within months, they had dozens of operatives spying on the enemy and began relaying their findings to London, first through couriers and later by radio. Their Interallié network kept the British well informed on German strength in France at a time when they had few spies of their own there.

In late 1941, Carré and Garby-Czerniawski were betrayed by one of their agents and seized by Sgt. Hugo Bleicher, a cunning Abwehr counterintelligence officer. He not only made Carré talk and expose others in the network but also seduced her and turned her into a double agent, transmitting deceptive messages to London. "I hated myself for my weakness," she wrote, "and as a result of my abasement I hated the Germans even more." By her own account, she escaped

Bleicher by persuading him to send her to England with Pierre de Vomécourt, a French-born SOE agent who asked her to serve as his radio contact with London. Bleicher expected her to spy on the SOE there, but she confessed to British authorities and said she wanted to rejoin the Allies. Unfortunately for Carré, Bleicher had recently freed Garby-Czerniawski on condition that he too would spy for the Abwehr in England. He persuaded British intelligence officers that he never intended to aid the Germans and denounced her for betraying agents and doing Bleicher's bidding. He became a double agent for MI5, while she spent the rest of the war in a British prison and was later incarcerated in France as a traitor. Spurned after being released, she told of her travails in a book entitled *I Was the Cat.* ○

CODE NAME: LA CHATTE

SPIED FOR: BRITAIN, GERMANY

SPIED AGAINST: GERMANY, BRITAIN

THE CAT'S COMPANIONS Mathilde Carré, pictured here in 1940, first became involved in espionage with Roman Garby-Czerniawski (above, left), a cat lover who dubbed her La Chatte. Their network spied on German forces in France until broken up by Sgt. Hugo Bleicher (center). Her stint as Bleicher's lover and double agent ended after she met the SOE's Pierre de Vomécourt (right) and went with him to England, where she was jailed.

to the British. Pujol first offered his services to an MI6 officer at the British Embassy in Madrid but was shown the door. He concluded that he would be of more interest to the Allies if he first gained access to the Abwehr, which enrolled him as an agent under the code name Arabel in early 1941 on his assurance that he could reach Britain by way of Portugal. Instead, he remained in Portugal and composed fictional intelligence reports that supposedly emanated from England. Submitted in writing using invisible ink, they were then relayed by his controller in Spain to his superiors in Germany by radio—transmissions intercepted and decoded by the British, who worried that an elusive spy named Arabel might indeed be in England, where he claimed to have recruited three subagents.

When Pujol tried again to join the Allied cause—this time through the American Embassy in Lisbon, which notified British officials there—MI5 realized that he was deceiving the Abwehr with his con-trived reports as Arabel and recognized his great potential as a double agent. In one instance, he informed the Germans that a fictional subagent of his in Liverpool had observed the departure of a powerful British convoy from that port, destined for Malta, a beleaguered Brit-ish base in the Mediterranean. The Germans dispatched U-boats and torpedo planes in pursuit of that imaginary convoy—just the sort of diversion of enemy resources that MI5 hoped to achieve on a grand scale as the war progressed. Pujol soon joined the agency's roster of double agents under the code name Garbo (as in Greta), a tribute to his skill at role-playing. Tutored by his handler, Tomás "Tommy" Harris, who was half Spanish but raised in England, Pujol avoided the gaffes

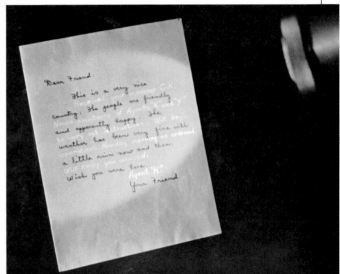

that MI5 detected in some of his earlier reports to the Abwehr—including a reference to dockworkers in Glasgow drinking wine by the liter when in fact they guzzled beer by the pint—and added new names to his list of notional subagents while doing away with others. His spy in Liverpool would not long remain credible to the Germans unless he reported accurately on warships departing there, information that had to remain secret. So Garbo informed the Abwehr that the man had fallen ill and later sent along an obituary for the imaginary subagent that MI5 planted in a Liverpool newspaper.

Unlike Pujol, who operated behind the scenes, the flamboyant Dusko Popov conducted espionage in person while posing as an international playboy. That role came naturally to him. Born wealthy in Dubrovnik, he was educated in France, England, and Germany and was well acquainted with casinos, fast cars, and beautiful women. His carefree man-ner helped disguise his deep-seated contempt for the Nazi regime, which he disdained even before Germany invaded Yugoslavia in April 1941 and blasted its capital, Belgrade, in murderous air raids. A year earlier, Popov had been approached by Johann Jebsen, a friend and former classmate of his at the University of Freiburg in Germany who had since joined the Abwehr to avoid regular military service. Jebsen would eventually turn against the Nazis and may have known where Popov's true loyalties lay when he recruited him to serve as an Abwehr agent in Britain. Popov accepted that assignment only after contacting an MI6 officer at the British passport control office in Belgrade. Urged to play along with the Germans, he traveled to London with the knowledge and assistance of MI6, which

OPERATION NORTH POLE

While German agents were being turned by MI5, the British too were being double-crossed by a shrewd Abwehr counterintelligence officer in the Netherlands, Maj. Hermann Giskes (top right). On the lookout for spies and saboteurs infiltrating Holland, he seized Hubert Lauwers (bottom right), who had fled the German occupation of his country in 1940, joined the SOE in England, and returned as a covert radio operator for his fellow resisters in the Netherlands, where he was captured in March 1942. Intent on turning Lauwers, Giskes avoided what he called the "cruel methods that were the nightmare of such agents when caught by the Germans." Lauwers realized he was being lulled into betraying the British. Although he agreed to send them messages scripted by Giskes, he lied to the major about his security check—a small error inserted in each message to confirm the sender's identity and indicate that all was well—and used the wrong security check to alert London that he was under duress. His warning signal was missed by the SOE, which then informed Lauwers of plans to send more agents, who were arrested by Giskes. Code-named Operation North Pole, the scheme expanded to include scripted messages from other captured radio operators, seizures of British weapons and explosives air-dropped in Holland, and minor acts of sabotage staged by Giskes to create the impression that the SOE's Dutch network remained intact. In all, he seized 52 SOE agents, many of whom were executed, and over 300 Dutch resisters. ○

SEIZED A dark-coated informant stands by as Germans seize British weapons meant for Dutch resisters. Giskes made many such hauls before he wrapped up North Pole by informing the SOE on April Fools' Day in 1944 that he and his forces had enjoyed acting "as your sole representatives in this country."

continued to oversee him when he ventured abroad in years to come, even though he did so as a double agent for MI5.

To enhance Popov's credibility with the Abwehr officers he met with periodically, MI5 assigned him two subagents who were real rather than notional, including Friedl Gartner, an Austrian socialite in London who was linked romantically to Popov and had friends in high places. She obligingly wrote notes to him in invisible ink that were scripted by MI5 and contained tidbits of misinformation about British leaders and their plans that he passed along to the Germans. A big wheel backed up by two small wheels, Popov received the code name Tricycle.

Popov later drew Johann Jebsen into MI5's web. Jebsen was one of a number of Abwehr officers secretly at odds with their own regime, including such prominent figures as Admiral Canaris and his chief of staff and fellow conspirator against Hitler, Maj. Gen. Hans Oster. Among those dissident spymasters—characterized later by British intelligence analysts as "good Germans, but bad Nazis"—was Herbert Wichmann, head of the Abwehr's Hamburg office, from which many ill-prepared agents recruited for Operation Lena were dispatched and fell into MI5's hands. Did Wichmann and others responsible for German military intelligence sabotage that operation because they considered Hitler's war on Britain a disastrous blunder and hoped to come to terms with the Allies after toppling the Führer? No such conspiracy was apparent to Abwehr case officer Nikolaus Ritter, who ran Arthur Owens and other agents from the Hamburg office, or to the MI5 officers who turned them against the Reich. All those who infiltrated agents into enemy territory were vulnerable to being double-crossed, including the British, who suffered bitter setbacks on more than one occasion when their operatives were seized in occupied countries and induced to send back deceptive radio messages scripted by the Germans. Negligence by British officers was partly to blame, but they did not conspire to cause those disasters. If Abwehr officers contributed to the success of MI5's Double Cross system, it was most likely through sheer carelessness or their stubborn refusal to admit the possibility that they were being fooled by the enemy.

Conspiracies were often suspected but seldom involved when drastic wartime intelligence breakdowns occurred, such as the American failure to anticipate the Japanese attack on Pearl Harbor. Popov himself traveled to the U.S. in the summer of 1941, with evidence suggesting that such an attack might soon take place, only to meet with skepticism from intelligence officers who were on the lookout for enemy agents operating on American soil but not yet fully alert to the threat posed by enemy forces within striking distance of American territory.

SPIES IN AMERICA

The U.S. entered the war officially in December 1941 after being attacked by Japan. But by then, the U.S. Navy was already supporting Britain against Germany by guarding merchant ships destined for British ports from U-boat attacks. The Anglo-American military alliance was concluded at the highest level, through personal diplomacy between Prime Minister Churchill and President Franklin D. Roosevelt. Before those leaders first conferred aboard the cruiser USS *Augusta* off Newfoundland in August 1941, however, the foundation for a

"Strategy, without information upon which it can rely, is helpless. Likewise, information is useless unless it is intelligently directed to the strategic purpose."

WILLIAM DONOVAN IN A 1941 REPORT TO FDR ON STRATEGIC INTELLIGENCE

transatlantic strategic partnership was laid by two dynamic spymasters—William Stephenson of MI6, the British security chief in America, and William Donovan, future founder of the Office of Strategic Services (OSS).

Raised in a gritty Irish Catholic ward in Buffalo, New York, Donovan became a classmate of Roosevelt's at Columbia Law School, earned the Medal of Honor for gallantry in World

War I leading troops who called him "Wild Bill," and served as assistant attorney general in Washington before FDR called on him to gather intelligence and direct secret operations. His impressive résumé was rivaled if not surpassed by that of the Canadian-born Stephenson, a champion boxer who enlisted in the Royal Air Force (RAF) in 1917 and won the Distinguished Flying Cross, escaped from a German prisoner of war (POW) camp, invented a process for transmitting photographs over the airwaves, made a fortune as an industrialist, and spied on Hitler's rearmament program during business trips to Germany in the 1930s. When Stephenson arrived in New York City in June 1940 to oversee the British Security Coordination Office, his duties included thwarting German spies and their paid informants in America. According to Ian Fleming, a great admirer who may have exaggerated his exploits, Stephenson once tracked down a British sailor in New York who was selling information to the Germans that helped them target Allied convoys and killed the traitor with a karate chop to the neck. "There was overwhelming evidence against the seaman," Fleming remarked. "Killing him quickly perhaps saved hundreds of sailors' lives and precious supplies." Whatever the truth of the matter, Fleming viewed Stephenson as a real-life model for James Bond, equipped with a license to kill.

Stephenson had another covert assignment that was more significant for Britain strategically than his counterespionage. He was sent to America by Churchill to counter the political influence of isolationists in the America First movement and to help draw the U.S. into the war. Stephenson reached out to Donovan as a partner in that effort and helped him advance from one of Roosevelt's advisers on national security to the president's intelligence chief. In July 1940, Roosevelt sent Donovan to England to assess whether the British could hold out against the Germans. FDR was inclined to offer Churchill military aid, but many Americans feared entanglement in the European war and thought the British would be crushed unless they came to terms with Germany. Joseph Kennedy—U.S. ambassador to Britain and father of future president John F. Kennedy—favored appeasing Hitler and opposed Donovan's visit. But Stephenson assured London that Donovan was Roosevelt's "most trusted" adviser on the war, an overstatement that brought him royal treatment, including

brief meetings with King George VI and Churchill. Intelligence chiefs gave him top secret briefings based on breakthroughs by British cryptanalysts, who were cracking German codes. Impressed with British defiance and defenses, Donovan assured the president that American aid could help turn the tide in Europe. Columnist Walter Lippmann wrote that he "almost singlehandedly overcame the unmitigated defeatism which was paralyzing Washington."

Donovan was not working alone, however. The campaign for American military support was led by Churchill, who appealed personally to Roosevelt in writing and influenced him indirectly through Stephenson and Donovan, who became fast friends and cohorts known to acquaintances as Big Bill (for the taller, stouter Donovan) and Little Bill. In December 1940, after FDR gave the Royal Navy 50 old American destroyers in exchange for long-term leases to British bases in the Atlantic, the two Bills traveled together to England. They stopped along the way in Bermuda, where Stephenson showed an admiring Donovan how British agents opened, inspected, and resealed supposedly inviolable diplomatic pouches that were sent between Germany, Italy, and other European countries and their embassies in the Western Hemisphere on flying boats that docked in Bermuda to refuel. Then the two spymasters went on to London, where Churchill met at length with Donovan and discussed plans to conduct secret operations against the Germans around the Mediterranean using the SOE, which would serve as a model for Donovan's OSS. After their talk, Churchill sent word to British military commanders and intelligence officers that Donovan had "great influence with the President" and should be "taken fully into our confidence."

Donovan's influence at the White House was confirmed in mid-1941 when Roosevelt asked him to draw up a plan for a centralized strategic intelligence service. With input from Ian Fleming and his chief, British Admiral John Godfrey, Donovan proposed a service that would have access to intelligence acquired by the U.S. Army, Navy, and FBI—which was responsible for counterespionage—and would combine those findings with its own intelligence to inform the president of enemy plans and capabilities, and devise strategies for subverting, demoralizing, and defeating the enemy. "Strategy, without information upon which it can rely, is helpless," Donovan's report began. "Likewise, information is useless unless it is intelligently directed to the strategic purpose." Elements of his ambitious plan would later be incorporated in the OSS, founded in 1942, but powerful figures such as FBI Director J. Edgar Hoover and Army Chief of Staff George Marshall strongly objected to having Donovan meddle in their affairs. Roosevelt compromised by appointing him Coordinator of Information (COI), with whom other agencies were supposed to share intelligence, in return for which he would not interfere with their operations. His responsibilities were vague, but Stephenson expressed satisfaction on behalf of the British that "our man is in such a position of importance to our efforts."

Donovan was not really Stephenson's man any more than Roosevelt was Churchill's man. The president and his newly appointed COI favored an Anglo-American military alliance—which was well under way in the North Atlantic by late 1941—because they considered defeating Nazi Germany absolutely essential

(continued on page 50)

SPYING ON THE NORDEN BOMBSIGHT

To the architects of America's strategic bombing program, the Norden bombsight was a technological marvel that would allow high-altitude bombers to strike enemy targets with unprecedented precision. Secrecy was paramount. Reportedly, the bombardier carried the top secret sight under guard to his aircraft before takeoff and swore an oath, in the event of a crash landing, to shield the mechanism with his life. Designed by engineer Carl Norden, the sight contained a mechanical computer that combined such factors as the plane's speed and altitude to determine when bombs were to be released to hit the target. In tests under ideal conditions in the Nevada desert, half the bombs dropped landed within 75 feet of the target from an altitude of 20,000 feet, close enough to damage or destroy large strategic objectives like enemy factories.

Despite security precautions, plans for the Norden found their way into the hands of German agents. In 1938, Hermann Lang, a German-born machinist employed by Norden's firm and a member of the so-called Duquesne spy ring in America, passed drawings of individual components to Abwehr officer Nikolaus Ritter, who traveled to New York to handle the case. Ritter later brought Lang to Berlin to reconstruct drawings of missing components, which the Carl Zeiss firm then used to improve the Luftwaffe's Lotfernrohr 7C bombsight. In actual combat, however, the often cloudy weather over northern Europe and unpredictable high-altitude winds severely reduced the accuracy of the Norden and the similar Luftwaffe bombsight. ☉

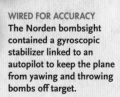

WIRED FOR ACCURACY
The Norden bombsight contained a gyroscopic stabilizer linked to an autopilot to keep the plane from yawing and throwing bombs off target.

FDR'S SECRET WAR

Franklin Delano Roosevelt was a secretive man who seldom revealed his true feelings and often disguised his intentions. As he said soon after the U.S. entered the global struggle against the Axis, "I am perfectly willing to mislead and tell untruths if it will help me win the war." That was his policy even before America joined the conflict. "I couldn't come out and say a war was coming," he told his son James, "because the people would have panicked and turned from me."

FDR firmly believed that America's fate was linked to that of its ally Great Britain and formed a close, confidential relationship with Winston Churchill that encouraged the president to nudge the U.S. toward war with Nazi Germany even as he publicly denied seeking conflict. Months before Churchill advanced from Lord of the Admiralty to become prime minister of embattled Britain in May 1940, Roosevelt initiated a secret correspondence with him. "You can always send sealed letters through your pouch or my pouch," he wrote. By the time the two leaders met at sea in August 1941 (below), they were united in their resolve to defeat Hitler. FDR considered American participation in that fight essential and inevitable, and began mobilizing the country for conflict not just by ordering the Navy to defend Atlantic sea lanes against U-boat attacks but

by publicizing potential German threats to the Americas. When Hitler's deputy, Rudolf Hess, flew away to Britain in May 1941, FDR wrote a letter (opposite) addressed to "former naval person"—his pet name for Churchill—urging him to keep the story "alive" in the press as long as possible and play up anything Hess might say "about the Americas" and Nazi intrigue there. In October, Roosevelt emphasized that menace in a speech he delivered on Navy Day. "I have in my possession a secret map," he declared, "made in Germany by Hitler's government . . . It is a map of South America and a part of Central America as Hitler proposes to reorganize it . . . The geographical experts of Berlin have ruthlessly obliterated all the existing boundaries; they have divided South America into five vassal states." Questions were later raised about that map (below, right), which was furnished by William Stephenson and may well have been forged. If FDR suspected as much, he was willing "to mislead and tell untruths" to prevent what he truly feared might happen if the British were defeated and the U.S. remained passive, allowing Hitler to spread terror across the Atlantic. ✪

PEN PALS FDR and Churchill, meeting here in 1941, exchanged notes like the one opposite concerning Rudolf Hess, which was routed through the American Embassy in London. British spymaster Stephenson provided Roosevelt with the map at right, depicting Nazi designs on South America and air routes.

SECRET

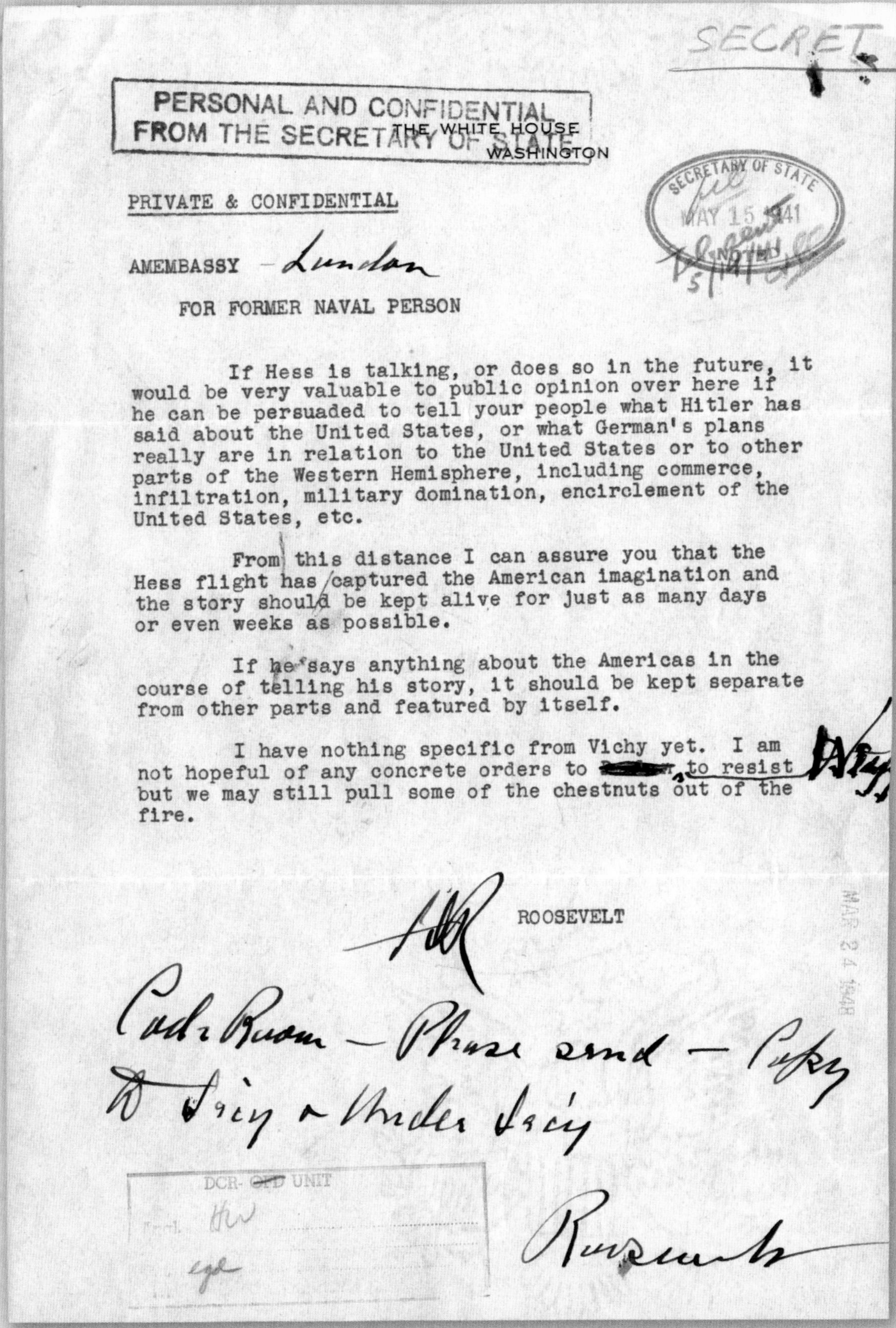

PERSONAL AND CONFIDENTIAL
FROM THE SECRETARY OF STATE

THE WHITE HOUSE
WASHINGTON

SECRETARY OF STATE
MAY 15 1941

PRIVATE & CONFIDENTIAL

AMEMBASSY – London

FOR FORMER NAVAL PERSON

If Hess is talking, or does so in the future, it would be very valuable to public opinion over here if he can be persuaded to tell your people what Hitler has said about the United States, or what German's plans really are in relation to the United States or to other parts of the Western Hemisphere, including commerce, infiltration, military domination, encirclement of the United States, etc.

From this distance I can assure you that the Hess flight has captured the American imagination and the story should be kept alive for just as many days or even weeks as possible.

If he says anything about the Americas in the course of telling his story, it should be kept separate from other parts and featured by itself.

I have nothing specific from Vichy yet. I am not hopeful of any concrete orders to [redacted], to resist but we may still pull some of the chestnuts out of the fire.

FDR ROOSEVELT

Code Room – Phrase and – Copy to Secy & Under Secy

DCR- UNIT

Roosevelt

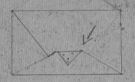

to American security. But they knew that American and British interests did not always coincide and that their transatlantic partners were not yet prepared to share with the U.S. everything they gleaned through code breaking and espionage. "Are we going to throw all our secrets into the American lap?" Churchill asked an aide before the U.S. officially joined the war. "It would be very much better to go slow, as we have more to give than they."

Nonetheless, Stephenson and MI6 shared secrets with Donovan more freely than the FBI and other American agencies did. And MI5 sent Dusko Popov to the U.S. with a document that could have helped alert American commanders to a dire threat had they possessed an overarching intelligence service of the sort Donovan envisioned—one capable of weighing all such evidence and providing clear and timely warnings of enemy intentions.

Popov arrived in the U.S. in August 1941, having been sent there by the Abwehr to organize a spy ring and gather military intelligence for the Germans—a trip welcomed by MI5 and the Twenty Committee, which hoped to exploit Popov's assignment by further deceiving the enemy. Popov brought with him a long list of questions, supplied by his Abwehr handlers and concealed on microdots, which German technicians produced by photographing documents with a camera equipped with a lens that functioned as a microscope in reverse, reducing a full page of text so that it fit within a dot no larger than a period in type. Easily concealed, microdots could be read through a conventional microscope and constituted a significant advance in spycraft over invisible ink. German microdot technology was of interest to British intelligence officers, but they found the content of Popov's questionnaire even more revealing. Roughly a third of the questions related to Pearl Harbor, where the U.S. Pacific Fleet was based. That target was beyond the range of either the small German surface fleet or the more formidable German U-boat fleet. The only Axis nation with a navy capable of attacking Pearl Harbor was Japan.

MICRO-MESSAGES The round handle of the latchkey at top could be unfastened to hide a microdot, which when placed on a slide like the one above and viewed through a microscope revealed an entire page of text. MI5 double agent Dusko Popov received messages on microdots from the Abwehr and notified a subagent of his code-named Balloon that he too would receive microdots stuck inside an envelope, as sketched here in a note from Popov using his German code name Ivan. Like Popov, Balloon was in fact working for the British, but Popov addressed him as one Abwehr spy communicating with another.

Popov could not operate as a spy in the U.S., even as a double agent working against the Germans, without the consent of counterespionage chief Hoover and his FBI, which had Popov under surveillance. He hoped to gain Hoover's gratitude and cooperation by revealing the microdots and their contents to him, but their meeting did not go well. According to a colorful account of his wartime adventures that Popov published in later years, Hoover greeted him with a scowl so menacing he looked like a "sledgehammer in search of an anvil." Fully informed of Popov's ongoing romance with film actress Simone Simon, with whom he had recently visited Miami, Hoover accused him of violating a federal statute called the Mann Act by crossing state lines with a woman for illicit purposes. Popov's explanation that posing as a playboy provided him with cover for espionage failed to soothe Hoover, whose suspicions about the double agent extended to the German questionnaire he provided. "It all looks too precise, too complete, to be believed," Hoover remarked by Popov's account. Hoover was more interested in the microdot technology employed by the Germans—and passed that information along to President Roosevelt without mentioning the contents of the questionnaire. Hoover later published a misleading article in *Reader's Digest,* claiming that he and his agents obtained the microdots by searching a German spy they caught, identified as the "playboy son of a millionaire."

Popov, in his account, was no less dismissive of Hoover, stating that by ignoring the questionnaire, he handed the Axis "a victory of incalculable proportions." Looking back on this episode years later, Twenty Committee chairman John Masterman reached a similar conclusion, stating that "the questionnaire indicated very clearly that in the event of the United States being at war, Pearl Harbour would be the first point to be attacked, and that plans for this attack had reached an advanced state by August 1941." Yet clues as to enemy intentions often appeared more obvious to analysts after an attack than beforehand. Hoover passed the questionnaire along to U.S. Army and Navy intelligence officers, and they did not infer that an attack on Pearl Harbor was imminent. As war loomed, commanders often sought information on enemy assets and targets that they did not end up attacking. Popov's questionnaire was just one suggestive piece in a puzzle that no single agency was able to solve at a time when American intelligence gathering was highly compartmentalized. Theoretically, coordinating and assessing information relating to national security was Donovan's job, but the FBI and armed services shared so little of significance with him in the months leading up to the attack on Pearl Harbor that he could hardly be blamed afterward.

Popov derided Hoover for snooping on him, but the FBI director had reason to be suspicious of a double agent who was not his man and, for all he knew, might be serving the Germans despite his professed loyalty to the British. Hoover trusted only those spies he controlled and kept on a short leash. One such agent, William Sebold—who had left Germany as a young man to work in the U.S. and obtained American citizenship—fell into Hoover's net after traveling in 1939 to Hamburg, where Abwehr officer Nikolaus Ritter pressured him to spy on the U.S. under threat of imprisonment. Sebold agreed but informed U.S. consular officials of Ritter's plans for him and was met by FBI agents when he returned to America. Hoover had leverage over Sebold—who risked being tried and executed for treason if he failed to cooperate—but assigned a man to live with him and follow his every step to make sure he toed the line. Meanwhile, the FBI rigged the office in Manhattan where Sebold met with other Abwehr agents, who were

(continued on page 54)

"It all looks too precise, too complete, to be believed."

FBI DIRECTOR J. EDGAR HOOVER, UPON REVIEWING POPOV'S QUESTIONNAIRE

Translation

Naval Information. Reports on enemy shipments (material foodstuffs - combination of convoys, if possible with names of ships and speeds).

Assembly of troops for oversea transports in U.S.A. and Canada. Strength - number of ships - ports of assembly - reports on ship building (naval and merchant ships) - wharves (dockyards) - state and privately owned wharves - new works - list of ships being built or resp. having been ordered - times of building.

Reports regarding U.S.A. strong points of all descriptions especially in Florida - organisation of strong points for fast boats (E-boats) and their depot ships - coastal defense - organisation districts -

Hawaii:
1) Ammunition dumps and mine depots. Details about the naval ammunition and mine depot on the Isle of Kushua (Pearl Harbor). If possible sketch.
2) Naval ammunition depot Lualuelei. Exact position? Is there a railway line (junction)?
3) The total ammunition reserve of the army is supposed to be in the rock of the Crater Aliamanu. Position?
4) Is the Crater Punckbowl (Honolulu) being used as ammunition dump? If not, are there other military works?

Aerodromes:
1) Aerodrome Lukefield: Details (sketch if possible) regarding the situation of the hangars (number?), workshops, bomb depots and petrol depots. Are there underground petrol installations? Exact position of the seaplane station? Occupation?
2) Naval air arm strong point Kaneohe: Exact report regarding position, number of hangars, depots and workshops (sketch). Occupation?
3) Army aerodromes Wicham Field and Wheeler Field. Exact position? Reports regarding number of hangars, depots and workshops. Underground installations? (Sketch).
4) Rodger's Airport: In case of war, will this place be taken over by the army or the navy? What preparations have been made? Number of hangars? Are there landing possibilities for seaplanes?
5) Airport of the Panamerican Airways: Exact position? (If possible sketch). Is this airport possibly identical with Rodger's Airport or a part thereof? (A wireless station of the Panamerican Airways is on the Peninsula Mohapuu).

Naval strong point Pearl Harbor:
1) Exact details and sketch about the situation of the state wharf, of the pier installations, workshops, petrol installations, situation of dry dock No. 1 and of the new dry dock which is being built?
2) Details about the submarine station (plan of situation). What land installations are in existence?

WAR WARNINGS **Before flying to America in August 1941, Popov received a questionnaire from the Abwehr seeking information about defenses at Pearl Harbor, attacked by Germany's ally Japan on December 7, 1941. Concealed on microdots, the questionnaire was translated by the British, who produced this top secret transcript, covering several pages. Queries regarding air bases at Pearl Harbor and "torpedo protection nets" for U.S. warships aroused little concern among American officials.**

THE WARTIME CARTOONS OF DR. SEUSS

Before Theodor Geisel, better known as Dr. Seuss, won fame as an author and illustrator of children's books, he practiced his craft as a political cartoonist. Many of his cartoons appeared in the magazine *PM* (inset) beginning in early 1941, when opposition to entering the war was widespread among Americans, including some who were openly or secretly pro-Nazi. An interventionist who despised Hitler and his ilk, Geisel skewered prominent isolationists like aviator Charles Lindbergh, who visited Nazi Germany and praised its "organized vitality" under "dictatorial direction."

Geisel's sympathy for Jews targeted by the Nazis and African Americans subject to discrimination did not extend to Japanese Americans, whom he grossly misrepresented in early 1942 as fifth columnists (covert enemy sympathizers), awaiting a "signal from home" to launch acts of sabotage—a jaundiced view shared by government officials who interned Japanese Americans as enemy aliens. Yet many of Geisel's other cartoon figures were drawn with a wry sense of humor, including his isolationist ostrich and American eagle, puffed up with pride after finding the guts to "punch Hitler in the snoot." Such playful images foreshadowed later Dr. Seuss illustrations that delighted the children of those who waged the war he supported and defeated the fascists he lambasted. ✪

WAR WORK Cartoons by Dr. Seuss ranged from scathing portraits of Axis brutality to sarcastic views of bumbling fascists, including a Nazi riding a mini-sub to meet a collaborator, French Adm. Jean Darlan.

RETALIATION

'To my secret meeting with Admiral Darlan in the duck pond in Central Park!'

By Dr. Seuss

Mein Early Kampf   by Adolf Hitler

June 5, 1889
I reject milk from Holstein cows as Non-Aryan

Waiting for the Signal From Home . . .

WASHINGTON
OREGON
Honorable 5th Column
CALIFORNIA

I WAS WEAK AND RUN-DOWN

I had circles under my eyes. My tail drooped. I had a foul case of Appeasement . . . .

. . . THEN I LEARNED ABOUT

"GUTS"

that amazing remedy
For all Mankind's Woes

NOW

I AM TAKING IT DAILY
and today

BEFORE

I FEEL STRONG
ENOUGH TO

AFTER

PUNCH MISTER HITLER RIGHT IN THE SNOOT!

"Only God can make a tree
To furnish sport for you and me!"

The Old Run-Around

U.S. WAR INDUSTRIES

NEGRO JOB-HUNTERS ENTER HERE

recorded and caught on camera. Among them was Frederick "Fritz" Duquesne, who had spied for Germany since the early 1900s and assumed numerous aliases and disguises over the years. Hoover scored his greatest coup as a spycatcher in late June 1941 when he arrested 33 German agents linked to Sebold, including Duquesne and Hermann Lang, a German immigrant who several years earlier had delivered to Ritter plans for the American-made Norden bombsight, which was then considered the most accurate device for delivering bombs on target. Not until 1940 did the British obtain the Norden bombsight for use against the Germans, a deal arranged by Stephenson through Donovan.

The Sebold sting put a damper on German espionage in America, but the U.S. remained under surveillance by agents of another foreign power notorious for snooping on allies and enemies alike—the Soviet Union, which sponsored an international communist movement from which many of its spies were drawn. Unlike Abwehr recruits in the U.S., who were mostly of German birth or ancestry, Americans spying for the Soviets often had no family ties to Russia and were hard to spot. Some believed that by divulging American secrets, they were fostering cooperation between their country and Mother Russia. That excuse became more credible when Hitler scrapped his nonaggression pact with Stalin and invaded the Soviet Union in June 1941, an offensive that led to SS atrocities far worse than those committed against Polish civilians in 1939. Soon the U.S. and U.S.S.R. were allied against the Axis, and Americans who served the Soviets could pretend that they were simply helping their friends. But once lured into the web of the GRU or NKVD—both of which ran spies in the U.S.—many found it hard to wriggle out. Some became committed Soviet operatives, who felt no shame in betraying their country because they had switched allegiance to Moscow.

ENEMY AGENT Josef Klein, pictured with his German shepherd and a shortwave radio set he built and operated as a German spy in the U.S., was one of 33 Abwehr agents nabbed by the FBI in 1941 with the help of double agent William Sebold. A mug shot of Klein appears opposite (third row from the top, second from left) in a gallery of the Duquesne Spy Ring, so named for its most notorious member, Fritz Duquesne.

One such convert to the Soviet cause was Martha Dodd, whose father, William Dodd, served as U.S. ambassador to Germany in the mid-1930s while she was in her 20s. After consorting with several prominent Nazis in Berlin, she grew disenchanted with their cause and fell passionately in love with Boris Vinogradov, an NKVD agent attached to the Soviet Embassy who had orders to recruit her. She hoped to marry him, but he was recalled to Moscow and executed during the Great Terror that Stalin launched in 1937. She never learned that he was a victim of the Soviet regime, and having offered herself to the NKVD under his influence, she remained faithful to the agency and the Communist Party thereafter. "It goes without saying that my services of any kind and at any time are proposed to the party for its use at its discretion," she wrote her NKVD

PAUL BANTE

MAX BLANK

ALFRED E. BROKHOFF

HEINRICH CLAUSING

CONRADINE DOLD

FREDERICK DUQUESNE

RUDOLPH EBELING

RICHARD EICHENLAUB

HEINRICH CARL EILERS

PAUL FEHSE

EDMUND CARL HEINE

FELIX JAHNKE

GUSTAVE KAERCHER

JOSEF KLEIN

HARTWIG KLEISS

HERMAN LANG

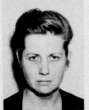
EVELYN CLAYTON LEWIS

RENE EMANUEL MEZENEN

CARL REUPER

EVERETT ROEDER

PAUL SCHOLZ

GEORGE GOTTLOB SCHUH

ERWIN WILHELM SIEGLER

OSCAR STABLER

HEINRICH STADE

LILLY STEIN

FRANZ JOSEPH STIGLER

ERICK STRUNK

LEO WAALEN

ADOLF WALISCHEWSKI

THE
33 CONVICTED MEMBERS
OF THE
DUQUESNE
SPY RING

ELSE WEUSTENFELD

AXEL WHEELER-HILL

BERTRAM W. ZENZINGER

MUG SHOTS German spies caught by the FBI included Fritz Duquesne (top right) and Hermann Lang (third row, third from right), who betrayed the Norden bombsight.

SECRET PREPARATIONS FOR INVASION

Adolf Hitler's directive of December 18, 1940, for Operation Barbarossa, the invasion of the Soviet Union, set in motion one of the most ambitious military operations in history. The plan called for 190 German divisions—approximately 3.3 million German soldiers—and an additional one million allied troops, mostly from Italy and Romania, to attack on a front nearly 1,000 miles long extending from the Baltic to the Black Sea. To prepare for that vast offensive, German intelligence agencies were tasked with secretly gathering information about Joseph Stalin's tightly veiled Soviet state.

While the Abwehr and SD conducted espionage, the intelligence staffs of the various armed forces gleaned what they could from open sources such as newspapers, journals, radio broadcasts, and government reports and speeches. The obsessive secrecy of Stalin's totalitarian state made it difficult to assess the accuracy of those open sources. All Russian news organs and publications were heavily controlled, and even maps were restricted. Reports on Soviet infrastructure—ports, cities, roads, and railways—often proved untrustworthy. To fill gaps in the emerging German intelligence picture of Russia, a covert Luftwaffe observation squadron flew long-range, high-altitude reconnaissance missions over Soviet territory using specially modified Dornier Do 17 aircraft and photographed airfields, railheads, and transportation systems.

As the fateful invasion loomed, German intelligence agencies published maps, guides, and reports covering the Soviet frontier and regions behind it. Those classified documents were disseminated to the headquarters of armies and divisions that would carry out the operation. Convinced that the Red Army and the Communist regime it served would easily fall before their vaunted war machine, Germans entered into the campaign in June 1941 expecting to achieve victory within a matter of months. That confidence crumbled when their advance stalled on the outskirts of Moscow as winter closed in and Stalin began drawing on deep reserves of Russian manpower and willpower that his foes failed to anticipate. ✪

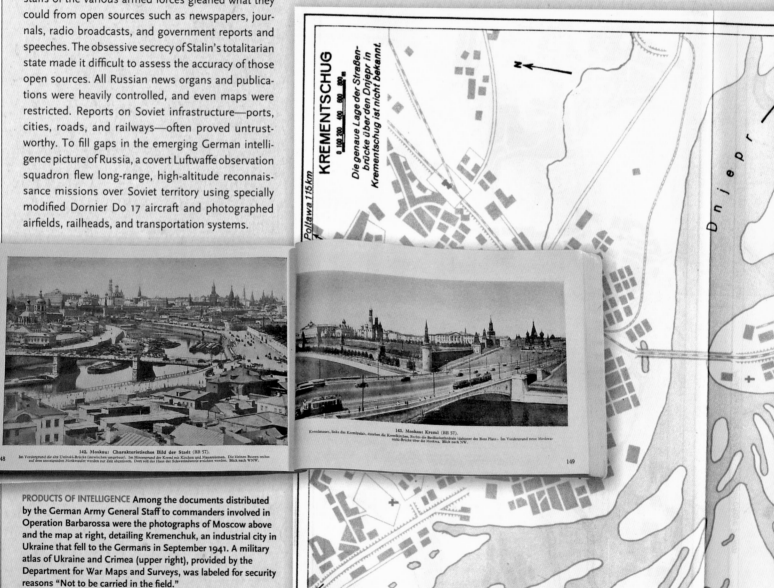

PRODUCTS OF INTELLIGENCE Among the documents distributed by the German Army General Staff to commanders involved in Operation Barbarossa were the photographs of Moscow above and the map at right, detailing Kremenchuk, an industrial city in Ukraine that fell to the Germans in September 1941. A military atlas of Ukraine and Crimea (upper right), provided by the Department for War Maps and Surveys, was labeled for security reasons "Not to be carried in the field."

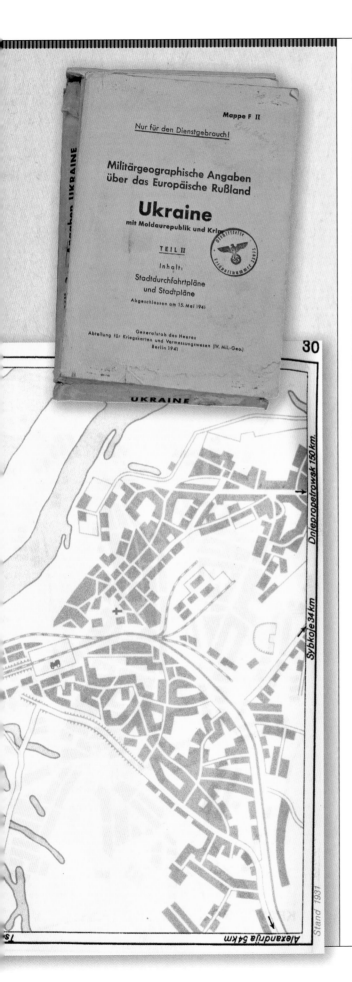

overseer when the State Department relieved her father as ambassador for denouncing Hitler. "Currently, I have access to the personal, confidential correspondence of my father with the U.S. State Department and the U.S. President," she added. If there was any particular American diplomat that Moscow favored as William Dodd's successor in Berlin, she promised, "I will persuade my father to promote his candidacy."

After returning to America with her father, Martha Dodd wed Alfred Stern, a New York millionaire, and eventually recruited him as a Soviet agent as well as her brother, William Dodd, Jr., who ran unsuccessfully for Congress with a secret $1,000 contribution from the NKVD. A source in the Justice Department later furnished him a report on J. Edgar Hoover that Dodd's Soviet handler then relayed to Moscow: "Hoover is keeping files on almost all major political figures: Congressmen, Senators and businessmen. He gathers compromising material on everybody and uses it for blackmail." Representatives who opposed full funding for the FBI, Moscow was told, risked having their sexual indiscretions disclosed by

"Tokyo Expects Hitler to Move Against Russia."

NEW YORK HERALD TRIBUNE HEADLINE, MAY 31, 1941

Hoover. The fact that the FBI director kept files on influential Americans—and sometimes used embarrassing information he acquired to pressure them—later became public knowledge. But during the Roosevelt administration, what William Dodd, Jr., revealed to the NKVD was only whispered about in Washington.

Hoover may not have learned about that particular disclosure, but he kept a close eye on would-be Congressman Dodd. The FBI investigated his communist activities in 1943, at which point the NKVD dropped him. Martha Dodd remained a Soviet agent until she and her husband were exposed in the 1950s. Like most spies, they were useful but not indispensable to those who employed them. Intelligence officers recruited scores of agents in the hope of finding one or two aces who could penetrate enemy defenses in depth and uncover secrets of the utmost significance. Those rare spies like Richard Sorge who mastered their deceptive craft and practiced it to the hilt could be worth more to their masters in wartime than an entire division of soldiers.

INTRIGUE IN TOKYO

On May 31, 1941, an article appeared in the *New York Herald Tribune* headlined "Tokyo Expects Hitler to Move Against Russia." Its author was Joseph Newman, the *Tribune*'s correspondent in Tokyo, but the unnamed source who provided Newman with his scoop was Sorge, who knew from

INVADERS' EMBLEMS Among the relics
of the calamitous German invasion of
the Soviet Union are these belt buckles
recovered on Russian ground, stamped
with a swastika (top), a German eagle,
and the lightning-strike insignia of the
Hitler Youth SS.

his Japanese informants and from German Ambassador Eugen Ott that the Wehrmacht would soon invade the Soviet Union. Sorge could not reveal that intelligence in his official role as a journalist, because the German press for which he worked was tightly controlled to prevent the disclosure of military secrets. And his covert attempts to alert Moscow to the German threat in his capacity as a GRU spy were dismissed by Stalin, who received many such warnings in the spring of 1941 and discounted them all. Morbidly suspicious, he thought rival powers such as Britain, America, and Japan were scheming to turn him against Hitler and push him into a war with Germany for which his Red Army was ill prepared—in part because he had eliminated many of its veteran officers in murderous purges during the 1930s. Such was his paranoia that he ignored an authoritative report that came from the very heart of the Reich by way of Ambassador Ott in Tokyo and his confidant Sorge, who signaled Moscow on May 30: "Berlin informed Ott that German attack will commence in latter part of June. Ott 95 percent certain war will commence."

When the German invasion occurred as predicted—on June 22, 1941—Stalin was staggered and revised his opinion of Sorge, whom he had earlier cursed for peddling foreign lies and propaganda. Sorge was now in a unique position to answer a question of enormous consequence not just for Stalin but for his foes in Berlin and his newfound friends in London and Washington: Which way would Japan turn? The Tripartite Pact that allied Japan with Germany and Italy in 1940 did not require the Japanese to join an offensive launched by the Germans, but Ott was urging officials in Tokyo to attack Russian forces in Siberia and earn a share of the spoils when the Soviet Union collapsed. Sorge exploited his credentials as a well-informed journalist to warn contacts in the Japanese military and Foreign Ministry that the Germans were downplaying Soviet military power to lure Japan into the war. Meanwhile, his influential Japanese confederate, Hotsumi Ozaki, now a full-fledged member of Sorge's spy ring, learned that a consensus was emerging among the military chiefs who dominated the government to avoid challenging the Soviets unless they were about to be defeated by the Germans. "If the Red Army stops the Germans short of Moscow," Sorge secretly reported in late July, "Japan will not make a move."

Sorge himself proved instrumental in stopping the Germans short of Moscow by providing Stalin with assurances he needed to shift numerous Soviet divisions and hundreds of tanks and warplanes away from Siberia, where they were guarding against a Japanese attack, to defend the Russian capital. That redeployment began after Sorge disclosed that instead of invading Russia, Japan would soon launch a sweeping offensive in Southeast Asia and the Pacific that would include assaults on British and American bases. Japan's "war with the United States," he informed Moscow in early October, "will begin in the near future, this month or next."

When that explosive conflict erupted at Pearl Harbor on December 7, Soviet forces bolstered by reinforcements from Siberia were driving German troops back from the outskirts of Moscow. Sorge was not at liberty to celebrate his notable contribution to Russia's military resurgence. On October 18, he had been arrested by agents of the Tokko, a secret police force responsible for tracking down spies and subversives. Hotsumi Ozaki and others in the spy ring were hauled in around the same time. After confessing to espionage under duress, Sorge was visited in prison by Ambassador Ott. Mitsusada Yoshikawa, the officer

who rounded up the spy ring and interrogated Sorge, noticed that he seemed reluctant to face Ott after deceiving him. Their "political opinions differed," Sorge remarked, but they were "personally good friends." Like a great actor, Sorge had not simply posed as Ott's confidant. He had thrown himself into that role so completely that he truly befriended the ambassador, who tolerated his anti-Nazi outbursts and harbored doubts of his own about Hitler's agenda. "I don't like this war any more than you do," he told Sorge as German forces bogged down in Russia, "but what can I do?"

Sorge seemed so distraught after that final meeting with Ott in prison that Yoshikawa feared he might commit suicide and had him watched. In the end, his divided heritage as the child of a German father and a Russian mother made him both an exceptional spy and a lost soul, with no country to call his own. There was bitter irony in the fact that a German official he betrayed took the trouble to visit and ask after him while the Soviets he served at the cost of his life disclaimed any responsibility for him. The Japanese long delayed carrying out Sorge's death sentence, hoping to trade him for one of their own agents in Russian custody. "Three times we proposed to the Soviet Embassy in Tokyo that Sorge be exchanged for a Japanese prisoner," Maj. Gen. Kyoji Tominaga said after Sorge was executed in November 1944. "Three times we got the same answer: 'The man called Richard Sorge is unknown to us.'"

LOST AND RECOVERED Dejected Russian prisoners lie in the rubble of Sevastopol, a strategic Black Sea port captured by the Germans in 1942. Despite intelligence from Sorge that helped Stalin reinforce Moscow and push the invaders back from the capital in December 1941, Soviet troops suffered costly defeats elsewhere in Russia the following year before besieging their foes at Stalingrad in late 1942 and ultimately recovering Sevastopol and other lost ground.

THE GLOBAL NEED FOR SECRECY

Keeping secrets and maintaining security became pressing concerns in many countries as World War II ignited in Europe and spread like fire around the globe. Agencies ranging from the Office of War Information in Washington to the Propaganda Ministry in Berlin commissioned talented artists to produce posters like those shown here and on the following pages, many of which warned people against speaking carelessly in the possible presence of enemy spies or informants. Idle remarks, the posters cautioned, could transform otherwise patriotic citizens into unwitting collaborators whose loose lips could sink ships and send soldiers to their doom.

Some artists designed alluring images that discouraged viewers from making indiscreet comments without trying to scare them, but the most conspicuous posters were ominous and menacing, revealing the dark side of the wartime obsession with national security. People had to watch what they said because they were being watched, not just by spies but also by agents of their own government responsible for guarding secrets. Such surveillance was especially strict in totalitarian states like Nazi Germany, where block wardens reported to the Gestapo people who made careless or unpatriotic remarks. Civilians often came under similar scrutiny from neighbors, police, or security forces in Italy, Japan, and the Soviet Union. But even in democratic nations where freedom of speech was cherished and protected under the law, war posters pointed accusing fingers at those who spoke too freely. Such images warned implicitly that those who violated the wartime code of silence and divulged secrets risked being exposed and called to account by their fellow citizens, if not by watchful authorities. ✪

SILENCERS The warning from Uncle Sam in the American poster at lower left is echoed in Russian at lower right and in German opposite, where an antiaircraft gunner demands silence *("Schweig!")*. In Nazi Germany and the Soviet Union, penalties for those in the know who did not keep their lips sealed could be severe.

SOMEONE MAY BE LISTENING

ENEMY EAVESDROPPERS
German posters above and at far left warn that anything said in public might be overheard by an enemy *(feind)* or spies *(spione)*. A similar message issued in France (near left) cautions that a seemingly innocent bystander in whom one confides could be an enemy agent. A poster made in the United States portrays a helmeted Nazi spying on Americans (above left), and another crafted in Britain shows a German officer assuming the guise of a civilian (opposite) to trick people into sharing secrets with him.

GRAPHIC WARNINGS

LOOSE LIPS MIGHT Sink Ships

QUIET!

LOOSE TALK CAN COST LIVES

DISTRIBUTED IN THE INTEREST OF NATIONAL DEFENSE, AND AS A MEANS OF OBTAINING FUNDS FOR AMBULANCES WHEREVER NEEDED. BRITISH AND AMERICAN AMBULANCE CORPS, INC., 450 LEXINGTON AVENUE, NEW YORK CITY

RISKY DISCLOSURES Artists came up with many ways to drive home the danger of divulging critical war information, including a fresh take on the old warning about loose lips (above), a comic view of a tattler being muzzled by the long arm of Uncle Sam, and a sentimental depiction of a dog mourning a sailor doomed by a thoughtless remark. Other posters opposite portray those who made reckless disclosures as accessories to murder or collaborators playing into the enemy's hand, shown offering Germany's prized Iron Cross, inscribed with a swastika, to those who aided Hitler with their "careless talk."

DIARY

DON'T keep a diary
it might get into the enemy's hands

...because somebody talked!

WANTED!

FOR MURDER

Her careless talk costs lives

AWARD

FOR CARELESS TALK

DON'T DISCUSS TROOP MOVEMENTS · SHIP SAILINGS · WAR EQUIPMENT

TELLING *a friend may*

mean telling THE ENEMY

BITS OF CARELESS TALK
ARE PIECED TOGETHER BY THE ENEMY

Convoy sails for England tonight

DIRE CONSEQUENCES

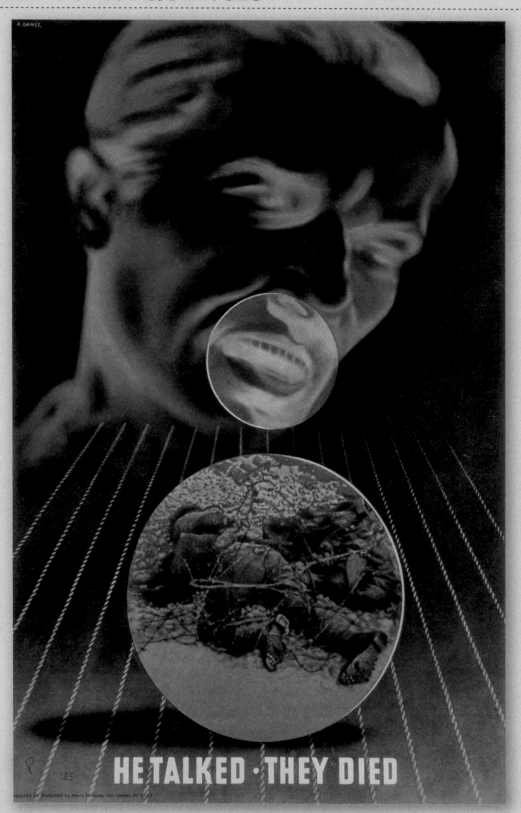

HE TALKED · THEY DIED

CONDEMNED BY CHATTERERS
Two riveting posters depict a fallen soldier and a drowning sailor (opposite) as victims of loose talk. Such alarming images played on the guilt civilians felt about remaining safe at home while those in uniform were risking their lives in battle and reinforced wartime codes of silence and secrecy that discouraged people who did war work from confiding too freely in others.

DAY OF INFAMY Pearl Har
comes under assault on S
December 7, 1941. Althou
deciphered Japanese mes
warned of hostilities, U.S
here were caught by surp

SURPRISE ATTACKS IN THE PACIFIC

fficers gathering military intelligence acquired new tools in the 20th century as technology advanced, but their objective was the same as ever, summed up by the time-honored maxim: "Know your enemy." Few Japanese commanders knew America better as war approached in the Pacific in 1941 than 57-year-old Adm. Isoroku Yamamoto. He had twice visited the United States, first as a staff officer studying English and later as a naval attaché at the Japanese Embassy in Washington, where his duties included monitoring developments in the U.S. Navy and American industry. Some military attachés engaged in espionage at the risk of being caught and expelled, but Yamamoto's surveillance was transparent and tolerated by American authorities because they did not want restrictions placed on their own attachés in foreign nations. A keen observer could learn more about his host country through authorized channels—including meeting with other officers, attending air shows and military reviews, touring factories, and reading newspapers and technical journals—than some spies learned working undercover.

Altogether, Yamamoto spent nearly four years in the U.S. between the two World Wars and came away with a healthy respect for its military and industrial capacity. Unlike some Japanese who considered Americans soft and lacking in resolve, he knew otherwise. "It is a mistake to regard Americans as

MASTERMIND A former naval attaché in Washington, Adm. Isoroku Yamamoto (opposite) commanded Japan's Combined Fleet and made headlines with his attack on Pearl Harbor.

||||||||||| **CHRONOLOGY** |||||||||||

CARNAGE IN CHINA This photo of a bloodied infant in a Shanghai railway station bombed by the Japanese in 1937 shocked Americans, who grew increasingly opposed to Japan as its punishing invasion of China continued.

luxury-loving and weak," he told former classmates at a reunion in his hometown of Nagaoka in September 1941. "I can tell you that they are full of spirit, adventure, fight, and justice. Their thinking is scientific and well advanced . . . Remember that American industry is much more developed than ours, and—unlike us—they have all the oil they want. Japan cannot vanquish the United States. Therefore we should not fight the United States."

What Yamamoto did not say—and could not reveal for reasons of national security—was that Japan was preparing for war with the U.S. and that he himself, as commander in chief of the Combined Fleet, was plotting a surprise attack on the Pacific Fleet at Pearl Harbor. Yet he was sincere when he warned against challenging America. He had offered a similar warning to his country's prime minister, Prince Fumimaro Konoe, after Japan concluded the Tripartite Pact with Germany and Italy in late 1940. If Japan ended up at war with the U.S. and its allies, Yamamoto said, his fleet would "run wild for the first six months or a year, but I have utterly no confidence for the second or third year."

Emperor Hirohito had similar concerns about a prolonged conflict, and negotiations to avert war with the U.S. continued until late 1941. But hopes for a settlement dwindled after Japanese troops—already involved in a brutal war in China—occupied all of French Indochina in July and President Roosevelt responded by imposing an oil embargo on Japan. Reluctant to bow to American demands that it withdraw its invasion forces from China and Indochina, Japanese chiefs made plans to secure oil and other strategic resources by seizing vulnerable British and Dutch colonies in Southeast Asia and the Pacific as well as the Philippines, an American protectorate that lay within the zone Japan intended to occupy. If conflict with the U.S. could not be avoided, Yamamoto hoped to smash the Pacific Fleet before it posed a threat to Japanese forces engaged in that planned offensive or Japanese civilians in the home islands.

Yamamoto had to maintain strict secrecy while assembling a formidable strike force that included battleships, cruisers, destroyers, oil tankers to refuel the ships as they advanced across the North Pacific—and six big aircraft carriers that would launch more than 400 warplanes against Pearl Harbor. The risk that such a buildup might be detected was considerable, for the U.S. had intelligence assets around the Pacific, including military attachés in Tokyo who were as diligent in sizing up Japan as Yamamoto was in assessing America. Since the early 1920s, promising American officers had been sent to Japan to study the language there. Some of those language officers became cryptanalysts who worked to decode Japanese military signals that were sent by radio and picked up at American listening stations in Hawaii, the Philippines, and elsewhere. Others served as attachés at the U.S. Embassy in Tokyo, where they came under surveillance as tensions between Japan and America increased. At one point, a large vehicle with curtains on its windows parked across from the embassy in Tokyo and remained there. A press photographer approached that suspected "spy wagon" and was shooed away by Japanese agents who emerged from the van in their underwear, having stripped down because it was so hot inside.

Despite being watched, American attachés acquired much useful intelligence in Japan, often by sharing notes with those on similar assignments from other nations. A prewar group of naval attachés formed a club—whose members came from countries that would soon be allied with Japan like Germany and Italy as well as from rival nations like the U.S., Britain, and Russia—and met periodically for lunch in Tokyo to share what they knew or suspected about Japanese naval developments, including the construction of superbattleships that far exceeded the 35,000-ton limit set by an international treaty that Japan renounced. In the late 1930s, an American naval attaché in Tokyo informed Washington that Japan was constructing two such superbattleships and was "planning to lay down a third and possibly a fourth."

Officials at the American Embassy also received tips from foreign diplomats, including the Peruvian ambassador in Tokyo, who in early 1941 passed along information he

LINE OF ATTACK This postwar American map derived from a Japanese original uses Tokyo time to chart the movement of the naval task force dispatched by Yamamoto as war loomed. Designated the First Air Fleet, it set out on November 26 (November 25 in the U.S.)—before talks in Washington to avert conflict had concluded—and bombed Pearl Harbor on December 7 (December 8 in Japan).

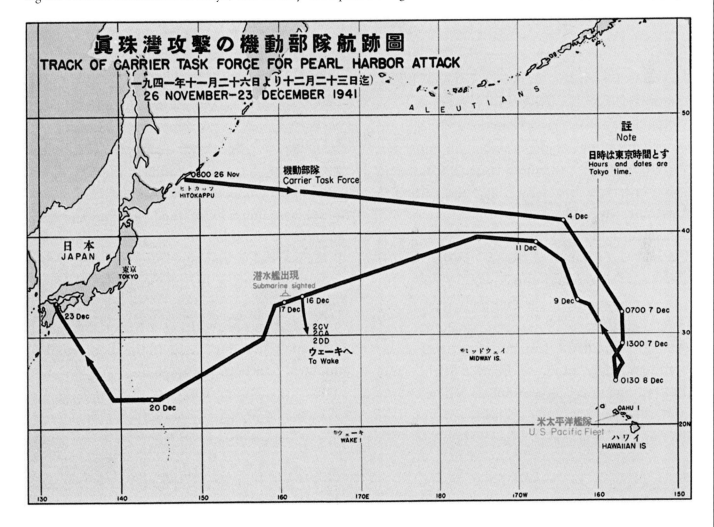

received from a Japanese employee that an attack on Pearl Harbor was being planned. U.S. Ambassador Joseph Grew and his naval attaché, Cmdr. Henri Smith-Hutton, had received such reports before and did not put much stock in this one, which received little

credence when they passed it along to Washington. As the year progressed, however, Smith-Hutton became convinced that Japan was preparing for a major offensive. He and other American intelligence officers predicted that Japanese forces would advance southward against British-ruled Singapore on the Malay Peninsula, the Dutch colonies of present-day Indonesia, and possibly the Philippines. But Smith-Hutton saw no signs that distant Pearl Harbor would be among the targets—a testament to Yamamoto's success in keeping his momentous operation under wraps.

The U.S. Navy compiled a dossier on Yamamoto, which indicated that he loved to gamble and might take risks that other commanders would shun. The confidence with which he played his hand helped him overcome opposition from Japanese officers who feared his attack might fail. But there was also a risk if he succeeded that irate Americans would spare no effort to rebuild their fleet and avenge the attack. Yamamoto's superior, Adm. Osami Nagano, chief of the Imperial Japanese Navy, had also spent several years in the U.S. and doubted that smashing the Pacific Fleet would stop America from striking back. "Even if our Empire should win a decisive naval victory," he warned in September 1941, "we will not thereby be able to bring the war to a conclusion. We can anticipate that America will attempt to prolong the war, utilizing her impregnable position, her superior industrial power, and her abundant resources." Japan, he concluded, did not have the means to make Americans "give up their will to fight."

Despite that bleak prognosis, Nagano approved Yamamoto's bold plan and thought it was better to fight America sooner rather than later when its armed forces were stronger. Unable to dissuade Japan's leaders from defying the U.S., Yamamoto sought to neutralize the Pacific Fleet and so demoralize Americans that they might come to terms. But by extending his nation's fateful offensive from the Philippines—which harbored U.S. troops but had been promised independence—to Hawaii, a territory permanently attached to America, he raised the stakes. If he did not force his foes to back down, hitting them close to home might make them more determined to recoup their losses and crush Japan.

For all the intelligence that astute Japanese observers like Yamamoto and their American counterparts acquired about each other before the war, they had little idea how their opponents would respond when challenged. American officials underestimated Japanese pride and determination when they applied economic pressure to induce Hirohito and his chiefs to abandon their imperial ambitions. And with few exceptions, U.S. officers failed to credit the Japanese military with the capacity to carry out an audacious offensive of epic proportions, extending from Southeast Asia to Hawaii, over 6,000 miles away. That intelligence failure was galling because American cryptanalysts had penetrated Japan's diplomatic communications and obtained evidence hinting at an attack on Pearl Harbor. But the setback would be temporary because they were beginning to unlock Japanese naval

JAPAN'S ENVOY Ambassador Kichisaburo Nomura (above) presented Japan's final peace proposal to Secretary of State Cordell Hull and President Roosevelt, who learned from decrypts of intercepted Japanese communications that leaders in Tokyo had set an ominous deadline of November 30 for a settlement.

"The deadline absolutely cannot be changed. After that things are automatically going to happen."

TOKYO'S DIRECTIVE TO AMBASSADOR NOMURA IN WASHINGTON

codes as well, which would allow U.S. commanders to read Yamamoto's plans as the war progressed and ultimately bring down that daring admiral.

COUNTDOWN TO CONFLICT

When Kichisaburo Nomura arrived in Washington in early 1941 to serve as Japan's ambassador there, he hoped to avert war with America and negotiate a settlement. A retired admiral who had preceded Yamamoto as a naval attaché in Washington, he became a celebrity of sorts when he was portrayed on the cover of *Time* magazine in September 1941 above the caption: "Japan's Nomura: Between a tough Army at home and a tough President in Washington." That was an apt description, for army chiefs in Tokyo were intent on war and insisted on deploying troops for battle in November 1941 even as Nomura presented peace proposals to a skeptical President Roosevelt and his tough secretary of state, Cordell Hull. They offered Nomura little encouragement and held back when he pressed them for a quick response. That was not because Roosevelt wanted war. As he told Churchill, conflict with Japan in the Pacific would be "the wrong war in the wrong ocean at the wrong time." But his qualms about negotiating increased when he received alarming decrypts—deciphered messages from Tokyo to Nomura and other diplomats, indicating that Japan was preparing to attack even as its ambassador in Washington held out an olive branch.

AXIS ALLIANCE Japanese-American relations deteriorated when officials in Tokyo endorsed the Tripartite Pact with Germany and Italy on September 27, 1940, and celebrated the agreement by toasting their Axis partners (above). Gen. Hideki Tojo, Japan's future prime minister and war leader, stands at center during the ceremony, flanked at far right by Eugen Ott, German ambassador to Japan, whose disclosures to Soviet spy Richard Sorge kept Moscow informed of Axis war plans.

THINK

NO ADMITTANCE

WASHINGTON'S WIZARDS U.S. Army code breakers led by William Friedman, standing at center here with his team, solved the Japanese cipher machine dubbed Purple and built the analog below to decipher its messages.

Roosevelt and Secretary Hull knew what Japan was offering—to refrain from further military advances and pull back some of its troops if the oil embargo was lifted—before Nomura presented those proposals. And they soon learned from decrypts that Japan had set a deadline of November 30 for a negotiated settlement. "The deadline absolutely cannot be changed," Nomura was informed by his superior in Tokyo. "After that things are automatically going to happen." Roosevelt feared that Japan might attack as soon as that deadline passed, and he was further alarmed by an intelligence report that may have come from the British, revealing that Japanese forces were already on the move. He concluded that making concessions to Japan under such pressure would amount to appeasement and encourage further aggression. On November 26, Hull declined the terms Nomura proposed but left the door open for a settlement if Japan agreed to withdraw its forces from China and Indochina by a date to be negotiated. Hideki Tojo—an army commander committed to imperial expansion who had recently become Japan's prime minister—dismissed the American response and sought permission to commence hostilities, which Hirohito granted him at a conference in Tokyo on December 1. Up until then, the naval strike force dispatched by Yamamoto under the command of Vice Adm. Chuichi Nagumo and other Japanese units heading for battle could have been recalled, but there was no stopping them now.

Roosevelt knew of Japan's ominous deadline

because American cryptanalysts had constructed an analog of the cipher machine used for Japanese diplomatic communications worldwide. That breakthrough, accomplished without any prior knowledge of the machine or its components, was achieved by a team headed by William Friedman of the U.S. Army's Signal Intelligence Service (SIS), aided by cryptanalysts from the Navy's code-breaking unit, OP-20-G. A geneticist by training who had taken up cryptography during World War I, Friedman helped transform code breaking from an art to a science, based on mathematical principles. Although the cipher machines devised for military use by the time the war began were so intricate that some considered them impenetrable by cryptanalysts, they substituted one letter or character for another in ways that were subject to mathematical analysis and other decryption techniques, which offered clues as to how such machines were designed and wired. They could be set to decipher an incoming message from senders using the same device. That made constructing an analog—which was not identical to the machine but duplicated its functions—of enormous value to intelligence officers, government officials, and military commanders.

The first Japanese diplomatic encryption device, introduced in the mid-1930s and known as the Red machine, was among several cipher machines in use then that contained one or more wheels that rotated like clockwork to alter how each successive letter or character in a message was enciphered. American cryptanalysts were familiar with such rotors and were further aided by the fact that the Red machine always substituted a vowel for a vowel and a consonant for a consonant. Not long after they solved that puzzle, however, Japan's Foreign Ministry introduced a new cipher machine, which the Americans dubbed Purple. For some time beginning in 1939, Japanese diplomatic messages were sent using both the Red and Purple machines for the benefit of those who had not yet received the new device. That overlap helped Friedman's team make headway with Purple, but its operating principles remained mysterious until they determined that it substituted one character for another using stepping switches like those designed to route telephone calls without going through operators at switchboards. Solving Purple and constructing an analog was a nerve-wracking challenge for Friedman, who suffered a breakdown as a result. But he and his wizards succeeded in 1940, and the top secret decrypts provided by their coup became known as Magic.

By 1941, Japanese diplomatic messages enciphered on Purple machines and transmitted by radio were being intercepted at far-flung American listening posts and relayed to Washington to be deciphered and translated. The workload was so heavy that OP-20-G shared the task with the SIS by producing decrypts in English on alternate days. Tokyo did not reveal specific military plans to its diplomats abroad, but some messages to embassies or consulates included requests for military intelligence that indicated possible Japanese targets as war loomed. In late September 1941, Nagao Kita, the Japanese consul general in Honolulu, received a message from Tokyo seeking information on U.S. Navy vessels at Pearl Harbor. "With regard to warships and aircraft carriers," it stated, "we would

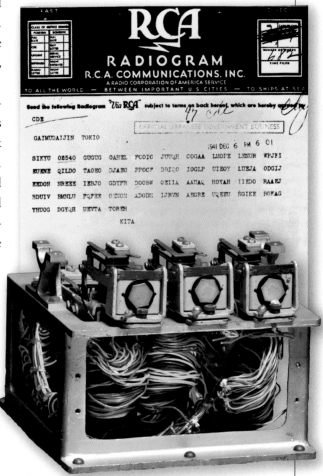

SIGNALING TOKYO The message at top from Nagao Kita, Japanese consul general in Honolulu, was encrypted on a Purple machine—whose circuits are shown above—and sent as a commercial radiogram on December 6, 1941, to alert Tokyo that much of the Pacific Fleet remained anchored at Pearl Harbor. The message was intercepted and deciphered, but it was not translated in Washington until after the attack.

DIPLOMATIC COVER Japanese naval officer Takeo Yoshikawa arrived under an assumed name in Honolulu in April 1941 to serve as a vice consul there and secretly report on the Pacific Fleet at Pearl Harbor. Following the attack on December 7, he was arrested along with others at the Japanese consulate by FBI agents but was later released in a diplomatic prisoner exchange.

like to have you report on those at anchor . . . tied up at wharves, buoys, and in docks. (Designate types and classes briefly . . . make mention of the fact when there are two or more vessels alongside the same wharf.)"

That message and other decrypts of military significance reached Adm. Harold Stark, chief of naval operations, and Gen. George Marshall, Army chief of staff, both of whom issued general warnings of possible Japanese attacks to commanders at Pearl Harbor and elsewhere in the Pacific. But they were careful not to mention details that might reveal the existence of Magic to Japanese listeners and code breakers. As it happened, the Japanese were unable to read U.S. military messages enciphered using SIGABA, a machine equipped with rotors that was developed jointly by SIS and OP-20-G. But American officers could not be certain their communications were inviolable. Because of those security concerns, neither Adm. Husband Kimmel, commander of the Pacific Fleet at Pearl Harbor, nor Lt. Gen. Walter Short, U.S. Army commander in Hawaii, had access to Magic. Not until after the attack in December did they learn of Tokyo's worrisome message to the Japanese consulate in September, which Short later described as "a bombing plan for Pearl Harbor."

Short and Kimmel would have been even more alarmed had they known the lengths to which Japanese agents went to fulfill Tokyo's request for information on Pearl Harbor. Chief among those spies was Takeo Yoshikawa, an ensign in the Imperial Japanese Navy who arrived at the consulate in Honolulu in April 1941 under the assumed name Tadashi Morimura. Although he was assigned by the Japanese naval intelligence agency known as the Third Bureau to conduct surveillance without breaking any laws and risking arrest, entering Hawaii under a false name and passport would have been sufficient grounds for American authorities to detain and interrogate Yoshikawa had they suspected him. He knew that the consulate in Honolulu was bugged by the FBI and did much of his spying from a Japanese tearoom overlooking Pearl Harbor. Yoshikawa picked up tips from geishas who entertained U.S. naval officers there but did not recruit Japanese Americans in Hawaii, whom he found "essentially loyal to the United States." A similar assessment of Japanese Americans living on the West Coast was contained in a confidential report President Roosevelt received in November 1941. "There is no Japanese 'problem' on the coast," it concluded, "there will be no armed uprising of Japanese." That did not stop Roosevelt from authorizing the internment of more than 100,000 Japanese Americans as enemy aliens after war was declared.

Yoshikawa's espionage intensified in early November when the Japanese liner *Taiyo Maru* arrived in Honolulu. The ship had taken a long route to Hawaii across the North Pacific to reconnoiter the stealthy path that the strike force dispatched by Yamamoto would follow a month later. Aboard was Lt. Cmdr. Suguru Suzuki, a naval aviation expert who hoped to survey Pearl Harbor's defenses personally but was urged by Consul General Kita to leave that sensitive task to Yoshikawa, who received a list of 97 questions on crumpled rice paper to be answered before the ship returned to Japan. Some were easy enough for the spy to handle. When asked on "what day of the week would the most ships be in Pearl Harbor on normal occasions?" he readily answered "Sunday." Other questions

(continued on page 82)

THE KUEHN FAMILY, GERMAN AGENTS IN HONOLULU

Takeo Yoshikawa was not the only one who spied on the Pacific Fleet as Japan prepared to attack Pearl Harbor. Also supplying intelligence on the fleet to the Japanese was Bernard Julius Otto Kuehn, aided by his wife Friedel and their adult daughter Susie Ruth. Otto, as he was known, was born in Germany in 1895 and joined the Nazi Party in 1930. His daughter later became involved with Propaganda Minister Joseph Goebbels, who had numerous extramarital affairs. Goebbels then proposed that the Kuehns serve the Reich by spying for Japan, a potential ally of Nazi Germany. After being indoctrinated in Japan, the family settled in Honolulu in 1935. Friedel Kuehn returned to Japan several times in years to come and received large amounts of cash in American dollars to support their intelligence gathering, which included lavish parties attended by American servicemen, with whom Susie Ruth fraternized. She also gleaned information on the comings and goings of the fleet by eavesdropping on officers' wives who frequented a beauty parlor she operated. When Otto Kuehn visited Pearl Harbor to reconnoiter, he took along his young son Hans, dressed in a sailor's suit to make the surveillance look like an innocent outing to admire warships.

By 1941, Japan was formally allied with Germany and Otto was sharing results of his family's espionage with the Japanese consulate in Honolulu. That proved dangerous because the Kuehns had drawn the attention of FBI agents and armed forces intelligence officers. They were closing in on Otto when he made his last contact with the consulate in early December. At that time, he submitted a list of ships at anchor in Pearl Harbor and proposed to alert Japanese submarines off Oahu to fleet movements with visual signals, including lights in the window of two houses he owned on the coast. Arrested soon after the attack on the seventh, he confessed and was then placed in a cell next to that of his wife, where their conversation was taped as she scolded him for confessing and incriminated herself in the process.

Otto Kuehn was convicted and condemned to death by firing squad, a sentence that was later commuted to 50 years' hard labor. His wife and daughter received lighter sentences. All three members of the Kuehn spy ring were eventually paroled and deported to postwar Germany. ⊗

NAME: OTTO KUEHN
SPIED FOR: JAPAN, GERMANY
SPIED AGAINST: UNITED STATES

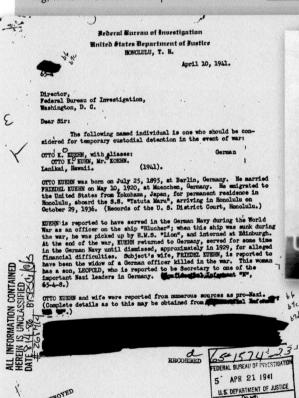

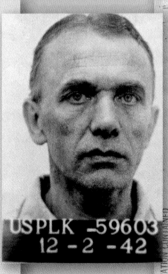

TRACKED DOWN Otto Kuehn (above) and his wife were arrested on December 8, 1941, as documented at right in an FBI memo. Eight months earlier, FBI Director Hoover had been notified in writing that the Kuehns were "pro-Nazi" (left).

CHARTING THE ATTACK

On December 1, 1941, in Tokyo, Emperor Hirohito gave the Imperial General Staff final authorization for war against the United States. Using the code words "Climb Mount Niitaka," Admiral Yamamoto signaled his First Air Fleet—which was already at sea and constituted the most powerful naval force in the Pacific—to proceed with his plan for a surprise attack on Pearl Harbor. Meticulous preparations had been under way since April, when Yamamoto gave the order to organize the First Air Fleet and his staff began fleshing out details of the operation, which included midget submarines assigned to enter the harbor and launch torpedoes. For the audacious plan to succeed, pilots and crewmen needed charts showing the location of warships of the U.S. Pacific Fleet. Such classified information was not indicated on commercial navigation charts like those obtained by Japanese naval attachés in Washington, but officers there helped track the Pacific Fleet by following announcements and press releases by the U.S. Navy and combing newspapers for notices of ships arriving and departing.

More precise intelligence on the situation at Pearl Harbor came from Japanese spies in Honolulu, notably Takeo Yoshikawa, and from naval listening posts located near Tokyo and on various Japanese-held islands. Those stations picked up radio transmissions from Pearl Harbor and used radio direction finding and signal analysis to pinpoint ships that were approaching or leaving the base. As the First Air Fleet neared its launching point off Hawaii, it maintained strict radio silence but carefully monitored incoming signals. A radio intelligence team on the *Akagi*—flagship of Vice Adm. Chuichi Nagumo, assigned by Yamamoto to command the strike force—received coded reports from Tokyo on what listening stations had detected and also picked up American naval communications and commercial broadcasts from Honolulu. By the time the six aircraft carriers of Nagumo's fleet turned into the wind to launch their warplanes, the pilots had been thoroughly briefed and provided with charts reflecting the most current Japanese naval intelligence on targets that would soon be within their sights. ✪

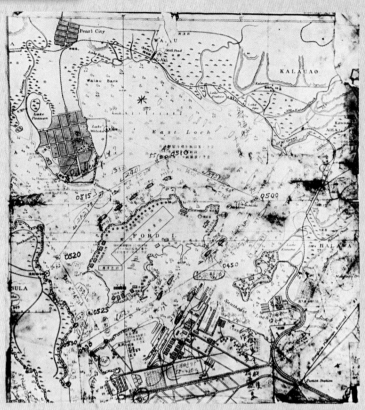

SUB'S CHART This map of Pearl Harbor, annotated with the locations of American warships, was recovered from the captured Japanese midget submarine *Ha-19*, which failed to enter the harbor as planned and was found beached on Oahu.

ALTERNATE ANCHORAGE Recovered from a Japanese aircraft shot down during the attack, this chart of Lahaina Roads anchorage off the island of Maui identifies mooring locations using a radial grid with sectors and distances from shore. The Japanese mapped this location in case some warships of the Pacific Fleet were anchored there on December 7.

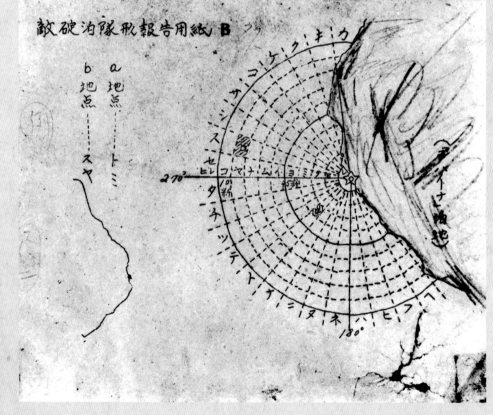

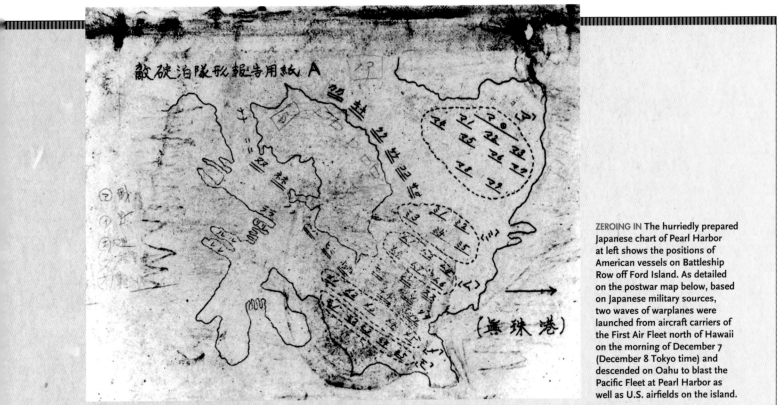

ZEROING IN The hurriedly prepared Japanese chart of Pearl Harbor at left shows the positions of American vessels on Battleship Row off Ford Island. As detailed on the postwar map below, based on Japanese military sources, two waves of warplanes were launched from aircraft carriers of the First Air Fleet north of Hawaii on the morning of December 7 (December 8 Tokyo time) and descended on Oahu to blast the Pacific Fleet at Pearl Harbor as well as U.S. airfields on the island.

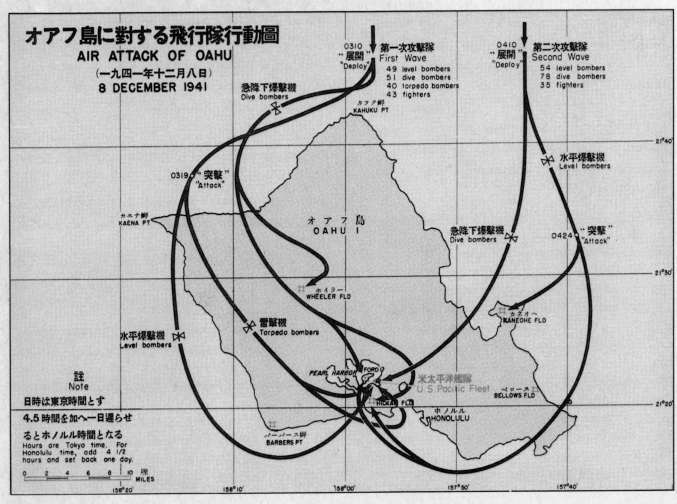

were harder to resolve. He was unable to determine if an antisubmarine net guarded the entrance to the harbor, but his naval superiors rightly concluded that such a barrier existed and added secret weapons to the attack—five two-man midget subs, small enough to slip in behind American ships when the net was raised, enter the shallow harbor, and fire two torpedoes. Suzuki headed home on the *Taiyo Maru* with maps and aerial photographs of Pearl Harbor, taken by Yoshikawa from a tourist plane.

After Emperor Hirohito authorized the Japanese offensive on December 1, coded messages exchanged between Tokyo and the Honolulu consulate indicated that an attack on Pearl Harbor was likely. Yoshikawa reported the departure from Pearl Harbor of the aircraft carriers U.S.S. *Enterprise* and U.S.S *Lexington*—bad news for Yamamoto, for those ships were the Pacific Fleet's chief assets along with a third carrier, U.S.S. *Saratoga,* which was in San Diego Harbor after being overhauled. Yoshikawa also informed Tokyo that battleships docked at Pearl Harbor were not shielded by torpedo nets and added that there was "considerable opportunity left to take advantage for a surprise attack." Those revealing messages were intercepted and deciphered, but they were not translated until after Pearl Harbor was attacked on Sunday, December 7.

Although leaders in Washington did not know where Japanese forces would strike, they

(continued on page 86)

MODELING THE ATTACK This large-scale model of Pearl Harbor was built after the attack for a Japanese propaganda film. American intelligence officers who later recovered the model initially thought it was used to plan aerial torpedo attacks in the shallow waters of Pearl Harbor, but that problem was solved by tests in Kagoshima Harbor, a Japanese naval base.

From: Tokyo
To : Washington
7 December 1941
(Purple-Eng)

#902   Part 14 of 14

(Note: In the forwarding instructions to the
radio station handling this part, appeared the
plain English phrase "VERY IMPORTANT")

7. Obviously it is the intention of the American
Government to conspire with Great Britain and other countries
to obstruct Japan's efforts toward the establishment of
peace through the creation of a New Order in East Asia,
and especially to preserve Anglo-American rights and interests
by keeping Japan and China at war.   This intention has
been revealed clearly during the course of the present
negotiations. Thus, the earnest hope of the Japanese
Government to adjust Japanese-American relations and to
preserve and promote the peace of the Pacific through
cooperation with the American Government has finally been
lost.

The Japanese Government regrets to have to notify
hereby the American Government that in view of the attitude
of the American Government it cannot but consider that it is
impossible to reach an agreement through further negotiations.

WAR SIGNALS Among the messages sent to signal the outbreak of war in the Pacific was part 14 of a long, ominous statement from Tokyo to Washington (left). Deciphered and translated just hours before the attack on Pearl Harbor, it said that Japan was breaking off talks with the U.S. and ending efforts to "adjust Japanese-American relations." A pilot involved in the attack carried the handmade leaflet below, showing ships exploding and conveying threats in Japanese and in English: "You damned! Go to the devil!" When incoming Japanese warplanes were spotted that morning by American reconnaissance pilots, their commander issued the warning at bottom: "Air raid on Pearl Harbor. This is no drill."

RA 12 TR 14 V AC   COMMANDER AIRCRAFT, SCOUTING FORCE

Heading: L Z F5L Ø71830 C8Q TART O

AIRRAID ON PEARL HARBOR X THIS IS NO DRILL

		ACTION	TT/1911/7 DEC/WU-PF			
Originator	Date-Time Gr. Ø71830	Date 7 DEC 41	System TT	Super PF	C.W.O.	Number 338
CINCPAC		Action ALL U S NAVY SHIPS PRESENT HAWAIIAN AREA		Info.		
Classification Precedence URGENT						

AD	CS	OP	FS	FLT	GUN	MAT	ENG	SUP	SDO			COM	ACO

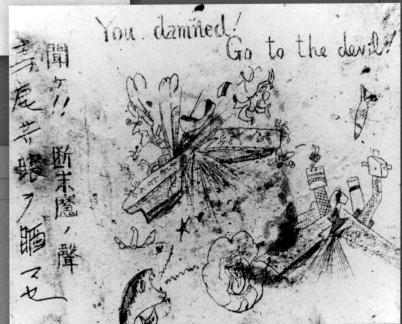

聞ケ!!
断末魔ノ聲
青鹿芒眼
ヲ晒マセ

You damned!
Go to the devil!

"Listen to the voice of doom.
Open your eyes, blind fools."

JAPANESE INSCRIPTION
ON THE LEAFLET ABOVE

CONFIDENTIAL VIEWS OF A SURPRISE ATTACK

Many photographs of the stunning Japanese assault on Pearl Harbor were not made public until long after the event. Some shots by press photographers of the mayhem on Battleship Row were withheld from publication because American officials considered them too demoralizing. Other images like the U.S. Navy photo of a stranded Japanese midget submarine assigned to the attack (opposite) were restricted for security reasons. The Japanese carefully documented their operation on film, not for publicity purposes but for official review and analysis afterward. Several of the pictures featured here were discovered in Japanese military archives as U.S. forces reclaimed ground lost to their foes and went on to occupy their homeland. These confidential views offer a more complete picture of the raid that ignited war in the Pacific than was available to civilians on either side during the conflict. ✪

WAR FILM In this frame from film shot by a Japanese motion-picture cameraman to document the attack, an officer briefs pilots aboard their aircraft carrier shortly before they took off for Pearl Harbor.

ARMED AND READY Among the warplanes pictured by Japanese military photographers as the operation unfolded on December 7 were dive-bombers revving up on one carrier (above) and a Mitsubishi Zero fighter lifting off from the *Akagi* (inset top right).

SET ABLAZE A Navy photographer standing on shore when the Pacific Fleet came under fire took this grim picture of black smoke billowing from the doomed battleship U.S.S. *Arizona* (center) and nearby airfields.

SECRET WEAPON The Japanese midget submarine *Ha-19*, which went aground soon after the attack, was one of five mini-subs, each carrying two men and one torpedo, assigned to enter Pearl Harbor and target warships there.

SITTING DUCKS Bombs strike targets on Battleship Row in a shot snapped by a Japanese aerial observer during the attack. Warships at Pearl Harbor were moored side by side, which shielded those landward from incoming torpedoes but left them exposed to falling bombs.

were alerted by Magic decrypts that an offensive was imminent. One dispatch from Tokyo on November 30 to Japan's ambassador in Berlin, Lt. Gen. Hiroshi Oshima, warned that "war may suddenly break out between the Anglo-Saxon nations and Japan . . . this war may come quicker than anyone dreams." That was followed by a lengthy message from Tokyo to Ambassador Nomura in Washington, meant to be delivered to Secretary of State Hull at 1 p.m. in Washington on December 7, just before the attack on Pearl Harbor. The last part of that message was transmitted to the Japanese Embassy in Washington early that Sunday morning and was deciphered and distributed in English to American officials before the short-staffed Ambassador Nomura was able to translate and hand it to Hull. Nomura did so at 2:20 that afternoon in Washington, nearly an hour after the first bombs fell in Honolulu. Hull already knew the gist of the message when Nomura presented it to him and declared that he had never seen "a document that was more crowded with falsehoods and distortions." His indignation was genuine, but he too engaged in deception by concealing from Nomura his prior knowledge of Japan's intentions. By then, Hull and others in Washington were better informed on the Japanese offensive than Nomura, who was unaware that war had begun in the Pacific when he delivered Tokyo's message severing relations with the U.S.

ATTACKING THE CODES

If any American at Pearl Harbor had the training and expertise to anticipate the assault there, it was Lt. Cmdr. Edwin Layton, intelligence officer for the Pacific Fleet. He and Lt. Cmdr. Joseph Rochefort—who directed Station Hypo, a secret combat intelligence unit at Pearl Harbor responsible for analyzing and deciphering Japanese naval signals—had studied in Japan together as promising young language officers. Rochefort then applied his knowledge of Japanese as a naval code breaker at OP-20-G in Washington, learning his craft under the tutelage of Agnes Meyer Driscoll. A former math teacher who had joined the Office of Naval Intelligence during World War I and set out to demonstrate that "any man-made code could be broken by a woman," she imparted her expertise to Rochefort and other cryptanalysts who would figure prominently in the next world war. Layton, meanwhile, became an attaché in Tokyo, where he met Yamamoto and other commanders and gained valuable insights into Japanese naval and security operations, including efforts by agents of the Kempeitai (Japanese military police) to penetrate the U.S. Embassy and gain access to American codes.

When Layton and Rochefort came back together at Pearl Harbor in early 1941, they formed a formidable tandem but faced a daunting challenge. Unlike Japanese diplomats, who relied on their cipher machine, Japanese naval officers used codebooks to disguise their messages. Each word or name was represented in the book by a five-digit number, to which another five-digit number was added from a cipher table, making the message even harder to penetrate for those without access to the documents. Furthermore, the Japanese

CALL TO ARMS Soon after the attack on Pearl Harbor, Japan issued this official declaration of war "on the United States of America and the British Empire." The declaration portrayed the Americans and British as aggressors, intent on denying imperial Japan its place in the sun: "Our Empire for its existence and self-defense has no other recourse but to appeal to arms and to crush every obstacle in its path."

THE KEMPEITAI: JAPAN'S GESTAPO

Organized in the late 19th century as an elite corps of military police for the Japanese Army, the Kempeitai evolved into a dreaded imperial security force, whose duties went far beyond policing the military. Among their responsibilities was enforcing conscription, which met with some resistance in Japan when it was introduced, especially in rural areas where drafting able-bodied young men caused hardship for farm families. The Kempeitai also conducted military espionage and counterespionage, which meant that they sometimes pursued the same spies as the Tokko, the so-called Thought Police who cracked down on subversive activities in Japan and arrested Soviet agent Richard Sorge and members of his spy ring. In other cases, the Kempeitai often took precedence over the Tokko and the regular police force because Japan was so militarized by the time World War II began that many breaches of law and order came under the jurisdiction of the military police. More than 10,000 Kempeitai officers and enlisted men operated within the borders of wartime Japan, keeping a close watch on civilians as well as soldiers.

The Kempeitai maintained an even tighter grip on people in Japanese-occupied countries, including Korea, Manchuria, China, Indochina, and other places overrun during the sprawling offensive launched in December 1941, which vastly expanded the Japanese Empire. That expansion was overseen by Gen. Hideki Tojo, who commanded the Kempeitai in Manchuria before becoming Japan's prime minister in 1941. In occupied territory, Kempeitai officers had sweeping powers, including the right to arrest, condemn, and execute suspect civilians—many of whom were interned as enemy aliens by the Japanese—as well as defiant prisoners of war who refused orders from commandants or tried to escape.

A Kempeitai handbook authorized the use of torture, including "kicking, beating, and anything connected with physical suffering." Torture was supposed to be applied only "when everything else has failed," according to the handbook, but the Kempeitai were often quick to torture suspects and kept it up until they confessed.

One Dutch civilian at a Japanese internment camp for women on Sumatra was accused of organizing an escape attempt and jailed with several other women in a filthy cell with no toilet. (Elsewhere, suspects were often crammed into cages.) The next morning, she was taken to a room at the rear of the prison. "Two members of the Kempeitai were there," she later testified. "I saw lying on a table a selection of weapons, cudgels, belts, and whips and in the center of the floor a lighted brazier with irons heating in it. I realized I was in the torture chamber . . . Pointing to the instruments, one of the Kempeitai threatened me with torture unless I pleaded guilty." When she refused to do so, her wrists were tied behind her back and raised by a pulley until her arms were "nearly pulled out of their sockets." She remained defiant and was placed before a firing squad, only to be spared execution and returned to prison.

Many others who fell into the hands of the military police in Japanese-occupied territory were not granted reprieves. Some were beheaded by sword-wielding Kempeitai officers, who were among the fiercest exponents of *bushido,* a code that originated among samurai warriors and required that Japanese soldiers not only fight to the death for their emperor but also put to death those who subverted or defied his imperial regime. Regular Japanese officers also embraced that code and dealt harshly with Allied troops who surrendered rather than fight to the death. But the Kempeitai were the empire's ultimate enforcers. They compelled women in occupied countries to serve as prostitutes for Japanese soldiers and used some civilians and prisoners of war as guinea pigs in dangerous medical experiments. The Kempeitai functioned much like Gestapo agents did in German-occupied territory but had broader authority because they policed the army as well as people under military authority. They could arrest officers who were superior to them in rank and used their clout to ensure that Japanese forces bore down hard on the soldiers they held in captivity and the civilians they held in thrall. ⊙

MILITARY POLICE Kempeitai like those pictured here wore regular Japanese Army uniforms and were distinguished only by their armbands and other insignia.

Navy changed their codes and ciphers before launching their offensive in late 1941, and Rochefort's team had to start over from scratch. The U.S. Navy did manage to track the movements of various Japanese warships through traffic analysis, which involved using radio direction finders at several listening posts to determine the approximate location of a ship, which could then be identified through aerial reconnaissance and traced by its distinctive call signal. But the strike force that Yamamoto launched in late November observed radio silence and evaded reconnaissance. All Layton could tell Admiral Kimmel at Pearl Harbor was that the whereabouts of Japan's six big aircraft carriers were unknown.

"You mean they could be coming around Diamond Head, and you wouldn't even know it?" Kimmel asked.

"Yes sir," Layton replied, "But I hope they'd have been sighted before now."

Chiefs in Washington who had access to decrypts that Kimmel and Layton were denied reckoned that Pearl Harbor was a far less likely target than American bases closer to Japan, including those in the Philippines and on Wake and Midway Islands. The aircraft carriers *Enterprise* and *Lexington* escaped the carnage at Pearl Harbor not because that attack was anticipated but because they were sent to deliver fighter planes to Wake and Midway. Layton, for his part, knew that Pearl Harbor was at some risk but had no reason to question the intelligence assessment of his superiors. When he received a call on the morning of December 7 at his home on Oahu, some distance from the harbor, and was told the Pacific Fleet was under attack, he was as shocked as anyone. It was, he wrote later, "the most stunning message of my life."

The staggering assault on Pearl Harbor was followed within hours by air raids on American bases on Guam (which fell to Japan on December 10), Wake Island (seized on December 23), and the Philippines, where American and Filipino troops led by Gen. Douglas MacArthur retreated to the Bataan Peninsula and were besieged by Japanese invasion forces. The massive offensive continued into 1942 and forced the British to abandon Hong Kong, Singapore, and much of Burma to Japanese troops, who also invaded the Dutch East Indies and New Guinea and threatened Australia. Allied hopes of weathering the Japanese onslaught rested on shielding Australia and the surviving U.S. bases at Midway and Pearl Harbor and preserving the capacity to strike back.

When Adm. Chester Nimitz arrived at Pearl Harbor a few weeks after the attack there to replace the ill-fated Kimmel as commander of the Pacific Fleet, Layton recalled, bloated corpses were "still surfacing from submerged wrecks," including the doomed battleship U.S.S. *Arizona,* which accounted for nearly half of the 2,400 or so lives lost there on December 7. It was a "terrible sight," Nimitz remarked, but he knew that the damage to the fleet could have been far worse had its aircraft carriers and fuel depots been destroyed. He was confident that he could defend against further attacks and begin taking the fight to the enemy as long as he had carrier-based airpower—and timely intelligence on enemy plans and movements from Layton, Rochefort, and Station Hypo.

Housed in a windowless basement at the 14th Naval District headquarters to avoid notice, Hypo was known to its inhabitants as the dungeon. Rochefort worked there for days on end, sleeping intermittently on a cot and seldom emerging into the light of day. He was always "nearly fully dressed," wrote his aide, Lt. Cmdr. W. Jasper Holmes, and "ready at a

JAPANESE CODE JN-25

The Japanese Imperial Navy used codebooks filled with five-digit numbers representing words such as those below. The code numbers shown here were then altered using a cipher table, so that when a word appeared a second time in the message, it was represented by a different five-digit number.

attack (ing, ed)	73428
battleship (s)	29781
cruiser (s)	58797
destroyer (s)	36549
enemy	38754

CODE BREAKERS Lt. Cmdr. Joseph Rochefort (above), an expert linguist and cryptanalyst, led secret efforts at Station Hypo to unlock the JN-25 code, used in conjunction with cipher tables to conceal Japanese naval messages, as explained at top right. Rochefort was aided by Capt. Thomas Dyer (right), the senior member of his code-breaking team, and by personnel who entered intercepted Japanese signals as numerical sequences on punch cards and ran them through IBM tabulators (below).

SIFTING FOR CLUES Tabulating numerical Japanese messages helped code breakers at Station Hypo detect and interpret the underlying code numbers.

moment's notice to roll out and jump into carpet slippers and an old, red smoking jacket." A sign on the cluttered desk of Capt. Thomas Dyer, who served as the senior cryptanalyst under Rochefort and often worked more than 24 hours at a stretch, summed up the spirit of Station Hypo: "You don't have to be crazy to work here—but it helps." Knowledge of what went on there was limited to senior officers, who were often skeptical of the arcane calculations of code breakers until their efforts paid off. As Holmes put it, many considered Hypo's inmates "to be a bunch of nuts, in a basement, dreaming up wild hallucinations."

Similarly claustrophobic conditions prevailed at the station's separate listening post on Oahu, where radiomen adept at Morse code as employed by the Japanese—whose kana script had many more characters than the 26-letter Roman alphabet—recorded signals they picked up. Listeners at such posts sometimes transcribed voice messages from Japanese pilots or signals sent in plain text (Morse code that was not enciphered) by other servicemen who did not have the time or means to disguise their communications. But more often, radiomen at Oahu and other Allied listening stations that remained in operation after war erupted in the Pacific transcribed numerical sequences produced using the Japanese naval codebook and cipher table. Those puzzling intercepts were then passed along to Rochefort and his team, who labored tirelessly to solve them, aided by traffic analysis and tips from the listeners, who became so familiar with the "signature" of various Japanese telegraphers—who had distinctive ways of pressing the key—that they could often tell which ship sent the message without knowing its contents.

As the intercepts poured in and the work load increased, Rochefort asked that bandsmen from the wrecked battleship U.S.S. *California,* put out of action on December 7, be assigned to Station Hypo. "Rochefort and Dyer believed that their musical ability might be useful in working out the chords and syncopations of codes and ciphers," Layton recalled. Some of them went on to serve as cryptanalysts, but their main task was running IBM tabulating machines and entering enciphered code groups from intercepts onto punch cards. "Their labor was considerable," Layton noted, "since each Japanese message required anywhere from seventy-five to one hundred IBM cards." Punch cards and tabulators proved crucial in speeding laborious searches such as scanning for telltale errors made by Japanese cipher clerks, who sometimes used the same sequence of numbers from the table day after day to encipher the same basic information, revealing the underlying code numbers for significant details such as the ship's destination.

Those IBM tabulating machines were forerunners of electronic computers but lacked the essential component that would allow those computers to store information and be programmed—an internal memory. Station Hypo relied primarily on Rochefort's own

LOST IN BATTLE All 21 bandsmen of the U.S.S. *Arizona* (above) died when the battleship sank in Pearl Harbor on December 7, 1941. One former member of the band, William Harten, Jr., survived because he was reassigned to the U.S.S. *West Virginia* shortly before the attack, during which that battleship also sank but most of its crew escaped. A diver later retrieved Harten's damaged cornet (top), an enduring emblem of the battered but unbowed Pacific Fleet.

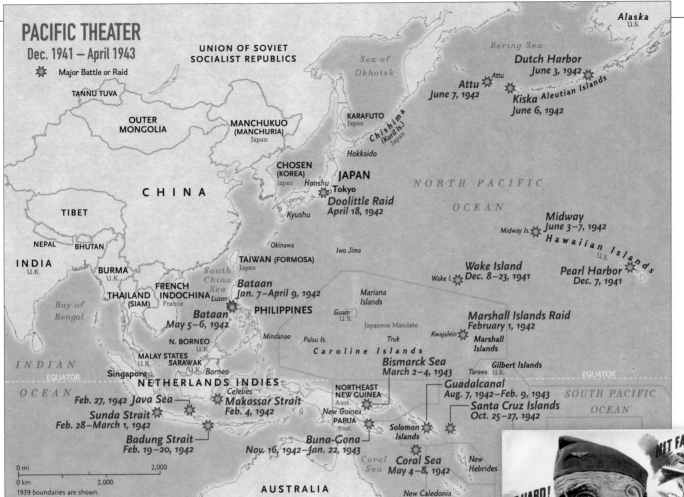

PACIFIC THEATER
Dec. 1941 – April 1943

✯ Major Battle or Raid

UNION OF SOVIET SOCIALIST REPUBLICS

Alaska
U.S.

Sea of Okhotsk

Bering Sea

TANNU TUVA

OUTER MONGOLIA

MANCHUKUO (MANCHURIA)
Japan

KARAFUTO
Japan

Chishima (Kuril Is.) Japan

Dutch Harbor
June 3, 1942

Attu
Attu
June 7, 1942

Kiska Aleutian Islands
June 6, 1942

CHINA

TIBET

CHOSEN (KOREA)
Japan

Honshu

JAPAN

Hokkaido

NORTH PACIFIC OCEAN

Tokyo
Doolittle Raid
April 18, 1942

Kyushu

Midway
Midway Is. June 3–7, 1942

Hawaiian Islands
U.S.

NEPAL BHUTAN

Okinawa

Iwo Jima

INDIA
U.K.

BURMA
U.K.

South China Sea

TAIWAN (FORMOSA)
Japan

Wake Island
Wake I. Dec. 8–23, 1941

Pearl Harbor
Dec. 7, 1941

THAILAND (SIAM)

FRENCH INDOCHINA
France

Bataan
Jan. 7–April 9, 1942

Luzon

Mariana Islands

Bataan
May 5–6, 1942

PHILIPPINES

Guam
U.S.

Japanese Mandate

Marshall Islands Raid
February 1, 1942

Bay of Bengal

Mindanao

Palau Is.

Truk

Kwajalein

Marshall Islands

N. BORNEO
U.K.

Caroline Islands

MALAY STATES
U.K. SARAWAK
U.K.

Bismarck Sea
March 2–4, 1943

Gilbert Islands

INDIAN

EQUATOR

Singapore

Borneo

Tarawa U.K.

EQUATOR

OCEAN

NETHERLANDS INDIES

Celebes

NORTHEAST NEW GUINEA
Aust.

Guadalcanal
Aug. 7, 1942–Feb. 9, 1943

SOUTH PACIFIC OCEAN

Feb. 27, 1942 Java Sea

Makassar Strait
Feb. 4, 1942

New Guinea

Santa Cruz Islands
Oct. 25–27, 1942

Sunda Strait
Feb. 28–March 1, 1942

PAPUA
Aust.

Solomon Islands

Badung Strait
Feb. 19–20, 1942

Buna-Gona
Nov. 16, 1942–Jan. 22, 1943

Coral Sea
Coral Sea May 4–8, 1942

New Hebrides

0 mi   2,000
0 km   2,000
1939 boundaries are shown.

AUSTRALIA

New Caledonia

memory. Without referring to notes or looking though files, he could fill in gaps in a partially deciphered intercept by recalling a message from the same source that he had puzzled over several months earlier. Aside from a keen memory, Rochefort had what Layton called a "sixth sense when it came to assembling seemingly unrelated information in partially decrypted enemy messages and turning the puzzle into an accurate picture of enemy plans and intentions." Layton collaborated with Rochefort in assembling that picture by combining partial decrypts from Station Hypo with battle and reconnaissance reports from around the Pacific and his own insights into Yamamoto's tendencies to provide Nimitz with increasingly reliable forecasts of his opponent's next moves.

Although Rochefort and his team could read less than 15 percent of any given intercept in January 1942, they doubled that capacity over the next few months because the Japanese continued to use the same naval codebook and cipher table until late May. Their warships were now widely dispersed, and introducing new books and tables took time. That delay and the tracking of Japanese ships through radio direction finding, traffic analysis, and aerial and submarine reconnaissance enabled Rochefort and Layton to begin furnishing Nimitz with actionable intelligence—good enough for him to risk his diminished fleet in action against a much larger one—within two months of the attack on Pearl Harbor.

Informed that no further naval assault on Pearl Harbor was imminent and that most of Yamamoto's fleet was operating in the southwest Pacific and Indian Ocean, Nimitz

HIT HARD!
HIT FAST!
HIT OFTEN!

Produce for Your Navy
VICTORY BEGINS AT HOME!

PACIFIC THEATER Mapped at top are battles and raids conducted around the Pacific from the attack on Pearl Harbor until Yamamoto's death in April 1943. Many of the naval battles pitted Yamamoto's Combined Fleet against the U.S. Pacific Fleet, led by Admiral Nimitz, who dispatched keen commanders like Vice Adm. William "Bull" Halsey, portrayed in the war poster above. Halsey assisted the Doolittle Raid against Tokyo in April 1942 before taking part in the hard-fought Battle of the Coral Sea in May.

HEADQUARTERS
UNITED STATES ARMY FORCES IN THE FAR EAST
OFFICE OF THE COMMANDING GENERAL
MANILA, P.I.
Fort Mills, P. I.

IN REPLY REFER TO:

Special Order)
No.   66)   11 March, 1942.

E X T R A C T

1.   The following named officers, Headquarters United States Army Forces in the Far East, will proceed by the first available transportation from Fort Mills, Philippine Islands, to destination described in letter of instructions:

General Douglas MacArthur, (O-57) USA
Major General Richard K. Sutherland, (O-4623) USA
Brigadier General Spencer B. Akin, (O-2915) USA
Brigadier General Richard J. Marshall, (O-4635) USA
Brigadier General William F. Marquat, (O-5535) USA
Brigadier General Hugh J. Casey, (O-2298) USA
Colonel Charles A. Willoughby, (O-4615) GSC
Colonel Charles P. Stivers, (O-4687) GSC
Lt. Col. Francis H. Wilson, (O-6701) Inf., ADC
Lt. Col. Joe R. Sherr, (O-14587) SC
Lt. Col. LeGrand A. Diller, (O-15078) Inf., ADC
Lt. Col. Sidney L. Huff, (O-890004) Inf., ADC

The Quartermaster Corps will furnish the necessary transportation. The travel directed is necessary in the military service. FD 1401 P 1-06 A 0410-2.

X   X   X

By command of General MacARTHUR:

R. K. SUTHERLAND,
Major General, G. S. C.,
Chief of Staff.

OFFICIAL:

CARL H. SEALS,
Brigadier General, U. S. A.,
Adjutant General.

BESIEGED Gen. Douglas MacArthur, shown smoking his famous corncob pipe, was hemmed in by Japanese invasion forces and evacuated from the Philippines to Australia along with several of his officers in March 1942 under the secret order at right. American and allied Filipino troops who remained behind on the Bataan Peninsula surrendered to the Japanese in April and were herded to a distant prison camp (below) on the infamous Bataan Death March.

BURIAL GROUND American POWs carry remains of their dead to be buried at Camp O'Donnell, a former Allied base converted to a Japanese prison camp.

launched the carriers *Enterprise* and *Yorktown* on raids in late January against the Japanese-occupied Marshall Islands in the central Pacific. Station Hypo provided the commander of the *Enterprise,* Vice Adm. William "Bull" Halsey, with a mobile intelligence unit consisting of three radio operators and a language officer. As their carrier approached the island of Kwajalein, they intercepted and translated a message from a Japanese reconnaissance pilot that he had "nothing to report." Reassured, Halsey moved in close and launched warplanes that pounded enemy headquarters on Kwajalein, killed the admiral in command there, and dropped leaflets on the island with taunting words from Halsey in Japanese: "Thank you for not spotting us." He kept up his air strikes and eventually came under attack but escaped without major damage to the *Enterprise,* prompting overenthusiastic newspaper editors in the U.S. to proclaim that the attack on Pearl Harbor had been avenged.

In truth, Nimitz's initial raids were not much more than pinpricks in the enemy's hide. But they worried Japanese commanders, who were further alarmed in April when the U.S.S. *Hornet,* a new carrier in the Pacific Fleet, advanced with the *Enterprise* to within 670 miles of Tokyo and launched a squadron of 16 B-25s commanded by Lt. Col. James Doolittle that succeeded in bombing the Japanese capital. Damage was slight, but the Doolittle Raid boosted morale in the U.S. in the bitter aftermath of the Japanese conquest of the Philippines, when American and Filipino captives were herded to wretched prison camps in the notorious Bataan Death March. Their commander, General MacArthur, had been ordered to abandon his headquarters on the island of Corregidor, off the Bataan Peninsula, and depart for Australia aboard a PT boat. That escape, arranged without alerting the Japanese because they could not decipher radio signals sent to and from Corregidor, was well publicized after MacArthur landed safely. Kept secret was a larger evacuation from Corregidor, involving all those employed at Station Cast, which like Station Hypo included listeners, traffic analysts, cryptanalysts, and translators. If they were captured and forced to talk, Yamamoto would learn that his fleet's signals were being read and Nimitz would lose his edge in the intelligence war. On April 8, the last of some 50 officers and enlisted men at Station Cast boarded a submarine for Australia, where they continued to monitor and interpret enemy communications.

Following the Doolittle Raid, Yamamoto won approval for an ambitious new offensive designed to eliminate such threats to Japan by extending its defensive perimeter far across the Pacific. His plan called for diversionary assaults on U.S. bases on the Aleutian Islands, followed quickly by an attack on Midway. He expected that Nimitz would then rush to defend Midway, giving Yamamoto—who would be laying in wait with the remainder of his forces—another chance to shatter the Pacific Fleet, including its vital aircraft carriers. If he achieved that objective, Hawaii would be vulnerable to invasion. Loss of the fleet and its base at Pearl Harbor might force the U.S. Navy to pull back to the West Coast and concentrate on countering the German threat in the Atlantic, which was President Roosevelt's priority.

(continued on page 96)

DOOLITTLE RAID At top, Lt. Col. James Doolittle stands beside Capt. Marc Mitscher (right), commanding officer of the aircraft carrier U.S.S. *Hornet*. Escorted by Halsey's *Enterprise,* the *Hornet* launched Doolittle's squadron of 16 B-25 bombers in a surprise attack on Tokyo on April 18, 1942. The big planes managed to take off (center) but were too heavy to land on the *Hornet*. After bombing Tokyo, the airmen continued on to China, where most were rescued but some were seized by Japanese troops (bottom).

FEAR AND SUSPICION ON AMERICA'S WEST COAST

Early on February 23, 1942, a Japanese submarine surfaced off Santa Barbara, California, and briefly shelled fuel storage tanks before slipping away. Little damage was done, but the incident unnerved Californians. On the night of February 24, air raid sirens blared in Los Angeles and antiaircraft batteries blazed away following reports of unidentified planes approaching the city. There were no Japanese aircraft carriers within range of the West Coast, and the supposed enemy raid that drew headlines in Los Angeles (right) may have amounted to nothing more than a stray blimp or wayward weather balloons, mistaken for aerial intruders. Yet fear of attack, whipped up by the assault on Pearl Harbor, swept the coast like a tidal wave and imperiled Japanese Americans there, who were often suspected of being spies or potential saboteurs. In fact, most agents operating for Japan in the U.S. were not naturalized Japanese Americans but Japanese citizens under orders from Tokyo, including a naval officer who visited America to learn English and was charged with espionage.

Japanese Americans had long faced bias and

PHANTOM RAID This edition claimed that "foreign aircraft" were spotted over Los Angeles, but added that "no bombs were reported dropped."

resentment in the U.S., which prohibited further immigration from Japan and other Asian nations in 1924. After war erupted in the Pacific in 1941, Earl Warren—the attorney general of California and future chief justice of the U.S. Supreme Court—called for interning those of Japanese ancestry living on the West Coast, a drastic step that President Roosevelt authorized in February 1942. Warren argued for keeping those detainees in camps even after fears of a Japanese attack subsided. "If the Japs are released," he said in 1943, "no one will be able to tell a saboteur from any other Jap . . . We don't want a second Pearl Harbor in California." Late in life, Warren admitted that Japanese Americans had been wrongly confined without evidence that they were disloyal. He wrote that he "deeply regretted the removal order and my own testimony advocating it, because it was not in keeping with our American concept of freedom and the rights of citizens." ✪

CIVIL DEFENSE Responses on the West Coast to the Pearl Harbor attack ranged from using floodlights to spot enemy aircraft at night (above) to shielding a telephone company building in San Francisco against bombardment with a huge pile of sandbags (left).

WESTERN DEFENSE COMMAND AND FOURTH ARMY
WARTIME CIVIL CONTROL ADMINISTRATION
Presidio of San Francisco, California
May 6, 1942

INSTRUCTIONS
TO ALL PERSONS OF
JAPANESE
ANCESTRY
Living in the Following Area:

All of the County of Kings, State of California.

Pursuant to the provisions of Civilian Exclusion Order No. 45, this Headquarters, dated May 6, 1942, all persons of Japanese ancestry, both alien and non-alien, will be evacuated from the above area by 12 o'clock noon, P. W. T., Wednesday, May 13, 1942.

No Japanese person living in the above area will be permitted to change residence after 12 o'clock noon, P. W. T., Wednesday, May 6, 1942, without obtaining special permission from the representative of the Commanding General, Northern California Sector, at the Civil Control Station located at:

Hanford Civic Auditorium,
Civic Center,
Hanford, California.

Such permits will only be granted for the purpose of uniting members of a family, or in cases of grave emergency.

The Civil Control Station is equipped to assist the Japanese population affected by this evacuation in the following ways:

1. Give advice and instructions on the evacuation.
2. Provide services with respect to the management, leasing, sale, storage or other disposition of most kinds of property, such as real estate, business and professional equipment, household goods, boats, automobiles and livestock.
3. Provide temporary residence elsewhere for all Japanese in family groups.
4. Transport persons and a limited amount of clothing and equipment to their new residence.

The Following Instructions Must Be Observed:

1. A responsible member of each family, preferably the head of the family, or the person in whose name most of the property is held, and each individual living alone, will report to the Civil Control Station to receive further instructions. This must be done between 8:00 A. M. and 5:00 P. M. on Thursday, May 7, 1942, or between 8:00 A. M. and 5:00 P. M. on Friday, May 8, 1942.
2. Evacuees must carry with them on departure for the Assembly Center, the following property:
(a) Bedding and linens (no mattress) for each member of the family;
(b) Toilet articles for each member of the family;
(c) Extra clothing for each member of the family;
(d) Sufficient knives, forks, spoons, plates, bowls and cups for each member of the family;
(e) Essential personal effects for each member of the family.

All items carried will be securely packaged, tied and plainly marked with the na[me]
in accordance with instructions obtained at the Civil Control Station. The size
ited to that which can be carried by the individual or family group.

3. No pets of any kind will be permitted.
4. No personal items and no household goods will be shipped to the Assembly
5. The United States Government through its agencies will provide for the stora[ge]
of the more substantial household items, such as iceboxes, washing machines, pia[nos]
Cooking utensils and other small items will be accepted for storage if crated, pack[ed]
name and address of the owner. Only one name and address will be used by a gi[ven]
6. Each family, and individual living alone, will be furnished transportation t[o]
authorized to travel by private automobile in a supervised group. All instructions
be obtained at the Civil Control Station.

**Go to the Civil Control Station between the hours of 8:0[0]
Thursday, May 7, 1942, or between the hours of 8:[00]
Friday, May 8, 1942, to receive further instructions.**

J. L
Lieutenant G[eneral]
Co[mmanding]

SEE CIVILIAN EXCLUSION ORDER NO. 45

FORCED OUT The evacuation notice at left, issued in San Francisco, called on those of Japanese ancestry to report with personal belongings, excluding pets, for removal to internment camps. The order applied to both aliens and "non-aliens," meaning American citizens of Japanese ancestry. Among them was a Japanese-American grocer who declared his loyalty on his storefront (below) but was ousted from his home and business and interned by the nation to which he pledged allegiance.

Yamamoto's new plan was even bolder than his opening attack on Pearl Harbor—and even harder to coordinate and disguise. Although unaware of recent advances by American code breakers, who first obtained clues as to his intentions in late April, Yamamoto knew that fleet movements could be detected through traffic analysis because his own listeners were using similar techniques. According to Layton, the Japanese radio intelligence center at Owada, near Tokyo, "achieved a good record in deducing whenever our task forces sortied from Pearl Harbor from the increased radio activity," including voice messages from pilots, which could be picked up much farther away than thought possible when the war began. The only way to avoid radio detection was to observe strict radio silence, as the strike force dispatched by Yamamoto against Pearl Harbor did. That was not feasible when assembling a widely dispersed fleet for a sprawling offensive. Silence would be maintained only after Yamamoto's warships left their staging ground off the island of Saipan and moved into position to attack. He did not underestimate his opponents, but his assurance that he could prevail at Midway, even though his forces would be divided and his signals might alert the enemy that he was up to something, was symptomatic of what the Japanese called "victory disease," or the overconfidence that afflicted those of all ranks following their dramatic advances in the war's first months.

Before Nimitz knew the targets or timing of Yamamoto's forthcoming offensive, he had to deal with an imminent threat to Port Moresby on New Guinea and other Allied bases around the Coral Sea, which if seized by the Japanese could be used to attack American supply ships bound for Australia and might serve as platforms for bombing and invading that country. In late April 1942, Yamamoto dispatched a task force that included two big aircraft carriers, *Shokaku* and *Zuikaku,* and the small carrier *Shoho* to shield Japanese troops who would land on New Guinea and Tulagi, a small island off Guadalcanal in the Solomons. Based on decrypts provided by Rochefort, Layton concluded that Yamamoto's task force would be stretched thin attempting "to cover both the Moresby landing and an occupation of the Solomon Islands." That intelligence assessment prompted Nimitz to take a calculated risk by sending a task force including the *Yorktown* and *Lexington* to the Coral Sea.

The fierce contest waged there over several days in early May was the first battle between aircraft carriers, which remained far apart but traded deadly blows delivered by the warplanes they launched. Both American carriers were battered, and the *Lexington* eventually went down after most of its crew was rescued. But their fighters and bombers, guided by combat intelligence units that picked up enemy signals, took a heavy toll in return by sinking the *Shoho* and forcing the *Shokaku* and *Zuikaku* out of action. Japanese forces seized Tulagi—from which they went on to occupy Guadalcanal—and invaded

BATTLEGROUND Midway Atoll was hotly contested in June 1942 because of the crucial airfield that U.S. forces held there. Rochefort and his team determined that the objective designated "AF" in coded messages sent by Admiral Yamamoto's fleet was Midway, enabling Admiral Nimitz to anticipate and counter the Japanese offensive there.

New Guinea but failed to oust Australian troops from Port Moresby. Neither of the big Japanese carriers engaged in the Battle of the Coral Sea would be available to Yamamoto when he next challenged the Pacific Fleet.

FORECASTING MIDWAY

Like earlier contests in the Pacific, the Coral Sea battle provided Rochefort's team at Station Hypo with a bonanza by allowing them to review coded Japanese radio messages concerning plans, movements, and ships involved in operations that were now a matter of record. Interpreting a message in which only one word in four words had been deciphered could be fiendishly difficult, but it was possible to fill in gaps when one looked back after the event and knew the identity, course, and destination of the sender. Solving the codes for destinations or targets was of utmost importance because Nimitz could not hope to counter the forthcoming offensive by Yamamoto's larger fleet—which had eight operational aircraft carriers after the Coral Sea battle to the Pacific Fleet's three—unless he knew where that blow would fall and had the advantage of anticipating it. Rochefort detected a pattern in which the decoded Japanese words *koryaku butai* (meaning "occupation force" or "invasion force") were followed by two letters, the first of which designated a zone in the Pacific and the second a place within that zone. "MM," for example, represented the Philippine zone and the capital city of Manila. All two-letter codes beginning with "A" were in the American-controlled zone.

Soon after the Battle of the Coral Sea, Rochefort hit the jackpot. "I've got something so hot here it's burning the top of my desk," he told Layton. Rochefort showed him a partial decrypt of a message containing the phrase "*koryaku butai* AF." That meant AF would be invaded in Yamamoto's upcoming offensive, and Rochefort concluded from other intercepts—one of which referred to Japanese ground crews destined for AF—that the target was Midway, which had an air base the Japanese could use to attack the Pacific Fleet. Layton and Nimitz were sure he was right, but naval intelligence officers at OP-20-G in Washington were skeptical and thought the target might be Johnston Island, closer to Pearl Harbor. Station Hypo settled the argument through a classic ruse suggested by Jasper Holmes, who knew that the base at Midway depended on a desalination plant for fresh water. Rochefort arranged for Midway to broadcast an emergency message in plain language that the plant had broken down. American listening posts soon picked up coded Japanese messages requesting water supplies for occupation forces destined for AF, which could only be Midway.

By late May, when the Japanese finally instituted new naval codes and ciphers to

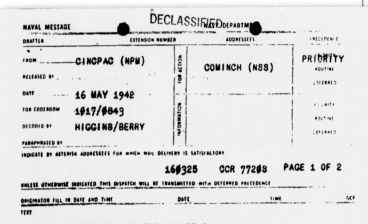

TIMELY WARNING This secret dispatch—sent to Washington on May 16, 1942, by Nimitz, designated CINCPAC (Commander in Chief Pacific)—reflected intelligence he received from Rochefort and Layton, who accurately forecast the offensive that Yamamoto would launch in early June, including an assault on the Aleutian Islands and a major attack on Midway. They did not yet know when that attack would occur, but Nimitz ordered Halsey to return to Pearl Harbor from the southwest Pacific with a task force including the *Enterprise* to prepare that aircraft carrier to counter Yamamoto's thrust toward Midway.

VICTORY AT MIDWAY At left, SBD Dauntless dive-bombers from the aircraft carrier *Hornet* swoop down on the burning Japanese cruiser *Mikuma*, pictured below shortly before it sank. This action occurred on June 6, 1942, as Japanese forces were withdrawing from Midway after suffering the devastating loss of four aircraft carriers.

safeguard their communications, Rochefort and Layton had uncovered Yamamoto's plan in remarkable detail. The date for the attack on Midway was one of the last puzzles to be solved because the Japanese superenciphered dates in their messages using a grid that had 12 rows for the months of the year and 31 columns for the days of the month. Thanks to Lt. Joseph Finnegan, a cryptanalyst at Station Hypo who figured out that scheme and constructed the grid, Rochefort was able to fill in crucial gaps in decrypts, including one revealing that the invasion force would reach AF "at 1900 June 6." Layton reckoned that the attack on Midway would begin a day or two earlier because Japanese troop transports would not risk approaching the island until the American air base there had been neutralized by warplanes from Yamamoto's carriers. Furthermore, decrypts and traffic analysis enabled him to inform Nimitz that the attack would be led by a strike force containing four big aircraft carriers: *Akagi, Kaga, Hiryu,* and *Soryu.* By rushing repairs on the damaged *Yorktown* and dispatching it to Midway along with the *Enterprise* and *Hornet,* Nimitz would have a fighting chance against that force while other elements of Yamamoto's fleet followed behind or attacked in the Aleutians. When pressed by Nimitz to be specific, Layton told him that the four Japanese carriers would approach Midway on June 4 "from the northwest on a bearing of 325 degrees. They could be sighted at about 175 miles from Midway at around 0700 local time."

That precise forecast, made possible by the relentless efforts of Rochefort's team and naval analysts at other stations, was borne out when a reconnaissance aircraft spotted the strike force at almost the exact time and place that Layton predicted. As Nimitz put it, he was "only five minutes, five degrees, and five miles out." That foreknowledge transformed a battle that could have been disastrous for Nimitz had he rushed belatedly to Midway's defense into a closely fought contest, in which daring American commanders and airmen capitalized on the fact they knew what they were up against while their opponents remained unaware of the threat they faced for a few crucial hours that morning. When Vice Adm. Chuichi Nagumo—assigned to lead the assault on Midway as he did the attack on Pearl Harbor—learned from one of his own reconnaissance aircraft that enemy carriers were approaching, he was caught in a bind. After clearing his carrier decks to allow warplanes that had bombed Midway at dawn to land, he then had a second wave of bombers destined for Midway rearmed with torpedoes for attacks on American ships. His foes had the jump on him, and before Nagumo could launch those strikes, his carriers were targeted by American torpedo planes, many of which were shot down, followed by dive-bombers that released their payloads on decks lined with highly combustible Japanese aircraft, fueled and armed for takeoff. Nagumo's flagship *Akagi* erupted in flames along with the *Soryu* and *Kaga.* All three went down, leaving only the *Hiryu,* which launched an attack on the *Yorktown* that caused captain and crew to abandon that stricken carrier before the *Hiryu* too was blasted from above and sank.

> ## "Well, you were only five minutes, five degrees, and five miles out."
>
> ADM. CHESTER NIMITZ TO LT. CMDR. EDWIN LAYTON, WHO PREDICTED WHEN AND WHERE JAPANESE CARRIERS WOULD APPEAR OFF MIDWAY

EVASIVE ACTION The Japanese aircraft carrier *Hiryu* turns to avoid bombs dropped by Midway-based B-17 bombers on June 4, 1942, the first day of the Battle of Midway. Hit and set aflame during a second attack later that day, the *Hiryu* went down on June 5, sharing the fate of the Japanese carriers *Akagi, Kaga,* and *Soryu,* destroyed on the fourth.

Word of the devastating outcome reached Yamamoto at his mobile headquarters aboard the superbattleship *Yamato,* a 72,000-ton behemoth that some thought invincible but that he and other advocates of naval airpower considered no match for the destructive power and range of warplanes unleashed by aircraft carriers. Yamamoto knew that occupying a few islands in the Aleutians, as Japanese forces succeeded in doing while the fighting raged off Midway, was paltry compensation for the loss of all four carriers in the strike force, which compelled him to withdraw and ensured that Japan now faced the long war he dreaded. He later learned that the *Akagi* had broken radio silence as it approached Midway on June 2 to summon oil tankers for ships that needed to be refueled. That seemingly explained the uncanny ability of the Pacific Fleet's carriers to be in the right place at the right time on June 4. What Yamamoto did not know was that his opponents had refined signals intelligence and cryptanalysis into secret weapons that could penetrate his plans weeks before they unfolded. Without the early warning that code breaking provided, Nimitz told his officers as they celebrated a victory even more stunning and significant than the defeat suffered at Pearl Harbor six months earlier, "the Battle of Midway would have ended differently."

COASTWATCHERS ON THE SOLOMONS

Victory at Midway altered the course of the war in the Pacific and allowed U.S. troops shielded by the Pacific Fleet to challenge Japanese forces on strategic islands around the Coral Sea. While General MacArthur prepared to dispatch American soldiers to Port Moresby to help Australian troops reclaim New Guinea, Admiral Nimitz sent aircraft carriers, battleships, cruisers, and destroyers to support U.S. Marines as they invaded Japanese-occupied Guadalcanal and Tulagi in August 1942 and faced blistering counterattacks in the months that followed. That marked the beginning of a long and bloody campaign for control of the Solomon Islands—a struggle in which American forces were aided mightily by Allied spies called coastwatchers. They included British officials on the islands as well as planters and missionaries from Australia and New Zealand who secretly reported on Japanese movements by radio to Lt. Cmdr. Eric Feldt of the Royal Australian Navy. Anticipating hostilities, Feldt had expanded the number of coastwatching stations in the Solomons to over 60 by the time the war began. Many of his agents went into hiding to avoid arrest and possible execution by the Japanese and employed native islanders as scouts to track the enemy.

Before American troops landed on Guadalcanal, coastwatchers on that island had to contend with Japanese forces who were alerted to their presence by an informant. F. Ashton "Snowy" Rhoades, the Australian manager of a coconut plantation, camped with his radio equipment along the Hylavo River near Guadalcanal's west coast until a scout told

SOLOMON ISLANDS
April 1943

CONTESTED ISLANDS In August 1942, U.S. troops landed on Guadalcanal, launching a campaign to retake the Solomon Islands from Japanese occupiers, who also came under attack on New Guinea and New Britain. Yamamoto's fateful flight from Rabaul to Bougainville in April 1943 was intercepted by fighter pilots flying from Guadalcanal.

him that the Japanese knew his whereabouts and planned to cut off his hands and feet when they caught him. "That's when I decided to sleep with a pistol under the pillow," recalled Rhoades, who moved deep into the jungle to a new hideout. Martin Clemens, the British district commissioner on Guadalcanal, took refuge with his scouts atop Gold Ridge, overlooking Lunga Point, where the Japanese began building an airstrip in June. His report on that alarming development helped prompt the American invasion, which came none too soon for Clemens, who had to shift base frequently to avoid being tracked by Japanese technicians using radio direction finders. Shortly after the Marines landed on August 7, he marched into their camp and placed his team at their service. Jacob Vouza, a sturdy islander who had cracked down on offenders as a constable before joining forces with Clemens, went on to spy for American commanders at great risk and was seized, bayoneted, and left for dead by Japanese troops—an ordeal he survived.

As the Marines transformed the Japanese strip at Lunga Point into their own air base, Henderson Field, their opponents launched furious efforts by land, sea, and air to dislodge them. Vital warnings of those attacks came from coastwatchers on islands to the northwest, including Bougainville, located roughly midway between Guadalcanal and the Japanese stronghold of Rabaul on New Britain, from which many air raids and naval sorties were launched. At the north end of

(continued on page 104)

ALLIED AGENTS At left, Martin Clemens—the British district commissioner on Guadalcanal, who remained there as a coastwatcher following the Japanese invasion—stands at center with islanders who served as scouts, helping gather intelligence that he transmitted to Allied listening posts by radio. After U.S. troops landed on Guadalcanal in August 1942, Clemens joined them and briefed American officers on Japanese positions and movements (above).

THE DANGEROUS LIVES OF JUNGLE SPIES

Few coastwatchers who observed enemy movements for the Allies in the South Pacific required training for their perilous assignment. Most were accustomed to hazards and hardship before they began spying and risked being caught and executed by the Japanese. Such was the background of Leigh Vial (inset), who served before the war as an Australian patrol officer on New Guinea, pursuing hardened criminals through dense jungle. When that island was invaded, he joined the Royal Australian Air Force and set up an observation post from which he peered through binoculars and reported by radio on Japanese warplanes aloft, ships at sea, and troops on the ground. Vial moved his post repeatedly to avoid capture and said later that he had a "bad scare" nearly every week. But he continued to supply intelligence of such value to Allied forces that the Americans awarded him the Distinguished Service Cross. Granted a few months' leave in late 1942, he wrote a manual on how to survive in the jungle, then

SENTINEL Vigilant and brave, Leigh Vial was a consummate coastwatcher.

returned to action as a flight lieutenant and perished in a crash in 1943.

Other coastwatchers were government officials or plantation managers in peacetime who undertook their dangerous wartime task because they were as attached to their island and fellow islanders as captains were to their ship and crew. Like captains, they had no intention of abandoning ship when the enemy bore down and instead kept up the fight as best they could. Most eluded capture by exercising caution and exploiting their knowledge of the terrain, but they endured more than a few close calls. Snowy Rhoades, who had occasion to use the pistol he carried while serving as a coastwatcher on Guadalcanal, often asked himself why he risked his life when war broke out by remaining at the plantation he managed and spying on the Japanese. The answer he arrived at was simple: "Here I was at this place, responsible for it, and nobody to look after it or the people if I left. So I stayed." ✪

SCANNING THE SKIES At left, a coastwatcher uses binoculars to search for Japanese warplanes aloft (above). Many Japanese squadrons on bombing raids were spotted and reported to Allied defenders before the planes reached their targets.

SPYING ON SHIPS Charts like that below helped coastwatchers identify Japanese warships and warn distant Allied commanders by radio of their approach. Some observation posts were fortified against attack like the one at bottom, maintained by coastwatchers on New Britain.

SIGNALING ALERTS Coastwatchers like the two men above communicated with signalmen at stations such as that at Henderson Field on Guadalcanal (top right) by sending coded telegraphic messages on radios similar to the set at right.

NAVIGATORS An Australian coastwatcher wearing a sailor's cap sits beside his comrade in a small boat used to travel between islands. Typically, such agents moved quietly under sail or under their own power, wielding oars or paddles, and used a compass like the one above to navigate when land was not in sight.

Bougainville, W. J. "Jack" Read, the island's assistant district commissioner, watched for Japanese warplanes heading toward Guadalcanal and reported by radio nearly two hours before they reached their targets. Terse messages such as this one he dispatched on August 31—"18 twin-engine bombers, 23 fighters now en route yours"—enabled fighter pilots at Henderson to take off before the attack and reach high altitude from which they descended like hawks on their prey. Read's timely warnings became legendary on Guadalcanal and inspired gallows humor among Marines there, who responded to repeated Japanese assaults and other travails of life in the jungle with the catch phrase: "Forty bombers heading yours."

Meanwhile, Paul Mason—who like Snowy Rhoades was a veteran plantation manager from Australia who knew his island as well as some who were born and raised there—sent increasingly accurate reports on Japanese naval movements from the south end of Bougainville by keeping close watch and studying *Jane's Fighting Ships*. Such visual surveillance by coastwatchers and reconnaissance aircraft was essential because traffic analysis was negated when Japanese warships maintained radio silence and cryptanalysts at Station Hypo and elsewhere could not yet quickly decipher messages sent using the most recent Japanese naval codes and ciphers. In early November, Mason reported 33 destroyers and more than two dozen other Japanese vessels assembling off Bougainville for a concerted attack on Guadalcanal. Forewarned, Admiral Halsey—now serving as commander in the South Pacific Area—went all out to meet that threat. His losses in the explosive Naval Battle of Guadalcanal waged in mid-November were steep, but he thwarted the last big Japanese push to retake the island by sinking 10 troop transports and several warships. "The coastwatchers saved Guadalcanal," he said later, "and Guadalcanal saved the Pacific."

Coastwatchers on the Solomons also rescued downed American pilots and shipwrecked sailors. Scores of seamen from the cruiser U.S.S. *Helena,* torpedoed off the island of Vella Lavella in 1943, were harbored by Reverend A. W. E. Silvester at his Methodist mission there until they could be safely evacuated by the Navy. Silvester had no radio transmitter but observed Japanese movements and sent reports by canoe to his fellow New Zealander and coastwatcher, Donald Kennedy, a district administrator on the island of New Georgia who held the rank of captain in the British Solomon Islands Protectorate Defence Force. He recruited and armed over 70 islanders at his station at Segi, on New Georgia's southern tip, and attacked Japanese soldiers who intruded on what he called his "forbidden zone."

A former schoolmaster, Kennedy was a stern disciplinarian who punished scouts for insubordination and other offenses by flogging them over a barrel. Yet one islander who felt his wrath called him "the right man at the right time." Native inhabitants of the Solomons and other war zones around the Pacific often had to choose between familiar colonial overseers like Kennedy and Japanese invaders who were strangers to them and could be even more demanding and punishing than white colonizers. Despite his strict regimen, Kennedy retained the support of islanders because he knew them and their terrain far better than the Japanese did. "I was able to fight and able to lead them," he later remarked of his

"The coastwatchers saved Guadalcanal and Guadalcanal saved the Pacific."

ADM. WILLIAM HALSEY,
U.S. NAVY COMMANDER,
SOUTH PACIFIC

SPYING IN STYLE **Donald Kennedy (left) dines comfortably with a visiting American intelligence officer at the remote coastwatching station Kennedy maintained under armed guard on the Japanese-occupied island of New Georgia.**

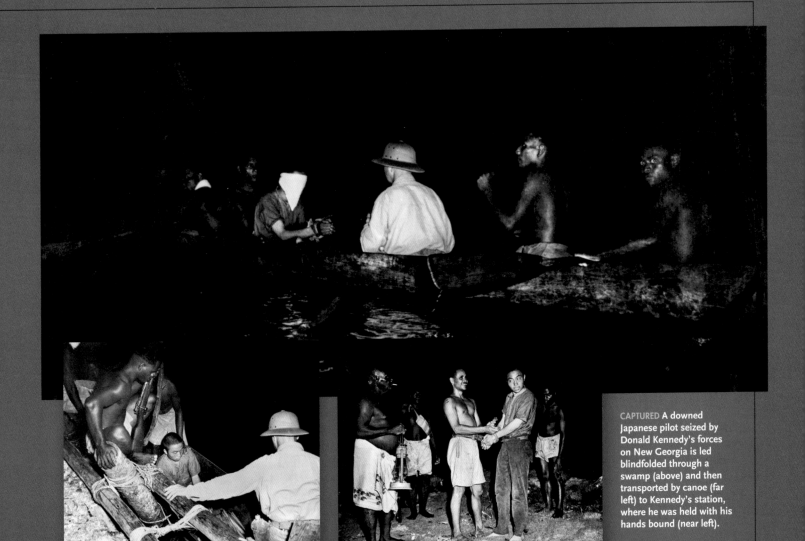

CAPTURED **A downed Japanese pilot seized by Donald Kennedy's forces on New Georgia is led blindfolded through a swamp (above) and then transported by canoe (far left) to Kennedy's station, where he was held with his hands bound (near left).**

STANDING GUARD **More than just scouts or observers, the islanders recruited by Kennedy served as soldiers and guards, including these men armed with British rifles.**

THE LAST DAYS OF COLONIAL GLORY

The thinly veiled secret behind the war waged against imperial Japan was that the Allies were fighting for their own colonial interests and possessions. Although Americans called the Philippines a protectorate, it was essentially a colony, seized from Spain in 1898 by U.S. forces, who went on to wage a fierce campaign against Filipino guerrillas seeking freedom for their country. Americans shocked by that conflict asked why their nation, founded in rebellion against an empire, was now acting like one. Congress eventually responded to pressure from American anti-imperialists and Filipino nationalists by promising in the mid-1930s to grant independence to the Philippines within a decade while retaining military bases there. No such pledges were offered to India, Burma, or other British colonies in Asia by avowed imperialists like Winston Churchill who argued that British rule helped civilize people not deemed ready to rule themselves.

Among the chief beneficiaries of imperialism were Westerners who resided in Far Eastern colonies, including French Indochina and the Dutch East Indies, and profited from cheap labor there. Planters and officers who might not have been conspicuously wealthy back home lived as colonial grandees, with plenty of servants to ease their existence and "coolies" to bear their burdens. Some colonizers were conscientious and earned the respect of native people, who aided them during the war against Japanese invaders. But the main obstacle Japan faced when imposing on those under military occupation in its so-called Greater East Asia Co-Prosperity Sphere was not the loyalty of indigenous people to Westerners in their midst but their loathing for Japanese imperialists, whose grim reputation in Korea, Manchuria, and China followed them to lands they seized and exploited beginning in 1941. All those who sought to achieve or perpetuate colonial glory during the war were fighting in vain. Contestants on both sides would lose their colonies in the postwar era, not to other imperial powers but to the inhabitants themselves, unwilling to wait until their colonial masters considered them ready for independence. ◗

SPECIAL TREATMENT Pictured in the 1920s when much of Asia was dominated by imperial powers, a dozen waiters attend a few privileged white guests at a hotel in the Dutch East Indies, later occupied by Japanese forces during World War II. The independent nation of Indonesia emerged here following the conflict.

AMERICAN OCCUPIER A veteran of the Civil War and the Apache Wars, Maj. Gen. Henry Lawton was sent in late 1898 to pacify the Philippines, where this picture of him was taken. He was killed in December 1899 while battling Filipinos opposed to the American occupation.

HEAVY BURDEN A native bearer carries a French official across a river in colonial Indochina, which France reclaimed from Japan when World War II ended but later relinquished as Vietnam, Cambodia, and Laos broke free.

scouts, and success in battle convinced them that "they were on the right side." In addition to providing Allied commanders with timely radio reports on enemy sorties, Kennedy and his men killed nearly 120 Japanese soldiers, captured 20 more, and rescued nearly two dozen American servicemen.

In March 1943, Halsey sent a team led by an intelligence officer on his staff to reconnoiter New Georgia, the next target in the relentless Allied campaign to secure the Solomons and New Guinea and evict Japanese forces from Rabaul. Donald Kennedy hosted those Americans in style at Segi. Houseboys in jackets served them dinner at a table covered in linen, and they were joined by an attractive young island woman who was part of Kennedy's retinue. He was master of his tropical domain, but he would not preside over it much longer. In a few months, his private war against the Japanese on New Georgia would give way to a massive assault by U.S. troops, and his station would be bulldozed to provide a runway for American warplanes. As the conflict in the Pacific intensified, it was sweeping away not only Japanese imperial ambitions but also the colonial traditions of officers like Kennedy whose ancestors had fanned out from the British Isles around the world and forged an empire on which the sun was now setting.

DOWNING YAMAMOTO

April 4, 1943, was Admiral Yamamoto's 59th birthday. It was also the day on which he planned to launch Operation I-Go, during which warplanes from five Japanese aircraft carriers would join fighters and bombers taking off from Rabaul in blasting American bases on New Guinea and the lower Solomon Islands. Stormy weather forced postponement of the offensive, adding to the tension and foreboding that gripped Yamamoto and left him in no mood to celebrate his birthday. The operation that would begin belatedly on April 7 was not one he undertook gladly. He and other naval commanders had argued for concentrating the attacks on the Solomons, but army chiefs insisted on extending them to New Guinea, where their forces were under mounting pressure from MacArthur's troops and Maj. Gen. George Kenney's Fifth Army Air Force. Expanding the operation increased the risks

"There was no doubt in my mind that shooting down Yamamoto would be a vital and serious blow to the Japanese."
LT. CMDR. EDWIN LAYTON

for Yamamoto's naval airmen, who had suffered substantial losses at Midway and other battles since then. By necessity, the training time for Japanese naval pilots was being reduced from the 18 months they received before the war began to shorter stints. Some of those who would take part in Operation

I-Go possessed more enthusiasm than expertise. Yamamoto's outlook would have been even gloomier had he known the full range of intelligence assets arrayed against him. In addition to the advance warnings provided by coastwatchers, reconnaissance aircraft, submarines, and new radar installations, American commanders in the southwest Pacific were now receiving timely decrypts from Navy code breakers—who were back up to speed—and from Army cryptanalysts, aided by breakthroughs made at an Allied signals intelligence station in New Delhi, India, where coded radio messages from Japanese forces in Burma were intercepted and analyzed.

When Operation I-Go unfolded, American airmen knew what to expect and downed more incoming planes than they lost—a fact not readily apparent to Yamamoto because his pilots overstated their kills. Yet he knew that even a successful series of air raids would not evict enemy forces from New Guinea and Guadalcanal or end the threat to Rabaul, the stronghold from which he directed the strikes. On April 13, he decided to fly to air bases around Bougainville, whose proximity to Rabaul made that island pivotal, and encourage his forces there to keep up the fight. Yamamoto's aides were concerned for his safety, but he felt obliged to make a personal appeal to officers, visit the sick and wounded at hospitals, and salute men who would have to pay dearly to resist further American advances up the Solomon chain to New Georgia and Bougainville.

A staff officer drew up an itinerary for Yamamoto's quick trip, which called for him to depart Rabaul at six in the morning on April 18 and visit three bases before returning that afternoon. The details were then enciphered using the latest naval codebook and cipher table and transmitted by radio on the evening of April 13 to Japanese commanders at those bases. American listeners "were keeping a special watch on the Rabaul radio circuits," wrote

YAMAMOTO'S VISION: SUBMARINE AIRCRAFT CARRIERS

In early 1942, Admiral Yamamoto proposed to take the war to the U.S. mainland with an innovative fleet of supersubmarines that could serve as aircraft carriers and penetrate American coastal defenses. He ordered the construction of 18 *I-400*-class *Sen Toku* (Special Attack) submarines, each capable of launching three floatplane bombers, housed in a watertight hangar when the vessels were submerged. The fleet would approach an American coastal city undetected and surface to launch dozens of bombers that would carry out a surprise attack and return to land alongside the subs, which had cranes to retrieve them. The first submarine of the Special Attack class, *I-400*, was 400 feet long—nearly twice as long as some older American subs in service then. It could dive to a depth of 330 feet and had a phenomenal globe-spanning range of 37,500 nautical miles.

Targeted by the U.S. in April 1943, Yamamoto did not live to fulfill his plan, which proved too ambitious for an empire increasingly on the defensive as the war went on. By January 1945, only two of the big subs—*I-400* and *I-401*—had been completed, and work on the rest had been canceled. Desperate Japanese naval planners considered using the two *I-400*s to bomb the Panama Canal or wage biological warfare on the West Coast. Instead, they were dispatched in August 1945 on a kamikaze attack against an American fleet anchored at Ulithi Atoll in the Caroline Islands. The war ended before the *I-400*s reached that objective and they were surrendered intact to the U.S. Navy, which studied the prodigious submersible aircraft carriers and eventually scuttled them. ✪

CAPTURED GIANT At bottom, the Japanese submarine aircraft carrier *I-400* arrives under control of the U.S. Navy at Sasebo, Japan, shortly after the war ended. The massive vessel had a 115-foot-long, 12-foot-wide hangar located beside its conning tower that could house three Aichi M6A1 Seiran floatplane bombers like the one pictured below once their wings were folded. Launched by pneumatic catapult, each plane could carry a torpedo or 1,800 pounds of bombs and had a range of 740 miles.

Edwin Layton, who remained at Pearl Harbor as chief intelligence officer for Nimitz and received a partial decrypt of Yamamoto's itinerary from Station Hypo within 36 hours of the time it was dispatched. Hypo was no longer directed by Joseph Rochefort, who had been denied credit for his achievements by rival officers in Washington and reassigned. But cryptanalysts he instructed and inspired were still there and provided Layton with all he needed to determine that Yamamoto's forthcoming flight from RR—the letter code for Rabaul—would bring him within range of American fighter planes based on Guadalcanal.

"There was no doubt in my mind that shooting down Yamamoto would be a vital and serious blow to the Japanese," Layton recalled. "There was no one of the same stature to replace him." Nimitz agreed and secured approval for an attack on Yamamoto from Navy Secretary Frank Knox, who may have sought Roosevelt's consent without leaving any record of the conversation that would implicate the president. Aware that the attack risked alerting the Japanese that their codes were being broken, Layton drafted instructions from Nimitz that "all personnel concerned, particularly the pilots," be told that intelligence on Yamamoto's flight came from Australian coastwatchers near Rabaul. Nimitz sent the order to Halsey with his compliments: "Best of luck and good hunting."

Instructions to target Yamamoto went from Halsey at his headquarters on New Caledonia, south of the Solomon Islands, to Rear Adm. Marc Mitscher, commanding on Guadalcanal. He assigned the task to Maj. John Mitchell, an Army Air Force pilot whose 339th Fighter Group flew P-38 Lightnings, the swiftest and deadliest fighters in the American arsenal. To steel Mitchell and his men for their dangerous mission and give them time to prepare, they were told that Yamamoto was their target, which blew the cover story contrived by Layton because coastwatchers had no way of anticipating the admiral's flight. At 7:10 a.m. on April 18, 17 P-38s took off from Henderson Field, one of which turned back a short time later when an engine malfunctioned. Drop tanks carrying extra fuel extended the squadron's range, and Mitchell led pilots on a circuitous course to Bougainville, flying perilously low over the Coral Sea to make their aircraft harder to spot from a distance and invisible to Japanese radar. Based on the decrypt, Mitchell planned to intercept Yamamoto's plane and its accompanying fighters shortly before 10 a.m. along the west coast of Bougainville. Most of the P-38s would then climb to high altitude to deal with the Japanese fighters while the four pilots Mitchell assigned to the "killer flight" would go straight for the bomber carrying Yamamoto and his staff. As it turned out, Yamamoto divided his staff among two bombers to reduce the risk that all of them would be lost in an accident or attack.

Around 9:45, Mitchell encountered those bombers near the coast, escorted by six Mitsubishi Zeros. Three Zeros and one P-38 went down in the ensuing dogfight while kill shots sent Yamamoto's plane plunging into the jungle and the other bomber crashing into the sea. Vice Adm. Matome Ugaki survived that crash, swam ashore, and was rescued by a Japanese search party, who found Yamamoto dead amid the wreckage of his aircraft. All Major Mitchell knew for sure when he returned to base was that his squadron had downed the bombers and accomplished its mission. Halsey received word from Guadalcanal that evening: "Pop goes the weasel . . . April 18 seems to be our day." Officers at his headquarters cheered the apparent demise of Yamamoto, but Halsey, whose hatred for the Japanese knew no bounds, complained that he had lost the chance to take him alive: "I'd hoped to lead

"Best of luck and good hunting."

ADMIRAL NIMITZ TO ADMIRAL HALSEY, ORDERING AN ATTACK ON YAMAMOTO

"Tallyho. Let's get the bastard."

HALSEY'S COMMENT ON NIMITZ'S ORDER

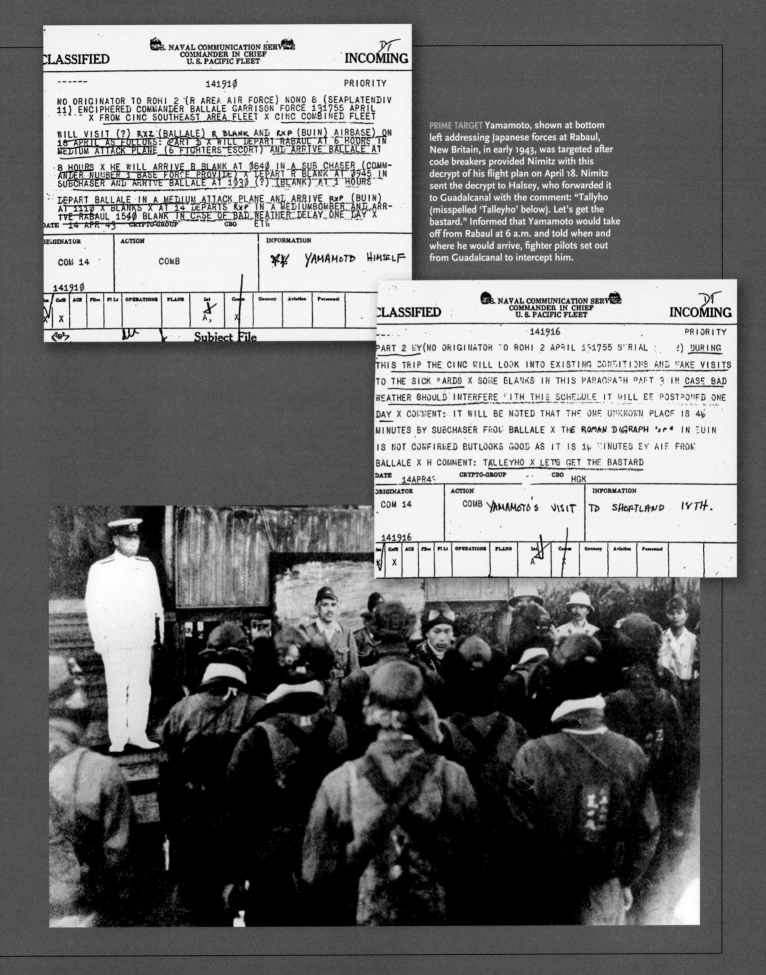

CLASSIFIED — U.S. NAVAL COMMUNICATION SERVICE
COMMANDER IN CHIEF
U. S. PACIFIC FLEET — **INCOMING**

141910 — PRIORITY

NO ORIGINATOR TO ROHI 2 (R AREA AIR FORCE) NONO 8 (SEAPLATENDIV 11) ENCIPHERED COMMANDER BALLALE GARRISON FORCE 131755 APRIL X FROM CINC SOUTHEAST AREA FLEET X CINC COMBINED FLEET

WILL VISIT (?) RXZ (BALLALE) R BLANK AND RXP (BUIN) AIRBASE) ON 18 APRIL AS FOLLOWS: PART 1 X WILL DEPART RABAUL AT 6 HOURS IN MEDIUM ATTACK PLANE (6 FIGHTERS ESCORT) AND ARRIVE BALLALE AT 8 HOURS X HE WILL ARRIVE R BLANK AT 0840 IN A SUB CHASER (COMMANDER NUMBER 1 BASE FORCE PROVIDE) X DEPART R BLANK AT 0945 IN SUBCHASER AND ARRIVE BALLALE AT 1030 (?) (BLANK) AT 1 HOURS DEPART BALLALE IN A MEDIUM ATTACK PLANE AND ARRIVE RXP (BUIN) AT 1110 X BLANKS X AT 14 DEPARTS RXP IN A MEDIUMBOMBER AND ARRIVE RABAUL 1540 BLANK IN CASE OF BAD WEATHER DELAY ONE DAY X

DATE 14 APR 43 — CRYPTO-GROUP — CBO ETH

ORIGINATOR: COM 14 — ACTION: COMB — INFORMATION: YAMAMOTO HIMSELF

141910

Subject File

PRIME TARGET Yamamoto, shown at bottom left addressing Japanese forces at Rabaul, New Britain, in early 1943, was targeted after code breakers provided Nimitz with this decrypt of his flight plan on April 18. Nimitz sent the decrypt to Halsey, who forwarded it to Guadalcanal with the comment: "Tallyho (misspelled 'Talleyho' below). Let's get the bastard." Informed that Yamamoto would take off from Rabaul at 6 a.m. and told when and where he would arrive, fighter pilots set out from Guadalcanal to intercept him.

CLASSIFIED — U.S. NAVAL COMMUNICATION SERVICE
COMMANDER IN CHIEF
U. S. PACIFIC FLEET — **INCOMING**

141916 — PRIORITY

PART 2 BY (NO ORIGINATOR TO ROHI 2 APRIL 131755 SERIAL 2) DURING THIS TRIP THE CINC WILL LOOK INTO EXISTING CONDITIONS AND MAKE VISITS TO THE SICK WARDS X SOME BLANKS IN THIS PARAGRAPH PART 3 IN CASE BAD WEATHER SHOULD INTERFERE WITH THIS SCHEDULE IT WILL BE POSTPONED ONE DAY X COMMENT: IT WILL BE NOTED THAT THE ONE UNKNOWN PLACE IS 40 MINUTES BY SUBCHASER FROM BALLALE X THE ROMAN DIGRAPH 'XP' IN BUIN IS NOT CONFIRMED BUT LOOKS GOOD AS IT IS 10 MINUTES BY AIR FROM BALLALE X H COMMENT: TALLEYHO X LETS GET THE BASTARD

DATE 14APR43 — CRYPTO-GROUP — CBO HGK

ORIGINATOR: COM 14 — ACTION: COMB YAMAMOTO'S VISIT TO SHORTLAND 18TH.

141916

A RISKY MISSION TO KILL YAMAMOTO

On April 17, 1943, Capt. Thomas Lanphier, Jr., learned that the target of the secret mission he and other Army Air Force fighter pilots on Guadalcanal would fly the next day was Admiral Yamamoto. Lanphier knew he was making history and began keeping a journal (below). He was called on to lead the "killer flight" of four P-38s that would go after Yamamoto's plane while other pilots dueled with fighters escorting the admiral to Bougainville on a schedule that U.S. Navy cryptanalysts had decoded. Success, Lanphier wrote, depended on Yamamoto "arriving on time as we had only 15 minutes over the target area." His timely arrival doomed him, and Lanphier could not resist berating the fallen admiral afterward, declaring by radio that the "son of a bitch" would never again threaten America.

Lanphier's words, if picked up by Japanese listeners, could have alerted them that the attack was not a lucky strike by pilots who had no way of knowing whose plane they downed but a deliberate assault on Yamamoto, based on decrypts. Disclosing that Japanese naval plans were being decoded could do even more harm to the American war effort than Yamamoto might do as a strategist if he remained alive. Nimitz was mindful of that risk and hoped to keep the objective secret, but security was compromised when pilots were told in advance that Yamamoto was their target. Nimitz was further alarmed when he read—and promptly suppressed—a story by a reporter who interviewed Lanphier and others after the mission and wrote that the U.S. had tracked Yamamoto before he was killed. When Nimitz complained of "flagrant disregard" for security, Admiral Halsey berated pilots for speaking about the mission. "He accused us of everything he could think of, from being traitors to our country to being so stupid we had no right to wear the American uniform," recalled Lt. Rex Barber, who shared credit with Lanphier for downing Yamamoto. Yet Halsey and other commanders had also been lax when they made thinly disguised references to killing Yamamoto in encrypted radio messages without knowing for sure that they were indecipherable by the Japanese. Had such lapses betrayed the Navy's code-breaking capability to the enemy, what was later hailed as an intelligence coup would have been an intelligence failure. ✪

KILLER FLIGHT Tom Lanphier sketched on the right page of this entry from his journal the path he and other pilots followed on April 18, 1943. Departing from Guadalcanal, they swung west of the Solomons to avoid detection before downing Yamamoto's plane over the coast of Bougainville and returning directly to Henderson Field.

that scoundrel up Pennsylvania Avenue in chains, with the rest of you kicking him where it would do the most good!"

Reaction in the U.S. was much the same as Halsey's after Yamamoto's fate was confirmed through intercepts of secret communications between Japanese authorities, who did not make his death public until May 21. Since the attack on Pearl Harbor, he had been demonized in America as a warmonger who once stated that the only way for Japan to defeat the U.S. was to capture the White House and force the president to capitulate. As Capt. Thomas Lanphier, one of the pilots credited with downing Yamamoto, radioed to Guadalcanal after the attack: "That son of a bitch will not be dictating any peace terms to the White House." In fact, Yamamoto's point—which he made before the war to a Japanese militarist—was that conquering the U.S. and seizing the White House was a fantasy, beyond Japan's means. The best it could hope for was to deprive America of the naval capacity to oppose Japanese expansion in Southeast Asia and the Pacific. Yamamoto reckoned he had a year at most in which to achieve that objective. If his codes had not been broken and his plans penetrated, he might have succeeded. By the time he died, however, he faced a desperate struggle that those who knew America's strength as he did feared might end with Admiral Nimitz or General MacArthur dictating terms to Emperor Hirohito in Tokyo.

"I am looking forward to dictating peace to the United States in the White House at Washington"
— ADMIRAL YAMAMOTO

What do YOU say, AMERICA?

PILLORIED Contrary to this war poster, Yamamoto never proposed to invade the U.S. and seize Washington. He was a dreaded foe of American forces in the Pacific, however, and downing him brought credit to Lt. Rex Barber and Capt. Tom Lanphier, shown standing at right beside Barber.

ENTER THE OSS

When Franklin Roosevelt was asked by William Donovan to place the civilian intelligence office he directed as COI (Coordinator of Information) under the Joint Chiefs of Staff, FDR was wary. "They'll absorb you," he cautioned Donovan, who replied firmly: "You leave that to me, Mr. President." Donovan knew that some commanders resented him for treading on their turf and hoped to abolish or neutralize his agency. But other officers recognized that Donovan's keen recruits, including civilians as well as volunteers with military experience, could perform tasks for which regular soldiers were ill suited, including helping partisans conduct sabotage, assassinations, and other unconventional acts of war against enemy occupation forces. Donovan was confident his organization could serve the armed forces without being absorbed and welcomed the letter he received from Roosevelt in June 1942 (below left), stating that the agency would operate under the

BADGE OF HONOR
Sworn to secrecy during the war, each OSS employee received this pin when the agency disbanded in late 1945.

Joint Chiefs and be known thereafter as the Office of Strategic Services (OSS).

Close ties to the military gave the OSS an active role in the war effort. Although many in the agency remained civilians, among them scholars in Research and Analysis who provided confidential assessments of Axis leaders and capabilities, others involved in covert combat operations were commissioned as officers. Donovan ended the war as a major general and often conferred in uniform with OSS subordinates like those who organized guerrilla warfare against the Japanese in China (opposite). All those serving in OSS operational groups wore uniforms, which did not spare some who were captured from being shot to death. Secret agents like Virginia Hall (bottom right) who operated for the OSS behind enemy lines without military credentials were in even greater danger if they fell into enemy hands, which exposed them to torture and execution. ✪

FOREWARNED Some who enlisted under Donovan (seated at center opposite) after FDR authorized the OSS (far left) knew from experience that intelligence work was "no picnic," as stated on the agency's training manual (near left). Virginia Hall, shown on a driver's license issued in Estonia in 1938, went on to aid French resistance fighters at great risk for the SOE and later the OSS.

COMMANDO TRAINING

Combat training procedures of the OSS owed much to the British, who had begun preparing recruits to operate behind enemy lines long before the U.S. entered the war. Some OSS officers who trained recruits had themselves been trained at Camp X, established along Lake Ontario in Canada by William Stephenson, British security chief in America and a confidant of William Donovan, who sent prospective OSS instructors there to learn lessons in stealth from British paramilitary officers.

As the OSS expanded, it set up training camps at sites around Washington, D.C., including the Congressional Country Club in Bethesda, Maryland, whose manicured greens were pockmarked with divots gouged by grenades hurled by secret warriors. Few OSS trainees would soon forget instructor William Fairbairn, a British expert in close combat and "gutter fighting," which he said had "no rules except one: *kill or be killed*." He and Eric Sykes—who like Fairbairn had honed his skills as a police officer in Shanghai and drilled both British and American recruits—taught trainees how to wield concealed weapons and eliminate foes quickly and quietly. Recruits adept at such dark arts, including planting explosives and landing at night by parachute, were ready to fulfill Donovan's master plan for covert operations, carried out by agents possessed of "disciplined daring," as he put it, and "trained for aggressive action." ✪

TARGET PRACTICE An instructor shows OSS recruits in training camp how to aim and fire a pistol with a steady hand.

TRADECRAFT OSS trainees exercise as climbers to prepare to scale towers and sabotage power lines and other lofty targets in enemy territory. Those entering combat were issued weapons that were easy to carry and conceal like the knife below. Held in a sheath disguised as a spatula whose slots allowed it to be attached to any belt, the weapon was developed by Eric Sykes and William Fairbairn, shown demonstrating how to wield the knife at right.

Fighting Stance

INTELLIGENCE AND ESPIONAGE

Some of the heftiest contributions to the war effort by the OSS came from men and women trained not in camps but in colleges and universities, where they acquired knowledge and skills with strategic applications. Historian William Langer (top right), director of OSS Research and Analysis (R&A), recruited hundreds of scholars and assembled a comprehensive map collection to provide commanders and officials with charts and intelligence reports on the various countries, cultures, friends, and foes encountered by Allied forces. Among those academic recruits was his brother, psychologist Walter Langer, whose team produced a psychoanalytic study of Hitler (below), drawing on disclosures from informants like Ernst "Putzi" Hanfstaengl, who fled Germany after serving as the Führer's foreign press secretary. The report predicted that Hitler would never surrender and, if not assassinated before Allied troops closed in on him, would wait "until the last moment" to commit suicide.

Many OSS researchers and analysts schooled in ivory towers ended up working near war fronts as Amer-

IVIES **William Langer** from Harvard (above) and **Sherman Kent** from Yale (below) supervised R&A at the OSS.

ican armies advanced. Sherman Kent, who oversaw R&A for Europe and Africa, had 31 people reporting to him from Paris soon after that city was liberated in September 1944. Espionage was undertaken by a separate OSS branch designated Secret Intelligence (SI). Most of those spying for the OSS in Axis territory were residents of occupied countries or émigrés who returned there and communicated with their SI case officers through coded radio messages or other channels. OSS agents did not penetrate Germany until late in the war, but some Germans opposed to the Nazi regime entered neutral Switzerland earlier in the conflict and provided vital intelligence to Allen Dulles (below), the agency's preeminent spymaster. No one outside the Reich was better informed than he was on secret efforts to topple Hitler, thanks largely to Hans Gisevius, a German intelligence officer who met covertly with Dulles prior to a failed attempt on Hitler's life in 1944 and escaped arrest and execution for his role in that plot when Dulles helped him reach safety in Switzerland. ✪

ANALYZING HITLER **William Donovan** ordered this psychological profile because he wanted to "know what Hitler was thinking before he thought it."

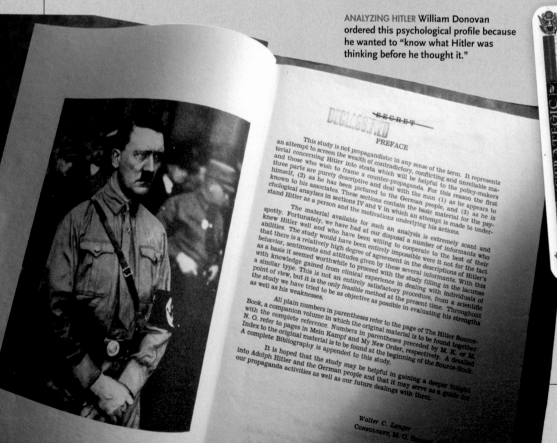

FUTURE DIRECTOR **Allen Dulles,** shown on his ID card, was one of several adept OSS officers who later directed the Central Intelligence Agency (CIA).

CHARTING THE WAY This map of the Solomons was one of thousands collected or produced for the government and armed forces by the busy OSS map department (above), which received a million requests for charts from officers or officials in 1944 alone.

GADGETS FOR ARMED INFILTRATORS

When chemist and inventor Stanley Lovell (right) was asked to take charge of OSS Research and Development (R&D) and design secret weapons for use in hostile territory, William Donovan told him he wanted someone as crafty as Professor Moriarty, the sinister adversary of Sherlock Holmes. "I'd relish the assignment," Lovell said, "but dirty tricks are simply not tolerated in the American code of ethics." Donovan replied that if he was so naïve as to think that Americans would disdain any trick that might help them defeat their mortal enemies, then "you're not my man." Lovell took the job and went on to develop the baseball-shaped BEANO hand grenade (below) for those adept at America's national pastime along with stealthy sidearms, truth potions, and poison pills. Lovell's message to his staff was just what Donovan ordered: "Throw all your normal law-abiding concepts out the window. Here's a chance to raise merry hell."

Proposals for exotic new weapons came not just from Lovell but

R&D CHIEF A chemist and inventor before he joined the OSS, Stanley Lovell led the agency's innovative Research and Development office.

also from President Roosevelt, who passed along to Donovan a letter from a dentist in Pennsylvania suggesting that bats be harnessed with small incendiary devices and released over Japan, where they would nest in wooden buildings and set them ablaze. Those so-called bat bombs were tested with mixed results before the project was abandoned in 1944. Other brainstorms never got beyond the laboratory, including Lovell's suggestion to inject female hormones into vegetables that Hitler consumed so he would lose his moustache and exhibit other humiliating symptoms. Several weapons designed or commissioned by OSS R&D, however, proved well suited for covert warfare like the High Standard .22-caliber pistol (opposite), with a built-in silencer. According to Lovell, his boss demonstrated that gun in the Oval Office by firing it into a sandbag while FDR's back was turned. Duly impressed, Roosevelt told Donovan, who belonged to the opposing party: "You're the only wild-eyed Republican I'd ever let in here with a weapon." ✪

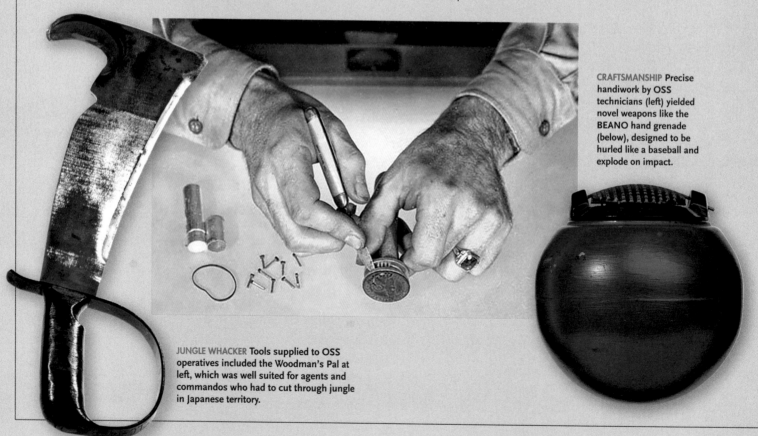

CRAFTSMANSHIP Precise handiwork by OSS technicians (left) yielded novel weapons like the BEANO hand grenade (below), designed to be hurled like a baseball and explode on impact.

JUNGLE WHACKER Tools supplied to OSS operatives included the Woodman's Pal at left, which was well suited for agents and commandos who had to cut through jungle in Japanese territory.

ROAD HAZARD R&D designed this caltrop so that when tossed onto a road, one of its four steel spikes would always point upward to puncture enemy tires.

STARS AND STRIPES This blood chit—carried by those entering hostile territory to signal their nationality and seek help in various languages if wounded—was issued to OSS operatives in the China-Burma-India Theater.

QUIET THREAT Manufactured for the OSS by High Standard Firearms, this .22-caliber pistol equipped with an integral silencer combined power with stealth.

CONCEALED COMPASS Lovell's team designed a uniform button (above) that could be opened to reveal a miniature compass (top) for use by escapees or those stranded in enemy territory.

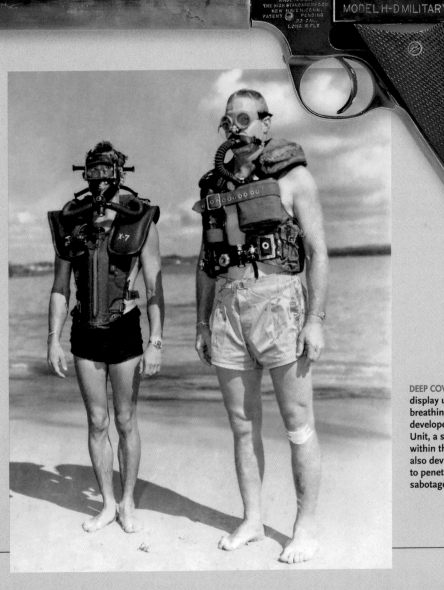

DEEP COVER OSS frogmen display underwater breathing apparatuses developed by the Maritime Unit, a separate branch within the agency that also devised watercraft to penetrate harbors and sabotage enemy ships.

UNDERMINING ENEMY MORALE

Unlike the Office of War Information, which dealt in overt propaganda such as broadcasting American news and views to occupied territory, the OSS specialized in black propaganda, disguised so that it appeared to originate within enemy territory. OSS agents assigned for that purpose to Morale Operations (MO) sought to demoralize opposing soldiers and civilians by sending them subversive messages in their own language, including broadcasts aimed at German troops by the station Soldatensender ("Soldiers' Radio") West, which originated as a British operation. Among that station's featured performers was German-born singer and actress Marlene Dietrich (below), whose rendition of "Lili Marlene," about a soldier separated from his sweetheart, struck a chord in war-weary men who longed to return home. Nazi authorities banned the song and warned Germans against tuning in but could not stop them from listening to OSS shows that sounded much like their own programs.

Few MO schemes were more ingenious than Operation Cornflakes, carried out late in the war when Germans were losing faith in their Führer. Following a bombing raid that wrecked a German mail train, Allied aircraft dropped mailbags along the tracks containing copies of *Das Neue Deutschland* ("The New Germany"), an anti-Nazi newspaper that was seemingly of German origin but produced by the OSS. The papers were sealed in envelopes bearing forged postage stamps (opposite), most of which showed Hitler properly in profile above the words *Deutsches Reich* ("German Reich"). Some, however, portrayed him with a skeletal death's head above the words *Futsches Reich* ("Ruined Reich"). The mailbags were picked up and delivered in Germany, disseminating seditious propaganda that appeared to come from within Hitler's crumbling Reich. ✪

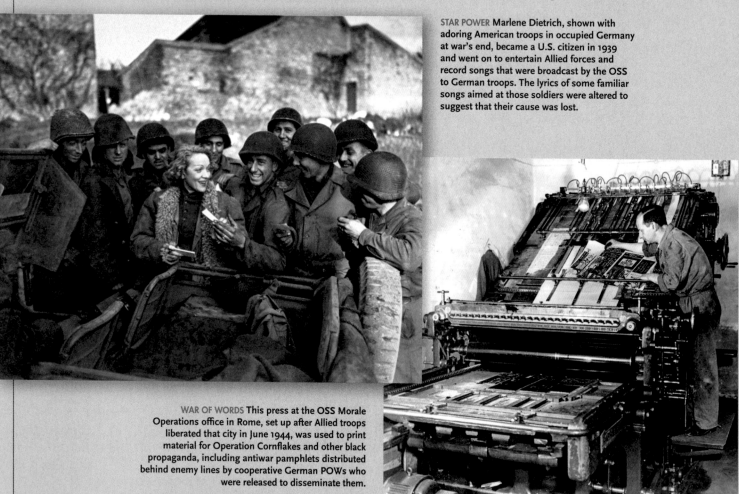

STAR POWER Marlene Dietrich, shown with adoring American troops in occupied Germany at war's end, became a U.S. citizen in 1939 and went on to entertain Allied forces and record songs that were broadcast by the OSS to German troops. The lyrics of some familiar songs aimed at those soldiers were altered to suggest that their cause was lost.

WAR OF WORDS **This press at the OSS Morale Operations office in Rome, set up after Allied troops liberated that city in June 1944, was used to print material for Operation Cornflakes and other black propaganda, including antiwar pamphlets distributed behind enemy lines by cooperative German POWs who were released to disseminate them.**

12 12

FUTSCHES REICH

DEUTSCHES REICH

POSTAL ASSAULT Forgers involved in Operation Cornflakes produced thousands of 12-pfennig stamps like the one at left, copying an authentic stamp honoring Hitler. They were placed on anti-Nazi propaganda and infiltrated into Germany along with some parcels stamped with a skeletal image of Hitler (above), adding insult to the injury done to German morale.

BEHIND ENEMY LINES

No branch of the OSS did more to answer William Donovan's call for "aggressive action" than Special Operations (SO), modeled after Special Operations Executive (SOE), which Churchill authorized to "set Europe ablaze." Like SOE agents, SO recruits operated behind enemy lines, often aiding or organizing attacks by partisans on Axis occupation forces. In Yugoslavia, OSS special operatives helped resistance fighters combat German forces and evacuated downed Allied pilots harbored by those partisans. In Burma, officers of OSS Detachment 101 armed and trained Kachin guerrillas (below), who were credited with killing two dozen Japanese occupiers for every one of their own losses. In Norway, OSS commandos led by William Colby (opposite) descended by parachute and advanced on skis to sabotage rail lines and keep German divisions penned up in Norway as Allies invaded the Reich. Supreme Allied Commander Dwight Eisenhower declared at war's end that the value of such operations by the OSS had been "so great that there should be no thought of its elimination." Despite that endorsement, the agency was disbanded in late 1945, but it helped foster the CIA, led in years to come by proven OSS veterans like Colby. ✪

SERBIAN CONNECTION OSS officers and Serbian fighters called Chetniks make their way in 1944 to the camp of Chetnik leader Draza Mihailovic, whose forces helped the OSS rescue downed Allied pilots in Yugoslavia.

JUNGLE PATROL Warriors of the Kachin tribe, including the watchful men at left on patrol in Burma in 1944, were recruited and equipped by OSS Detachment 101 to fight Japanese forces there. Wading along streams enabled such guerrillas to move quietly without leaving tracks that enemies might use to pursue them.

PARATROOPERS Maj. William Colby stands behind his uniformed OSS commandos in the photograph opposite, taken in early 1945 as they prepared to parachute into German-occupied Norway, the ancestral home of most of the men in Colby's outfit.

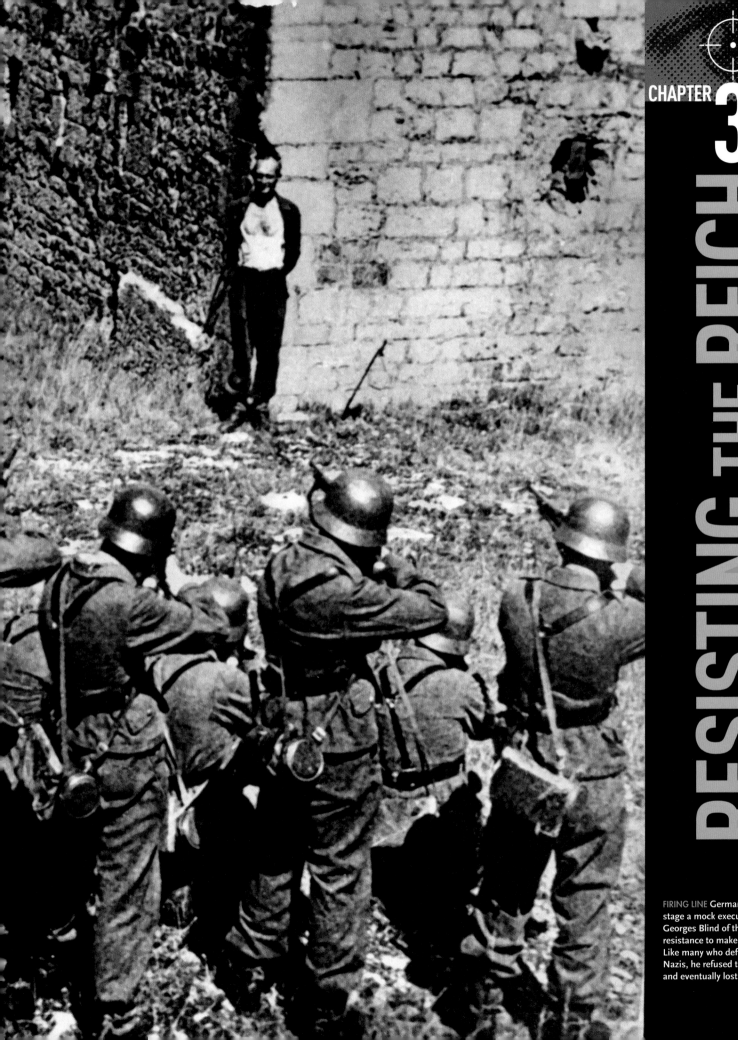

RESISTING THE REICH

FIRING LINE German troops
stage a mock execution of
Georges Blind of the French
resistance to make him talk.
Like many who defied the
Nazis, he refused to collaborate
and eventually lost his life.

SECRET WARRIORS

Noor Inayat Khan seemed an unlikely candidate for secret service. Earnest and soft-spoken, she was the daughter of Hazrat Inayat Khan, a descendant of Indian royalty who taught Sufism, a mystical form of Islam, and preached nonviolence. Educated in Paris, she became an accomplished musician and author of children's stories before fleeing the German invasion of France in 1940 and settling in London with her widowed mother, an American by birth. After she underwent training as a wireless radio operator with the Women's Auxiliary Air Force (WAAF), her technical skill and fluent French brought her to the attention of Vera Atkins, who supervised female agents for Section F, the French section of Special Operations Executive (SOE). Beginning in 1942, Atkins and Maurice Buckmaster, her chief at Section F, assigned women as couriers to networks in France that were involved in sabotage and other forms of resistance. Although those female couriers were less likely than men to be stopped and searched, they still ran great risks, and Section F was now preparing to use women in an even more dangerous role—as radio operators, whose signals could be monitored by the Germans and tracked to their source. Noor Inayat Khan would be the first woman to serve the SOE in that capacity in France. Before she

WELL CONCEALED SOE agent Noor Inayat Khan (opposite), who infiltrated France in 1943 to serve as a clandestine radio operator for a resistance network there, carried her equipment from one hiding place to another in a suitcase like that below, made to conceal a British Type A Mark III radio set, which was capable of transmitting and receiving signals within a range of 500 miles.

NAME: NOOR INAYAT KHAN
OCCUPATION: BRITISH AGENT
ASSIGNMENT: OCCUPIED FRANCE

CHRONOLOGY

DECEMBER 1941 German troops are driven back from Moscow and dig in for a lengthy struggle in Russia that will drain the Reich and increase its demands on occupied countries for labor and other resources.

JANUARY 1942 SS security chief Reinhard Heydrich lays out the "Final Solution"—the secret Nazi plan to exterminate European Jews—at the Wannsee Conference in Germany.

APRIL 1942 The SOE is authorized to infiltrate women as British agents into occupied France to aid and arm resistance groups.

JUNE 1942 Reinhard Heydrich assassinated by Czech commandos in Prague in a covert operation run by the Czech government-in-exile in London and the SOE.

AUGUST 1942 German counterintelligence officers break up a spy ring in Berlin known as the Red Orchestra for its links to Moscow.

NOVEMBER 1942 Allied troops invade French North Africa, prompting Hitler to occupy the Vichy zone in southern France and take full control of that country.

JUNE 1943 French resistance leader Jean Moulin seized by SS officer Klaus Barbie and tortured to death.

set out on that perilous assignment in mid-1943, Atkins had to be quite sure that she was up to the challenge.

Reports Atkins received on the 29-year-old recruit from her SOE trainers raised doubt as to whether someone so honest and scrupulous could function undercover and deceive the enemy. "She confesses that she would not like to have to do anything 'two-faced,'" remarked one instructor. "Pretty scared of weapons but tries hard to get over it," wrote another. Atkins did not consider that a great liability in a recruit whose job was to learn codes and send radio messages quickly and accurately using a telegraph key—tasks that her musical skill as a harpist helped her master. The crucial question for Atkins was whether Noor was fully committed to an assignment that would probably not involve shooting anyone but could be fatal for her if she were caught. Nearly one in four female SOE agents serving in occupied Europe lost their lives, and their risk of being seized, tortured, and executed was even greater in places riddled with Gestapo agents and other German security forces like Paris, where Noor would be operating. The peril SOE agents faced was made clear to them when offered cyanide pills that they could use to commit suicide if captured.

Noor had volunteered to work undercover because she wanted to do "something more active in the prosecution of the war, something which would demand more sacrifice." As her training concluded and her departure loomed, however, she grew anxious. Two female agents close to her wrote Atkins, urging that Noor be spared from duty that appeared to weigh heavily on her. Atkins met with her privately and told her that it was not too late to withdraw and she could do so without any blot on her record. But Noor had no intention of backing down. What troubled her, she explained, was not the risk of losing her life but how that loss might affect her family. Since her father's death, she had felt responsible for her younger siblings and her mother, who was told only that she would soon be serving abroad, supposedly in Africa. Noor asked that in case she went missing in action in France, her mother not be informed of her fate unless her death was confirmed.

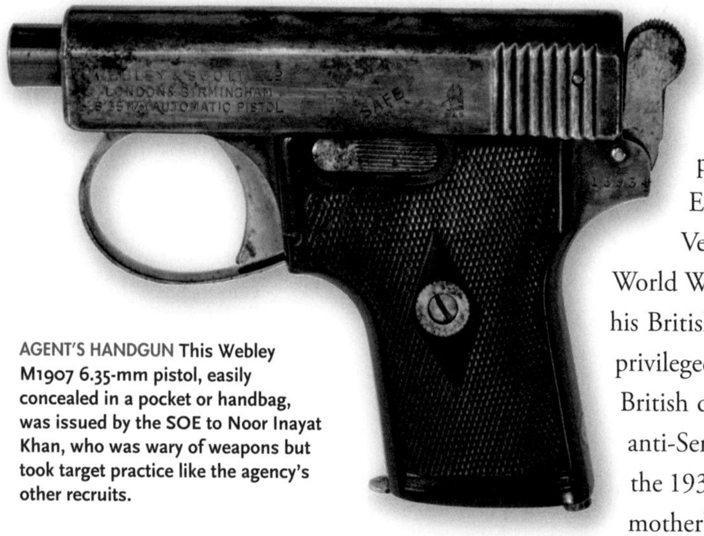

AGENT'S HANDGUN This Webley M1907 6.35-mm pistol, easily concealed in a pocket or handbag, was issued by the SOE to Noor Inayat Khan, who was wary of weapons but took target practice like the agency's other recruits.

Atkins granted that request and concluded that Noor was ready for service and any sacrifice that might require. It helped in this case that the agent and her controller had similar backgrounds, having both arrived in England as refugees. Few people acquainted with the 34-year-old Atkins, who spoke perfect English and appeared British to the core, knew that she was born Vera Rosenberg in Romania, which sided with Germany during World War II. The daughter of a prominent German businessman and his British South African wife, both of whom were Jewish, she lived a privileged life in Bucharest—where her friends and admirers included British diplomats and spies as well as the German ambassador—until anti-Semitic fascists of Romania's Iron Guard gained strength there in the 1930s. In 1937, she fled with relatives to London and adapted her mother's maiden name of Etkins to become Vera Atkins. Because of her Romanian birth, she was unable to find war work until Maurice Buckmaster took notice of her linguistic skills—which included fluent French acquired while studying at the Sorbonne in Paris—and hired her in 1941 as his secretary, from which she advanced to become his trusted aide. Following the death of a British airman to whom she was close, she remained wedded to her work and lived with her widowed mother, who like Noor's mother knew nothing of her daughter's secret life.

Atkins looked after all her "girls" (some of whom were in their 30s or 40s) and made a point of seeing them off on their perilous assignments. But she had reason to be particularly concerned for Noor while accompanying her on June 16, 1943, to Tangmere, an airfield near England's south coast where a single-engine Lysander that could set down on short landing strips in the French countryside would deliver her and three other agents to their destinations. The network that she would join was SOE's largest in France, and its ringleader, Francis Suttill, code-named Prosper, feared for its security, having suffered losses recently that he thought might be caused by carelessness or by a traitor within the ranks. Born in France to a French mother and English father, Suttill had been educated in England and no longer spoke flawless French when he returned to his native country as an SOE operative in 1942 to organize resistance to the German occupiers. He relied to a great extent on Andrée Borrel, an anti-Nazi refugee from France who enlisted as one of Section

DEADLY DOSE SOE technicians designed the necklace above to hold the cyanide capsule at right. Such pills were routinely issued to agents, but many who were seized in enemy territory were prevented by their captors from committing suicide or chose not to.

SPECIAL DELIVERY An RAF pilot boards a Lysander, used by the SOE to land agents in occupied Europe because it could set down on remote landing strips too short or rough for larger planes. Its rear cockpit was meant for one passenger, but two or three agents sometimes crammed in there.

"ATKINS'S GIRLS" IN ACTION

During the war, Section F of the SOE sent 39 women to France to aid those resisting German occupation forces. The first such volunteer was an American, Virginia Hall, who went there on her own initiative for the SOE before it was authorized in 1942 to enlist women as agents. Those who followed in her path, including the six women at far right, were known as Atkins's girls for Vera Atkins (inset), an imposing figure at Section F. She was concerned for all 400 or so SOE agents assigned to France but felt personally responsible for her "girls," some of whom were mothers with boys and girls of their own. Atkins always saw them off, keenly aware of the danger they faced. Those SOE women were in fact far less likely to survive the war than men serving in the British armed forces.

Atkins and her superior, Maurice Buckmaster, sought recruits who spoke flawless French. Many who qualified had been raised in France or studied there before leaving for Britain as war loomed. Some then joined the Women's Auxiliary Air Force or the First Aid Nursing Yeomanry (FANY), which included ambulance drivers as well as women in a secret unit that handled coded radio communications with SOE agents abroad. Eileen Nearne, for example, was educated in France and returned to England in 1940 to work for FANY's secret branch before she joined Section F. By then, her older sister Jacqueline was an SOE courier in France and did not want her put in jeopardy there. Eileen insisted on doing her part as a radio operator, however, and was seized, tortured, and sent to a concentration camp, from which she emerged so traumatized that she would long remain under Jacqueline's care. Most SOE radio operators in France lasted

only a month or two before they were arrested or relieved. But Yvonne Cormeau kept up that perilous task for over a year. After leaving her young daughter with caretakers and parachuting into southwest France in 1943, she avoided being tracked and captured by keeping her messages brief and moving often with her suitcase radio until her sector was liberated.

Some women were already adept as secret agents when recruited by the SOE. Christine Granville served as an SOE courier in France after acting as a conduit between the resistance in her native Poland and British intelligence officers. Nancy Wake, born in New Zealand and raised in Australia, was living with her French husband in Marseille when the war erupted and helped downed Allied pilots and anti-Nazi refugees escape to neutral Spain before she herself fled to elude the Gestapo. Sent back to France by the SOE to arm tough resistance fighters called the Maquis, she won their respect by wielding weapons with them. In battle, one of them said, she fought "like five men."

Courier Odette Sansom, born in France, was arrested there in 1943 with SOE officer Peter Churchill. She told her captors that he was her husband and an influential nephew of Winston Churchill, a lie that helped induce German commandants who feared Allied reprisals to spare both of them. No such reprieve awaited Violette Szabo, seized in 1944 after holding off pursuers with gunfire long enough for the Maquis leader she was aiding to escape. Executed in January 1945, she was one of 13 SOE women sent to France who never returned. After the war, Vera Atkins investigated their fate and that of over 100 Section F men lost in action, and amassed evidence against German officers who were tried for war crimes. ✪

VERA ATKINS
Maurice Buckmaster's "right-hand woman" at Section F, Atkins was a role model for female recruits.

CHRISTINE GRANVILLE
Born in Warsaw, she lost her Jewish mother to the Nazis and paid them back.

EILEEN NEARNE
Just 22 when she enlisted, Nearne barely survived her brutal captivity.

NANCY WAKE
Tough Maquis who battled the Germans considered Wake "one of their own."

ODETTE SANSOM
Her undercover work with the SOE's Peter Churchill inspired the film *Odette*.

VIOLETTE SZABO
Sansom called this agent who died for her native France "the bravest of us all."

YVONNE CORMEAU
One of the finest "pianists" ever to tap out coded radio signals for the SOE.

F's first female agents and joined Suttill in Paris as his courier and aide. Posing as his sister, she accompanied him and did much of the talking as they sought French recruits. By mid-1943, his network had grown so large that Suttill could not be sure that all its members were capable and trustworthy. Shortly before Noor departed, two French sisters who operated a safe house for him were arrested, heightening concerns for the Prosper network at Section F. It was not easy for Atkins to expose someone who trusted and confided in her to such danger. She sent Noor off with a gift—a silver brooch in the shape of a bird, for a fledgling agent who was bravely taking flight and might never return.

THE ROOTS OF RESISTANCE

The SOE and other Allied agencies that penetrated occupied Europe could have accomplished little there without the help of homegrown resistance movements in France and many other countries. For the French and neighboring Belgians, the German invasion in 1940 had aroused bitter memories of a similar onslaught in 1914 at the start of World War I. But Hitler's offensive was far broader and more devastating than that earlier invasion and brought much of Western Europe, from Norway down through central France, under German occupation. Hitler left southern France to be administered by the compliant Vichy government, led by Marshal Philippe Pétain, who announced that to maintain French unity, he would follow "the path of collaboration." In truth, he and other Vichy authorities bitterly divided wartime France by legitimizing collaboration and setting those who deferred to the Germans and did business with them against those who despised and defied the occupiers.

French resistance began with small, symbolic acts. In Paris, a merchant slyly skewered the Vichy regime by displaying in the window of his shop a handsome portrait of Pétain labeled "Sold." No amount of intimidation or surveillance stopped resisters from defacing German posters overnight or plastering walls with patriotic slogans like "Vive de Gaulle," in honor of Gen. Charles de Gaulle, leader of the Free French government in exile in London. His supporters and other French foes of the Reich took as their insignia the Cross of Lorraine, an emblem dating back to the Crusades that came to symbolize resistance to Germany, from which France had reclaimed the lost province of Lorraine at the end of World War I. An anonymous pamphlet that was distributed covertly in Paris warned French patriots to avoid fraternizing with German soldiers. "They are not tourists, they are conquerors," it declared. "If one of them speaks to you in German, shrug helplessly and go quietly on your way."

> **"They are not tourists, they are conquerors . . . If one of them speaks to you in German, shrug helplessly and go quietly on your way."**
> RESISTANCE PAMPHLET DISTRIBUTED IN GERMAN-OCCUPIED PARIS

Violent resistance in the form of sabotage or attacks on German authorities increased in France as pressure mounted on people to work for the Reich and support its war effort. In exchange for the release of French prisoners of war, nearly 600,000 French workers were conscripted and sent to labor in Germany, and many others were forced to help build the Atlantic Wall—coastal fortifications intended to prevent Allied forces from landing. Thousands of Frenchmen evaded forced labor, banded together, and waged guerrilla warfare against German and Vichy forces. Known as Maquisards or Maquis for the tangled bush or thickets where many of them hid out, they obtained weapons and agents trained in sabotage from the SOE. Various French resistance groups received messages from London through BBC radio broadcasts, which included seemingly trivial announcements that signaled in code when and where an agent or arms shipment would be dropped. The Germans searched homes and confiscated radios, but resisters were adept at disguising radios, weapons, and other tools of their trade within common household items.

Belgians were subjected by German occupiers to the same demands and indignities as the French, including forced labor and the siphoning off of fuel, food, and other resources to sustain the Reich and its armed forces. A vital form of resistance in Belgium—over which Allied bombers flew frequently to target German cities and war industries—involved harboring downed Allied airmen and helping them escape through France to Spain, where

GERMAN DOMINATION OF EUROPE

December 1941

- German Reich and organized territories
- German Allies or dependent states
- Under German military administration
- Under military administration of German Allies or dependent states
- Allied states
- Allied-held areas
- Neutral states

IRELAND
UNITED KINGDOM
London
NORWAY Oslo
FINLAND
Helsinki Leningrad
Eastern Karelia
Finnish military admin.
North Sea
SWEDEN
Stockholm
DENMARK
Copenhagen
Baltic Sea
Riga
Reichskommissariat Ostland
SOVIET UNION
Moscow
Minsk
Eastern Front at the end of Operation Barbarossa Dec. 5, 1941
NETHERLANDS
Arnhem
Antwerp
BELGIUM
Cologne
Berlin
GERMAN REICH
Warsaw
General Government
Reichskommissariat of Ukraine
Kiev
Stalingrad
Paris
Occupied Zone
Protectorate of Bohemia and Moravia
Munich
Vienna
SLOVAKIA
FRANCE
SWITZ.
Vichy
Free Zone
Milan
Budapest
HUNGARY
ROMANIA
Sevastopol
Rostov
Eastern Front at the end of Operation Case Blue Nov. 24, 1942
Bordeaux
Vichy France
CROATIA
Belgrade
Territory of the Military Commander in Serbia
Bucharest
Black Sea
Marseille
Florence
ITALY
MONTENEGRO Italy
Sofia
BULGARIA
Istanbul
TURKEY
ATLANTIC OCEAN
PORTUGAL
Lisbon
Madrid
SPAIN
Corsica Vichy France
Rome
Sardinia Italy
ALBANIA Italy
GREECE
German and Italian military administration, Bulgarian annexation
Athens
Dodecanese Italy
SYRIA Free France
0 mi 400
0 km 400
Tangier
SPANISH MOROCCO Spain
FRENCH MOROCCO Vichy France
ALGERIA Vichy France
TUNISIA Vichy France
MALTA U.K.
Mediterranean Sea
CYPRUS U.K.
LEBANON
IRAQ U.K.

A CONTINENT SUBDUED By late 1941, much of Europe lay under the Nazi swastika, having been absorbed or occupied by Germany. Many other countries were allied with or subservient to the Reich, and even neutral nations like Sweden and Spain could ill afford to defy Hitler openly.

PATRIOTS Resistance fighters gather around a sign inscribed with the Cross of Lorraine and the slogan: "French We Are, French We Shall Remain." A symbol of French pride and defiance during the German occupation, the Cross of Lorraine was drawn on the French national flag at top.

dictator Francisco Franco deferred to Hitler but remained officially neutral, enabling British diplomats to take charge of the men and ship them home by way of their base in Gibraltar. A single Belgian family, including Andrée "Dédée" de Jongh, her father Fréderic de Jongh, and other relatives, was largely responsible for an elaborate escape route called the Comet Line that conducted hundreds of airmen to Spain. Dédée was the instigator and began by arranging safe houses in Belgium, where downed airmen received civilian clothing and forged identity papers. To reduce the risk that one arrest would lead to others along the escape route, the Comet Line consisted of numerous links whose guides were unknown to one another and dropped their "packages" (escapees) at cutoffs, where they were later picked up by the next guide in the relay.

Dédée herself often conducted men over the Pyrenees into Spain, aided by a sturdy Basque named Florentino. As one RAF pilot they escorted recalled, Florentino set "a murderous pace and we began to fall further and further behind. In the end, Dédée and Florentino were carrying all our packs. She was very annoyed that we simply could not keep up; she was only a slip of a girl, but she had enormous strength and courage." Michael Creswell of MI9—a British agency established soon after the war began to help downed Allied airmen and POWs escape from the Germans—provided financial aid to the Comet

MAJOR ESCAPE
ROUTES
1940–1942

— O'Leary Lines
--- Comet Lines
☐ Occupied by Germany

1939 boundaries are shown.

ESCAPE ARTIST Dédée de Jongh was in her early 20s when she organized the Comet Line with the aid of her father and other family members and began helping downed Allied airmen in Belgium escape German-occupied territory. She personally escorted more than 100 of those fliers over the Pyrenees to neutral Spain.

DELIVERANCE As shown on this map tracing the various routes of the Comet Line (dashed lines) and the O'Leary Line (solid lines), both operations extended from Belgium or northern France—areas where many Allied airmen sent to bomb Germany were shot down—to Spain, where British consular officials quietly took charge of the escapees and sent them home by way of Gibraltar.

INCOGNITO Belgian Albert-Marie Guérisse, pictured here in Marseille, France, in 1941, had by then assumed a new identity as Patrick O'Leary and was running an escape line to Spain. He expanded his operation in 1942 by arranging for Royal Navy trawlers to pick up escapees at night along the French Mediterranean coast and deliver them safely to Gibraltar.

Line and often took charge of those "packages" after Dédée and others delivered them to Spain. Spanish police sometimes arrested escapees and their guides, but Creswell's official position as an undersecretary at the British Embassy in Madrid provided him with diplomatic cover as he escorted servicemen to Gibraltar and freedom.

MI9 played an even larger role in sustaining the O'Leary Line, led by Albert-Marie Guérisse, a Belgian medical officer who had been evacuated from Dunkirk in 1940 to England, where he took the name Patrick O'Leary. After volunteering to serve in the Royal Navy, he was captured by Vichy forces while carrying out a clandestine mission along the south coast of France. Interned with other British prisoners, he escaped with the help of Capt. Ian Garrow, a Scottish officer who went underground in the southern French city of Marseille and inaugurated the escape line that O'Leary later took charge of when Garrow was arrested by Vichy police in October 1941. MI9 sent O'Leary a radio operator and arranged an additional method of extracting escapees. Rather than crossing the Pyrenees into Spain at some peril, they waited in a safe house near Perpignan on the Mediterranean coast and were evacuated by ship at night. The O'Leary Line was more vulnerable than the Comet Line because many of its agents knew each other and a single defector could potentially expose dozens of people to the enemy. Eventually, both lines would be penetrated by the Germans and suffer grievous losses, but together they rescued nearly 1,500 people, many of them airmen who returned to action and helped loosen Hitler's grip on the occupied countries.

All along the western flank of what Nazis called Festung Europa (Fortress Europe), German occupiers faced resistance to their military presence, economic exploitation, and venomous racial policies. In the Netherlands, roughly 35,000 of the country's 140,000 Jews were either helped to escape or hidden by resisters, who if caught would often meet the same grim fate as those they harbored. Johannes Bogaard, who hid Jews on his farm near Amsterdam and helped others find refuge with neighbors, recalled that when there were no longer hiding places for entire families, parents left children to be harbored without knowing if they would ever see them again. "Can you imagine what that meant to the parents?" Bogaard said later. "Their grief was worse, much worse, than all the danger I ran."

In Denmark, which fell to Germany in short order, efforts by Nazi authorities to arrest Jews there and deport them to concentration camps met with concerted opposition. Danes learned of that roundup in advance and succeeded in hiding and conducting to safety in neutral Sweden more than 7,500 of the nation's 8,000 or so Jews. That successful rescue effort galvanized resistance in Denmark, which included frequent acts of sabotage and a general strike in Copenhagen that led to clashes in the streets between troops and protesters and prompted the Germans to cut off water and electricity there for nearly a week. Before the war ended, some 2,000 Danish policemen who refused to cooperate with the occupiers were sent to concentration camps.

Resistance to the Reich was never without risk, but it was especially dangerous in Eastern European countries that fell under German occupation, like Poland. After Hitler turned on Stalin in June 1941, SS security forces bore down relentlessly on any real or presumed enemies of the Reich operating between Germany and the Soviet Union. Hitler's determination

(continued on page 141)

"In the end, Dédée and Florentino were carrying all our packs. She was only a slip of a girl, but she had enormous strength and courage."

A DOWNED RAF PILOT WHO ESCAPED ON THE COMET LINE

INGENIOUS WAYS TO HIDE OBJECTS AT HOME

Anyone living under the heavy hand of German occupation faced severe restrictions on their personal liberties and constant scrutiny of their daily lives. Resistance groups throughout occupied Europe were dogged by agencies of the Reich's massive security service—the Sicherheitsdienst or SD—and were often pursued by their own police forces as well. To avoid detection and execution, resistance members devised ingenious methods of concealing weapons, cameras, and other tools of their secret trade within inconspicuous household items like books, cans, or matchboxes that authorities might not expect to contain anything of significance.

In addition to hiding weapons and gear for sabotage and espionage, resistance groups devised ways of concealing information or the means of obtaining it, including anti-Nazi newspapers or pamphlets and radios that could be used to transmit and receive secret messages or pick up broadcasts. With radio stations closed or heavily censored by German authorities, Allied radio broadcasts like the BBC's foreign language service and the shortwave "Voice of America" served as lifelines for people starved for news or views other than what Nazi propagandists doled out. When the Germans confiscated radio sets, resistance fighters became adept at building radios from scrounged components and contriving clever ways to hide them. ✪

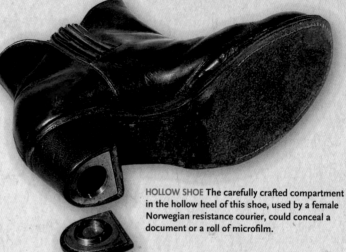

HOLLOW SHOE The carefully crafted compartment in the hollow heel of this shoe, used by a female Norwegian resistance courier, could conceal a document or a roll of microfilm.

MINI-CRYSTAL SETS Matchboxes (left) and a German thumbtack box (below) conceal miniature crystal radio receiving sets, which could be used to listen to Allied news broadcasts.

HIDDEN NEWS Underground newspapers published by the Norwegian resistance were transported for distribution in this hollowed-out log that could be concealed in a shipment of firewood.

CANNED GOODS Norwegian resistance agents concealed microfilm in this fish-roe can—cut away to reveal a hidden compartment—for delivery to Britain via neutral Sweden. If opened, the can would appear to contain its proper contents.

UNDERCOVER GUN A Dutch resistance fighter adapted a time-honored concealment device, the hollowed-out pages of a book, to hide a small pocket revolver, which could then be carried in public without drawing attention.

SPY'S RAZOR The hollow handle of this ordinary safety razor, with its blade-opening gear removed, contains a document detailing German military map symbols.

CONCEALED RADIO Norwegian resisters concealed a radio transmitter/receiver in a can for commercial varnish. The body of the can (right) could be lifted off the base, allowing the radio to be connected to a power source and fitted with a pair of headphones (below).

POISON PEN Danish technicians converted this fountain pen to conceal a vial of poison, the "last friend" of a captured spy or resistance agent. The poison label was probably added after the war.

Alf Bjerckes
Fernissfabrikk
OSLO

XYLIN-SIKKATIV 542ᵡ

JOSEPHINE BAKER

Applauded and elevated to stardom in France, Josephine Baker returned the favor by serving her adopted country as a spy and courier during World War II. Born in St. Louis, Missouri, in 1906, Baker was a 19-year-old vaudeville dancer in Harlem when a French talent agent spotted her and brought her to Paris, where she raised exotic dancing to an art form, performed in films, and was embraced as a celebrity in a way that few African Americans were in the racially divided United States until several decades later. In 1937, she became a French citizen. Two years later, as war loomed, she was approached by Capt. Jacques Abtey, an intelligence officer for the Deuxième Bureau, the French secret service, who asked her to exploit her access to social circles that included officers and diplomats from various countries by spying on those who might be Axis agents or French traitors. The assignment would be dangerous for her if the Germans invaded, but she accepted it readily. "France made me what I am," she told Abtey. "The people of Paris have given me everything. They have given me their hearts, and I have given them mine. I am ready, Captain, to give them my life."

Baker and Abtey grew close, and he did not ask her to risk her life by remaining as an agent in Paris when German troops occupied the city in June 1940. Nazi racial policies would have ended her career there, in any case, and she fled to the Vichy zone in southern France, where she continued to perform in public occasionally while working secretly with Abtey for Charles

> **"The people of Paris have given me everything . . . I am ready, Captain, to give them my life."**
>
> JOSEPHINE BAKER

G.L. Manuel fr

CODE NAME:	NONE
SPIED FOR:	FRANCE
SPIED AGAINST:	GERMANY

de Gaulle's Free French resistance movement. In early 1941, they departed for French North Africa by way of Spain. Abtey traveled under an assumed name, posing as her press agent, and she smuggled documents across the border to Free French agents in Lisbon, including photos hidden under her clothing and messages written in secret ink on sheet music. She continued to serve now and then as a courier for the French resistance in North Africa until American forces landed there in late 1942 and then entertained Allied troops until her beloved Paris was liberated in 1944.

After the war, Josephine Baker was wrongly suspected of being an agent of a different sort. In 1948, she visited the U.S. with her white husband and spent the next few years there, often speaking out against racial segregation and refusing to perform in segregated nightclubs. When denied service at a soda fountain in Washington, D.C., she told the manager that Washington was "the capital of the world and should be an example of a living democracy." Black soldiers, she added, were "dying in Korea for a democracy that their people cannot enjoy." Columnist Walter Winchell accused her in print of being an anti-American "riot inciter" and urged FBI Director Hoover to investigate rumors that she was a communist agitator. While visiting Cuba in 1953, she was detained and interrogated by Cuban military police, who said they did so after being informed by the FBI that she "might be an active Communist." The FBI eventually concluded that she was not "pro-communist" but "pro-Negro." She was later heartened by gains made by the civil rights movement in the U.S. but remained a proud citizen of France, which in 1961 admitted her to the Legion of Honour and awarded her the Croix de Guerre for her wartime service. ☉

to guard his eastern flank and eradicate opposition there was signaled a few months after the invasion of Russia began when he sent his top enforcer to root out resistance among neighboring Czechs, setting the stage for the most daring and dramatic attack on the Nazi leadership undertaken in any occupied country.

ASSASSINATION IN PRAGUE

In September 1941, SS security chief Reinhard Heydrich arrived in Prague to serve as Reich Protector of Bohemia and Moravia in what is now the Czech Republic. His task was not to protect the inhabitants but to protect the Reich by cracking down on Czechs and boosting their already substantial contribution to the German war effort. Beginning in 1938, Hitler had dismantled the fragile, ethnically diverse nation of Czechoslovakia by annexing the Sudetenland along Germany's border, inducing Slovakia to secede and submit to the Reich, and occupying the Czech provinces of Bohemia and Moravia, which he planned to incorporate in the Reich. German troops entered Prague unopposed in March 1939 after Hitler bullied President Emil Hacha into backing down and announcing that he "confidently placed the fate of the Czech people and country in the hands of the Führer." Hacha remained in Prague as a figurehead, but real power lay with the 37-year-old Heydrich, who replaced Reich Protector Konstantin von Neurath, an elderly diplomat Hitler considered too weak to whip recalcitrant Czechs into line.

Heydrich had schemed against Neurath to obtain this appointment because he wanted to emerge from the shadows and play a more visible and commanding role. As chief of the Reich Security Main Office (RSHA)—which included the Gestapo (secret state police) and the Kripo (criminal police) as well as the Nazi Party's Sicherheitsdienst (SD), responsible for foreign and domestic intelligence operations—he uncovered not just the plots of subversives but the dirty secrets of rivals in the German hierarchy. Some suspected that his ultimate goal was to surpass his SS boss, Heinrich Himmler, and other top Nazis and succeed Hitler as Führer. Already one of the Reich's most dangerous and dreaded men behind the scenes, Heydrich hoped to enhance his power and prestige by entering the public arena and forcing Czechs to do his bidding.

He set out to transform his protectorate into a compliant and productive SS state by subjecting the populace to what he called his "whip and sugar" policy. The sugar consisted of increased rations, wages, and benefits for Czech workers, whose output at factories like the sprawling Skoda munitions plant helped sustain the ongoing German offensive in Russia. Industrial sabotage declined under Heydrich and production increased, in part because those incentives appeased workers but also because they feared the whip he wielded. After taking power, he declared martial law and had thousands of people arrested over the next few months. Some were active resisters, loyal to the Czech government-in-exile in London, but many were simply influential figures who might potentially cause trouble and encourage opposition. Here as in Poland, the SS systematically eliminated those who were capable of exercising independent leadership, leaving only collaborators in office. Over 400 Czechs were executed during Heydrich's crackdown, and several thousand others were sent to concentration camps.

DEATH THREAT This miniature wooden coffin and others like it were crafted by members of the French resistance and were used to warn those who collaborated with the Germans that they were betraying their country, an offense punishable by death.

Heydrich did not hide such purges from the public because he wanted Czechs to conclude that resistance was futile and suicidal. But he kept secret other aspects of the sinister Nazi agenda. While serving as Reich Protector, he remained SS security chief and assumed responsibility for administering the so-called "Final Solution to the Jewish Question." Heydrich was tasked not just with organizing the extermination of Jews in occupied territory but with keeping that vast atrocity under wraps. The fiction devised to conceal the Holocaust was that Jews would be "resettled in the East," which made them less likely to resist being rounded up, and kept other non-Aryans, including millions of Slavic Czechs, Slovaks, and Poles, from recognizing that they too were menaced by their Nazi overseers, who viewed them as subhuman. After more than 100,000 Czech Jews had been confined to Theresienstadt—a ghetto that also served as a concentration camp, located in the city of Terezin, northwest of Prague—Heydrich and his SS underlings began surveying the racial makeup of the remaining population. Heads of households were asked to fill out forms listing their ancestors, and young people underwent physical exams by doctors who could supposedly identify those who exhibited Aryan traits and might be successfully integrated into the Reich. As Heydrich remarked privately, "We will try to Germanize these Czech vermin." Those who were too racially impure to be Germanized would be kept laboring for the Reich until the war ended and would then be removed. Hitler proposed giving them "special treatment," meaning extermination.

Heydrich's success at suppressing resistance, enhancing war production, and concealing the grim fate awaiting Czechs who could not be Germanized made him a prime target for Edvard Benes, former president of Czechoslovakia, who led the government in exile. Benes had fled to London in 1938 as Hitler prepared to carve up his country and had struggled since then to gain recognition from the Allies, on whom his hopes of reconstituting Czechoslovakia at war's end depended. He had two assets that gave him some leverage with Allied leaders—a small army-in-exile, consisting of about 3,000 soldiers who were eager to strike a blow against the forces occupying their country, and a military intelligence unit that controlled a well-placed German spy named Paul Thümmel. An Abwehr officer in Prague whose reputation as an ardent Nazi helped him avert suspicion, Thümmel betrayed German war plans for small payments, raising questions in London as to his true motive. Some suspected he was a double agent, feeding the Czechs false leads. But his reports—including one in May 1941 detailing German preparations for the invasion of Russia—proved so accurate and valuable that the Allies concluded he was a real catch and gave Benes credit for hooking him.

A few days after Heydrich became Reich Protector, coded radio signals relaying reports from Thümmel to London ceased. Benes hoped to restore contact with him and his handlers through an operation launched earlier that year in conjunction with the SOE, which was training Czech soldiers as parachutists to return covertly to their country with radio equipment and weapons for sabotage. But Benes needed something more dramatic than

DEADLY FOE Wearing a fencing outfit with the SS insignia on his sleeve, Reinhard Heydrich cracked down on dissident Czechs after being sent to Prague in late 1941 by Hitler, who lauded him as "one of the greatest opponents to all enemies of the Third Reich."

furtive acts of sabotage or espionage to highlight Czech resistance and gain credibility among the Allies. He proposed "a spectacular action against the Nazis—an assassination carried out in complete secrecy by our trained paratroop commandos." The target was Heydrich, and secrecy was essential not just to avoid alerting the enemy but to conceal the involvement of the SOE and the government in exile. Neither Benes nor the British wanted this to be seen as a plot concocted in London, even if it succeeded. The Germans had recently avenged the assassination of a local commandant in France by killing 50 hostages. They were sure to exact a much heavier toll for an assault on Heydrich. Any credit or blame for the operation would be assigned by the organizers in London to homegrown Czech patriots, acting spontaneously in defense of their country.

That was in fact a fairly accurate description of the two men chosen to carry out the attack, Jozef Gabcik and Jan Kubis. Both had fled their homeland when Hitler dismantled Czechoslovakia and had fought German troops in France in 1940 before they and other Czech soldiers were evacuated to England. By the time the plot against Heydrich, code-named Operation Anthropoid, was conceived in October 1941, Gabcik and Kubis had completed a rigorous SOE commando course in the Scottish Highlands—which included lessons in silent killing techniques from Eric Anthony "Bill" Sykes, formerly of the Shanghai Police—and were training as parachutists. Kubis was selected only after the candidate who was supposed to accompany Gabcik made a hard landing and suffered a concussion. Like Gabcik, Kubis readily volunteered for the risky operation. Shortly before they departed on their mission, armed with SOE-supplied weapons, they met with Benes and his intelligence chief, Lt. Col. Frantisek Moravec, who recalled that Benes "stressed the historical importance" of what the two soldiers were undertaking: "He knew that this was a do-or-die mission and I could see that—like me—he was affected by the moving simplicity with which they accepted their lot. When he said goodbye to them, there were tears in his eyes."

On the night of December 28, 1941, a long-range Halifax bomber modified to deliver parachutists flew the would-be assassins— along with two other teams of (continued on page 146)

OPERATION BERNHARD

The idea of flooding Britain with forged currency to wreck its economy was first proposed to Reinhard Heydrich in 1940 by Alfred Naujocks, who had led the 1939 attack on the Gleiwitz radio station near Germany's border with Poland, staged so Hitler could blame Polish commandos for his invasion of their country. After Naujocks demonstrated that it was possible to produce convincing forgeries of British banknotes, Operation Bernhard was launched in 1942 by SS Maj. Bernhard Krüger, who drew forgers from various concentration camps, including Sachsenhausen, where he set up a workshop and printing press for them. Aware that failure meant being thrown back with other doomed inmates, they turned out exquisite copies of British banknotes in denominations of 5, 10, 20, and 50 pounds (below). The notes could not be introduced directly to Britain, so they were circulated instead in occupied countries and used to pay German agents. Some found their way to the Bank of England—which declared the forgeries "the most dangerous ever seen"—but their economic impact on Britain was negligible. In May 1945, after producing banknotes worth nearly 135 million pounds, the Sachsenhausen forgers were about to be put to death by the SS when Allied troops freed them. Having bought time with their bogus currency, they now had a new lease on life. ✪

CUNNING COUNTERFEIT Despite the care that went into producing such expertly forged banknotes, Operation Bernhard faltered because Germany lacked the means to flood Britain with counterfeit currency.

SECRET PLANS FOR THE "FINAL SOLUTION"

In January 1942, Reinhard Heydrich briefly set aside his duties as Reich Protector in Prague and traveled to Wannsee, outside Berlin, to inform high-ranking German officials and SS officers of a drastic measure instigated by Hitler—the so-called "Final Solution of the Jewish Question." Banishing Jews from German territory had long been an objective of Hitler, but his obsession with those supposed enemies of the Reich turned deadly when he set out to dominate Europe. "The world war is here," he told like-minded Nazi leaders in 1939. "The annihilation of the Jews must be the necessary consequence."

Initial efforts by the SS to fulfill Hitler's murderous agenda in occupied Poland and Russia were flagrant and chaotic. By late 1941, nearly a million Jews had been massacred in occupied Russia, most of whom were shot to death and buried in mass graves (opposite). That mayhem could not be concealed from the Russian populace or from German officers, some of whom cooperated with the SS and approved of the massacres while others were appalled. The Final Solution that Heydrich laid out at Wannsee depended on a quieter means of mass murder—gas chambers, first applied using motorized vans in Russia and now being installed in death camps to which Jews in Polish ghettos would soon be deported. That hid the genocide from view and allowed for secrecy, imposed to lessen resistance from the intended victims as well as from those who were not targeted but might defy the Nazis if their atrocities came to light. The cover story used to mask the Final Solution was that those herded into boxcars (below) and destined for the camps were being resettled in the East. At Wannsee, Heydrich made no mention of gas chambers or extermination. But when he announced that 11 million Jews in areas under German occupation or control were subject to the Final Solution and would be deported to the East, those in attendance knew what that meant: Hitler's sweeping death sentence for European Jews was being systematically carried out. ☉

HOLOCAUST Above, Jews from the Warsaw Ghetto are forced into boxcars in 1942. Most were sent to death camps that, unlike concentration or slave labor camps where some able-bodied Jews and other captives toiled for years, were designed to kill people as quickly as possible. The SS secretly instituted death camps to avoid open massacres like that in the photo opposite, showing a noncommissioned SS officer in Russia shooting a Jewish man at a burial pit.

commandos assigned to reestablish radio communications with Czech resisters—to separate drop zones. Gabcik injured his foot when he landed and had to be helped along in the dark by his partner. They were fortunate not to be spotted by police before they found shelter in a rock quarry. Czech resisters learned of their whereabouts and escorted them to a safe house in Prague. Although they had orders not to reveal their mission to anyone, they had little choice but to confide in Ladislav Vanek, head of the network that harbored them. Only with his help and that of other resisters in Prague could they avoid detection and learn enough about Heydrich's movements to target him.

Meanwhile, one of the two radio teams had made contact with London and been instructed to locate the Anthropoid team. Gabcik still had difficulty walking when those commandos caught up with him and Kubis in late February 1942. As he recuperated, reports from Czech informants—including workers in the castle that served as Heydrich's headquarters—disclosed that the SS security chief was lax about his own security. To reach the airport where he boarded a private plane to confer with Himmler or Hitler, he often traveled in an open car, accompanied only by his driver. That was typical of Heydrich. A skilled pilot and Luftwaffe reserve officer, he had flown combat missions at considerable risk before Himmler put a stop to that. Confident that he had crushed opposition to the Reich, Heydrich did not want to be seen traveling under armed guard.

By May, Gabcik and Kubis were ready to strike, but some of their fellow commandos as well as resistance leader Vanek feared that their attack would only make a bad situation worse. In the past few months, Paul Thümmel had been arrested and the last Czech agent in contact with that spy had died in a shoot-out. Several more teams of parachutists had landed with radio equipment or weapons, and most of those commandos were now dead, in custody, or laying low. Czech resisters were under siege, and their surviving networks might collapse if the attack on Heydrich brought massive retaliation. Vanek sent a coded message by radio in early May urging that Operation Anthropoid be scrubbed or shifted to a lesser target such as a Czech official collaborating with the Nazis. Thousands of lives would be at risk if the attack went ahead as planned, he warned, and the Nazis would "wipe out the last remainders of any organization. It would then be impossible for the resistance to be useful to the Allies."

Vanek's appeal failed to sway the organizers in London, and Gabcik and Kubis remained committed to their assignment. "The killing is necessary," Gabcik insisted, "and for my part I shall obey the orders I have been given." When he and Kubis were informed that Heydrich was scheduled to depart by plane on the morning of May 27 to confer with Hitler—and might soon be reassigned to occupied France to take charge there—they saw it as their last chance. They had scouted Heydrich's route to the airport through the outskirts of Prague, and they awaited his car that morning where a bend in the road required drivers to slow down. Gabcik opened his briefcase and assembled a compact Sten submachine gun beneath a raincoat he carried. Kubis stood across from him on the far side of the road, packing two bombs that resembled oversized hand grenades and would detonate on impact.

When Heydrich's car rounded the bend at half past 10, Gabcik pressed the trigger on his Sten gun, which jammed. Heydrich then drew his pistol and ordered the driver to stop.

> ## "The killing is necessary, and for my part I shall obey the orders I have been given."
>
> JOZEF GABCIK, CZECH COMMANDO

FREEDOM FIGHTERS Commandos Jan Kubis (left) and Jozef Gabcik (right) were trained in Britain by the SOE but owed allegiance to Edvard Benes, the exiled president of Czechoslovakia. Benes proposed assassinating Heydrich to show the Allies that Czechs were determined to defy the Nazis and free their country, which he hoped to reconstitute at war's end.

22/1/42.

OPERATION ANTHROPOID.

The operation ANTHROPOID, consisting of 2 agents was despatched by parachute on the night of 28/29th December, 1941. They carried with them a package containing two metal boxes, the contents of which are shown in the attached schedule.

The object of the operation is the assassination of Herr HEYDRICH, the German Protector in Czechoslovakia and the small box contains equipment for an attack on him in car on his way from the Castle in Prague to his office. The larger box contains assorted equipment for alternative attacks by:-

(a) Getting into the castle,
(b) Getting into his office,
(c) Placing a bomb in his car or in his armoured railway train.
(d) Blowing up his railway train,
(e) Mining a road along which he is going to travel.
(f) Shooting him when he is appearing at some ceremony.

The time and place of this operation will be decided on the spot but the two agents concerned have been trained in all methods of assassination known to us. They intend to carry out this operation whether or not there is any opportunity of subsequent escape.

This project is not known to the Czech organisation within the Protectorate.

H Herketh Prichand
Capt

ENCL.

EQUIPMENT TAKEN WITH ANTHROPOID.

Samll box:	2........38 Supers & shoulder holsters.
	4........Spare magazines.
	100........Rounds ammunition.
	6........Percussion bombs with plastic.
	2........Detonator magazines.
	2........4 second Mills bombs.

Large box:	1........Tree spigot.
	1........Coil trip wire.
	2........Igniters.
	1........Spigot bomb.
	4-hour time delay for use with 2-lb. P.E. charge.
	4........Medium magnets.
	4........Electric detonators & 30" wire & battery.
	1........Sten gun.
	100........Rounds ammunition for Sten gun.
	32-lbs. P.E.
	10-lbs. Gelignite.
	2 yards Cordtex (new).
	4........Fog Signals.
	3........Time pencils.
	1........Lethal hypodermic syringe.

Abb. V

V. Sprengkörper.   VI. Fahrrad.

DOCUMENTING THE ATTACK Operation Anthropoid, code name for the assault on Heydrich, was well documented in both British and German files. A British report composed after Gabcik and Kubis set out on their mission described various ways in which they might target Heydrich (top left) and listed the weapons issued to them (above). Following the attack, a photo of Josef Valcik (top center), who served as a lookout for the assassins, was reproduced on a poster offering a reward for his capture. Among the evidence obtained by German investigators were a hat and coat worn by one of the commandos (top right), a pistol, a hand grenade (far left), and a bicycle used to flee the scene.

Seconds later, a bomb hurled by Kubis struck the vehicle, wounding Heydrich in the spleen. He staggered from the car and collapsed after firing several errant shots at Gabcik, who fled on foot while Kubis escaped on a bicycle after dodging shots fired by the driver. Heydrich underwent an operation and clung to life, but his wound festered. He died on June 4, 1942.

By then, Gabcik, Kubis, and five commandos on other teams—including Josef Valcik, who served as a lookout for the assassins on May 27—had found sanctuary in the catacombs beneath an Orthodox church in Prague. Hitler wanted 10,000 Czechs arrested and held as hostages—and anyone suspected of aiding the assassins executed along with family members. On June 9, Gestapo agents and SS security police entered the town of Lidice, which was under suspicion because a Czech parachutist had been captured carrying addresses of two families there with sons in the Czech army-in-exile. No evidence was found that they or anyone else in Lidice had aided the assassins, but all adult males in town—nearly 200 men in all—were shot to death on the spot or executed after being detained and interrogated. Several women were killed as well, and the rest were sent to Ravensbrück, a concentration camp for women in Germany, after being separated from their children. A small number of those children were spared to be Germanized, but more than 80 were sent to Chelmno, a death camp in Poland.

MISSION ACCOMPLISHED Armed with a Sten submachine gun like the one above, Jozef Gabcik targeted Heydrich as he was being driven to the Prague airport in an open Mercedes Benz Cabriolet (below) on the morning of May 27, 1942. When the gun jammed, Gabcik's fellow commando Jan Kubis hurled a powerful hand grenade that hit the right side of the vehicle and mortally wounded Heydrich.

The Nazi-controlled press publicized the massacre at Lidice, which was reduced to rubble, and warned Czechs to denounce all suspects before "Reich justice punishes the whole nation." Furious that the culprits were still at large, Hitler now wanted 30,000 Czechs executed. But on June 13, before reprisals escalated to that level, authorities in Prague offered amnesty to anyone who betrayed the assassins within the next five days. On June 16, commando Karel Curda—who had landed by parachute in March and linked up with Gabcik and Kubis in April before taking refuge with his mother and sister—entered Gestapo headquarters in Prague and sold out his comrades in exchange for amnesty for himself and his family and a hefty reward. Curda did not know the location of the fugitives, but he directed Gestapo agents to the home of a woman active in Vanek's resistance network. When they arrived there on June 17, she killed herself by swallowing a cyanide capsule. Her son, who had served as a courier in the network, was tortured and broke down when shown his mother's severed head, immersed in a fish tank. He confessed that she had advised him to seek refuge in the church where the commandos were hiding. Within hours, hundreds of policemen and Waffen-SS troops had them surrounded.

When Himmler learned that they were trapped, he cabled Prague urging that they be captured alive to prove that the British were behind the assassination plot. The message arrived too late, and in any case the Czech soldiers in the church were determined to fight to the death. Kubis and two others had left the gloomy catacombs and were up in the choir loft with weapons in hand when the attack began around dawn on June 18. They were the first of the commandos to die that day after battling SS troops. Gabcik and three others held out in the catacombs for several hours and left more than a dozen Germans dead before using their last bullets to take their own lives.

Gruesome reprisals for the killing of Heydrich continued after the assassins perished. On June 24, all 52 adults in the small town of Lekazy—where a radio

ANNIHILATION In retaliation for the assassination of Heydrich, German forces wiped out the town of Lidice, killing the men and a number of women (bottom) and sending most of the children to death camps. Little remained after Lidice was torched other than the sign below.

transmitter belonging to one of the commando teams had been found—were shot to death. Two children there were spared to be Germanized, and 11 others died at Chelmno. In all, more than 5,000 Czechs were killed in retaliation for the attack on Heydrich, including 3,000 Jews who had nothing to do with the plot but were deported from Terezin to death camps as scapegoats. Organizers in London had been warned that thousands of people would suffer and resistance would be crippled as a result of Operation Anthropoid, and such was the case. Czechs had reason to question whether eliminating Heydrich was worth that terrible price. Few Nazis were as ruthlessly efficient as he was, but his death did not stop the SS from pursuing its malevolent agenda in the Czech homeland or elsewhere in Europe. The Reich paid a substantial price as well, however. Heydrich's assassination deprived Nazi leaders of their aura of invincibility at a time when they seemed destined to dominate Europe. And by publicizing the Lidice massacre, the Germans lifted the veil of secrecy surrounding SS terror tactics and made the Allies more supportive of the Czech government in exile and more determined to seek unconditional surrender and bring Nazis to justice. "If future generations ask us what we were fighting for in this war," said U.S. Navy Secretary Frank Knox, "we shall tell them the story of Lidice."

Propaganda Minister Joseph Goebbels tried to score points for the Reich by offering evidence that the assassination plot was "made in England." But Goebbels was so notorious among non-Germans for lying that Allied propagandists easily deflected his assertions. "No order for Heydrich's murder was ever issued from London," the British Foreign Office claimed. "In fact the whole Nazi theory about a fight for freedom being conducted and ordered from London is false, as all acts of resistance in the homeland are directed and decided by its own headquarters there." In this case, truth was a necessary casualty of the Allied war effort. If Benes and the British had admitted responsibility for Operation Anthropoid, they would have aided the enemy and diminished the heroic efforts of Gabcik, Kubis, and other Czech patriots who made the ultimate sacrifice for their country. As the Gestapo chief in Prague remarked of 252 relatives and associates of the commandos who were arrested, beaten, and sentenced to death in September, many were heard to say, "We are proud to die for our country."

PARTNERS IN ESPIONAGE A magnetic couple, Harro and Libertas Schulze-Boysen attracted like-minded opponents of the Nazi regime to their Berlin home, some of whom joined them in a wartime spy ring that supplied the Soviets with German secrets, including military plans Harro obtained as a Luftwaffe intelligence officer. The Berlin ring was one of several such bands in Europe that communicated with Moscow by radio and were known collectively as the Red Orchestra.

RED ORCHESTRA IN BERLIN

In late October 1941, as the plot against Heydrich was taking shape in London, Lt. Harro Schulze-Boysen of the Luftwaffe, an intelligence officer at the German Air Ministry, was visited at home in Berlin by an agent who operated under the code name Kent but carried a passport identifying him as Vincent Sierra of Uruguay. He was in fact Anatoli Gourevitch of the GRU (Soviet military intelligence). For a Russian spy to make such a house call in the closely monitored German capital was highly irregular and insecure, but the Soviets were desperate to reach Schulze-Boysen, having not heard from him in months. The lieutenant, for his part, was so eager to betray the Reich's secrets and bring down Hitler's regime that he welcomed Gourevitch without qualms and spent hours briefing him on German plans and capabilities on the Eastern Front. Schulze-Boysen did not bother to hide this indiscreet rendezvous from his wife, Libertas, for she was privy to his espionage and his partner in high crimes against the Nazi state.

Harro Schulze-Boysen's personal vendetta against the National Socialists had begun when Hitler took power in 1933. Then in his mid-20s, Schulze-Boysen edited a journal called *Der Gegner* ("The Opponent"), which was not aligned with the outlawed German Communist Party but was far too critical of the brutal new regime in Berlin to be tolerated. Storm troopers broke into its offices, hauled him off along with his friend and co-editor, Henry Erlanger, and beat them so severely that Erlanger died and Schulze-Boysen had to be hospitalized. The ordeal transformed him from an open critic of the Nazis whose small journal posed little threat to them into something far more dangerous—a mole, who burrowed into the German military establishment and subverted the Reich from within. "I have put my revenge on ice," he confided to an acquaintance before joining the Luftwaffe, where doubts about his political loyalty were overridden by his admirable pedigree as the son of a German naval officer and the great-nephew of the celebrated Adm. Alfred von Tirpitz.

Like her husband, Libertas Schulze-Boysen came from a prominent family and had the blond hair and Nordic look that many Germans who subscribed to the myth of Aryan supremacy lacked and envied. She worked in the movie industry, first as a press agent for the Berlin office of Metro-Goldwyn-Mayer and later for Kulturfilm, a government agency that produced documentaries under the supervision of Joseph Goebbels. The social circle that formed around the fashionable Schulze-Boysens included actors, actresses, writers, and directors, but these were not carefree figures of stage and screen like those featured in Hollywood gossip columns. Many had Jewish friends, in-laws, or ancestors and were appalled by the Nazis' virulent anti-Semitism. Gifted acquaintances of the Schulze-Boysens like author and director Adam Kuckhoff struggled to find work worthy of their talents because they had been part of a vibrant German counterculture in the 1920s that included Jews and Communists and that the Nazis now denounced as degenerate. It was Kuckhoff who introduced Harro Schulze-Boysen to the man who helped transform this casual circle of anti-Nazis into an effective espionage ring—Arvid Harnack, whose responsibilities at the Economics Ministry in Berlin included monitoring German industrial output.

Unlike Schulze-Boysen, whose associates outside the Air Ministry were well aware of his hatred for Nazis, Harnack was circumspect and preferred to oppose the regime through covert channels. During the 1930s, he passed classified information on the Reich's economy and capacity to wage war to attachés at the American Embassy as well as intelligence officers at the Soviet Embassy. Harnack once described himself as "a bridge between the United States and the Soviet Union here in Germany" and may have hoped that those two powers would form an alliance against Hitler and hasten his downfall. The Hitler-Stalin Pact in 1939 seemingly dashed such hopes, and Harnack had no further contact with the Soviets until late 1940, by which time he knew that Hitler was planning to break the pact and invade Russia. Harnack not only shared that state secret with Soviet agent Alexander Korotkov

INSTIGATOR German official Arvid Harnack initiated contact between the Berlin ring and Soviet agents.

HELPMATE Devotion to her husband and contempt for the Nazis drew Mildred Harnack into the ring.

INTERMEDIARY Author Adam Kuckhoff introduced Harro Schulze-Boysen to Arvid Harnack and spied with them.

but also drew in as co-conspirators Kuckhoff and Schulze-Boysen, who provided details on German high-level aerial surveillance of Soviet territory and the Luftwaffe's war plans.

Like similar reports from Richard Sorge and other Soviet agents and informants, those warnings from Berlin went unheeded by Stalin. But intelligence officers in Moscow hedged their bets by sending the German spy ring radio equipment to use if the invasion took place and Korotkov was evicted from Berlin along with other Soviet officials. Korotkov urged the three ringleaders to sever ties with other German dissidents, who if captured and tortured might betray them, but they declined to do so and remained involved in resistance activities such as helping Jews flee Germany and printing and disseminating anti-Nazi flyers and pamphlets. Dozens of people knew they were foes of the regime, and a smaller number knew of their espionage and took part in it, including their wives. Unlike Libertas Schulze-Boysen and Harnack's American wife, Mildred—an English teacher who sometimes served as a courier for the ring—Greta Kuckhoff had a child to look after. Although her husband tried to shield her from involvement, he consented when Korotkov asked that she pick up a suitcase containing the radio equipment. Such deliveries were considered safer for women than for men, but Greta knew the task was treacherous and likened it to "sticking my head into the noose." To make matters worse, Korotkov dropped the suitcase before passing it to her and later had to retrieve and repair the fragile equipment before handing it over a second time.

After Germany attacked Russia in June 1941, the Soviets abandoned their embassy in Berlin and radio transmissions were the only means for the conspirators to communicate with Moscow. Hans Coppi, a young Communist who served as their radio operator, was inexperienced at the task, and the equipment he received may have been defective. His coded messages to Moscow were brief and fitful, and soon ceased altogether. That failure to communicate may well have spared the Berlin ring from being detected and destroyed in short order. German technicians monitored radio signals throughout occupied Europe and paid special attention to any transmissions on unauthorized frequencies emanating from Berlin, the Reich's nerve center. They picked up Coppi's messages but did not have time to determine the point of origin, which involved using several vans equipped with radio direction finders (RDFs), whose aerials rotated until they fixed on the signal. Three vans had to home in on the same signal before the approximate location of the transmitter could be triangulated and the area could be searched. Coppi did not transmit long enough for German counterintelligence officers to pinpoint him. But they suspected that this furtive agent with his finger on the key was sending signals to Moscow and might be one of several "pianists" performing for a far-flung Soviet espionage network they dubbed the Red Orchestra.

In fact, the Berlin ringleaders had no idea they were part of such an organization. They had never heard of Leopold Trepper, who had been recruited by the GRU several years earlier to establish an espionage network in Western Europe and now had bases in France and Belgium from which his agents sent coded messages to Moscow by radio. Trepper would later be touted by German spycatchers who nabbed him as the conductor or "Big Chief" of the Red Orchestra. But he had no control over a separate cell in Switzerland operated by Rudolf Rössler—an adept agent code-named Lucy who relayed by radio to Moscow military

"I have put my revenge on ice."

HARRO SCHULZE-BOYSEN, AFTER BEING ATTACKED FOR OPPOSING THE NAZIS WHEN THEY TOOK POWER

MONITORING SUSPICIOUS RADIO TRANSMISSIONS

On any given night in Nazi-occupied Europe, listeners with shortwave radios could hear mysterious messages, sent in Morse code after being encrypted as seemingly meaningless strings of letters or numbers. Some were transmitted by secret agents to Allied listening stations to be deciphered there. No covert means of communication was faster and more effective—or more vulnerable to detection. German agencies such as the Abwehr and Gestapo used special radio direction finding (RDF) units to track secret signals to their source and uncover spy rings or resistance cells.

The best defense against RDF was to give the enemy too little time to home in on signals. SOE agents in occupied Europe had standing orders to limit transmissions to no more than five minutes, but few agents were able to send a message of any length that quickly. Every additional minute gave German agents more opportunity to find their quarry using devices with antennas to determine the direction from which signals emanated. Fixed RDF stations first triangulated the approximate location of the transmitter, then mobile RDF equipment in vans called *Funkspielwagen* helped narrow the search. For a closer fix, an operator might walk the streets with a sensitive direction finder held in his hand or concealed under his coat to determine which block the signal was coming from, and police would then go house to house. Another technique used to narrow the search for hidden radio transmitters, which often used electrical power, was to cut electricity to one zone after another until the suspect signals went off. Despite precautions against RDF such as using a hard-to-detect low-frequency radio set, moving often, and transmitting briefly, the life expectancy of an active secret radio operator in occupied Europe was little more than a month. ✪

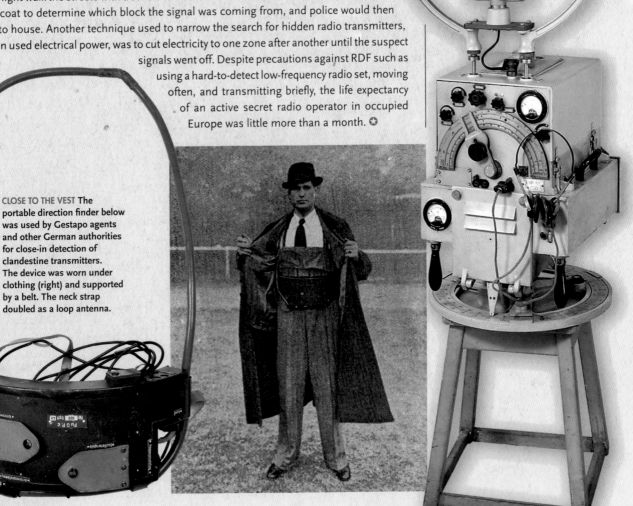

MOBILE DETECTOR This direction-finding radio receiver—a Nachfeldpeiler P57N with an integral loop antenna—could be concealed in a van or truck and was used to track signals sent by resistance groups in German-occupied Italy.

CLOSE TO THE VEST The portable direction finder below was used by Gestapo agents and other German authorities for close-in detection of clandestine transmitters. The device was worn under clothing (right) and supported by a belt. The neck strap doubled as a loop antenna.

WHITE ROSE RESISTANCE

Few German cities were more closely associated with the Nazis than Munich, where Hitler addressed his "Old Fighters" each year on the anniversary of his Beer Hall Putsch there in 1923. "Never before," he assured those Nazis on November 8, 1941, "has a giant empire been smashed and struck down in a shorter time than Soviet Russia." Even as he claimed victory, however, German forces were bogging down in Russia, and resistance to his regime was sprouting up at the University of Munich. Some students in that small but dedicated White Rose movement served as medics in Russia, where they witnessed bloody German setbacks and atrocities. By 1942, leaders of the movement—including medic Hans Scholl and his sister Sophie (below), who rebelled against their upbringing as Hitler Youth—were distributing anti-Nazi leaflets in Munich and other cities. One leaflet warned that Hitler's war would reduce German cities to rubble, and another stated that 300,000 Jews had been murdered in German-occupied Poland "in the most bestial way." Gestapo agents investigated those anonymous flyers, but White Rose members continued to urge resistance to the Nazis and their "abominable crimes." Some scrawled defiant messages on walls such as "Hitler the Mass Murderer." In February 1943, Hans and Sophie Scholl were arrested in Munich with leaflets in hand, charged with treason, and sentenced to death. Their friend Christoph Probst and others instrumental in the movement were also executed, but their message was not eradicated. One of the last White Rose leaflets was smuggled to Britain and reproduced for distribution by the RAF, which dropped hundreds of thousands of copies over Germany in mid-1943. ✪

DEFIANT TRIO Hans Scholl, in uniform at left, meets in Munich with his sister Sophie and their White Rose cohort Christoph Probst. After they were executed, leaflets in German supposedly inspired by their efforts—including a Munich student manifesto (top) and a flyer from the "Scholl-Bund" (bottom)—were produced by Allied propaganda units.

secrets supplied by German officers who shared Schulze-Boysen's contempt for Hitler's regime. Nor was Trepper involved with the Berlin ring until Moscow grew desperate and radioed his "Little Chief" in Brussels, Anatoli Gourevitch, instructing him to make contact with the Berlin spies. Trepper, operating in Paris, was appalled when he learned his superiors in Moscow had included the actual names and addresses of the Berlin spies in the message to Brussels. "It's not possible," he exclaimed. "They have gone crazy!"

His fears were well founded. German listeners had not yet pinpointed Gourevitch's location in Brussels, but they were picking up radio signals sent to and from that base and recording those coded messages. If counter-intelligence officers located the transmitter and broke the code, the Berlin ringleaders would be exposed. Broadcasting their names and addresses was a dreadful gaffe, but Soviet spymasters were desperate for intelligence from Berlin as German forces closed in on Moscow. Many seasoned Soviet intelligence officers had been purged by the morbidly suspicious Stalin in recent years, along with thousands of Red Army officers. Their replacements would do anything to satisfy Stalin's demands and were often reckless with the lives of those serving under them.

When Gourevitch met with Schulze-Boysen at home in October 1941 and the Berlin ring resumed spying for the Soviets, they compounded the risks they were already running through their resistance activities. They were informed of atrocities committed in Poland and occupied Russia by SS forces, sometimes with the assistance of regular German troops or police, and were seeking ways of revealing those crimes to the public. Adam Kuckhoff drew on accounts that Libertas Schulze-Boysen obtained from soldiers on leave to compose a letter describing a German police officer who broke down after participating in a mass execution of the sort that claimed the lives of vast numbers of Russian Jews: "The victims had to kneel. Then he walked along the row behind them, shooting each one in the back of the head at close range." Copies of this letter, said to be from a German officer to his son, were circulated among troops on their way to Russia. Such efforts by the Berlin ring had little impact on public opinion or the war effort as a whole, but knowledge of Nazi atrocities drove the inner circle of spies and the outer circle of resisters associated with them to risk their lives in defiance of Hitler. As Harro Schulze-Boysen said to a woman whose Jewish fiancé had been sent to a concentration camp: "This barbarity has to stop. We all have to work together to stop that devil."

For Schulze-Boysen and his co-conspirators, that meant betraying German military plans to the Soviets. Gourevitch returned from Berlin to Brussels with so much intelligence to convey to Moscow that his radio operators worked long shifts. That allowed Capt. Harry Piepe of the Abwehr—who had recently been

RUDOLF RÖSSLER

Operating from Switzerland under the code name Lucy, Rudolf Rössler sent highly accurate reports on German military plans by radio to Moscow. He was one of the war's most accomplished and discreet secret agents—so discreet that he never revealed much about his operation, raising questions as to the secret of his success. A German veteran of World War I acquainted with officers who shared his disdain for the Nazis, Rössler moved in 1934 to Switzerland, whose neutrality made it a hotbed of intrigue and espionage during World War II. He dealt with Soviet spies there but did not reveal his sources to them or to Russian military intelligence officers of the GRU, for whom he worked. His radio operator was Alexander Foote, a British expatriate who had fought alongside communists in the Spanish Civil War. In 1943, Rössler's reports on German preparations for the Battle of Kursk contributed to a crucial Soviet victory there.

CODE NAME:	LUCY
SPIED FOR:	SOVIET UNION
SPIED AGAINST:	GERMANY

One theory later advanced to explain Rössler's uncanny ability to forecast German moves was that Foote was a British intelligence agent, passing along information obtained by code breakers who solved the German Enigma machine and deciphered military messages encrypted on that device. That theory seemed plausible because the British wanted to see Russia prevail over Germany without revealing their Enigma breakthrough. But F. H. Hinsley, who took part in that top secret program and became official historian of British wartime intelligence agencies, denied that they used Lucy to "forward intelligence to Moscow." A more likely explanation for Rössler's success is that he had German informants with access to precious military secrets, including Abwehr officer Hans Gisevius and others so opposed to Hitler that they aided his Allied foes and plotted against him. ✪

"This death suits me."

CONDEMNED SPY
HARRO SCHULZE-BOYSEN

"And I loved Germany so much!"

MILDRED HARNACK'S LAST WORDS

DEATH CHAMBER Mildred Harnack and other women condemned for their involvement in the Berlin spy ring were beheaded by guillotine (opposite), a quicker execution than reserved for the men, who were slowly hanged to death.

shifted from German military duty to counterintelligence—to pinpoint one of three transmitters being operated by pianists for the Red Orchestra at different locations in Brussels. Had Piepe taken more time to investigate, he might have succeeded in shutting down all three simultaneously and arresting Gourevitch and perhaps even his "Big Chief" Trepper, who visited Brussels frequently to check up on operations there and remained at large until late 1942. But like Soviet intelligence officers, German spycatchers were under pressure to produce results. On December 14, 1941, Piepe's men stormed the one Red Orchestra hideout they had a fix on, at 101 Rue des Atrébates in Brussels, and seized several suspects, who were turned over to the Gestapo for "intensified interrogation." Radio operator Mikhail Makarov endured torture and revealed nothing of significance. Cipher clerk Sophie Poznanska knew details that would have allowed German cryptanalysts to decode messages sent between Brussels and Moscow but committed suicide rather than have those secrets extracted from her.

The only cooperative suspect was Rita Arnaud, the mistress of a Soviet courier, who seemingly knew little that would help her interrogators. Further investigation in months to come, however, indicated that Poznanska had encoded messages using a book that she and her counterpart in Moscow possessed, from which keywords were drawn, indicated by page number, line number, and word order within that line. Such codes were fiendishly difficult to break unless one knew which book among millions in print was being used for that purpose. Arnaud recalled the titles of several novels she had seen near the transmitter in Brussels, one of which contained the keywords that unlocked the case. Finally, in July 1942, that fatal message was decoded.

Gestapo agents in Berlin placed the ringleaders under tight surveillance, tapped their phones, and expanded the list of suspects. Harro Schulze-Boysen was the first to be arrested,

AMY THORPE PACK

Among the assets William Donovan obtained for the OSS through his partnership with British spymaster William Stephenson were the expert services of a seductive Anglo-American agent, Amy Thorpe Pack. Wed in 1930 at the age of 19 to British envoy Arthur Pack, the glamorous American-born debutante (shown here in her bridal gown) soon fell out with her husband but gained dual citizenship and access to diplomatic circles in Europe, where she obtained secrets for Britain from officials enthralled by her. As she later said of one such admirer: "I let him make love to me as often as he wanted, since this guaranteed the smooth flow of political information I needed."

After the war began, Amy Pack left her husband and returned to America, where Stephenson employed her as a secret agent in Washington under the code name Cynthia. Impressed by her work, he asked her in 1941 to penetrate the French Embassy, which represented a Vichy regime that was technically neutral but subservient to Nazi Germany. She promptly seduced the embassy's press attaché, Charles Brousse, who soon realized she was a spy but did as she asked because he adored her and disdained the Nazis. What Stephenson wanted most from the embassy were codebooks locked in the naval attaché's office, but he would not risk burgling a neutral embassy in Washington without American involvement. In 1942, he turned to Donovan, who would soon take charge of the newly formed OSS and would do anything to gather intelligence on Vichy forces before American and British troops landed in French North Africa later that year. Donovan agreed to share the take with Stephenson and conduct a break-in that might cause a diplomatic uproar if it went wrong.

The plan called for Brousse and agent Cynthia to gain access to the embassy late at night with the consent of the guard, who was told they were using Brousse's office for a clandestine affair. After a few fumbling

> "Life is but a stage on which to play. One's role is to pretend, and always to hide one's true feelings."
>
> AMY THORPE PACK

CODE NAME:	CYNTHIA
SPIED FOR:	BRITAIN, UNITED STATES
SPIED AGAINST:	VICHY FRANCE

efforts to fulfill their mission, they again entered the naval attaché's office, where they were joined by a wily ex-con dubbed the Georgia Cracker, whom they let in through the window. Hired by the OSS for his skill at breaking locks, he extracted the codebooks and took them to be photographed. Cynthia and Brousse were nervously awaiting the return of those documents when they heard the approaching guard, who was doing his rounds and was sure to talk if he found the couple making not love but mischief in the naval office. She hastily stripped and threw herself in Brousse's arms—a sight that caused the embarrassed guard to mumble his apologies when he intruded on them and hurry off. By dawn, the codebooks were back where they belonged and the perpetrators were out of danger.

Although Vichy French authorities were not alerted to the heist, it aroused the suspicion of FBI Director Hoover, whose agents were watching the embassies. After another OSS team was spotted breaking into the Spanish Embassy in Washington, Hoover complained to President Roosevelt that conducting covert operations against foreign agents or envoys in the U.S. was the FBI's business. Roosevelt agreed, so long as Hoover shared what he gleaned from any future break-ins with the OSS. Hoover and Donovan were now such bitter rivals, however, that they were more inclined to spy on each other than share intelligence.

The French Embassy heist was a hard act for Amy Pack and Charles Brousse to follow. Donovan considered sending them to spy on Vichy France but scrapped the plan when Brousse's wife discovered their affair. Agent Cynthia had once prided herself on remaining detached from her lovers. "Life is but a stage on which to play," she wrote. "One's role is to pretend, and always to hide one's true feelings." But her relationship with Brousse was too intense to be hidden. When they could no longer be spies together, they became husband and wife, a marriage that lasted until her death in 1963. ◗

in late August, and dozens more were swept up in weeks to come. Altogether, 117 people were seized, many of them resisters with no knowledge of espionage, hauled in after their names were divulged under torture. Hitler was aghast to learn that prominent Germans had conspired against his regime and ordered secret trials, which resulted in death sentences for 46 men and women, including the Schulze-Boysens, Harnacks, and Kuckhoffs, although Greta Kuckhoff was later spared and spent the remainder of the war in prison. Libertas Schulze-Boysen pleaded in vain for her life, but her husband remained defiant and unrepentant. "This death suits me," he said. Mildred Harnack's last words were for her adopted country, once so cultivated and accomplished and now demeaned and disgraced by the Nazis: "And I loved Germany so much!"

OSS IN NORTH AFRICA

When William Donovan took charge of the newly formed Office of Strategic Services in mid-June 1942, his main task was to gather intelligence and conduct covert operations in support of the forthcoming American invasion of French North Africa, whose Vichy overseers collaborated with the Germans. That invasion was less than five months away, but American agents had begun infiltrating North Africa and recruiting informants and Allied sympathizers even before President Roosevelt picked Donovan in mid-1941 to head the Office of Coordinator of Information. (Both the office and Donovan were designated COI.) His main assets when he assumed that post were the "twelve disciples," whose stated task was to ensure that oil, food, and other American goods purchased by Vichy officials did not end up in the hands of German or Italian troops fighting the British in North Africa. But those 12 officials also spied on Vichy forces and defenses, armed with diplomatic immunity as U.S. vice consuls. (Spies attached to embassies or consulates could be expelled but not prosecuted by their host country.) German agents in French Morocco, Algeria, and Tunisia knew what the twelve disciples were up to and considered them amateurs. "All their thoughts are centered on their social, sexual, or culinary interests," reported a German intelligence officer.

Donovan did not begrudge his spies some amusement in their spare time as long as they kept a sharp eye on Vichy installations and intentions. The twelve disciples kept him well informed while their chief, Robert Murphy, the U.S. Consul General in Algiers, made secret overtures to French commanders in North Africa who were disillusioned with Vichy and might prefer cooperating with the Allies to collaborating with fascists. Donovan prepared for covert operations in support of the American invasion by assigning Marine Col. William Eddy—born to missionaries in the Middle East and fluent in French and Arabic—to seek the cooperation of North African tribal leaders and enlist partisans and saboteurs to wreak havoc behind enemy lines.

Donovan also recruited Americans who had lived or studied in North Africa and had the local knowledge and language skills required to serve as agents under Eddy. Among

DIRE CONSEQUENCES Issued by the French Vichy regime, which collaborated with the Nazis, this poster condemns acts of sabotage using the proverb *"Les conseilleurs ne sont pas les payeurs"* ("The advisers are not the ones who pay"), meaning that those who urged resistance in the form of sabotage exposed people uninvolved in those attacks to fierce German reprisals.

"All their thoughts are centered on their social, sexual, or culinary interests."

A GERMAN INTELLIGENCE OFFICER DESCRIBING AMERICAN AGENTS IN NORTH AFRICA CALLED THE TWELVE DISCIPLES

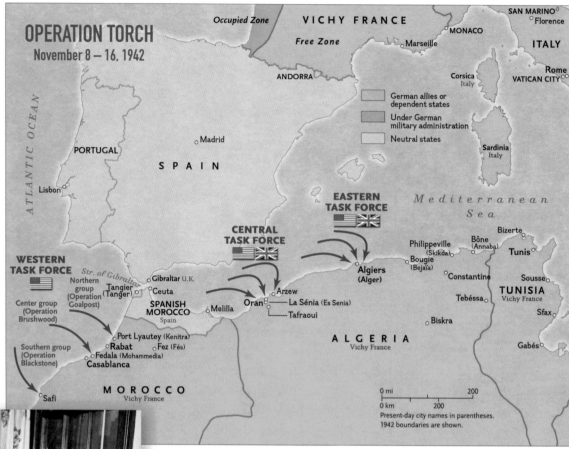

OPERATION TORCH
November 8 – 16, 1942

German allies or dependent states

Under German military administration

Neutral states

0 mi 200
0 km 200
Present-day city names in parentheses.
1942 boundaries are shown.

WESTERN TASK FORCE
Northern group (Operation Goalpost)
Center group (Operation Brushwood)
Southern group (Operation Blackstone)

CENTRAL TASK FORCE

EASTERN TASK FORCE

ATLANTIC OCEAN
PORTUGAL
Lisbon
Madrid
SPAIN
Str. of Gibraltar
Tangier (Tanger)
Gibraltar U.K.
Ceuta
SPANISH MOROCCO
Spain
Melilla
Port Lyautey (Kenitra)
Rabat
Fez (Fés)
Fedala (Mohammedia)
Casablanca
Safi
MOROCCO
Vichy France
Oran
Arzew
La Sénia (Es Senia)
Tafraoui
Algiers (Alger)
ALGERIA
Vichy France
Biskra
Constantine
Bougie (Bejaïa)
Philippeville (Skikda)
Bône (Annaba)
Bizerte
Tunis
TUNISIA
Vichy France
Sousse
Tébessa
Sfax
Gabès
Occupied Zone
VICHY FRANCE
Free Zone
Marseille
MONACO
ANDORRA
Corsica Italy
Sardinia Italy
SAN MARINO
Florence
ITALY
Rome
VATICAN CITY
Mediterranean Sea

TORCH Anthropologist Carleton Coon (above) began serving as an OSS officer in North Africa before Allied troops landed there in November 1942 in Operation Torch (map at top). They quickly took control of French Morocco and Algeria but had to battle Gen. Erwin Rommel's armored forces and other Axis troops in Tunisia before securing North Africa in mid-1943.

them was 38-year-old Carleton Coon, an anthropologist at Harvard who did field work in Morocco and was rejected for a naval commission because he was overweight and had high blood pressure. "I never took an oath for the COI or OSS," Coon recalled. "We were all gentlemen volunteers on our honor. We were never under orders. We were always asked, 'Would you like to . . . (e.g., get yourself killed)?' To which we always said 'yes.'" Before joining Eddy in North Africa, Coon underwent training in covert radio communications and sabotage. He considered himself fortunate to be fulfilling a boyhood dream "to travel in strange mountains, stir up tribes, and destroy the enemy by secret and unorthodox means."

Coon began serving undercover in Tangier, the capital of Spanish Morocco, which lay north of French Morocco and across from the British bastion of Gibraltar. His chief task was to induce tribal leaders to aid the Allies and defy the Germans if they occupied Spanish Morocco with Franco's consent and tried to close the strategic Strait of Gibraltar to Allied ships. Coon cultivated the support of an influential Moroccan mullah code-named Strings by donating 50,000 Francs to help him construct a mosque. "From that time on," Coon recalled, "Mr. Strings was our man" and offered "to hide us out in case the Germans surprised us in Tangier." Coon traveled frequently to Gibraltar, where British SOE officers gave him further training in explosives and demolition. In return, he and fellow agent Gordon Browne readily agreed when the SOE asked them to gather stones from Moroccan roads to serve as models for tire-puncturing bombs that could be deployed to stop German vehicles. "We discovered that there were very few stones along the roads," Coon related, "but that mule turds were to be found in abundance. So to our stone collecting, which filled the back seat, we added a few samples of local mule dung, and this was carefully packed and sent to London." SOE technicians "made up explosive turds from these samples," he added, "and we used them to good effect later in Tunisia."

As the American invasion loomed in the fall of 1942, Coon and other OSS agents spent long hours transmitting military intelligence by radio from North Africa to the headquarters of Lt. Gen. Dwight D. Eisenhower, commander of Operation Torch, who shifted base from London to Gibraltar shortly before the landings took place. In October, Eisenhower learned from Robert Murphy in Algeria that Maj. Gen Charles Mast of the Vichy high command wanted to meet secretly there with a senior American officer. Ike sent his top deputy, Maj. Gen. Mark Clark, who boarded the British submarine H.M.S. *Seraph* at Gibraltar and came ashore with other officers by kayak on the night of October 21 at the quiet Algerian port of Cherchell, where they were greeted by Murphy and met in a safe house with General Mast. Far from objecting to Operation Torch, Mast wanted the Americans to occupy not only French North Africa but also the Vichy zone in southern France to prevent a German takeover there. Clark explained that the Allies were not yet prepared to invade France but left with assurances from Mast that French troops would not resist

SWITCHING SIDES Adm. Jean Darlan—pictured at center facing Lt. Gen. Dwight Eisenhower—yielded as commander of French Vichy forces soon after Eisenhower's Allied troops landed in North Africa. Notorious for collaborating with the Germans, Darlan was assassinated in late December 1942, an attack that drew banner headlines (top) and ended his controversial arrangement with Eisenhower, who left Darlan in charge of Morocco and Algeria.

Torch and that only the Navy was likely to put up a fight. French naval officers had not forgotten or forgiven a blistering British attack on the Vichy fleet in July 1940, conducted to keep French warships out of German hands. Among those who remained suspicious of the Allies and reluctant to yield to them was Adm. Jean Darlan, the supreme Vichy commander.

Thanks to the diligent undercover work of Consul Murphy, Colonel Eddy, and the OSS, Eisenhower knew what to expect when his forces came ashore on November 8 in two waves, on French Morocco's Atlantic coast and Algeria's Mediterranean shore. Only the French Navy and scattered French Army units offered significant opposition, and that threat soon evaporated when Darlan agreed to a cease-fire, under pressure from American forces as well as anti-Vichy partisans, who were informed of the invasion in advance by Murphy and staged a simultaneous uprising in Algiers, where Darlan was visiting his ailing son in the hospital. The admiral then came to terms with Eisenhower, who left him to administer Morocco and Algeria while Ike's troops advanced eastward to challenge Axis forces in Tunisia.

SPY HANDLER OSS intelligence officer Allen Dulles was nearly stranded in enemy territory when Germany responded to the Allied invasion of North Africa by occupying the Vichy zone in southern France. Dulles made it over the French border into neutral Switzerland, where he dealt with Fritz Kolbe and other German spies who defied the Nazi regime by betraying its secrets to the Allies.

On December 24, Darlan was shot to death in Algiers. As it happened, his assassin was among a group of French volunteers who were being trained by Carleton Coon and other Allied agents to fight as commandos and commit sabotage. That operation was run by the SOE, with assistance from the OSS. Neither agency was linked to the assassination, but the trainers came under suspicion and had to disperse. Coon ended up at Cap Serrat in Tunisia, overseeing a motley crew of Arabs and former French Legionnaires who slipped through Axis lines, monitored troop movements, blew up bridges, and laid mule-turd bombs in the path of enemy vehicles.

A few days after American troops landed in North Africa, the Germans occupied Vichy France to secure that sector against Allied invasion. At the time, one of William Donovan's top aides, Allen Dulles, formerly of the State Department, was traveling from Spain through southern France on his way to Switzerland, where he would serve as a spymaster under diplomatic cover. His train reached the border on the eve of the German military takeover, and he barely escaped being detained by a Gestapo agent before crossing into Switzerland with the help of a sympathetic French policeman.

Dulles brought with him a one-million-dollar letter of credit, which he deposited in a Swiss bank. That was a hefty investment by the OSS, but it paid dividends. Diplomatic espionage involved setting oneself up in style, socializing with other diplomats and dignitaries, and gleaning intelligence from them—not to mention paying informants and couriers for their services or dispensing the occasional bribe. Dulles's most valuable source, however, betrayed precious secrets to him free of charge. One night in 1943, Fritz Kolbe, who worked in the Foreign Office in Berlin and reviewed daily dispatches from German embassies and military commands around the globe, appeared at Dulles's door in Berne with an intermediary who vouched for him and offered Dulles access to that treasure trove.

FRITZ KOLBE

Allen Dulles called Fritz Kolbe an "intelligence officer's dream," a fitting description of a man who held Nazis in contempt and refused to join their party but was granted access to secret German documents and shared them freely with the OSS. Born in 1900, Kolbe served briefly as a soldier before Germany was defeated in World War I. Unlike Hitler and other angry veterans who vowed to avenge that loss, Kolbe regarded the conflict as a tragic waste of life and opposed those who would lead Germans down that bloody path again. He went to work at the Foreign Office in Berlin several years before Hitler took power and remained entrenched there afterward because Nazis needed experienced civil servants like Kolbe who were not party members to help run agencies that grew rapidly as Hitler's Reich expanded.

In late 1941, Kolbe began reviewing sensitive diplomatic and military cables for Karl Ritter, who served as liaison between the Foreign Office and the Wehrmacht Supreme Command. "From the first day I found myself in touch with Nazi secrets," Kolbe said later, "I knew I would have to find a way, somehow, to get them out." He used various methods to gather intelligence that he would later deliver to Dulles, including copying reports by hand after hours, removing them to be photographed before returning them, and stashing away carbon copies of typed documents.

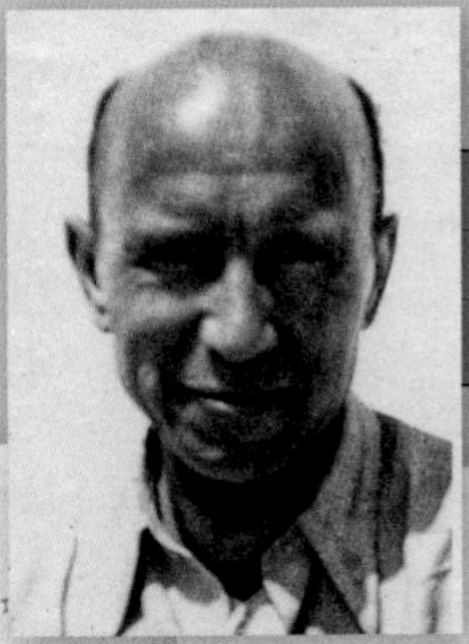

CODE NAME: GEORGE WOOD
SPIED FOR: UNITED STATES
SPIED AGAINST: GERMANY

In 1943, a friend of his at the Foreign Office helped Kolbe enter Switzerland as a courier, where he gave Dulles the first of several installments of pilfered documents.

With help from like-minded accomplices in Berlin, Kolbe passed more than 1,600 secret German communiqués to the OSS before the war ended. Among them were the three messages translated below—a summary of losses sustained by the Luftwaffe during a bombing raid on London (right), an assessment of Mussolini's sorry state of mind after Hitler installed the deposed dictator as his puppet in northern Italy (left), and a report in late 1943 from the German ambassador to the Vatican (center), who suggested that Pope Pius XII, by urging the Western powers to abandon "the formula of Unconditional Surrender," was seeking a settlement between the U.S., Britain, and Germany that would thwart Soviet expansion and contain communism. ✪

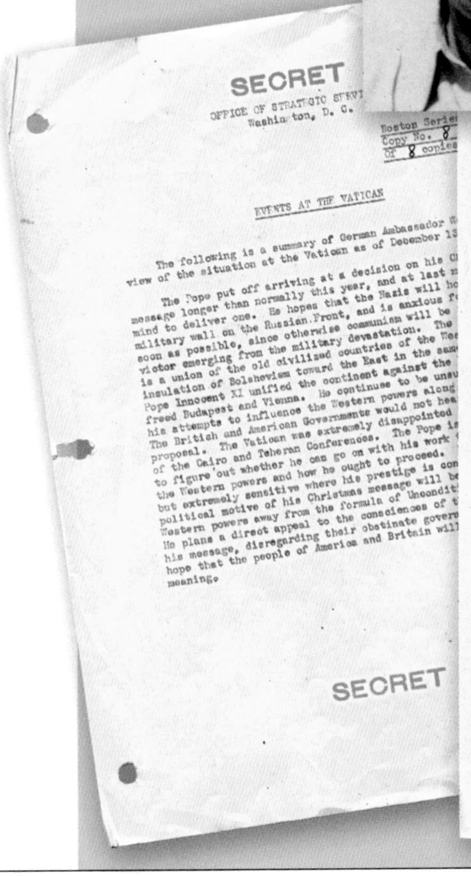
SECRET

OFFICE OF STRATEGIC SERVI
Washington, D. C.

Boston Serie
Copy No. 8
Of 8 copies

EVENTS AT THE VATICAN

The following is a summary of German Ambassador W
view of the situation at the Vatican as of December 13

The Pope put off arriving at a decision on his Cl
message longer than normally this year, and at last m
mind to deliver one. He hopes that the Nazis will ho
military wall on the Russian Front, and is anxious f
soon as possible, since otherwise communism will be
victor emerging from the military devastation. The
is a union of the old civilized countries of the Wes
insulation of Bolshevism toward the East in the same
Pope Innocent XI unified the continent against the
freed Budapest and Vienna. He continues to be unsu
his attempts to influence the Western powers along
The British and American Governments would not hea
proposal. The Vatican was extremely disappointed
of the Cairo and Teheran Conferences. The Pope is
to figure out whether he can go on with his work
the Western powers and how he ought to proceed.
but extremely sensitive where his prestige is con
political motive of his Christmas message will be
Western powers away from the formula of Uncondit
He plans a direct appeal to the consciences of t
his message, disregarding their obstinate govern
hope that the people of America and Britain will
meaning.

SECRET

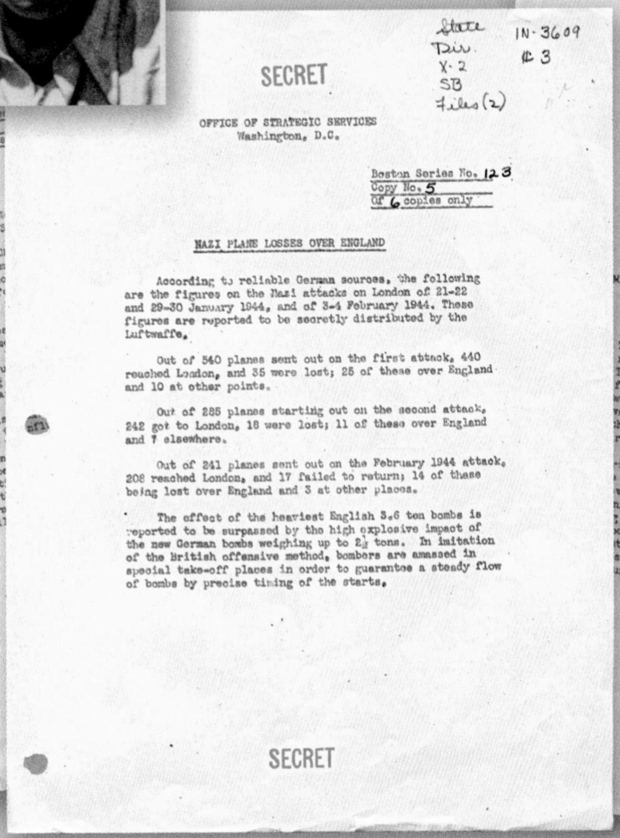
SECRET

State
Dir.
X-2
SB
Files (2)

IN-3609
3

OFFICE OF STRATEGIC SERVICES
Washington, D.C.

Boston Series No. 123
Copy No. 5
Of 6 copies only

NAZI PLANE LOSSES OVER ENGLAND

According to reliable German sources, the following are the figures on the Nazi attacks on London of 21-22 and 29-30 January 1944, and of 3-4 February 1944. These figures are reported to be secretly distributed by the Luftwaffe.

Out of 540 planes sent out on the first attack, 440 reached London, and 35 were lost; 25 of these over England and 10 at other points.

Out of 285 planes starting out on the second attack, 242 got to London, 18 were lost; 11 of these over England and 7 elsewhere.

Out of 241 planes sent out on the February 1944 attack, 208 reached London, and 17 failed to return; 14 of these being lost over England and 3 at other places.

The effect of the heaviest English 3.6 ton bombs is reported to be surpassed by the high explosive impact of the new German bombs weighing up to 2½ tons. In imitation of the British offensive method, bombers are amassed in special take-off places in order to guarantee a steady flow of bombs by precise timing of the starts.

SECRET

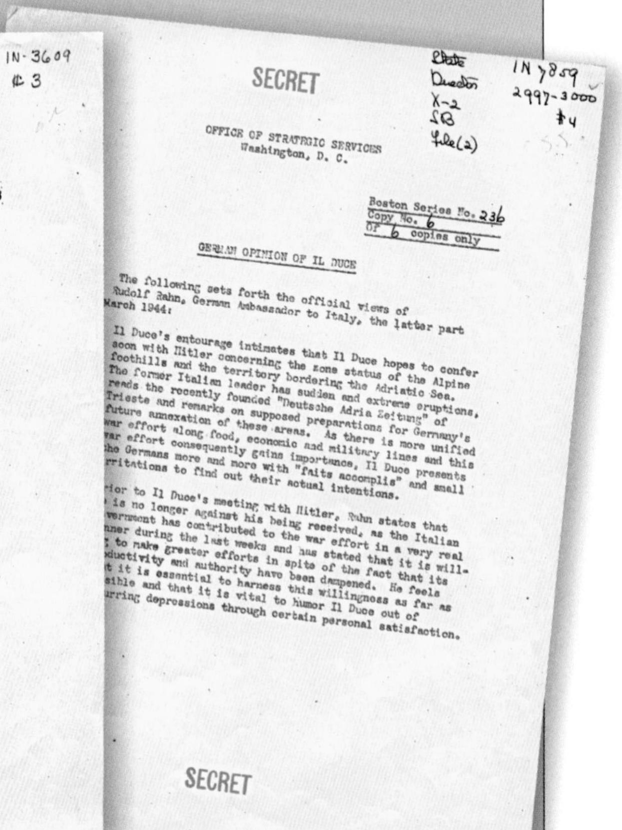
SECRET

State
Director
X-2
SB
File (2)

IN 7859
2997-3000
4

OFFICE OF STRATEGIC SERVICES
Washington, D. C.

Boston Series No. 236
Copy No. 6
Of 6 copies only

GERMAN OPINION OF IL DUCE

The following sets forth the official views of Rudolf Rahn, German Ambassador to Italy, the latter part March 1944:

Il Duce's entourage intimates that Il Duce hopes to confer soon with Hitler concerning the zone status of the Alpine foothills and the territory bordering the Adriatic Sea. The former Italian leader has sudden and extreme eruptions, reads the recently founded "Deutsche Adria Zeitung" of Trieste and remarks on supposed preparations for Germany's future annexation of these areas. As there is more unified war effort along food, economic and military lines and this war effort consequently gains importance, Il Duce presents the Germans more and more with "faits accomplis" and small irritations to find out their actual intentions.

rior to Il Duce's meeting with Hitler, Rahn states that
is no longer against his being received, as the Italian
vernment has contributed to the war effort in a very real
nner during the last weeks and has stated that it is will-
to make greater efforts in spite of the fact that its
oductivity and authority have been dampened. He feels
t it is essential to harness this willingness as far as
sible and that it is vital to humor Il Duce out of
urring depressions through certain personal satisfaction.

SECRET

Kolbe wanted nothing more than the satisfaction of subverting a Nazi regime that was disgracing and destroying Germany. He seemed too good to be true, but he would soon be recognized in Washington as a superspy, and his revelations would help propel Dulles to the top of his profession as future director of the Central Intelligence Agency.

CRACKDOWN IN FRANCE

For those considered enemies of the Reich, things went from bad to worse when Germans occupied the Vichy zone in southern France. The Vichy regime had authority over French officials and police nationwide and collaborated with German officers and Gestapo agents throughout France by helping them register and round up Jews and apprehend resisters. But people targeted by the Nazis were at greater risk of being arrested in the occupied north than in the south until the Germans intervened there as well and cracked down on spies and dissidents.

TREACHEROUS TRADECRAFT A French resistance agent shows comrades how to operate a clandestine radio set of the sort used to arrange for the delivery of weapons by the SOE or OSS. Agents caught by the Germans were often tortured to induce them to talk and executed if they refused to cooperate. Hanging a captive upside down, the punishment inflicted on the French resistance fighter opposite, could prove fatal if prolonged.

The Mediterranean port of Marseille, the largest city in the south, was a hotbed of resistance and harbored thousands of people wanted by the Germans, including Jews who had eluded a roundup by Vichy police in August as well as anti-Nazi refugees from across occupied Europe. Belgian-born Patrick O'Leary, who helped hundreds of downed Allied airmen escape from enemy territory, was based in Marseille and aided there by Australian-born Nancy Wake, who served as a courier and conductor for escapees. Her wealthy French husband, Henri Fiocca, funded the operation and established safe houses. Soon after the German takeover, O'Leary learned from informants that Ian Garrow—who had originated the escape line and helped spring O'Leary from a POW camp in 1941—was about to be transferred from detention in southern France to almost certain death at Dachau. Nancy Wake visited Garrow in prison, posing as his cousin, while O'Leary posed as her husband and bribed a guard to smuggle a uniform to the prisoner. In early December, Garrow walked out dressed as a guard and was conducted by O'Leary's confederates to Spain, where British diplomats arranged for him to return to England and help MI9 coordinate escape operations.

In January 1943, Heinrich Himmler instructed Carl-Albrecht Oberg, the SS officer in charge of the Gestapo and other German security forces in France, to target the Old Port district in Marseille, whose winding streets and cramped tenements were hard to patrol and hid many refugees and resisters. Vichy police chief René Bousquet, who worked closely with Oberg, offered to conduct that massive search-and-destroy operation, during which 6,000 people were arrested and some 30,000 evicted before the district was leveled with explosives. Vichy authorities announced that they had "decided on the grounds of internal security to carry out a vast police operation to rid Marseille of certain elements," whose subversive

RESISTING THE REICH / SECRET WARRIORS ★ 165

EXPOSING THE TRUTH Jan Karski (top) and others in the Polish underground compiled evidence in 1942 that vast numbers of Polish Jews were being sent to death camps. A report based on their findings by the Polish government-in-exile in London (above) prompted the Allied-constituted United Nations to issue a joint declaration in December 1942 against the Nazi program to exterminate Jews, which extended far beyond Poland.

activities supposedly placed the entire population at risk. But some people were seized there not because of anything they did but simply because of who they were, including 2,000 Jews who were sent to French concentration camps and ultimately consigned to SS death camps.

Some Frenchmen who took part in such murderous roundups would later claim ignorance of the fact that Jews were slated for extermination. But that defense was crumbling by the time the crackdown in Marseille occurred. As announced by the BBC, which broadcast to Europe in French and other languages, Allied countries known collectively as the United Nations had issued a joint declaration on December 17, 1942, stating that German authorities were "now carrying into effect Hitler's oft-repeated intention to exterminate the Jewish people in Europe . . . In Poland, which has been made the principal Nazi slaughterhouse, the ghettos established by the German invader are being systematically emptied of all Jews except a few highly skilled workers required for the war industries. None of those taken away are ever heard of again."

That declaration was based partly on a report issued by the Polish government-in-exile in London, entitled "The Mass Extermination of Jews in German Occupied Poland." Among those who helped document that atrocity and dispel the secrecy surrounding the Final Solution was Jan Karski, a Polish officer who went underground in Warsaw after Germans occupied that city. In 1942, Karski slipped into the Warsaw Ghetto, where Jews were being deported by SS troops, and met with Jewish resistance leaders who had proof that those deportees were not being "resettled in the East," as the Germans claimed, but murdered in gas chambers at Treblinka and other death camps along with Gypsies, who were also targeted for extermination. Thousands of people who remained trapped in the Warsaw Ghetto and faced imminent deportation staged an armed uprising in April 1943 and died fighting the Germans. By then, few who helped the SS round up Jews in France—or made covert efforts to save them—were ignorant of the Holocaust. "We were facing a genocide," recalled one resister in southern France who helped Jews hide or escape to unoccupied countries. "Anyone taken by the Germans was dead."

Patrick O'Leary left Marseille before the crackdown there, but he and others operating escape lines that ran through southern France were now under constant threat from the Gestapo and its informants. Comet Line leader Dédée de Jongh was seized in January 1943 while escorting British pilots over the Pyrenees into Spain and was sent to Ravensbrück concentration camp, where she survived the war—in part because the Germans mistakenly considered her a less significant figure in that operation than her father, who was arrested and executed later that same year. Patrick O'Leary was lured to a meeting in March by a traitor within his ranks and collared by the Gestapo. He ended up in Dachau and avoided being put to death only because that camp was liberated by Allied troops before his sentence was carried out.

For all the damage done to escape lines in the months following the German occupation of southern France, the number of downed airmen and refugees being spirited out of the country increased during 1943 as the Comet Line revived under new leadership and smaller networks took shape that proved harder for the Gestapo to penetrate. The Germans served unwittingly as recruiting agents for the opposition in France. By overrunning

DEPORTEES Jews leave the burning Warsaw Ghetto at gunpoint in 1943. Most deportees were killed in death camps, and others who were sent to labor in concentration camps died in wretched conditions or were executed there. Avraham Neyer, pictured up front in a dark coat, was the only one in his family to survive.

THE WARSAW UPRISING

More than 400,000 Jews were confined by Nazi authorities to the cramped Warsaw Ghetto, covering just 1.3 square miles and enclosed by a wall topped with barbed wire. Entire families were packed into a single room, disease was rampant, and thousands were slowly starving to death. Few Jews resisted initially when SS forces and German police began deporting them from the ghetto in July 1942. They were told they were being resettled, and it was hard to imagine a place worse than the one they left behind. Some in the ghetto were secretly in contact with outsiders, however, and learned the truth about the murderous SS operation, dubbed Reinhard for the recently assassinated Heydrich. Word that most of the deportees were being transported to Treblinka, a death camp east of Warsaw, prompted resistance groups within the ghetto to organize for combat. By year's end, they had amassed enough weapons, some of them smuggled in by the Polish underground, to arm more than 700 fighters.

On January 18, 1943, after a lull of several months, German forces resumed efforts to deport the 60,000 or so remaining Jews. Fighting erupted as people were being rounded up, and the Germans pulled out under pressure three days later after hauling away 5,000 deportees. Resistance leaders then took control of the ghetto and executed Nazi agents who had infiltrated the compound as well as some Jews who had collaborated with them. Anticipating a renewed assault, inhabitants excavated bunkers in which to hide while others prepared to battle the enemy. On April 19, SS Gen. Jürgen Stroop launched a relentless campaign to clear out every last occupant. After losing a dozen men on the first day in clashes with defiant Jews, Stroop began setting fires to reduce the ghetto to rubble. Many people were smoked out of their hiding places and seized, but 7,000 died fighting or perished in bunkers. It took Stroop almost a month to raze the ghetto and deport nearly 50,000 survivors to camps, from which few emerged alive. He capped the atrocity by blowing up the Great Synagogue of Warsaw, the last monument of what was once the largest Jewish community in Europe. ✪

the Vichy zone, they deprived 87-year-old Marshal Pétain—now a mere figurehead—and his sinister successor, Pierre Laval, of any lingering legitimacy and drove more French patriots into the ranks of the resistance than the SS and its Vichy accomplices could capture or kill.

KLAUS BARBIE AND JEAN MOULIN

Nothing infuriated French foes of the Reich more than the shameful services that some of their own countrymen rendered to SS officers like Klaus Barbie, who took charge of the Gestapo in the southern city of Lyon in late 1942. A relatively obscure figure up until then, he now commanded a force of 200 men, most of them French recruits who sympathized with the Nazis or aided them opportunistically. "I was only a lieutenant," Barbie later boasted, "but I had more power than a general." Among his enforcers was Frenchman Francis André, known as the "bath attendant" because he wrung confessions from suspects by immersing them repeatedly in a tub, sometimes drowning them in the process. Barbie himself often tortured those he captured and enjoyed doing so. "My God, he was savage!" one man who survived enhanced interrogation by him recalled. "He broke my teeth, he pulled my hair back. He put a bottle in my mouth and pushed it until the lips split from the pressure."

Barbie had plenty of targets in Lyon, which rivaled Marseille as a center of resistance. Many underground newspapers were printed there by covert organizations that took root in the Vichy zone before the German takeover—notably Combat, a vigorous resistance movement led by Capt. Henri Frenay, who had escaped from a POW camp after being cap-

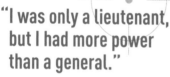

"I was only a lieutenant, but I had more power than a general."

SS OFFICER KLAUS BARBIE

tured by German troops in 1940 and then joined the French intelligence service, Deuxième Bureau, which continued to function under the Vichy regime. That gave Frenay cover as he reached out discreetly to other French officers disillusioned with Pétain and Laval and expanded his organization. Combat was the largest resistance movement in the south, but there were several others there and in the north—and one militant organization that was national in scope, the French Communist Party, which assassinated German soldiers and commandants and exposed the populace to deadly reprisals as a result.

Free French leader Charles de Gaulle, based in London, hoped to bring those Communists under his control and synchronize their efforts with those of other groups dedicated to liberating France, many of them led by men like Frenay who distrusted the Communists and

FREE PRESS Shown here are some of the many French resistance newspapers that were printed secretly and distributed covertly during the war. Many had titles that signaled defiance to the Nazi regime, including *La France Libre* (Free France), *La Résistance Ouvrière* (Worker Resistance), and *Juifs de France* (Jews of France). Ranging from single-sheet broadsides to multipage tabloids, hundreds of resistance publications were produced at great risk in France and other occupied countries.

> ## "My God, he was savage! He broke my teeth, he pulled my hair back. He put a bottle in my mouth and pushed it until the lips split from the pressure."
>
> A SUSPECT INTERROGATED AND TORTURED BY KLAUS BARBIE

BUTCHER OF LYON Klaus Barbie was notorious for torturing French resistance agents, Jewish fugitives, and others who fell into his grasp as an officer with the SD, the SS security service. "He had an extraordinary fund of violence," said one victim.

were reluctant to take orders from a general safely ensconced abroad while they faced lethal foes like Klaus Barbie. De Gaulle assigned the difficult and dangerous task of unifying the fractious French resistance movements to Jean Moulin, who bore a scar that testified to his commitment to the cause he served. In June 1940, while Moulin was administering the city of Chartres as prefect, Germans took control there after battling black troops from French Senegal on the outskirts and massacring many of those soldiers they captured. Moulin was then arrested and asked to sign a statement claiming that Senegalese troops had raped and murdered French civilians. He refused and was beaten for several hours, then taken to view the bodies of people who were supposedly killed by those soldiers but were plainly victims of an air raid. After undergoing further torture, he was locked in a room overnight. "I knew that I was at the end of my strength," he wrote afterward of his ordeal, "and that if it started again I would end up by signing." To avoid betraying Senegalese who had fought in defense of his country, he took a stray piece of broken glass and cut his throat.

When guards found Moulin alive but bleeding profusely, they took him to a German doctor, who stitched him up. He was left with a distinctive scar that he hid with a scarf when he later became a resistance leader and a target of the Gestapo. He was also targeted verbally by critics within his own ranks, including French resistance leaders who resented his efforts to force them into line behind de Gaulle. Henri Frenay, a conservative who suspected Moulin of being a Communist sympathizer if not actually a member of the party, balked at joining de Gaulle's proposed National Resistance Council, in which the entire political spectrum would be represented. Moulin then cut the flow of cash from Free French headquarters in London to Frenay, who responded by seeking support from Allen Dulles in Switzerland. Dulles reportedly pledged one million francs to Frenay's Combat movement, giving the OSS a stake in France. Dulles could do so without annoying President Roosevelt, who was no great admirer of de Gaulle.

Jean Moulin persisted with the Free French unity campaign and ultimately prevailed. Although Communist leaders opposed de Gaulle's insistence that there be no further armed resistance to the German occupiers except in direct support of an Allied invasion of France, they agreed under pressure from Moulin to attend the first meeting of the National Resistance Council, held secretly in Paris on May 27, 1943. Frenay did not attend, but Combat was represented, as were all other major French resistance movements. Debate was spirited, and Moulin had to warn the delegates to lower their voices to avoid being overheard.

Little was settled at the meeting, but it represented a triumph for Moulin. "He was very, very happy," a friend who dined with him afterward recalled. "That evening he was relaxed, which was extremely rare." It was only a brief respite for a man whose enemies were closing in on him. A series of arrests by the Gestapo and French police before and after the meeting brought resisters who were close to Moulin under grueling interrogation. He told his sister not to contact him even if his elderly mother died. "They would arrest me at her funeral," he said. "I will send you a note now and again, by courier. But you must not write to me."

On June 9, General Charles Delestraint, de Gaulle's candidate to head the Secret Army of resisters who would fight in support of the Allied invasion, was arrested outside a Metro station in Paris while awaiting René Hardy, who served under Frenay in Combat and had drawn up detailed plans to sabotage the French railway network. Hardy too was arrested while on his way to meet Delestraint in Paris and interrogated by the Gestapo before being released the following day. That should have caused him to be barred from any further involvement in resistance operations as a possible informant who agreed to cooperate with the Gestapo to avoid torture and execution, but Hardy concealed the fact that he had been detained. Moulin then arranged a meeting in the suburbs of Lyon to choose a replacement for Delestraint. It was held on June 21 in the house of a doctor who saw patients at home, allowing Moulin and other resistance leaders to arrive there during the day without arousing undue suspicion. Frenay sent a deputy, Henri Aubry, who brought along René Hardy. Moulin and two others arrived there belatedly. A few minutes later, Gestapo agents led by Klaus Barbie broke in the door and hand-cuffed all the men in the house except Hardy, who bolted as the suspects were being herded into a van and was grazed by a bullet fired at him as he fled.

Barbie did not know Jean Moulin by sight. But he knew from an informant that a ringleader code-named Max was at that meeting. He began the interrogation by lining up the suspects and asking each one to his face if he was Max. When that failed to produce results, he resorted to torture. One of the last witnesses to see Moulin alive was a resistance leader named Christian Pineau, who had been arrested earlier and saw Moulin stretched out on a bench half dead in a Lyon prison on June 24: "He had lost consciousness; his hollow eyes seemed to be sunk into his head. There was an ugly bluish wound on his temple. A soft, rasping sound escaped from his swollen lips. Without doubt, he had been tortured by the Gestapo." Barbie probably learned from others that this was the man he was looking for, but from "Max" himself he learned nothing. Had Moulin talked under duress, a devastating roundup of those at the highest level of the French resistance would have followed, and none ensued. He took his secrets with him to the grave.

René Hardy was widely suspected of betraying Jean Moulin and was tried for that offense after the war, but he was acquitted. There would be endless speculation about who within the resistance informed on Moulin. But there was no mystery as to who murdered him. He was tortured to death by the Gestapo, and if Klaus Barbie did not personally deliver the blows that killed him, he certainly had Moulin's blood on his hands—one of many crimes that earned Barbie the title "Butcher of Lyon."

Honored in postwar France as a national hero, Moulin joined a long list of men and women who resisted Nazi brutality to their last breath. While Gestapo agents were closing in on him, SS counterintelligence officers in Paris were breaking up the SOE Prosper network that Noor Inayat Khan joined as a radio operator after landing in France in the early hours of June 17, 1943. By month's end, Francis Suttill—the head of that network, established to support French resistance—and several of those working closely with him had been

MARKED MAN French resistance leader Jean Moulin covered his neck in public so that German authorities seeking him would not notice telltale scars from his attempted suicide while in custody early in the war. Seized and tortured by Klaus Barbie in June 1943, he refused to betray others wanted for resisting the Nazis and paid with his life.

"He had lost consciousness; his hollow eyes seemed to be sunk into his head ... A soft, rasping sound escaped from his swollen lips."

CHRISTIAN PINEAU, ONE OF THE LAST TO SEE THE TORTURED JEAN MOULIN ALIVE

arrested, including courier Andrée Borrel and veteran radio operator Gilbert Norman, who met briefly with Noor and helped her get started before he was captured. Henri Déricourt, a French pilot who oversaw landings by SOE agents in France and had extensive knowledge of the network, was suspected of betraying Suttill and his agents. But like René Hardy, Déricourt was later tried and acquitted, and the cause of the network's catastrophic collapse was never officially determined.

Noor eluded arrest for several months by moving frequently from one hideout to another, hauling her heavy equipment in a suitcase. By September, she was the last SOE operator still transmitting to London from Paris. Some other surviving members of the shattered Prosper network were recalled from France, but she was considered indispensable and left in place. German agents had learned enough from informants to post a description of her under the code name Madeleine, offering a hefty reward for her capture. Seized in October, she was interrogated by Hans Josef Kieffer, who served as chief in Paris for the SD—the SS intelligence agency founded by Reinhard Heydrich before he took on larger responsibilities. "She told us nothing," recalled Kieffer. "We could not rely on anything she said."

After refusing to cooperate and attempting to escape, Noor was subjected to increasingly harsh

PILLORIED Resistance fighters arrested after attacking Nazi officials in France are portrayed on this German poster as criminals rather than liberators.

treatment. Her ordeal ended at Dachau, where she and three other women who served as SOE agents in France—Yolande Beekman, Madeleine Damerment, and Elaine Plewman—were executed in September 1944. A jailer there said that Noor was severely beaten beforehand. Her last word as her executioner pressed a gun to the back of her head was *"liberté."* Perhaps she knew then, as news of Allied advances passed by word of mouth to dark cells in Nazi Germany, that the liberty she and other secret warriors fought for in France was now sure to prevail.

CITIZEN SOLDIERS French partisans at war with the Germans man a barricade with rifles in hand in 1944. Resistance groups supported by agents of the SOE and OSS stepped up their efforts to liberate France after Allied troops landed in Normandy on D-Day.

TOOLS FOR A DANGEROUS TRADE

To fulfill Winston Churchill's order to "set Europe ablaze," the SOE recruited top scientists and inventors to work at secret stations in Britain, where they designed innovative arms and equipment for sabotage and subversion. Station IX, set up in a converted hotel called the Frythe at Welwyn in Hertfordshire, supplied agents and resistance fighters with weapons and other gear, assigned the prefix "Wel-" as in the portable Welbike and the silenced Welrod pistol. Station XII, located at Aston House in East Hertfordshire, developed ingenious devices for commandos and saboteurs, including plastic explosives, magnetic limpet mines, pressure switches, time fuses, and incendiaries. According to Col. Leslie Wood, commanding officer of Station XII, Aston House also "designed and made up special explosive charges tailored for the job in hand," such as demolishing railroad tracks or blasting large facilities like a heavy water plant in Norway, targeted in early 1943 to prevent Germany from developing nuclear weapons. Devising cunning ways to assassinate or pulverize enemies "could sound a little grim," Colonel Wood remarked, "but I can truthfully say that we regarded the whole thing completely impersonally and as tremendously funny, the more hideous the devices we invented and made to confound the enemy—the funnier we thought it."

A similar spirit prevailed at the OSS Research and Development branch directed by Stanley Lovell. In keeping with his instructions from William Donovan to furnish the OSS with "every subtle device and every underhanded trick to use against the Germans and the Japanese," Lovell and his team devised miniature cameras, compasses disguised as uniform buttons, and a fountain pen that contained a single-shot pistol. During the war, the SOE and OSS supplied large amounts of arms and equipment, both conventional and specialized, to resistance groups in Europe and Asia. Before D-Day, more than 3,300 tons of supplies, including 35,000 grenades and 75,000 small arms, were air-dropped to resistance groups in France, Belgium, the Netherlands, Denmark, Poland, and Norway. ✪

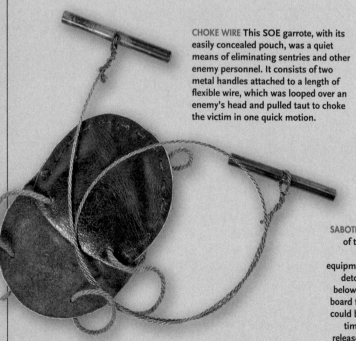

CHOKE WIRE This SOE garrote, with its easily concealed pouch, was a quiet means of eliminating sentries and other enemy personnel. It consists of two metal handles attached to a length of flexible wire, which was looped over an enemy's head and pulled taut to choke the victim in one quick motion.

SABOTEUR'S KIT Marcel Vandenberghe of the Belgian resistance used this violin case to conceal sabotage equipment. His kit contained trip wire, detonators, and the devices shown below the case, including a knife and board for cutting fuses and pliers that could be used to activate tubular SOE time pencils, which when crushed released acid, slowly eating away at a wire that broke and set off a bomb.

LIBERATOR The OSS Liberator pistol was a single-shot weapon for assassination and defense that fired a potent .45 ACP (automatic Colt pistol) cartridge and came with spare ammunition and a wooden dowel to eject spent cartridges. Most Liberators were sent to China and the Philippines.

PYRO ASSY
100 sec M68
LOT 3 ASM 71A

ARTIFACTS OF WAR

AIDING THE RESISTANCE

The SOE and OSS supplied eager but ill-equipped and often inexperienced resistance fighters in occupied Europe not just with weapons and equipment but with guidance from agents trained in covert operations. Many of those agents were instructed as parachutists like the SOE recruits above before they dropped into enemy territory from converted bombers such as the British Handley Page Halifax or the American Consolidated B-24 Liberator, which also delivered supplies for resistance groups by parachute. Gear designed for such drops included lights to mark landing zones, a collapsible motorbike packed in a container that protected it on impact with the ground, and camouflaged jumpsuits, which made agents descending by parachute harder for the enemy to spot and could be quickly discarded by those wearing civilian clothes underneath so as to blend in with the populace.

Through trial and error, Allied agencies refined the design and delivery of equipment and operatives to groups fighting German occupation forces. Those efforts culminated in Operation Jedburgh, a joint venture in which small teams of officers and radio operators from the SOE, OSS, and occupied countries landed by parachute behind enemy lines in 1944 and coordinated attacks by resistance groups as Allied troops invaded France and advanced into Belgium and Holland. ✪

JUMPSUIT SOE agents like those pictured at top during a training exercise and Jedburgh team members wore camouflaged jumpsuits such as this one when parachuting into enemy territory. Dubbed "striptease" suits, they were easily discarded after agents landed.

AGENTS' TOOL This standard British Army utility knife was supplied to both American and British agents for sorties into occupied France. The multipurpose tool could be employed as a weapon if required.

TAKING THE LEAP SOE agents began training as parachutists with static-line drops like the one above, in which a recruit jumps from a Handley Page Halifax bomber with a cord attached to his parachute that opens it automatically as he descends. Battery-powered landing lights such as the one at right were used by SOE "pathfinder" teams to mark night landing zones for agents or supply drops.

PORTABLE SCOOTER The SOE Welbike could be collapsed to fit into a parachute drop container. It was powered by a single-cylinder engine and had a range of 90 miles at 30 miles an hour. To deploy the bike, an agent lifted the handlebars into position, pulled up the seat, and folded out footrests.

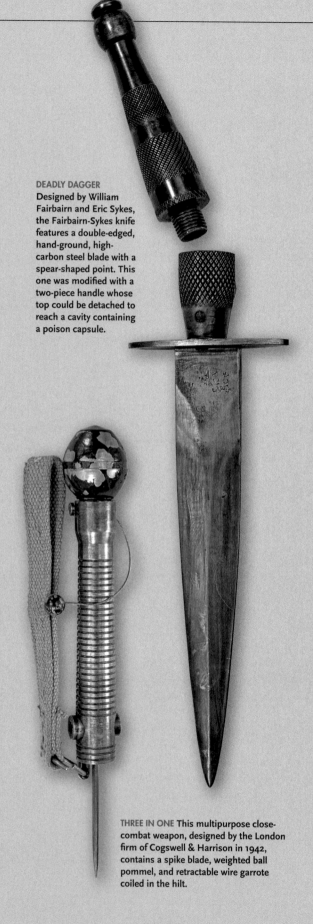

WEAPONS FOR CLOSE COMBAT

Men and women recruited as agents by the SOE and OSS, like British Commandos and American Rangers, were instructed in hand-to-hand combat and silent killing techniques. Their curriculum at training camps included communications, demolition, small group tactics, and practice with pistols. But the close combat course devised for the SOE by William Fairbairn, who also trained agents for the OSS, emphasized dispatching enemies with a knife like the one he and his colleague Eric Sykes designed (right). "The knife is a silent and deadly weapon" Fairbairn told trainees, one "that is easily concealed and against which, in the hands of an expert, there is no sure defense, except firearms or running like hell." Learning how to knife an opponent steeled recruits for challenges that lay ahead. "We practiced hand-to-hand combat using the famous Fairbairn knife under the guidance of the designer," recalled Robert Kehoe, who trained at an OSS base in Maryland that later became Camp David. "At the very least, this helped us develop a spirit of daring." Shown here are some of the deadly weapons designed for close combat by experts such as Fairbairn, who reminded recruits that this was "WAR, not sport. Your aim is to kill your opponent as quickly as possible." ✪

DEADLY DAGGER Designed by William Fairbairn and Eric Sykes, the Fairbairn-Sykes knife features a double-edged, hand-ground, high-carbon steel blade with a spear-shaped point. This one was modified with a two-piece handle whose top could be detached to reach a cavity containing a poison capsule.

PUT TO THE KNIFE A British Commando serving as instructor at an SOE training camp demonstrates how to dispatch an enemy sentry using a Fairbairn-Sykes knife.

THREE IN ONE This multipurpose close-combat weapon, designed by the London firm of Cogswell & Harrison in 1942, contains a spike blade, weighted ball pommel, and retractable wire garrote coiled in the hilt.

ESCAPE KNIFE Equipped with a sharp hook that parachutists could use to cut tangled shroud lines and free themselves, this small escape knife was easily concealed.

LAPEL KNIVES Allied weapons designers produced various lapel knives—which could be hidden under a lapel or elsewhere under clothing—including the sheathed dagger at left, which could be strapped around a leg, and the small, double-edged blade at far left, shown with its sheath and strap.

HIDDEN BLADES Concealed within French coins, these short, curved, retractable blades were issued by the SOE and had various uses, including puncturing the tires of enemy vehicles.

KNIFE AND HOOK The knife at left was designed to be hidden in a shoe. The hook at right, pictured atop its sheath, could be used as a tool or as a weapon to slash or stab an enemy.

DEADLY SKEWER The SOE spike dagger at right, hidden in a sheath attached to the forearm, was a formidable attack and self-defense weapon. The knob at top could be used to crack a skull or to withdraw the sharp end from a victim's body.

GUNS AND RIFLES

During the war, the SOE and OSS provided resistance groups with a wide assortment of firearms, ranging from standard Allied military arms to unconventional silenced weapons like the Welrod assassination pistol and small-caliber concealed devices such as pen and pipe guns. A favorite among resistance groups across Europe was the rugged and effective British-made Mk II Sten submachine gun (below), more than two million of which were manufactured during the conflict. Later versions, notably the heavier Mk V Sten, were also obtained by some resistance fighters. Modeled roughly after German MP 38 and MP 40 submachine guns, Stens fired standard 9-mm Parabellum cartridges and consisted of fewer than 50 stamped parts, which required minimal milling and welding and were quickly assembled in British factories or in secret workshops in Europe, where some resistance groups produced their own versions. Despite a tendency to jam or start firing spontaneously if they were dropped or jarred, they could be turned out so cheaply and efficiently that late in the war hard-pressed German arms makers, whose models had inspired the Sten, imitated it by manufacturing the MP 3008 submachine gun, which was almost indistinguishable from the Mk II Sten.

SOE and OSS agents inserted into enemy territory were generally armed with handguns, including American-made Colts and imports from neutral countries such as the .38-caliber Spanish Llama pistol. Some resistance groups, particularly in Eastern Europe, received no Allied weapons and were dependent on hidden stocks of civilian arms, local military rifles, captured Axis firearms, or crude but serviceable guns of their own making. British and American officials felt that firearms supplied to the resistance should not require extensive training or careful maintenance. Late in the war, however, when resistance groups began openly rebelling against German occupiers in several countries, Sten guns were supplemented by Bren light machine guns and other regular military weapons, including rifles and carbines. That helped raise morale among resistance fighters, who felt that the Allies now recognized them as real soldiers. ✪

ENHANCED FIREPOWER
A resistance leader in the Haute-Loire region of south-central France instructs fellow Maquis in the operation and maintenance of an MK II Sten submachine gun, which the SOE delivered by parachute in a canister.

REMOTE-FIRED MORTAR A mortar designed to be screwed into a tree trunk, this tree spigot gun was fired remotely or triggered by a trip wire and shot a three-pound armor-piercing projectile up to 150 yards. One such gun was included in equipment for the assassination of Reinhard Heydrich.

SOLDIERS' STANDBY The powerful Colt Model 1911A1, a .45-caliber semiautomatic pistol, was the standard sidearm of U.S. forces during World War II.

LOADED LIGHTER This custom-made cigarette lighter converted into a pistol, armed with a tiny 4-mm "gallery" cartridge that was designed for indoor target practice. It could be deadly when fired at very close range.

PEN GUN AND STINGER In 1943, the OSS contracted with the Rite-Rite Manufacturing Co., which made pens and pencils, to produce a single-shot .22-caliber gun disguised as a fountain pen (near right). A similar OSS weapon, known as the Stinger (far right), resembled a pen when clipped in an agent's jacket or shirt pocket.

HOLSTERED COLT This shoulder holster, which allowed an OSS agent to carry a gun concealed under his coat, contains a Colt Model 1908 Pocket Hammerless pistol, with a covered hammer that enabled it to be withdrawn from clothing without snagging.

PIPE PISTOL The stem of this pipe served as a gun barrel from which a small-caliber projectile could be shot with deadly force at very close range.

M1A1 A wartime version of the American-made Thompson submachine gun, the M1A1 was used by American Rangers, British and Canadian Commandos, and Jedburgh teams.

M1 CARBINE
A .30-caliber semiautomatic weapon designed for the U.S. Army, the M1 Carbine proved handy for OSS and SOE agents and was provided to Maquis fighters in France after D-Day.

SECRET SHOTS Dutch partisan Piet Nagel wraps two British Lee-Enfield rifles in a carpet (top) and carries them down an Amsterdam street (above) in pictures taken covertly by Charles Breijer, who registered with German authorities as a professional photographer for a labor journal and used that as cover to record activities of his comrades in the Dutch resistance. Breijer hid a Rolleiflex camera in his bicycle bag to capture Nagel as he walked down the street.

BREN A light machine gun adopted by Britain, the Bren was gas operated, using the gas produced when propellant in cartridges ignited, and fired up to 540 rounds a minute, fed from the magazine attached here.

DE LISLE CARBINE Designed by William G. de Lisle for the Sterling Armaments Co., the De Lisle carbine was a conversion of the Lee-Enfield No.1 Mk III rifle, fitted with a superb silencer that made it a stealth weapon for commandos.

LEE-ENFIELD Adopted in 1941, the Lee-Enfield No. 4 Mk1 bolt-action rifle was Britain's standard infantry small arm during World War II. It fired the British .303 Mark VII cartridge.

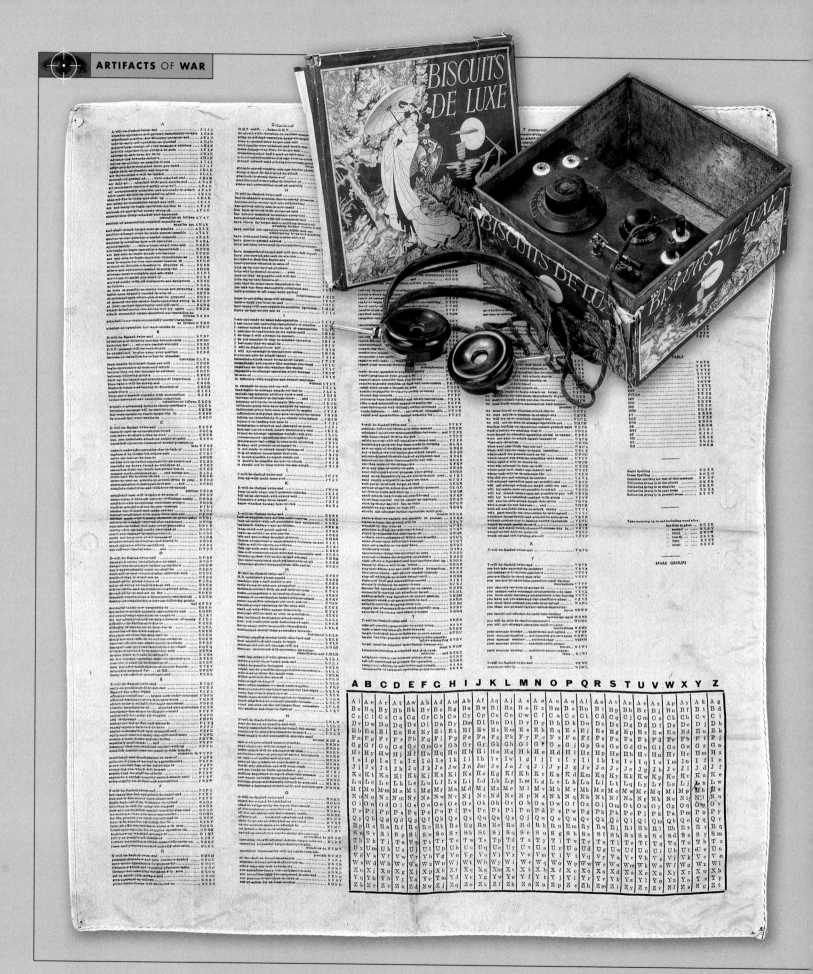

SHORTWAVE RADIOS

The radio transceiver, combining a shortwave transmitter and receiver in one set, was the primary link between agents in the field and their headquarters. Trained radio operators were an essential part of SOE and OSS networks in enemy territory, and each Jedburgh team included one. Operators were directed to send messages using Morse code over prearranged frequencies. Their messages had to be short, precise, and carefully encrypted using codes such as those printed on silk (opposite). Their wireless sets had to be light enough to be carried and were often concealed in suitcases to avoid attracting attention. The SOE produced suitcase sets that grew increasingly lighter and more portable during the war, trimming down from 42 pounds initially to just nine pounds for the Type A Mark III. Some resistance groups had operators who carried their own transceivers in cases like the one below, and most groups had radio receivers to monitor broadcasts from England that included coded phrases alerting resistance fighters to take action. Those radio receivers were disguised in various ways, like the one concealed in a French biscuit tin (opposite top) to avoid detection if Germans searched the premises. ✪

SENDING SIGNALS At top right, a commando uses a battery-powered transmitter in Norway. The French-made transceiver at right, concealed in a leather attaché case, was used by resistance agent Ernst Slain to report on German forces at Normandy before D-Day. As shown opposite, radio operators had codes for letters of the alphabet and for specific messages such as warning that Gestapo agents were searching an area.

HIDDEN LENS In these images taken by a Dutch resistance photographer, a woman carries a Rolleiflex camera concealed in her handbag (far left), with a lens exposed that can only be spotted up close (near left). To take a photograph, she would pretend to look for something in her bag and snap the shot.

SPY CAMERAS

As Allied agents and resistance forces struggled to loosen Hitler's grip on Europe, photography played an important role in subversion, surveillance, and various forms of spycraft. Taking pictures was not necessarily forbidden in Nazi-occupied territory, but recording on film anything that occupation authorities considered sensitive—military establishments, troop concentrations, dams, airfields, or rail and port facilities—could lead to arrest and severe punishment.

Clandestine cameras were essential tools for intelligence operatives performing military surveillance, enabling them to photograph enemy weapons, equipment, and military installations without being spotted. Agents working secretly against the Reich used cameras to detail fortifications of the Atlantic Wall and provide the first evidence of German rocket experiments. Cameras were also employed to expose collaborators and their activities on film and document atrocities that Axis leaders did not want revealed to the world, including attacks on Jews and other targeted groups in Eastern Europe and the brutal actions of occupation forces throughout the Third Reich.

Spies often relied on photography to copy clas-

MATCHBOX CAMERA **The Eastman Kodak Co. developed this miniature camera, which was small enough to fit in a matchbox, and manufactured more than 1,000 of them for the OSS during World War II.**

sified documents, using special cameras or regular commercial models with close-up lenses as well as stands that held cameras in place as one document after another was photographed. Compact, folding stands were produced that could be used during break-ins to photograph lengthy files or reports as quickly and precisely as possible. Large-format photos could then be converted to microfilm for covert transmission to Allied intelligence centers. Cameras were also useful for producing false papers and identity documents that mimicked genuine documents, for reproducing images on anti-Nazi posters and leaflets, and for photo-offset printing, employed by some underground newspapers

To perform such tasks, some partisans and resistance fighters hoarded prewar cameras and acquired scarce stocks of chemicals, film, and photographic paper. Others cobbled together cameras from scavenged lenses and spare parts. The SOE and OSS commissioned companies like Eastman Kodak, or employed experts at their own secret laboratories to design miniature cameras and the means to conceal them. Those clandestine cameras were not mere novelties but necessary tools in the secret war. ◌

HOMEMADE This camera was crafted by a French Resistance member from a telescope lens, an electrical box, and large bolts to advance the film. Although crudely constructed, it would have been serviceable.

INSTRUCTIONS FOR OPERATING CAMERA, SPECIAL, SMALL, 16 mm.

1. Hold camera with lens away from operator, instantaneous shutter release button to the right.

2. Push the right end of inner section of camera toward the left (so indented button will not scratch inner section).

...ve pressure plate from back of camera, exposi... ...ilm chambers, back of lens and winding or ...ancer spool. Remove winding spool.

...ve items so they may be located in total

...g operation of loading camera must be ... darkness.

...ainer. (Plus X for normal, clear da... ...ull, cloudy day). Cut off not m... ...om the roll of film. One foot of ... ...frames or images.

...ut not too tightly with the e... ...Do not pull roll of film ... ...n surface. Hold film by ed... ...s touch emulsion side, en... ...finished film will be da...

...chamber. Take free ... ...film chamber, hol... ...inding spool down ... ...rmly in slot.

...complete tur... ...e that film ...

10. ... of came...

11. In... ...n oute... ...ing ...s ma... on ... ...inter... clicks... ...tensi...

12. Unload... ...tal d... as num... ...d loose ... gently f... ...ol, coil, an... proof con... ...ng developm... by edges. ... ...oading and unl... pletely confident that operation ... total darkness.

13. The instantaneous shutter release ... film advancer disc are on the right. O... ... the lever for bulb exposure and button for diaphragm control. Pull out button for small aperture, f.11, for distant scenes and brilliant light; push home for full aperture, f.5, for dull light. Camera has fixed focus, everything 4 ft. to infinity in focus, instantaneous shutter speed of approximately 1/50th second. When not in use, carry in cloth case to prevent dust and cigarette scraps from jamming shutter.

BOXED UP A tiny camera, carried in the case above, was concealed in this matchbox and covered with matches so that it would not be visible even if the box was opened.

MINI MINOX Designed by Walter Zapp, an ethnic German born in Latvia, the Minox miniature camera, shown with its case and instruction sheet, entered production in 1937. The prototypical spy camera, it weighed less than a cigarette lighter and was procured by various intelligence agencies as the war unfolded.

INSTRUCTIONS FOR SABOTAGE

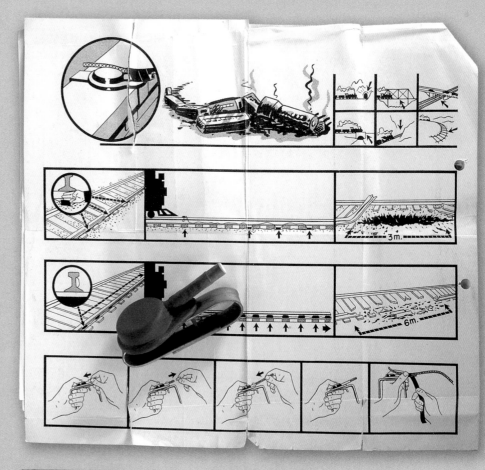

Any doubt that sabotage campaigns could effectively disrupt the German war machine in Europe was erased in June 1941, when Allied agents destroyed the Pessac power station near the French city of Bordeaux with well-placed demolition charges. The blast disrupted operations at a nearby U-boat base and halted the region's electric railways. Such sabotage figured prominently in the undercover war waged by resistance fighters, often supplied and instructed by SOE or OSS agents trained in using TNT or plastic explosives to destroy enemy equipment and installations. Those operatives furnished resistance groups not just with guidance and expertise but with a wide range of explosive devices devised in agency workshops, including coal bombs (opposite), used to sabotage coal-powered locomotives, ships, and power plants. Allied agencies also developed and distributed sophisticated time fuses, which detonated bombs when they would do the most harm and allowed saboteurs who planted them to escape injury and detection.

Anti-Nazi partisans and resistance fighters were not always dependent on Allied agents, and conducted numerous acts of sabotage on their own initiative. In one operation, a team of saboteurs from the University of Brussels blasted Belgian rail lines, canals, and power stations vital to the German war effort. By the end of 1942, nearly 200,000 attacks had been carried out against factories, military installations, railroads, and bridges in occupied Europe. ✪

TRACK WORK Saboteurs like the French partisan at right, wiring a demolition charge under a rail, often used the detonator pictured above with its illustrated instructions. Dubbed the "Clam," it resembled a harmless warning signal placed on tracks to alert engineers to reduce speed in fog or other unsafe conditions. When a locomotive ran over the Clam, the resulting explosion could derail the train.

WREAKING HAVOC Derailments like the one above in France in January 1942 often resulted when tracks were sabotaged. But agents could also wreak havoc by inserting in the fuel bin of a locomotive a coal bomb (right), filled with plastic explosives that detonated when shoveled into the fire. The OSS provided a kit containing instructions for priming the bomb and paints to match its color to the type of coal in use.

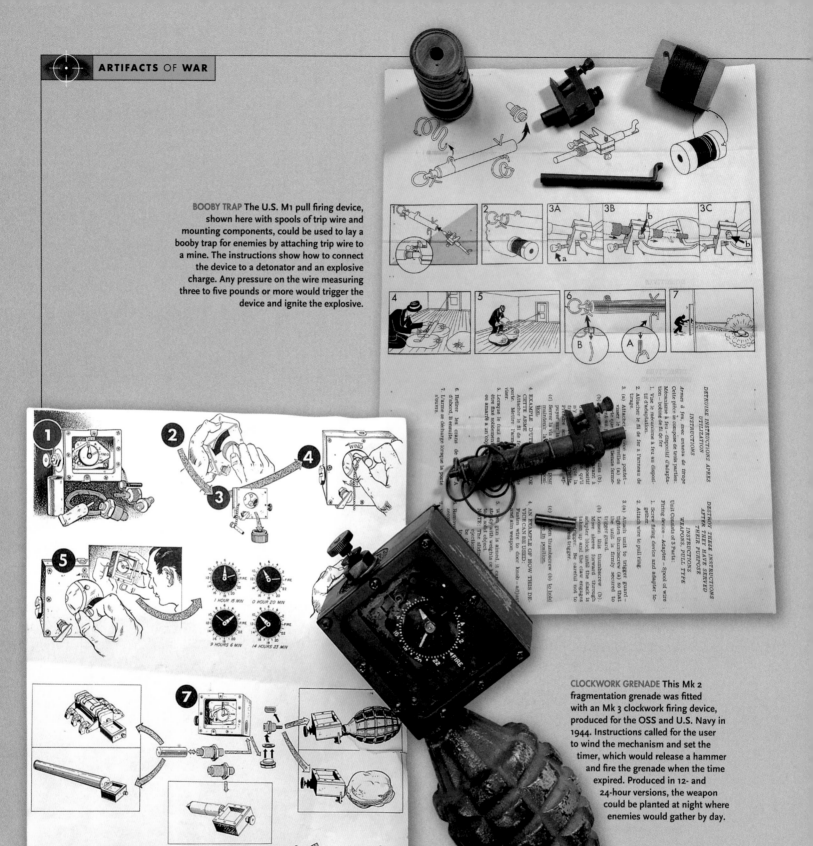

BOOBY TRAP The U.S. M1 pull firing device, shown here with spools of trip wire and mounting components, could be used to lay a booby trap for enemies by attaching trip wire to a mine. The instructions show how to connect the device to a detonator and an explosive charge. Any pressure on the wire measuring three to five pounds or more would trigger the device and ignite the explosive.

CLOCKWORK GRENADE This Mk 2 fragmentation grenade was fitted with an Mk 3 clockwork firing device, produced for the OSS and U.S. Navy in 1944. Instructions called for the user to wind the mechanism and set the timer, which would release a hammer and fire the grenade when the time expired. Produced in 12- and 24-hour versions, the weapon could be planted at night where enemies would gather by day.

TIMING THE BLAST Saboteurs who demolished the bridge above in France and other big structures survived by using fuses that gave them time to escape before the blast occurred. The SOE fuses at left, called time pencils for their shape, contained vials filled with acid that were crushed after the device was inserted in an explosive charge. The acid then came in contact with a wire and eroded it until it broke, releasing a striker that fired a percussion cap and detonated the bomb. The timing for such fuses ranged from 10 or 15 minutes to an hour or two and was indicated by the colored band on the tube.

ESCAPE AND EVASION

In December 1939, Maj. Norman Crockatt of the Royal Scots, the oldest regiment in the British Army, took charge of a new military intelligence agency designated MI9 at his office in Room 424 of the Metropole, a London hotel requisitioned for the war effort. Established to help downed British airmen evade capture in enemy territory and escape from prison if apprehended, MI9 upheld the doctrine that prisoners of war—particularly highly trained airmen—should try to escape to return to duty and force the enemy to expend military resources guarding POWs and pursuing escapees. To that end, Crockatt and his staff established secret means of communicating with POWs held in Axis camps, aided resistance groups in occupied Europe that ran escape lines, debriefed successful escapees to obtain intelligence, and provided airmen and other military personnel assigned to high-risk missions with maps, tools, and guidance to help them evade or escape captivity.

Nowhere in the German military prison system were escape techniques and equipment tested more fully than in Oflag IV-C (Officer Compound IV-C), located at Colditz Castle in eastern Germany. That brooding medieval fortress was designated a *Sonderlager*, or high-security camp, for officers classified as "anti-German" or inveterate escape artists. Concentrating so many determined individuals in one place made that seemingly inescapable prison the scene of some of the war's most ingenious and creative escape attempts. The inmates, who included officers from Great Britain, Canada, France, and other occupied countries, organized a central escape committee that obtained intelligence on a hidden radio receiver and oversaw units that forged documents, manufactured military and civilian clothing, and provided food for Colditz prisoners seeking freedom. Of the 130 or so who escaped, roughly one in four eluded pursuit and reached home. ◉

TUNNELING OUT In 1941, French officers gained access to the wine cellar at Colditz Castle and dug a tunnel (below) that extended some 50 yards to the castle wall before guards thwarted their escape attempt. The tin-can electric light fixture at left helped illuminate the tunnel as they worked.

TOWERING PRISON Colditz Castle, perched on a hilltop above the Mulde River in Germany, held captured Allied officers. Its imposing height and thick walls led some German authorities to consider it escape-proof.

DARING DESCENT In May 1941, two Polish officers descended from the roof of the castle down its 120-foot outer wall using knotted bed sheets (left) before being nabbed by a guard who heard the scraping of their boots. Playing cards that concealed maps helped guide escapees.

FOOLED BY DUMMIES Dutch Army officer Leo de Hartog holds "Moritz," one of two dummy wood-and-plaster heads, christened "Moritz" and "Max," that were propped up as shown here and used to fool guards at Colditz during the daily head count. The Dutch used the dummies to cover several escapes in the summer of 1941.

POINTERS Shown here on a 1944 cloth escape map are mini-compasses that could be hidden in buttons, badges, or pipe stems (far left), and strips of magnetized steel that pointed north when balanced on a belt buckle (left) or spike (above).

MAPS FOR DOWNED AIRMEN

An important tool in any POW's escape kit was a good map of the territory that had to be traversed to make a "home run" back to Allied territory. The task of providing those fell to Maj. Clayton Hutton, a former RAF pilot assigned to MI9. Hutton acquired his first maps from the venerable Scottish mapmaking company of John Bartholomew & Son, which published detailed tourist maps of Germany, Holland, Belgium, France, and other countries where Allied airmen were downed or held captive.

As a material for escape maps, Hutton selected silk, which was lightweight, durable, easily concealed, and silent when handled, unlike paper. He first obtained silk from stocks rejected for the making of parachutes. By 1943, as silk supplies from the Far East dwindled, MI9 shops began using rayon. Some specialized maps were concealed within playing cards included in POW relief packages. When soaked in water, the face of the card could be separated from the back to reveal a map section that could be assembled with others to form a regional map.

To make use of a map, an evader or escapee needed a compass that could be easily concealed. MI9 craftsmen fashioned tiny compasses that could be hidden in equipment or clothing, including cuff links, badges, and uniform buttons, some of which unscrewed clockwise rather than counterclockwise to thwart German searchers. ✪

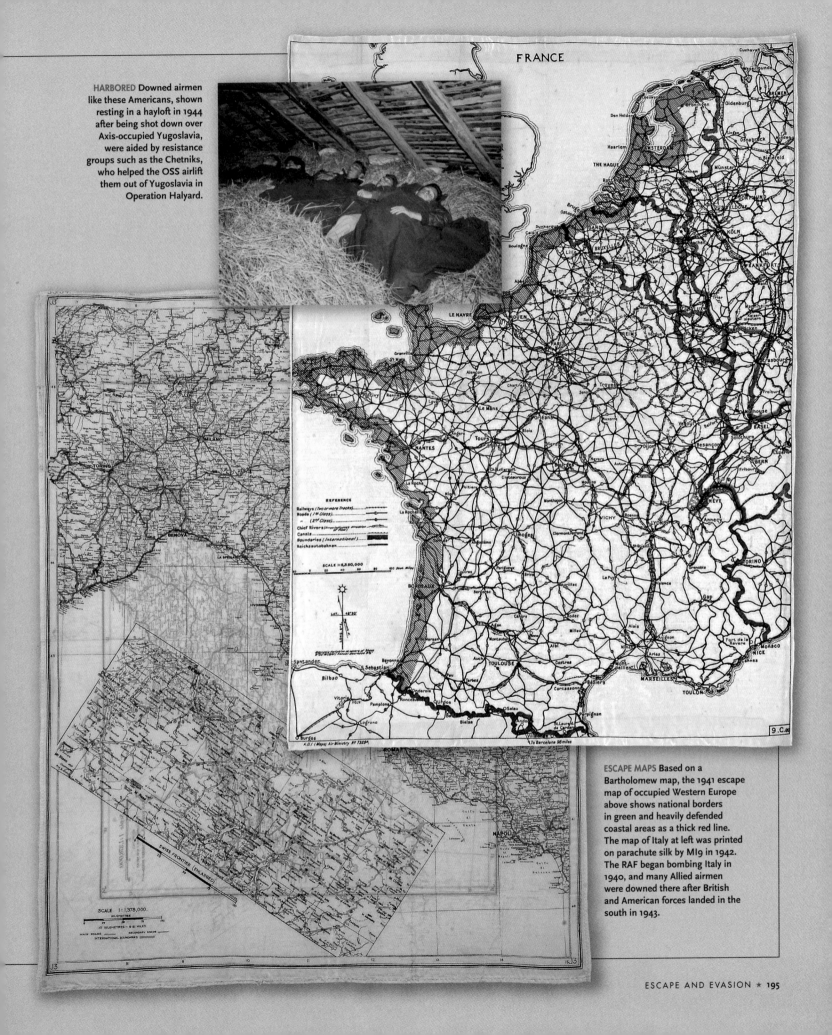

HARBORED Downed airmen like these Americans, shown resting in a hayloft in 1944 after being shot down over Axis-occupied Yugoslavia, were aided by resistance groups such as the Chetniks, who helped the OSS airlift them out of Yugoslavia in Operation Halyard.

ESCAPE MAPS Based on a Bartholomew map, the 1941 escape map of occupied Western Europe above shows national borders in green and heavily defended coastal areas as a thick red line. The map of Italy at left was printed on parachute silk by MI9 in 1942. The RAF began bombing Italy in 1940, and many Allied airmen were downed there after British and American forces landed in the south in 1943.

TOOLS TO PLAN AN ESCAPE

In addition to maps printed on silk and other equipment furnished by MI9 and smuggled in by POWs when they arrived at Colditz, determined inmates there secretly produced an astonishing array of escape and evasion gear. That equipment included civilian clothing and German military uniforms, complete with insignia, fashioned for escapees by prisoners working in a clandestine costume shop who succeeded in fabricating their own sewing machine. Prisoners in the forgery shop, often working by hand with pen, brush, and ink, turned out identity documents, ration cards, and travel permits. Maps were reproduced through an improvised mimeograph process, using rubbing alcohol and gelatin extracted from jelly that arrived in Red Cross packages. ✪

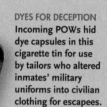

PICKS FOR PRISONERS This folding pocketknife containing a basic set of lock picks was made to be smuggled into prisons like Colditz to help inmates enter locked rooms and passageways.

BOGUS BADGE Inmates made this plaster mold to reproduce a Wehrmacht badge for those wounded in action, placed on uniforms for escapees posing as German soldiers.

DYES FOR DECEPTION Incoming POWs hid dye capsules in this cigarette tin for use by tailors who altered inmates' military uniforms into civilian clothing for escapees.

HANDMADE MAP This carefully rendered hand-drawn map, showing the region around the Swiss town of Schaffhausen near the German border, was found on a Colditz escapee when he was recaptured.

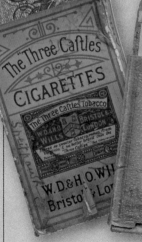

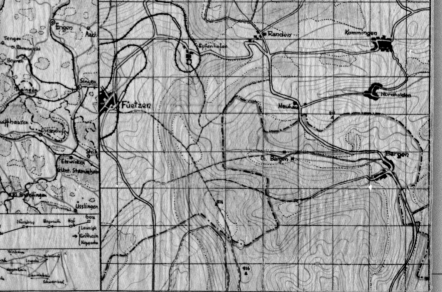

CONCEALED CASH Inmates escaping from Colditz used cigarette packs (above) to hide German marks. The funds came from cash contributed to the escape committee by airmen with concealed purses.

STEALTHY IMPRESSIONS
These blocks of soap were used to make impressions of keys or picks that could be copied and distributed, enabling prisoners to open locked doors.

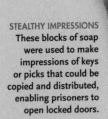

MIMICRY
Lt. André Pérodeau (near left) disguised himself as Colditz's electrician (far left) and tried to walk out the gate in December 1942 but was caught when he showed a forged pass to guards, who had this picture taken.

EMERGENCY FUNDS
An Allied pilot's survival kit contained these rings and gold coins, including British Sovereigns and French "Napoleons."

ARTFUL FORGERY
This travel permit and other identity cards forged at Colditz were painstakingly produced by hand. Later a smuggled camera was used, which expedited the process.

CAUGHT IN DRAG
Wearing his disguise in a photo taken by his captors, a French lieutenant identified as E. Boulé tried to walk out of Colditz dressed as a German woman in June 1941. He was caught when he dropped his watch and a German guard who retrieved it grew suspicious.

STAMPS OF APPROVAL
Inmates in the forgery shop made these official stamps for use on counterfeit German documents that escapees would show to guards or police.

SKELETON KEY
Filed from part of a metal bed frame, this skeleton key was produced by one of the many resourceful officers locked up at Colditz.

SPIKED PENCIL
Cut away to reveal a steel spike serving as a tool or weapon, this pencil was made to fool guards who searched POWs or comfort packages they received.

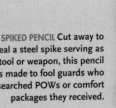

DARING ESCAPES

Capt. Reinhold Eggers, who became chief of security at Colditz, recalled in later years that the prison was not nearly as secure as it looked: "You might think at first sight that the place was impregnable . . . but apart from putting bars on the windows it had never really been built for the purpose of keeping people in. Breaking out was shown to be much easier than breaking in!" Faced with an inmate population of clever officers determined to break out, he and others who watched over Colditz kept a careful record of escape attempts and put evidence of them on display in a room called the "Commandant's Escape Museum." Eggers published case histories of those attempts in a newspaper for German POW guards, and a local photographer was assigned to take pictures of would-be escapees wearing their disguises or posing with their tools. Documenting past escape attempts did not halt future ones, but it preserved for posterity the resourceful efforts of POWs like those portrayed here, who refused to submit meekly to captivity and remained defiant. ✪

THEATRICAL EXIT On the night of January 5, 1942, four inmates, including British Lt. Airey Neave (top left) and Dutch Lt. Abraham Pierre Luteyn (above left), dropped through a hole cut in the floor of a theater for prisoners at Colditz and descended on a rope made of checkered blankets (right) into the empty room pictured above, which offered them a way out. They took off their own uniforms, under which they were wearing German Army uniforms atop civilian dress. Posing as German officers, they made their way past sentries through the main gate. They then assumed civilian dress and traveled in pairs to attract less notice. One pair was recaptured, but Neave and Luteyn, disguised as Dutch guest workers, reached neutral Switzerland.

BOLD IMPOSTOR A British officer with several escape attempts on record, Lt. Albert Michael Sinclair (near right) looked like a younger version of the senior German noncommissioned officer at Colditz, Fritz Rothenberger (far right), who held the rank of *stabsfeldwebel* (equivalent to master sergeant) and was known to prisoners as "Franz Joseph" for his imposing white moustache. In 1943, crafty inmates equipped Sinclair with a similar moustache and uniform, including the cap below, and carved a realistic wooden rifle and bayonet, shown here, for each of two men who would accompany him as sentries. Arriving at the gate at midnight, the disguised Sinclair announced that they had come to relieve the guards on duty. One guard asked to see his pass, which seemed to be in order, but he could not give the correct password. An argument ensued, which brought the real Rothenberger out to confront the impostor. Sinclair was shot through the chest—a wound he survived, only to be killed during another escape attempt in 1944.

OFLAG VII C 350

TIGHT FIT On September 8, 1942, prisoners in Colditz were ordered to store excess belongings in the three-foot-square wooden Red Cross crates (above). Diminutive RAF Flight Lt. Dominic Bruce (right) had himself packed inside one crate with a file and a 40-foot-long improvised rope. When guards spotted the rope hanging from the storeroom window, they searched and found an empty box inscribed: "The air in Colditz no longer agrees with me. Farewell!" It was signed, "Ex-PW Flying Officer Bruce." Bruce was recaptured a week later.

CHAPTER 4

UNLOCKING THE ENIGMA CODE

AT RISK Allied convoys like this one along the British coast in May 1942 were subject to devastating U-boat attacks until cryptanalysts broke the German naval Enigma code and helped win the Battle of the Atlantic.

MAN VERSUS MACHINE

WIZARD'S WAR A brilliant mathematician, Alan Turing (opposite) led British efforts to solve the German naval Enigma machine (below), one of the war's greatest challenges for code breakers.

Some letters written to Winston Churchill during the war never made it past his private secretary, who screened his mail. But this letter came from cryptanalysts at Bletchley Park, the top secret British code-breaking facility, and reached Churchill promptly. "Some weeks ago you paid us a visit," it began, "and we believe that you regard our work as important." That visit by Churchill in September 1941 was one of the few occasions when code breakers at Bletchley were officially recognized for their momentous contribution to the Allied war effort. For cryptanalyst Alan Turing, a prodigious 29-year-old mathematician who did as much to defend his embattled nation during the war as any British military officer but went unnoticed by the public, meeting the prime minister was a rare honor. Turing was far too nervous and reticent on that occasion to voice complaints about insufficient government support for operations at Bletchley Park. A month later, however, he joined his gifted colleague, Gordon Welchman, and two other cryptanalysts in writing to Churchill. Their urgent efforts to solve the Enigma machine used to encipher German military messages were being "held up," they told him, "and in some cases were not being done at all, principally because we cannot get sufficient staff to deal with it." They urged that skilled male staff who provided technical assistance to them and were subject to the draft be exempted from military service, as elite cryptanalysts at Bletchley were, and that more Wrens from the Women's Royal Naval Service be assigned to keep code-breaking machines running and perform other essential tasks.

NAME: ALAN TURING

OCCUPATION: MATHEMATICIAN

ASSIGNMENT: SOLVE THE ENIGMA

Turing's signature appeared first among the four on that letter to Churchill, who was one of the few people outside Bletchley Park who knew how important Turing was to the war effort. He led efforts to unlock the intricate Enigma codes and procedures that the German Navy used to conceal communications revealing the location of its U-boats, which were preying on Allied convoys in the Atlantic that brought food, fuel, and armaments from America and enabled Britain to keep fighting. As Churchill later remarked, "The only thing that ever really frightened me during the war was the U-boat peril." Anything that kept Turing and his colleagues from combating that peril and other military threats was of utmost concern to Churchill, who issued an emphatic order to his chief staff officer, Gen. Hastings Ismay: "ACTION THIS DAY: Make sure they have all they want on extreme priority and report to me that this has been done."

To casual observers, Turing hardly appeared to be someone on whom the nation's fate depended. A disheveled figure, he walked the halls at Bletchley Park with his eyes averted and spoke haltingly. Some thought he had a speech impediment because he often struggled to articulate thoughts and insights that came to his dazzlingly quick mind faster than words could convey. His great ambition was to design a machine that could solve problems the way the human mind did but more efficiently and accurately. He began theorizing about what he called a universal computing machine in a visionary article he wrote as a fellow at Cambridge University in 1936 entitled "On Computable Numbers." At that time, the term "computer" was applied to bookkeepers and other clerks who performed mathematical functions. Turing envisioned a computing machine that was universal, meaning that it could do everything a human computer could do, including following instructions as to which function to perform and how to carry it out. His hypothetical machine could accomplish

BLETCHLEY PARK During the war, this Victorian manor north of London was the hub of a sprawling code-breaking facility, crowded with makeshift huts for cryptanalysts, translators, technicians, and other personnel. Sworn to secrecy, they were described by Winston Churchill as "the geese who laid the golden eggs—and never cackled."

Hut 6 & Hut 8,
Room 47,
Foreign Office,
London, S.W.1.

21st. October 1941.   (Bletchley Park).

Dear Prime Minister,

Some weeks ago you paid us the honour of a visit, and we believe that you regard our work as important. You will have seen that, thanks largely to the energy and foresight of Commander Travis, we have been well supplied with the "bombes" for the breaking of the German Enigma codes. We think, however, that you ought to know that this work is being held up, and in some cases is not being done at all, principally because we cannot get sufficient staff to deal with it. Our reason for writing to you direct is that for months we have done everything that we possibly can through the normal channels, and that we despair of any early improvement without your intervention. No doubt in the long run these particular requirements will be met, but meanwhile still more precious months will have been wasted, and as our needs are continually expanding we see little hope of ever being adequately staffed.

We realise that there is a tremendous demand for labour of all kinds and that its allocation is a matter of priorities. The trouble to our mind is that as we are a very small section with numerically trivial requirements it is very difficult to bring home to the authorities finally responsible either the importance of what is done here or the urgent necessity of deal-ing promptly with our requests. At the same time we find it hard to believe that it is really impossible to produce quickly the additional staff that we need, even if this meant interfering with the normal machinery of allocations.

We do not wish to burden you with a detailed list of our difficulties, but the following are the bottlenecks which are causing us the most acute anxiety.

II

1. Breaking of Naval Enigma (Hut 8).

Owing to shortage of staff and the overworking of his present team the Hollerith section here under Mr. Freeborn has had to stop working night shifts. The effect of this is that the finding of the naval keys is being delayed at least twelve hours every day. In order to enable him to start night shifts again Freeborn needs immediately about twenty more untrained Grade III women clerks. To put himself in a really adequate position to deal with any likely demands he will want a good many more.

A further serious danger now threatening us is that some of the skilled male staff, both with the British Tabulating Company at Letchworth and in Freeborn's section here, who have so far been exempt from military service, are now liable to be called up.

2. Military and Air Force Enigma (Hut 6).

We are intercepting quite a substantial proportion of [wi]reless traffic in the Middle East which cannot be picked up [by] our intercepting stations here. This contains among other [thin]gs a good deal of new "Light Blue" intelligence. Owing [to sh]ortage of trained typists, however, and the fatigue of our [prese]nt decoding staff, we cannot get all this traffic decoded. [This h]as been the state of affairs since May. Yet all that we [need t]o put matters right is about twenty trained typists.

3. [Bo]mbe testing, Hut 6 and Hut 8.

[In] July we were promised that the testing of the "stories" [done] by the bombes would be taken over by the W.R.N.S. in [this] hut and that sufficient W.R.N.S. would be provided [for this p]urpose. It is now late in October and nothing has [been done]. We do not wish to stress this so strongly as the [preceding] points, because it has not actually delayed us in [producing th]e goods. It has, however, meant that staff in [those who] are needed for other jobs have had to do the

...lp feeling that with a Service
...e been possible to detail a
... if sufficiently urgent in-
...ight quarters.

...atters, there are a number of
... to us that we have met with
... take too long to set these
...ne of the matters involved
... effect, however, has been
...the importance of the work
...nt force upon those outside
...l.

...irely on our own initiative.
...sible for our difficulties,
...to be taken as criticising
...done his utmost to help us
...re to do our job as well as
...solutely vital that our
...promptly attended to. We
... felt that we should be failing in our duty if we did not draw your attention to the facts and to the effects which they are having and must continue to have on our work, unless immediate action is taken.

We are, Sir, Your obedient servants,

A. M. Turing
W. G. Welchman
C. H. O'D. Alexander
P. S. Milner-Barry.

ACTION THIS DAY

Secret
In a locked box

Gen. Ismay.
Make sure they have all they want on extreme priority & report to me that this has been done.

W.S.C.

CALL TO ACTION Alan Turing's signature appears first on the letter above, which he and fellow code breakers Gordon Welchman, Hugh Alexander, and P. S. Milner-Barry addressed to Churchill, seeking more staff support for efforts at Bletchley Park. Churchill responded promptly with the order at left, labeled "ACTION THIS DAY," directing that they be given all the help "they want on extreme priority."

that by reading a tape and distinguishing between spaces that were blank and those marked 0 or 1. The machine could also print or erase those digits. The digital options 0 and 1 constituted a binary code that could be used both to represent any number or letter, much as the dots and dashes of Morse code did, and to process those numbers or letters. Turing's article laid the theoretical foundation for digital, programmable computers because 0 and 1 could be represented electronically by an open or closed switch, and binary code could be used both for instructions to a computer and for the operations it performed.

Turing's paper had significance that went beyond the emerging field of computer science, for he demonstrated that there were some thorny mathematical problems that could not be solved even by a universal computing machine that functioned flawlessly. His awareness that mathematical logic had limits served him well as a cryptanalyst, for he and his colleagues often found themselves wrestling with problems that could not be solved without resorting to methods considered unscientific, such as educated guesswork or relying on cribs—phrases that often appeared in the sorts of messages they were trying to unscramble—or monotonously trying out one possible solution after another. One of Turing's major contributions at Bletchley Park was to show that such rote or intuitive methods of problem solving could be built into computing machines that would work tirelessly around the clock and arrive at solutions faster than he and his fellow wizards could. The battle of man versus machine that they waged was won by devising smarter machines, and that inventive process went back more than a decade to a time when the Germans refined the Enigma from a commercial device to a strategic asset that seemingly rendered their military secrets inviolable.

"The only thing that ever really frightened me during the war was the U-boat peril."

WINSTON CHURCHILL

FIRST ENIGMA This original version of the Enigma machine, introduced by German inventor Arthur Scherbius for commercial purposes in 1923, had a typewriter that printed the enciphered message. The typewriter was replaced in later models by a lamp board that lit up each of the enciphered letters in turn, which were transmitted in Morse code by radio to the recipient, who used an identical Enigma with the same setting to decipher the message.

POLISH PRECEDENTS

By the early 1930s, intelligence officers and cryptanalysts in several nations, including France, Britain, and Poland, were aware that an advanced version of the original Enigma machine, introduced in 1923 by German engineer Arthur Scherbius and marketed to banks and other businesses, was being used by German military and security services to disguise their communications. Messages enciphered on the advanced Enigma were transmitted by radio in Morse code and deciphered on identical machines operated by authorized recipients. Maj. Gwido Langer, chief of the Polish Cipher Bureau, was quick to recognize that solving the riddles posed by that Enigma was a task for mathematicians and began recruiting them at Poznan University. Three students who showed exceptional promise—Marian Rejewski, Henryk Zygalski, and Jerzy Rozycki—ended up working intensively on the Enigma in a basement office called the Black Chamber at the Cipher Bureau in Warsaw. Rejewski proved to be a genius on the order of Turing when it came to analyzing that machine and its output mathematically and using its own components and circuitry to solve the fiendish problems it presented.

Like Turing and his colleagues at Bletchley Park, Rejewski and company were aided by clandestine operations that gave them valuable insights into the Enigma's wiring and settings. The first of those breakthroughs came in late 1931 when Capt. Gustave Bertrand, a French intelligence officer, met covertly in Belgium with Hans-Thilo Schmidt, a clerk at the German Cipher Bureau in Berlin. Schmidt, who was living beyond his means, sold Bertrand access to top secret documents, which the captain photographed, and Schmidt then returned to the Berlin bureau. They included German manuals explaining how to encipher Enigma messages. Neither French cryptanalysts nor their British allies found those documents helpful in deciphering Enigma messages. But France was also allied with Poland, and when Bertrand shared the material provided by Schmidt with the Cipher Bureau in Warsaw, Major Langer was delighted. His goal was to solve Enigma messages by analyzing and replicating the advanced machine, much as William Friedman's American team later did by constructing an analog of the Japanese Purple machine. With the manuals in hand, Langer and his cryptanalysts had a better idea of what they were up against.

The Enigma's basic operating principle was deceptively simple. When the operator pressed a letter on the keyboard, an electrical impulse lit up another letter on a display called a lamp board, located above the keyboard (see the Enigma on page 214). Pressing the letter A would illuminate D, for example, and when a recipient of the message pressed the letter D on an identical machine with the same setting it would illuminate A. The complexity of the Enigma lay in its vast number of possible settings and in the way the machine altered the path of electrical impulses with each keystroke so that pressing A twice in succession, for example, would illuminate a letter other than A or D the second time. Typically, three rotors would be inserted by the operator atop the machine in a prescribed order, each

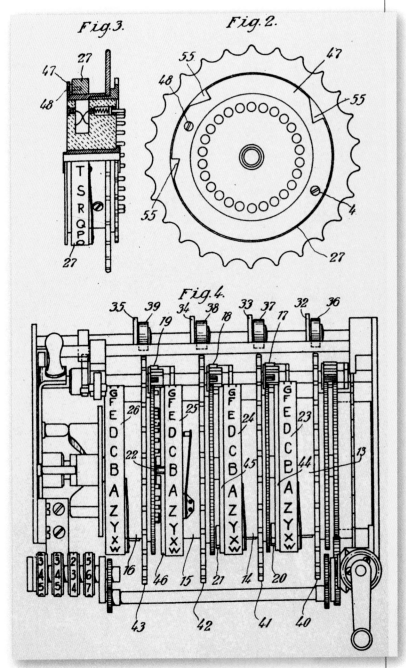

of which was wired in a different way to carry the electrical impulse from one of 26 contact points representing the letters of the alphabet to another contact point. Each rotor had a ring beside it that could be set at one of 26 positions and locked to the rotor so that they turned in tandem. There were 17,576 different three-letter settings for the three rotors, ranging from AAA to ZZZ. In addition, the advanced German Enigma had a plug board up front that resembled a telephone switchboard and increased the number of possible settings enormously. The path of the electrical impulse from one letter on the keyboard to another on the lamp board was altered by the way cables were attached on the plug board and by the wiring, order, and movement of the rotors, which turned at different rates. The rotor inserted in the fast position at right advanced a notch every time a key was pressed,

INNER WORKINGS A patent drawing for an Enigma developed by Scherbius in the late 1920s shows at bottom three rotors and a fourth wheel (far left) that reflected the electronic impulse back through the other rotors. A similar design was adopted by the Abwehr, but most German Enigmas used officially in the 1930s had three rotors and a fixed reflector disk. The reflector made identical Enigmas reciprocal, so that if the sender enciphered "A" as "D," the recipient would decipher "D" as "A."

completing one full rotation in 26 keystrokes. That triggered the middle rotor to advance, and when it completed one rotation after hundreds of keystrokes, the left rotor advanced.

For all its complexity, the Enigma operated according to mathematical principles, which Marian Rejewski reduced to equations. He then solved those equations with the aid of more documents from Schmidt, including a copy of instructions distributed to authorized Enigma operators for the months of September and October 1932, indicating the rotor order for those months as well as the daily plug board connections and daily ground setting for the rings and rotors. That ground setting was used to enter a unique three-letter rotor setting for each message, which the operator chose at random and typed twice at the start of the message, producing a six-letter indicator. Enciphering that random setting twice helped ensure that the sender and receiver had their rotors in identical positions, and the procedure was not immediately apparent to cryptanalysts because the first three letters of the enciphered indicator were not the same as the last three letters. But Rejewski was informed of that procedure by the manuals he received. Enciphering the same three-letter sequence twice at the start of each message helped him determine the wiring in the fast rotor, which he figured was the only one that rotated and altered the electrical path during those first six

TALENTED TRIO Polish cryptanalyst Marian Rejewski (right) and his colleagues Jerzy Rozycki (center) and Henryk Zygalski (left) used mathematical analysis to reconstruct the advanced Enigma employed by the German military in the early 1930s and decipher messages encrypted on it. When the Germans modified their Enigma to make it more secure, the Polish team devised techniques and machines to attack those defenses.

keystrokes. Furthermore, he knew from the documents Schmidt provided that operators changed the order of the rotors from September to October and placed a different one in the fast slot at right, which allowed him to determine the wiring of that second rotor as well. The known factors in his equations then enabled him to resolve an unknown factor—the wiring of the third rotor—and the documents told him how various cable connections on the plug board altered the electrical path from the keyboard to the lamp board. "Now all that had to be done was to build the machine," Rejewski recalled. By 1933, when Hitler seized power and Germans hailed him as their Führer, Rejewski and team had replicated the advanced Enigma and were reading the Reich's confidential messages.

Even with that machine in hand, deciphering Enigma intercepts was seldom quick and easy for the Warsaw cryptanalysts in years to come. Schmidt continued to provide settings periodically until 1936, when the French began paying him instead to provide intelligence on Hitler's plans to rearm Germany and expand the Reich. By then, Enigma procedures were being tightened considerably. For example, the rotor order, originally changed once every few months, was now altered daily. To keep up with such changes, Rejewski and his colleagues sought ways of sifting quickly through vast numbers of settings to find ones that worked. Henryk Zygalski devised an ingenious method of using large perforated sheets as punch cards and tabulating them manually to determine the rotor order and settings for those Enigma messages whose six-letter indicators contained the same letter twice separated by two other letters, a pattern that occurred on a daily basis among the many German messages intercepted by the Poles. Holes would be punched in sheets to represent all possible rotor orders and settings that could produce any of 26 letters twice in six keystrokes at three-letter intervals. When the sheets were stacked on a light box, holes through which light shined would reveal a small number of likely rotor orders and settings that would produce the specific repetition found in the indicator for that day's messages.

Preparing the sheets for those tabulations was a long, slow process. Before that task was completed, the Polish cryptanalysts came up with a faster way of conducting a similar search for likely rotor orders and settings. They built a machine incorporating the rotors from six Enigmas, all in the same order, and automated them so that they moved through thousands of settings in tandem until they happened on one that could produce the same repetition in the six-letter

ENIGMA AGENT Hans-Thilo Schmidt began spying for France in 1931 by selling secret Enigma documents taken from the Cipher Bureau in Berlin. He was later tracked down by the Gestapo during World War II and was executed or committed suicide under duress in 1943.

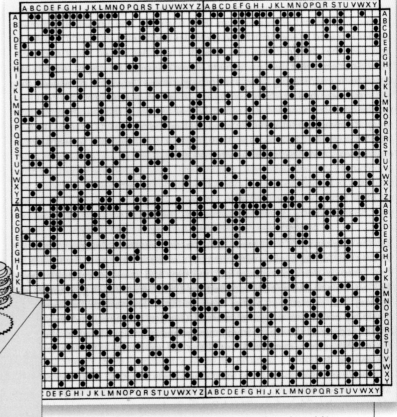

SEARCH MACHINES The Polish team developed perforated Zygalski sheets (above), which when stacked left holes through which light shined, revealing likely settings for the day's Enigma messages. They also built a bombe (left) that connected six sets of three rotors each—one of which is shown at top (1)—to a motor (2) and switches (3) and ran through three-letter settings until it found a combination that unlocked the day's messages.

THE FRENCH CONNECTION

I n November 1931, Capt. Gustave Bertrand of France (inset) made an investment that ultimately paid big dividends for his country and its allies. In charge of French radio intelligence, which meant investigating how rival nations enciphered radio signals, he met secretly in Belgium with an agent of his named Rodolphe Lemoine and Hans-Thilo Schmidt, a clerk at the German Cipher Office in Berlin. The German-born Lemoine served as interpreter in negotiations between Schmidt and Bertrand, who agreed to purchase coding instructions for a German military Enigma from Schmidt for 10,000 marks (about 4,000 dollars). The documents were photographed on the spot, and Schmidt then returned them to a safe at the Cipher Office without alerting his superiors.

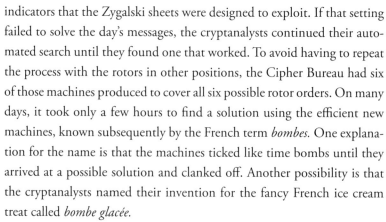

That and later purchases enabled Polish cryptanalysts, with whom Bertrand shared the documents, to decipher German Enigma messages. The French received intelligence reports on those decrypts and inherited the services of Marian Rejewski and fellow Polish cryptanalysts when Germany invaded Poland in 1939. Bertrand oversaw their work at a code-breaking facility near Paris designated PC Bruno, which served as the French connection between Polish and British efforts to solve Enigma procedures that were fast evolving. PC Bruno was disbanded as German troops approached Paris in June 1940, but Bertrand and members of his team secretly reassembled in Vichy-controlled southern France and broke Axis codes until the Germans occupied that zone in late 1942 and began closing in on his operation. Lemoine was arrested and forced to talk, and Schmidt committed suicide rather than face torture and execution. Bertrand was being pressured to cooperate with the Germans in 1944 when he arranged with Allied agents to convey him and his wife to England, where they arrived safely just before D-Day. ✪

indicators that the Zygalski sheets were designed to exploit. If that setting failed to solve the day's messages, the cryptanalysts continued their automated search until they found one that worked. To avoid having to repeat the process with the rotors in other positions, the Cipher Bureau had six of those machines produced to cover all six possible rotor orders. On many days, it took only a few hours to find a solution using the efficient new machines, known subsequently by the French term *bombes*. One explanation for the name is that the machines ticked like time bombs until they arrived at a possible solution and clanked off. Another possibility is that the cryptanalysts named their invention for the fancy French ice cream treat called *bombe glacée*.

Neither the bombes nor the Zygalski sheets proved effective against a major change in Enigma procedures introduced in December 1938, when German operators were issued two additional rotors. That brought the total to five, each wired differently, three of which would be inserted in the machine on any given day as specified in instructions to operators. Suddenly, the number of possible rotor orders rose from six to 60. The Polish cryptanalysts had neither the time nor the resources to construct 60 bombes. They knew that Hitler had his sights set on Poland and might soon invade their country. Polish authorities had long kept secret the technological advances they made in attacking the Enigma, providing the French only with intelligence they derived by reading German messages. Now that France and Britain were committed to opposing Hitler if he invaded Poland, however, they decided to reveal everything to their allies. At a meeting outside Warsaw in July 1939—less than two months before German troops overran Poland—Cipher Bureau chief Langer unveiled two advanced Enigmas to be offered to the French and British. "Where did you get these?" asked Gustave Bertrand of the Deuxième Bureau, to which Langer replied proudly: "We built them ourselves."

Representing Britain at the meeting were Alastair Denniston, head of the Government Code and Cypher School in London, and Dillwyn "Dilly" Knox, an accomplished cryptanalyst there who had been puzzling over the advanced Enigma for years. One element in the machine had stumped him—a disk through which the electrical impulse produced when the operator pressed a key entered the rotors. Knox had assumed that the entry disk was cross-wired like the rotors and would transpose an impulse that entered in position A, for example, to position D on the first rotor next to it. The solution Rejewski arrived at instead was so elementary that Knox could hardly believe it: The wiring in the entry disk went straight from A to A, B to B, and so on. Rejewski's success in solving the machine was humbling for Knox, but he soon realized that tackling the newly fortified Enigma would be a tremendous challenge for him and other British cryptanalysts as the effort shifted from Warsaw to Bletchley Park. Situated some 50 miles northwest of London, Bletchley became the new home for the Government Code and Cypher School just days before the war began. Its fast-expanding team of code breakers were soon joined there by many other specialists and technicians, including traffic analysts, translators, and intelligence officers who worked in hastily constructed buildings called huts. Relocating to remote Bletchley Park, a Victorian estate with spacious grounds, allowed a facility that would eventually employ over 8,000 people to preserve strict secrecy—which would have been difficult to maintain in London—and distanced its vital operations from German air raids that took a heavy toll on that city.

After Poland was invaded, Rejewski, Zygalski, and Rozycki escaped first to Romania and then to France with the help of French diplomats in Bucharest. Their accomplishments greatly facilitated code breaking at Bletchley, where cryptanalysts would soon design a more powerful bombe. The British also produced complete sets of Zygalski sheets, one of which was sent to the Polish team in Paris, where they deciphered German Enigma messages for the French. They were so highly regarded that Stewart Menzies, who oversaw intelligence operations at Bletchley as chief of MI6, wrote a letter in January 1940 to Louis Rivet, head of the Deuxième Bureau, asking that the three cryptanalysts be sent to England "for a short visit" to help British code breakers obtain "quick results." The trio were too valuable to the French to be lent out, however, and they ended up fleeing Paris when German troops occupied that city in June 1940. Rozycki perished while crossing the Mediterranean in a ship that went down in a storm, but Rejewski and Zygalski reached Spain by means of an escape line and landed safely in England, where they helped break a code used by the SS, whose despised Nazi agents did much to devastate their homeland.

SPY CHIEF Stewart Menzies, standing here beside his wife, took charge of MI6, the British service responsible for spying on foreign countries and their military forces, soon after WWII began. He oversaw relentless efforts at Bletchley Park to decipher German Enigma communications and produce Ultra, the ultrasecret classification for Enigma decrypts and intelligence assessments based on them.

BREAKTHROUGH AT BLETCHLEY

On September 4, 1939, one day after Britain declared war on Germany, Alan Turing reported to Bletchley Park, where he joined an elite team of cryptanalysts overseen by Dilly Knox. Turing had worked recently with Knox on the Enigma in London and knew that changes made by the Germans had rendered the Polish bombe obsolete. He soon began designing a new bombe that could cope with those Enigma advances and an upcoming change that he and Knox anticipated. They assumed correctly that as German security concerns mounted in wartime, operators would not continue enciphering the three-letter rotor setting twice at the start of each message, a clue largely responsible for the gains made by the Polish cryptanalysts. Turing would have to find a new way of arriving at settings that could solve the Enigma's riddles. He did so by devising a machine whose calculations mimicked the way cryptanalysts manipulated letters and words to find solutions.

One time-honored linguistic device that code breakers continued to rely on was a crib consisting of one or more words that they expected to find within a scrambled message. Without benefit of a bombe, cryptanalysts could make some headway against an Enigma intercept by lining up a crib such as the 14-letter German word *einsatzgruppen* ("task forces") below various 14-letter sequences in the enciphered text and looking for one where no enciphered letter lined up above the same letter in the crib. That was a possible match for the crib, whereas an enciphered sequence whose fourth letter was "s" as in *einsatzgruppen,* for instance, could be ruled out as a match because the Enigma never substituted the same letter for the one pressed on the keyboard. Turing could not design an efficient bombe to test all possible crib matches within a message on all possible Enigma settings. But like the Polish cryptanalysts who found a pattern within the six-letter indicators that allowed them to narrow their search, Turing found a pattern in places where likely crib letters lined up with different letters in the intercepts to form a closed loop. If, for example, H lined up with M, M with D, D with X, and X with H, he had a closed loop beginning and ending with the same letter, which could then be tested by wiring Enigma components together and running through various settings until the machine found one that accounted for the loop and offered a possible solution for the message as a whole.

CRIB MASTER Mathematician Gordon Welchman began working at Bletchley Park on traffic analysis, studying the frequencies, call signs, and other characteristics of Enigma radio signals to determine the sender, recipient, and possible subject matter of the message. That helped identify cribs—words or phrases that were likely to occur within a message and were used in searches conducted electronically by an improved bombe that Turing and Welchman developed to determine Enigma settings.

"He agreed that the improvement over the type of bombe that he had been considering was spectacular."

GORDON WELCHMAN DESCRIBING TURING'S REACTION TO HIS IDEA TO IMPROVE THE BOMBE

Turing's task was complicated by the many different plug board connections used by Enigma operators, whose instructions now called for them to connect 10 cables, which meant that impulses for 20 of 26 letters on the keyboard were rerouted in various ways on the plug board. The original bombe he designed incorporated components of 30 Enigmas, including 90 rotors in all, and could arrive at the right plug board connections for a crib through trial and error. But his machine was temperamental and balky. During tests, it was subject to many false stops, which did not yield solutions. Another cryptanalyst at Bletchley, Gordon Welchman—as fine an engineer as he was a mathematician—improved the bombe by taking advantage of a plug board feature that Turing's design did not fully exploit. Welchman proposed a way of wiring the reciprocal connections of the plug board into the machine so that if it tested a crib at various settings with a cable connection transposing the electrical impulse from A to D, for example, a cable connection transposing D to A would also be assumed and tested. Welchman's innovation promised to make the bombe faster and more accurate, greatly reducing the number of false stops. Although Turing was often described as a loner, he was quick to appreciate the insights of gifted colleagues at Bletchley. He soon became as excited about the proposal "as I was," Welchman recalled. "He agreed that the improvement over the type of bombe that he had been considering was spectacular."

The Turing-Welchman bombe that resulted from their collaboration—equipped with a device called the diagonal board that simulated various connections on the Enigma's plug board—proved to be one of the most powerful secret weapons in the Allied arsenal.

A number of those machines were produced, and they proved so quick and efficient that they did not have to be fed closed loops, which only certain cribs provided. They could often arrive at a solution in timely fashion by testing any good crib that had a high likelihood of occurring within a message. Those were furnished by specialists working in Bletchley's crib room, who pored over decrypts and extracted words and phrases that cropped up repeatedly in messages from various German services and agencies, each of which had their own Enigma procedures and were handled separately at Bletchley. Welchman was assigned to Hut 6, where cryptanalysts worked to solve Enigma messages sent by the German Army (Heer) and Air Force (Luftwaffe). Well before the Turing-Welchman bombe entered service in August 1940, Hut 6 succeeded in deciphering intercepts from the Luftwaffe, whose procedures were less varied and secure than those employed by the German Navy (Kriegsmarine). The sprawling nature of naval warfare across vast oceans made it crucial to disguise communications that might betray the location of warships or submarines and allow the enemy to attack or evade them. Unlocking the more secure German naval Enigma—and combating the U-boat peril that Churchill so feared—fell to Alan Turing and his staff in Hut 8.

(continued on page 216)

MEGA-BOMBE Shown at top in two black-and-white photographs taken at Bletchley Park in 1943 is a later version of the Turing-Welchman bombe developed there a few years earlier. The bombe pictured in those photos stood six feet high and had more than 100 rotors in front and extensive wiring in back. As shown above in a close-up of a reconstructed bombe, its rotors mimicked those on Enigma machines, with 26 positions for the letters of the alphabet.

ENIGMAS FOR EVERY SERVICE

Secure communications at all levels were vital to the successful operations of the German war machine. To guard their secrets, the Reich's armed forces used several types of Enigma machines to encrypt and decipher messages. In 1933, the Wehrmacht acquired exclusive manufacturing rights to a military version of the commercial Enigma developed in the 1920s. That military model, designated Enigma I (below), had three rotors and was produced in large quantities for the German Army and the Luftwaffe. Another version, Enigma G, was selected for military intelligence communications by the Abwehr, and the German Navy adopted the Enigma M1, a model compatible with the army's machines.

During World War II, the easily transported Enigma I remained the mainstay of German Army field commands. But the navy responded to concerns that the Allies were reading messages enciphered on their three-rotor Enigma by adopting the four-rotor M4 "Triton" Enigma (page 202), introduced in February 1942 to direct U-boat operations in the Atlantic. The M4 was issued with eight additional rotors that could be inserted in various orders, allowing for 26 times as many settings. Heavier, more complex cipher machines were introduced for the highest-level German wartime communications, including the massive 10-rotor T-52 *Geheimfernschreiber* ("secret teleprinter") and the 12-rotor "Tunny" machine, which also had a teleprinter and was used for Hitler's orders.

Throughout the war, most of the Reich's top commanders remained convinced that their Enigma codes were unbreakable. "Our ciphers were checked and rechecked," recalled Grand Adm. Karl Dönitz, who advanced from head of the U-boat fleet to become the navy's commander in chief in early 1943. Every time the security of Enigma messages was questioned and reviewed, he added, they were pronounced "impossible for the enemy to decipher." ✪

ENIGMA IN ACTION Pictured during the invasion of France in May 1940, Gen. Heinz Guderian stands in his special command half-track, equipped with a three-rotor Enigma I like the one shown at left to encipher and decipher radio communications with Guderian's panzer forces. Components of the Enigma at left include the plug board in front, and the keyboard, lamp board, and rotors on top.

EXTRA SECURITY The Luftwaffe, whose Enigma messages were readily deciphered at Bletchley Park earlier in the war, tightened security in 1944 by introducing the Enigma Uhr (clock device), shown at far left. It provided 40 different wiring combinations for the Enigma I plug board, which the operator could change by turning the knob in the center. The German Army made its Enigma I machines more secure in 1938 by providing operators with two additional rotors, issued in the carrying case at left.

SECRET TELEPRINTER The 10-rotor T52 expedited high-level communications using teletype technology. Messages typed in plain text (uncoded) were automatically enciphered, transmitted by radio, and deciphered by an identical machine that printed the message in plain text.

TIME-SAVER Some M4 Enigmas used on U-boats incorporated the Schreibmax device above, which was attached to the Enigma's lamp board and printed the enciphered or deciphered text on a narrow paper ribbon. By eliminating the need for operators to laboriously read and transcribe letters, this reduced the time it took for essential messages to reach U-boat captains and their commanders.

Turing was no administrator and left the running of Hut 8 largely to Hugh Alexander, a congenial chess champion popular with both his fellow cryptanalysts and their assistants, many of whom were Wrens or members of the Women's Auxiliary Air Force. Like the code breakers, those assistants were sworn to strict secrecy when they arrived at Bletchley. As one Wren recalled, "We were told that we would never be posted anywhere else, because the work was too secret for us to be released." Some of them socialized with the male cryptanalysts, while others kept their distance and were not overly impressed by those men. "They were weedy looking boffin types walking in pairs or on their own," another Wren remarked. Turing was one of those boffin types often seen walking alone. He paid little attention to the women employed at Bletchley, with one notable exception. In June 1940, mathematician Joan Clarke joined the cryptanalysts in Hut 8. She was paid far less than her male counterparts and classified as a linguist but soon demonstrated her talents as a code breaker, as did several other women at Bletchley. Mutual respect formed the basis for a friendship between her and Turing that endured after they became engaged and he backed out. Few people at Bletchley other than Clarke knew his reason for doing so. As one of his colleagues, Peter Hilton, later wrote, "we did not know during the war that Turing was a homosexual. This was not because Turing took elaborate steps to conceal his predilections; it was because such a matter wasn't an issue with us—the thought never entered our heads." The only issue that really mattered at Bletchley was winning the war, to which Turing made a hefty contribution.

He and his team in Hut 8 wrestled for years with the toughest of all Enigma riddles, posed by wary German naval commanders intent on staying one step ahead of Allied cryptanalysts. The Germans would rightly be faulted for trusting too much in their Enigma. But the fast-moving campaigns they waged on land and at sea—including closely coordinated attacks by U-boats pursuing Allied convoys in so-called wolf packs—made using such a device preferable to manual forms of encryption because cipher machines were quicker at the task. The fault lay not in employing a machine but in relying mightily on one with a long operational history that helped cryptanalysts overcome one refinement after another, often using the Enigma's own mechanisms to defeat it. Even so, the fortified naval Enigma remained inscrutable to some of Bletchley's brightest lights for months on end. Among the obstacles they faced was that the rotor setting chosen for each message was encoded before it was enciphered on the Enigma. Turing eventually broke that code, but Hut 8 produced so few decrypts in the war's early months that its wizards had few good cribs to feed to the bombe. They were desperately in need of a "pinch"—a naval operation that would seize an Enigma or its documents and give them keys they needed to overcome the machine's defenses.

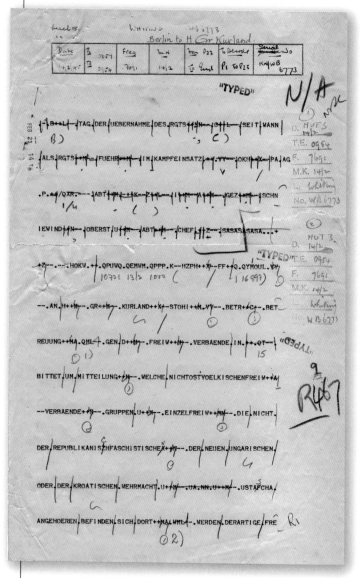

RAW DECRYPT This German Army Enigma message was deciphered in Hut 6 at Bletchley and translated and interpreted in Hut 3 by linguists and intelligence officers whose initials appear in the margins of the decrypt.

German naval officers were on guard against a pinch and had orders if their vessel was about to be boarded to jettison their Enigma and related documents, whose print was soluble in water. Those orders were not always carried out to the letter in emergencies, however. In April 1940, a German trawler carrying munitions to the port of Narvik for the invasion of Norway was boarded by crewmen of the British destroyer H.M.S. *Griffin,* who managed to salvage Enigma documents that helped Hut 8 produce its first few decrypts. But those keys were soon rendered obsolete when the Kriegsmarine altered its code and settings. As one member of Turing's team put it, the next several months produced "depressingly few results."

By September 1940, the British Office of Naval Intelligence was so hungry for a pinch that it approved a wild scheme by Lt. Cmdr. Ian Fleming, who proposed crash-landing a captured German bomber in the English Channel near a German trawler or some other vulnerable enemy naval vessel. The plane's British crew would wear Luftwaffe uniforms and would appear suitably bruised and bloodied when rescued by the Germans and taken aboard their ship, which the airmen would then commandeer at gunpoint, killing the seamen and tossing them overboard before pinching an Enigma and its operating instructions. Fleming volunteered for the raid because he spoke German and could communicate with the rescuers as a supposed Luftwaffe airman while others kept mum. Turing and Peter Twinn, his assistant and collaborator in Hut 8, had great hopes for Operation Ruthless, as Fleming's plan was christened. They were crestfallen when it was canceled after RAF reconnaissance flights detected no suitable target ship. Frank Birch, who directed naval intelligence at Bletchley in Hut 4, wrote that "Turing and Twinn came to me like undertakers cheated of a nice corpse two days ago, all in a stew about the cancellation."

The fall and winter of 1940–41 were bitter seasons for Allied convoys in the North Atlantic, which were stalked mercilessly by wolf packs. Beginning in March 1941, however, a series of pinches allowed Hut 8 to begin tracking U-boat movements consistently and providing convoys and the warships escorting them with timely warnings that substantially reduced losses. Francis Harry Hinsley, a young intelligence analyst in Hut 4 who later became the official historian of British intelligence operations during World War II, proposed targeting German weather ships off Norway and Iceland that used Enigmas to encipher their reports. Two such raids on those vulnerable ships yielded revealing documents that crewmen failed to jettison after throwing the machines overboard. Then in May 1941, an

(continued on page 220)

CODE BREAKER JOAN CLARKE

She would be remembered largely for her relationship with Alan Turing, but Joan Clarke (inset) made her own distinctive mark as a code breaker at Bletchley Park, where women constituted more than two-thirds of the staff but seldom advanced beyond the clerical level. She herself began working as a clerk in Hut 8, despite having graduated from Cambridge University with highest honors in mathematics.

Gordon Welchman, who had supervised her at Cambridge, recruited her for Bletchley, where her starting salary was lower than that of Wrens serving there in uniform. She soon began working as a cryptanalyst, albeit unofficially because that was considered a man's job. Classified instead as a linguist, for which she had no training, she later made light of that title by telling how she filled out a questionnaire, "Grade: Linguist, Languages: none!"

Joan Clarke and Alan Turing kept their brief engagement secret at Bletchley. Her success in Hut 8 was due not to any favors she received from him at work but to the aptitude she and other gifted mathematicians demonstrated for code breaking. She proved adept at a technique devised by Turing that he dubbed Banburismus for a factory in Banbury that produced long sheets in which holes were punched. Like Zygalski sheets, they helped cryptanalysts detect patterns in Enigma messages that indicated how the rotors were arranged and set. Using that method, she and her colleagues enabled Bletchley's bombes to reach solutions quicker, bolstering Allied efforts to track and target U-boats in the Atlantic.

After Turing moved on to other challenges, Joan Clarke became deputy director of Hut 8 in 1944. She was later named an MBE (Member of the British Empire), an honor she earned not as Turing's friend or former fiancée but as part of an elite team of code breakers who helped win the war. ✪

STEALTHY KILLING MACHINES

The U-boat peril that so alarmed Winston Churchill and made the Battle of the Atlantic an agonizingly close contest was sustained by encrypted Enigma communications between German submarines at sea and command centers on shore. Those signals allowed U-boats prowling separately to form devastatingly effective wolf packs when one of them spotted an Allied convoy, sent a coded report from its radio compartment (right), and shadowed the convoy until as many as a dozen or more submarines had moved into position to attack collectively. Their combined firepower was fearsome, considering that a single Type IX U-boat—the pride of Admiral Dönitz's submersible assault force—had four torpedo tubes at the bow and two at the stern. For sustained patrols, the Type IX carried six spare torpedoes internally and 10 more in watertight external containers on its upper deck. That allowed for prolonged attacks by those killing

NERVE CENTER **A signalman works in the radio compartment of *U-124* in March 1941, with an Enigma to his left.**

machines, which had a range of over 10,000 nautical miles. Each carried a powerful 105-mm deck gun in front of the conning tower and a 37-mm antiaircraft gun, and when threatened by Allied destroyers could dive to a depth of 750 feet without buckling.

Such defensive maneuvers were critical for U-boats like the Type IX and the smaller Type VII, which for all their offensive prowess were highly vulnerable to attack. The electric motors they used while submerged could not operate for too long without being recharged by the diesel engines that powered the subs at the surface, where they traveled most of the time and risked being tracked by radar and targeted by bombers as well as destroyers. And the radio signals that enabled them to hunt in packs exposed their movements to code breakers at Bletchley, who took on the advanced German naval Enigma M4 and eventually solved it, making U-boat operations in the North Atlantic too costly for Dönitz. ✪

TARGET IN SIGHT **A U-boat commander in his white-covered service cap gives orders while tracking a target through the attack periscope. That periscope fed the bearing of the target to an electromechanical computer that calculated when to fire the torpedo given other data such as the speed of the target and the torpedo.**

SHIP KILLERS Crewmen perform maintenance on a pair of torpedoes in a U-boat's forward torpedo compartment. The standard German torpedo was the ship-killing, 21-inch G7 electric torpedo armed with a 617-pound warhead. The photograph below left, taken through a periscope, shows a torpedo striking an Allied freighter.

MAKING SPEED A U-boat traveling at a fast clip leaves the wake shown in this photo taken in early 1944. U-boats generally operated on the surface under diesel power and submerged to attack. They might remain submerged up to 20 hours before resurfacing to recharge their batteries.

ROUGH SEAS A crewman hangs precariously from a safety wire on the deck of a German submarine in a heavy swell in April 1943. U-boats were unstable in rough seas, taking on water through open hatches and often subjecting the crew to injuries as they were tossed about in the boat's cramped interior. Even experienced sailors might become seasick in the foul atmosphere of the boat's interior.

PARTING SHOT A two-man crew trains their deck gun on a sinking freighter. Vessels damaged by torpedoes could be finished off by the deck guns on U-boats, but that happened less often as the war progressed and Allied convoys became better protected.

Enigma was recovered intact from the German sub *U-110,* which was disabled by depth charges off Greenland and forced to the surface, where it came under fire and was hastily abandoned by its crew. The commander assumed that his U-boat was about to sink, but it remained afloat long enough for a daring boarding party from the destroyer H.M.S. *Bulldog* to pinch the cipher machine and its documents, which added to a trove that helped Turing's team in Hut 8 give the Allies a boost in the Battle of the Atlantic.

Further seizures of German ships and the submarine *U-570* in months to come heightened concerns within the Kriegsmarine that its Enigma was insecure. Vice Adm. Erhard Maertens conducted an official inquiry in October 1941 and concluded that "our cipher does not appear to have been broken." Like their Japanese counterparts, German naval commanders were reluctant to admit that their indispensable encryption system might be vulnerable, but they guarded against that threat by continuing to enhance their Enigma and its operating procedures.

In February 1942, U-boats in the Atlantic were equipped with Enigmas containing four rotors instead of three—a major advance that Bletchley's bombes were not designed to handle. Soon afterward, a report from the British Admiralty stated ominously that "little can be said with any confidence in estimating the present and future movements of the U-boats." To make matters worse, German Navy cryptanalysts were breaking Allied codes, including the one used to direct transatlantic convoys. During 1942, U-boats would sink over 1,000 Allied and neutral ships in the Atlantic, surpassing the total for the two previous years combined.

While code breakers in Hut 8 struggled to overcome the enhanced German naval Enigma and help secure the transatlantic lifelines between America and Britain, others at Bletchley Park produced a wealth of decrypts—classified as Ultra for ultra-secret—that revealed enemy plans in Europe and North Africa. Armed with that intelligence, Allied

"Our cipher does not appear to have been broken."

VICE ADM. ERHARD MAERTENS REPORTING ON THE SECURITY OF THE GERMAN NAVY'S ENIGMA COMMUNICATIONS, OCTOBER 1941

ENIGMA RAID Led by Sub-Lt. David Balme (inset), a boarding party sent from the H.M.S. *Bulldog* in a whaler (right) approaches the German sub *U-110* in the North Atlantic on May 9, 1941. After boarding the U-boat, damaged by depth charges and abandoned by its crew, Balme's party retrieved an intact Enigma.

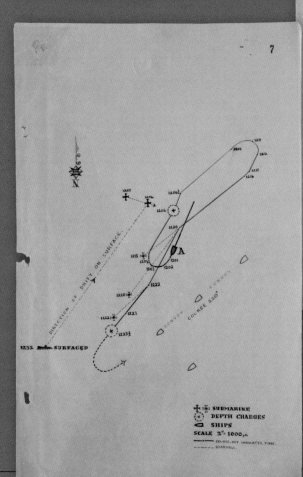

13

SECRET.

From.........Sub/Lieutenant.D.E.Balme. R.N.

Date.........11th May,1941.

To...........The Commanding Officer,H.M.S.Bulldog.

Subject......Boarding Primrose.

Submitted:-

At 1245 9th May, I left "Bulldog" in charge of a boarding party to board an enemy submarine which had surfaced. The crew consisted of 6 seamen, 1 telegraphist and 1 stoker. "Bulldog" was lying to windward of U boat and there was a heavy swell running so to save valuable time I made for the weather side (Port). There were numerous holes in the Conning Tower casing caused by "Bulldog's" 3" and Pom-pom.

As no small arm fire was opened up at the whaler from the U boat, I was fairly confident that there was no one in the Conning Tower. This proved correct after having entered conning tower through opening on starboard side. The hatch down was closed tight. (This hatch was 18" to 24" in diameter, spherical surface with wheel for screwing down; on unscrewing this the hatch sprung open as soon as a clip was released).

I went down the ladder to the lower Conning Tower where there was a similar closed hatch. On opening this hatch I found the Control Room deserted; hatches leading forward and aft were open and all lighting on. On the deck there was a large splinter from the conning tower. There was a slight escape of air in the control room but no sign of Chlorine so gas-masks which had been taken were now discarded. So also were revolers which now seemed more of a danger than an asset.

The U boat had obviously been abandoned in great haste as books and gear were strewn about the place. A chain of men was formed to pass up all books,charts,etc. As speed was essential owing to possibility of U boat sinking(although dry throughout) I gave orders to send up ALL books, except obviously reading books, so consequently a number of comparitively useless navigational books etc were recovered. All charts were in drawers under the chart table in the Control Room; there were also some signal books, log books etc here. The metal sheet diagrams were secured overhead.

Meanwhile the telegraphist went to the W/T office, just forward of control room on starboard side. This was in perfect condition, apparently no attempt having been made to destroy any books or apparatus. Here were found C.B.'s., Signal Logs,Pay Books and general correspondence, looking as if this room had been used as ships office. Also the coding machine was found here, plugged in and as though it was in actual use when abandoned. The general appearance of this machine being that of a typewriter, the telegraphist pressed the keys and finding results peculiar sent it up the hatch. This W/T office seemed far less complicated than our own-sets were more compact and did not seem to have the usual excess of switches, plug holes, knobs,'tally's' etc on the outside.

Forward of W/T office was the Hydrophone Office. This was about the same size as the W/T office and about twice as large as the A/S Cabinet in "Sealion", the only 1 have been out in.

CLOSED FILE David Balme's report on the boarding of *U-110* was contained in a top secret file on the incident (top left), labeled "Closed Until 1972" by authorities intent on withholding sensitive information about Enigma and Ultra long after the war ended. Accompanied by a map showing where the stricken U-boat surfaced (left), Balme's report tells how he entered the conning tower and formed a chain of men "to pass up all books, charts, etc." One member of his party, the *Bulldog*'s telegraphist, entered the W/T (wireless transmitter) office and came upon the Enigma: "The general appearance of this machine being that of a typewriter, the telegraphist pressed the keys and finding results peculiar sent it up the hatch."

commanders in those theaters were gaining the upper hand and setting German forces who once appeared unstoppable back on their heels.

ULTRA IN ACTION

In August 1942, Lt. Gen. Bernard "Monty" Montgomery took charge of the British Eighth Army in Egypt and began preparing his forces for battle against Lt. Gen. Erwin Rommel's

Panzer Army at El Alamein. Rommel was renowned as the Desert Fox for outmaneuvering foes with his agile panzers (armored units). Montgomery would soon be legendary as well for taking the measure of Rommel and meeting him head-on. Monty was portrayed in the press as something of a mind reader, who studied a portrait of Rommel each night before going to bed and asked himself: "What is in the mind of my adversary? What is he planning? How can I outwit him?" In fact, Monty's seemingly uncanny knowledge of Rommel and his plans came largely from the intelligence he received, often in the form of Ultra, which had helped sustain the British war effort at home and abroad against formidable odds over the past two years. Without the capacity to anticipate and counter enemy plans that code breaking provided, the British might not have withstood German assaults long enough for Montgomery to confront Rommel at El Alamein.

Beginning in 1940, when the Germans launched the intensive air campaign known as the Battle of Britain, Ultra decrypts of Luftwaffe messages helped Allied commanders prepare for attacks during that blitz and later bombing campaigns. Code breakers at Bletchley Park were aided by the lax procedures of Luftwaffe Enigma operators, such as using neighboring letters on the keyboard like WSX and EDC to encipher three-letter rotor settings. Early on, Ultra revealed that the Luftwaffe was planning to use radio beams to guide its bombers to targets at night and in bad weather. The first inkling of that new technology came soon after the war began in a document mailed to the British Embassy in Oslo, Norway, by a mysterious informant who identified himself only as a sympathetic German scientist. That Oslo Report mentioned several secret weapons under development by Germany, including guided missiles and radio guidance systems for warplanes flying at night or in bad weather.

DESERT WAR German commander Erwin Rommel (above) points the way during the campaign that brought his armored forces up against the British Eighth Army in Egypt, led by Bernard Montgomery (top). Rommel was aided by reports on British strength that were intercepted and deciphered by the Germans, but Ultra decrypts of messages to and from Rommel's headquarters provided an even bigger boost to Montgomery as battle loomed at El Alamein in October 1942.

British intelligence analysts were largely skeptical of the Oslo Report, with the notable exception of Reginald V. Jones of the Air Ministry. When he received an Ultra decrypt including directions for a technique the Germans dubbed *Knickebein,* he recognized that they were preparing to use radio beams to guide their bombers and warned Churchill, who ordered a crash program to develop countermeasures. Once the Luftwaffe began employing *Knickebein*—a system in which a bomber followed one radio beam until it intersected with another beam over the target and produced a distinct radio tone signaling bombs away—the RAF obtained further intelligence on the technique by interrogating downed German pilots. The British were soon able to jam the radio beams, often causing enemy aircrews to miss their targets.

When the Luftwaffe failed to bomb Britain into submission, the Germans and their Italian allies had to reckon with stubborn British opposition in the Mediterranean, made more formidable by Ultra. The Italian Navy enciphered messages on an Enigma without a plug board, for which Dilly Knox developed a manual form of decryption using cribs. Knox taught that method to a gifted young protégée, Mavis Lever, who was just 18 years old when she left London University and joined his team at Bletchley in 1940. After Italian naval Enigma operators were issued a new rotor for that machine, she helped solve its wiring by determining that an entire message in which not one L appeared was produced by enciphering L from start to finish. Such dummy messages were sent by operators who had nothing to report so that opponents could not tell which stations were more active and more likely to be involved in upcoming operations. A dummy message produced using a single letter, however, exposed the Enigma's circuitry to cryptanalysts.

Mavis Lever's breakthrough allowed Knox's team to decipher critical messages in early 1941, including one from "Supermarina" (naval headquarters in Rome) stating that "Today 25 March is day X-3." The code breakers were soon able to provide Adm. Andrew Cunningham, commander in chief of the Mediterranean Fleet, with details of an attack planned for March 28 on a British troop convoy bound for Crete, which was under assault by German paratroopers. The warning enabled Cunningham to waylay Italian warships before they reached the convoy and sink two destroyers and three cruisers. He later visited Bletchley Park to thank Knox, Lever, and others on their team for helping him win the Battle of Cape Matapan.

Despite Cunningham's victory in the Mediterranean, German forces conquered Crete in April 1941 and advanced in North Africa, where Rommel recouped recent Italian losses by driving British troops in Libya back toward Egypt. He was aided by cryptanalysts at the German Cipher Bureau, who succeeded in breaking the diplomatic code used by American ambassadors, consuls, and military attachés to encipher confidential messages before transmitting them by radio. That made Col. Bonner Frank Fellers, an attaché at the U.S. Embassy in Cairo who reported regularly to Washington on British military plans and preparations in North Africa, an unwitting spy for Rommel, who called Fellers his "good source." The colonel's reports were hailed in Washington

(continued on page 226)

DILLY KNOX'S SECRET SERVICE

In a field dominated by mathematicians and machines, Dilly Knox was something of a throwback—a linguistic cryptanalyst who began breaking codes during World War I using skills he honed while deciphering ancient Greek texts. But he kept up with technological advances as chief cryptographer of the Government Code and Cypher School, which provided the original brain trust for Bletchley Park, and offered encouragement to younger mathematical wizards like Turing and Welchman. While they designed a bombe to attack advanced Enigmas, he formed his own section at Bletchley called Intelligence Service Knox (ISK) to deal with basic Enigmas like those used by the Italian Navy that did not have plug boards and depended on their rotors to scramble letters. Knox devised a manual form of decryption for those messages called the rodding method, using rods that listed in sequence all ways that each rotor at each of 26 settings could transpose a letter typed into the machine. Rodding could be time-consuming, but Knox streamlined the process by using cribs.

Unlike many boffins at Bletchley who preferred working with men, Knox (sketched at top) staffed his secret code-breaking service with gifted young women like Mavis Lever (shown below Knox), a linguist who helped decipher Italian naval plans and later wrote an appreciative biography of Knox. His crowning achievement was solving the Abwehr Enigma, which had a reflector that served as a fourth rotor. That should have enhanced the machine, but he deduced that Abwehr operators were enciphering the rotor setting twice at the start of messages, which aided decryption. Knox died in 1943, but he bequeathed to the British the capacity to read the thoughts of German intelligence officers and perfect Double Cross deceptions that helped Allied forces prevail on D-Day. ◗

UNRAVELING THE MYSTERY OF THE OSLO REPORT

In November 1939, Capt. Hector Boyes, a naval attaché at the British Embassy in Oslo, Norway, received an anonymous letter, offering to disclose German scientific secrets if British authorities accepted by inserting a coded message at the start of a BBC German-language program: *"Hullo, hier ist London."* Soon after those words were broadcast, a parcel arrived for Boyes from a source who described himself as "well-wishing German scientist." It contained a vacuum tube for a proximity fuse—which if perfected would greatly increase the effectiveness of antiaircraft fire—and a report detailing several other weapons or devices under development in Germany, including radio beams to guide bombers at night, radar to detect incoming aircraft, torpedoes detonated by a ship's magnetic field, and guided missiles, tested at a site called Peenemünde on the Baltic Sea.

Most British intelligence officers doubted that any one scientist could have composed that wide-ranging Oslo Report and considered it a hoax, meant to mislead them. One analyst who thought otherwise was physicist Reginald Jones, a science officer at the Air Ministry with expertise in radar and radio waves. When the use of radio beams to guide German bombers was confirmed in 1940 by Ultra decrypts and the interrogation of downed Luftwaffe pilots (opposite), Jones and others at the Air Ministry quickly devised ways of jamming the radio beams and sending German bombers off target. That rapid response was due partly to the early warning provided by the Oslo Report, which also helped the British anticipate and counter the V-1, a guided missile deployed in 1944.

Who authored the report would long remain a mystery. Some thought it was leaked by an Abwehr intelligence officer who opposed the Nazi regime and had access to its secrets. Not until 1989 did Jones reveal that the source was in fact a German scientist—Hans Ferdinand Mayer, director of a research laboratory for the prestigious firm of Siemens, who was arrested in 1943 for making subversive remarks and survived internment in a concentration camp. Jones learned the truth in 1955 but waited until after Mayer died to disclose his authorship. Not all the devices divulged in his report were refined by the Germans, who failed to produce a proximity fuse while the Americans succeeded. But Jones considered it "probably the best single report received from any source during the war." ✪

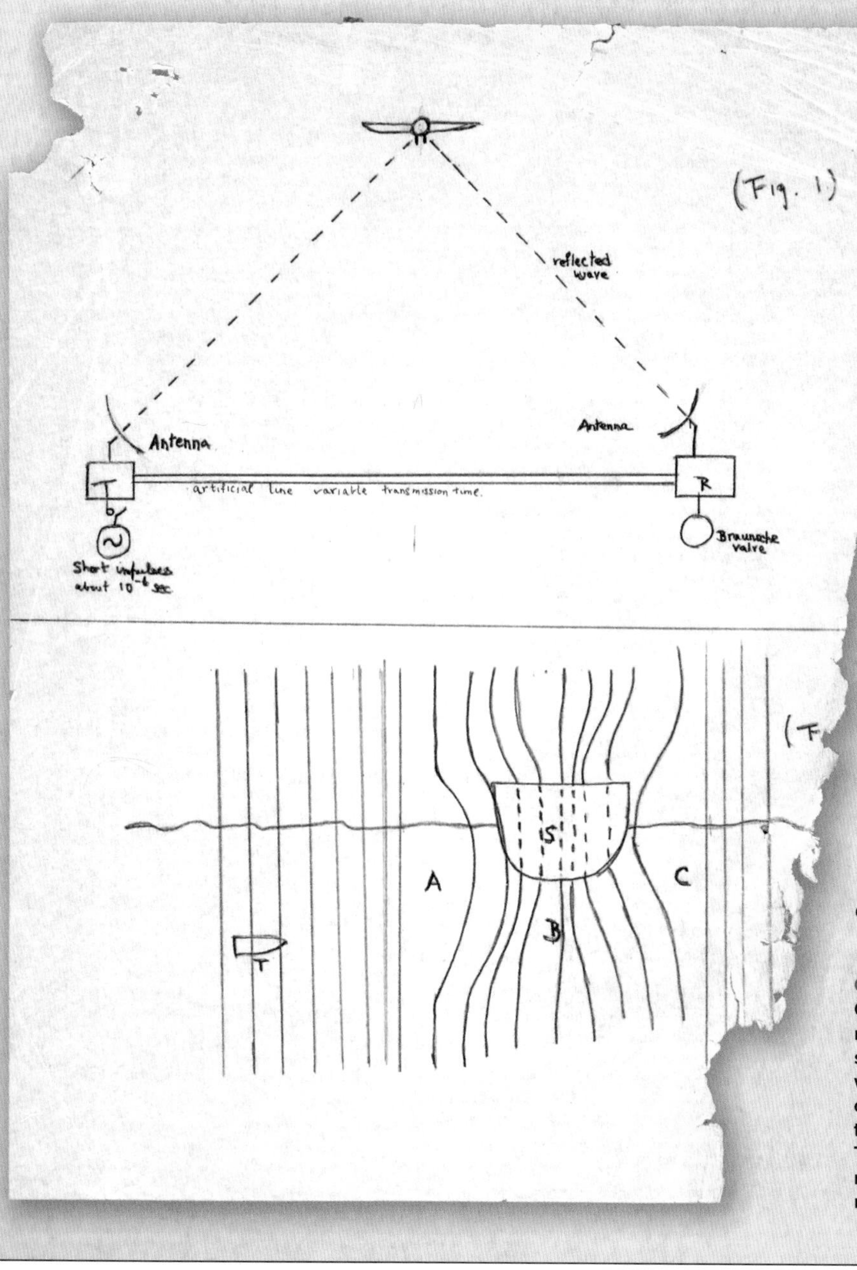

(Fig. 1)

reflected wave

Antenna

Antenna

artificial line variable transmission time.

T

R

Braunsche valve

Short impulses about 10⁻⁶ sec

A

B

C

S

T

GERMAN PLANS The sketch at top from the Oslo Report, illustrating a planned German radar installation, shows a transmitter (T) sending a radio beam toward an aircraft while signaling a nearby receiver (R) to turn on for an instant, just long enough to pick up the reflected beam with minimal interference. The sketch at bottom shows a torpedo (T) rigged to detonate when it enters the strong magnetic field (B) directly below a ship (S).

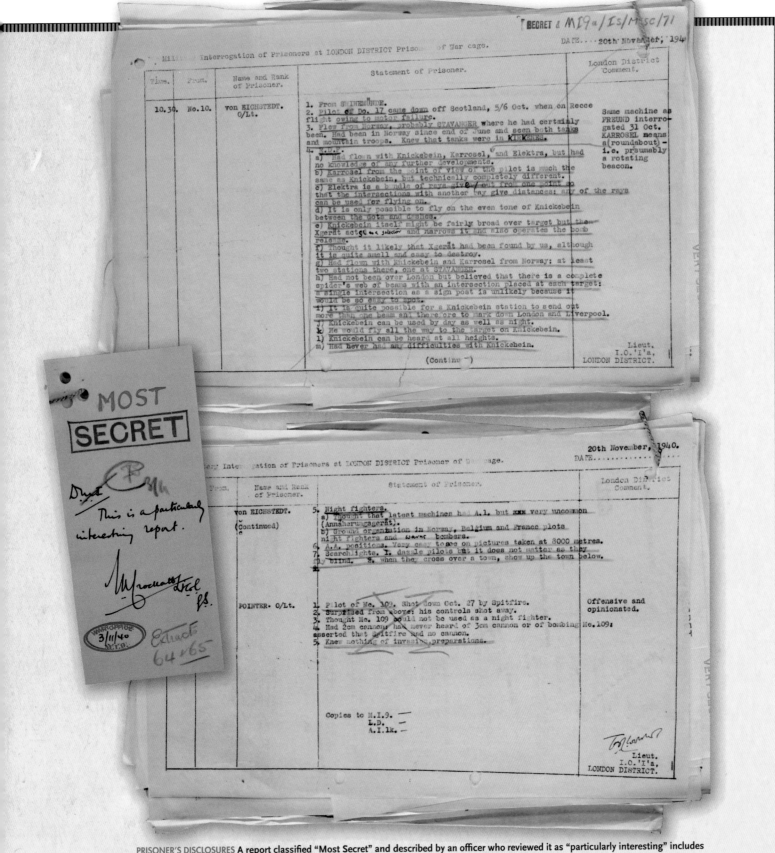

DATE.... 20th November, 1940

Military Interrogation of Prisoners at LONDON DISTRICT Prisoner of War cage.

Time.	From.	Name and Rank of Prisoner.	Statement of Prisoner.	London District Comment.

10.30.	No.10.	von EICHSTEDT. O/Lt.	1. From SWINEMÜNDE.
			 2. Pilot of Do. 17 came down off Scotland, 5/6 Oct. when on Recce flight owing to motor failure.
			 3. Flew from Norway, probably STAVANGER where he had certainly been. Had been in Norway since end of June and seen both tanks and mountain troops. Knew that tanks were in KIRKENES.
			 4. W.T.
			   a) Had flown with Knickebein, Karrosel, and Elektra, but had no knowledge of any further developments.
			   b) Karrosel from the point of view of the pilot is much the same as Knickebein, but technically completely different.
			   c) Elektra is a bundle of rays give/out from one point so that the intersections with another ray give distances: any of the rays can be used for flying on.
			   d) It is only possible to fly on the even tone of Knickebein between the dots and dashes.
			   e) Knickebein itself might be fairly broad over target but then Xgerät acts and narrows it and also operates the bomb release.
			   f) Thought it likely that Xgerät had been found by us, although it is quite small and easy to destroy.
			   g) Had flown with Knickebein and Karrosel from Norway: at least two stations there, one at STAVANGER.
			   h) Had not been over London but believed that there is a complete spider's web of beams with an intersection placed at each target: a single intersection as a sign post is unlikely because it would be so easy to spot.
			   i) It is quite possible for a Knickebein station to send out more than one beam and therefore to mark down London and Liverpool.
			   j) Knickebein can be used by day as well as night.
			   k) He would fly all the way to the target on Knickebein.
			   l) Knickebein can be heard at all heights.
			   m) Had never had any difficulties with Knickebein.
			
			 (Continued)
				Same machine as FREUND interrogated 31 Oct. KARROSEL means a (roundabout) - i.e. presumably a rotating beacon.
				
				 Lieut.
				 I.O.'I'a,
				 LONDON DISTRICT.

MOST
SECRET

Dept
This is a particularly
interesting report.

Brocklatt
Lt.Col.
fs.

WAR OFFICE
3/11/40
M.I.9.

Extract
64 + 65

20th November, 1940.
DATE.................

Military Interrogation of Prisoners at LONDON DISTRICT Prisoner of War cage.

Time.	From.	Name and Rank of Prisoner.	Statement of Prisoner.	London District Comment.

		von EICHSTEDT. (Continued)	5. Night fighters.
			   a) Thought that latest machines had A.I. but very uncommon (Annäherungsgerät).
			   b) Ground organisation in Norway, Belgium and France plots night fighters and bombers.
			 6. A.A. positions. Very easy to see on pictures taken at 8000 metres.
			 7. Searchlights. I. dazzle pilots but it does not matter as they fly blind. 8. when they cross over a town, show up the town below.	

		POINTER. O/Lt.	1. Pilot of Me. 109. Shot down Oct. 27 by Spitfire.
			 2. Surprised from above: his controls shot away.
			 3. Thought Me. 109 could not be used as a night fighter.
			 4. Had 2cm cannon: had never heard of 3cm cannon or of bombing: asserted that Spitfire had no cannon.
			 5. Knew nothing of invasion preparations.
			
			 Copies to M.I.9.
			   L.D.
			   A.I.1K.
				Offensive and opinionated.
				
				 Me.109:
				
				 Lieut.
				 I.O.'I'a,
				 LONDON DISTRICT.

PRISONER'S DISCLOSURES A report classified "Most Secret" and described by an officer who reviewed it as "particularly interesting" includes intelligence acquired by interrogating a captured German pilot who flew from occupied Norway in a Dornier 17 medium bomber in early October 1940 and ditched the plane off Scotland. The pilot had flown previous missions with the radio guidance system called *Knickebein,* which he noted could be used "by day as well as night." He also mentioned a new device called *X-Gerät* or the X-apparatus, which picked up radio beams that were harder to jam than those used for *Knickebein* and released bombs automatically when the beams intersected over a target.

as "models of clarity and accuracy," and Rommel was equally impressed with the valuable intelligence that Fellers provided. His messages—intercepted at a listening post in Germany equipped with six radio towers capable of picking up signals originating thousands of miles away—were deciphered and relayed to Rommel's headquarters within a matter of hours. Those decrypts kept the general so well informed, an official at the Cipher Bureau boasted, that each day at lunch, he "knew exactly where the Allied troops were standing the evening before."

In January 1942, after pulling back to be resupplied and reinforced in Libya, Rommel launched an offensive that he hoped would carry his forces all the way to Cairo and oust the British from North Africa. Frequent reports from Fellers kept him well informed on enemy strength and dispositions during that campaign. On January 23, he learned from his "good source" that 270 British military aircraft were being withdrawn from North Africa along with a number of antiaircraft batteries to bolster hard-pressed Allied forces battling Japanese troops in the Far East. Six days later, Rommel received a thorough briefing from Fellers on the location and strength of opposing motorized and armored units, revealing how many British tanks were out of order and how many were battle-ready. Those reports provided such a boost to the German advance that Hitler took notice, remarking on one occasion that he hoped Rommel's American informant in Cairo would continue sending "his badly enciphered cables." But that was not to be. Cryptanalysts at Bletchley Park broke into communications between the Cipher Bureau in Berlin and Rommel's headquarters and informed the Americans that the Germans were reading messages sent by Fellers from Cairo. In mid-1942, he was recalled to work for the OSS in Washington, and officials there furnished the embassy in Cairo with a Sigaba cipher machine to secure its signals.

Around the time that Rommel lost his good source, two Abwehr spies crossed the desert from Libya to spy on the British in Egypt, guided by Hungarian explorer Laszlo Almasy, who was awarded the Iron Cross for his wartime services to Germany. The agents he escorted, Johannes Eppler and Hans-Gerd Sandstede, infiltrated Cairo and sought the aid of Egyptians opposed to British rule, including a belly dancer named Hekmat Fahmy. All the while, Eppler and Sandstede were being tracked by British intelligence officers, who first learned of their venture from Ultra decrypts of Abwehr communications. The two failed to convey any British secrets to their superiors before they were arrested, bringing their venture, code-named Operation Condor, to an inglorious conclusion.

Meanwhile, Ultra was providing Allied commanders with voluminous intelligence on Rommel's situation and supply lines, which grew increasingly fragile as he advanced from Libya, where the shipments of fuel and munitions on which he depended arrived, into Egypt. Beginning in January 1942, a small team of intelligence officers met daily at British Middle East headquarters in Cairo to analyze Ultra and other reports on Rommel's supply lines and provide targeting information to the Royal Navy and Air Force. That allowed

ROMMEL'S SPIES German agents Johannes Eppler (right) and Hans-Gerd Sandstede (left) stand by a Ford truck in which they began a grueling desert journey in early 1942 from Libya to Egypt, where they conducted Operation Condor, seeking intelligence on British forces for General Rommel. Raised in Egypt by his German mother and Egyptian stepfather, Eppler disguised himself as an Arab during an earlier secret mission (top).

OPERATION CONDOR

Like many spy capers that went awry, Operation Condor was a failure that could also be viewed as a fantastic adventure, which is how Johannes Eppler portrayed it in a memoir he later published under the name John Eppler. After crossing the desert from Libya, he slipped into British-occupied Egypt in May 1942 as Hussein Gaafar (the name conferred on him by his Egyptian stepfather) while his fellow German spy and radio operator, Hans-Gerd Sandstede, posed as an American called Peter Monkaster. Aided by belly dancer Hekmat Fahmy (right), they targeted British officers who frequented the Shepheard Hotel (below) and other popular watering holes in Cairo. According to Eppler, she succeeded in seducing and drugging a staff officer from whose briefcase he extracted and copied a "Most Secret" document on British forces and dispositions that would have been of great value to Rommel. But they were unable to establish radio contact to convey that intelligence and were arrested the following night in a raid on their houseboat.

Other accounts of Operation Condor cast doubt on whether the two spies ever would have accomplished much. Future Egyptian president Anwar el-Sadat—whose help they sought because he belonged to a group of officers staunchly opposed to British rule and willing to work with the Germans—considered the pair frivolous amateurs. Their houseboat, he wrote, was "a place straight out of the *Thousand and One Nights,* where everything invited indolence, voluptuousness, and pleasure of the senses. In this dissolute atmosphere the young Nazis had forgotten the delicate mission with which they had been entrusted." Their carousing did not go unnoticed by authorities. Long before the two were arrested, they were under surveillance in Cairo by the British, who hauled in not just Eppler and Sandstede but also several of their associates, including Sadat and other suspected subversives. ✪

SEDUCTRESS An ardent Egyptian nationalist, belly dancer Hekmat Fahmy used her charms to extract intelligence from British officers who occupied her country and gathered at Cairo's fashionable Shepheard Hotel (left), a hotbed of intrigue during the war. After she was arrested for involvement in Operation Condor, she revealed her espionage technique to interrogators by remarking that an Englishman who has just made love to a woman "can't stop talking."

MOST SECRET.

TO BE KEPT UNDER LOCK AND KEY: NEVER TO BE REMOVED FROM THE OFFICE.

Date: 6th September, 1942.

From: Turkish Ambassador, LONDON.

To: Foreign Ministry, ANGORA.

No: 258.

Date: 3rd September, 1942.

According to information not published here and given to me privately and confidentially, the German armoured-division Commander, General von BISMARCK, has been killed in the Egyptian fighting, and Marshal ROMMEL is ill.

RAUF ORBAY.

Director.

DIPLOMATIC DISCLOSURE Intercepted and deciphered by the British, this message from the Turkish ambassador in London to the Foreign Ministry in Ankara (Angora), Turkey, reports on the death of Gen. Georg von Bismarck—killed in action in Egypt on August 31, 1942—and the illness that later forced Rommel to return to Germany for treatment before the Battle of El Alamein in October. An unnamed source shared that intelligence with the Turkish ambassador, whose neutral status did not stop the British from spying on him.

the British—who did not have many warships and submarines in the Mediterranean and whose air base on Malta was under frequent bombardment—to carry out precise attacks and sink nearly 100 Axis ships in the Mediterranean between January and August, when Montgomery took command at El Alamein. Ultra revealed the specific cargo carried by ships supplying Rommel's army, allowing the attackers to focus on those loaded with the goods he most required—oil and armaments. One German commander blamed spies in Italian ports for betraying those vital shipments and urged that security officers "get to work on this problem." In fact, the spying was being done a thousand miles away at Bletchley Park, where cryptanalysts were prying into Rommel's personal communications and those of his staff. Those Ultra decrypts revealed an army that was losing its vaunted mobility for lack of petrol—a situation made worse by the Allied Desert Air Force, which targeted German vehicles carrying fuel and other supplies between Libyan ports and Rommel's depots near El Alamein.

As Montgomery readied his forces for battle there, he exuded confidence that was based on detailed knowledge of his foe's strengths and weaknesses. He knew that Rommel's forces were hampered by attacks on their supply lines and that the general himself was ailing and had to return to Germany for medical treatment in late September. Rommel hurried back to the front soon after fighting erupted at El Alamein on the night of October 23, 1942. But he had little room to maneuver and was outgunned and outfoxed by Monty, who deployed combat intelligence units that eavesdropped on enemy voice communications—used in urgent situations when enciphering messages was too time-consuming—and employed traffic analysis and radio direction finders to fix the location of German armored units and provide targeting instructions. It was a long, grueling struggle, but Monty held firm, knowing that his opponent's resources were dwindling. On November 4, Rommel cut his losses. Abandoning many tanks that had not already been destroyed, he executed a skillful retreat to Libya.

Rommel was reinforced by way of Tripoli in early 1943. But continued attacks on Axis supply shipments from Italy, exposed by Ultra, left him with too little strength to contend both with Montgomery's pursuing army and with the Allied forces who had landed in Morocco and Algeria under Eisenhower's command soon after the fighting ended at El Alamein. Rommel launched his last North African attack on March 6, 1943, at Medenine in Tunisia. Ultra informed Monty of that thrust in advance, and he smashed it with artillery and armor.

As Rommel wrote afterward, "it became obvious the British were prepared for us." He left for Germany three days after suffering that defeat, physically ill and sick at heart. His successor, Gen. Hans-Jürgen von Arnim, was captured along with nearly 250,000 Axis troops when the Allies seized Tunis in May and took control of North Africa. They would soon invade Sicily and use it as their bridge to Italy, exploiting their strength not only in

TARGETS EXPOSED Ultra decrypts of Enigma messages sent in October 1942 provide departure times at right for Axis convoys and reveal below that as a result of attacks on ships supplying Rommel's forces in North Africa, "the fuel situation of the Panzer Army is dangerous and the ammunition situation strained." Informed by Ultra that Rommel's supplies were dwindling, General Montgomery fought a long, methodical battle at El Alamein in which many German tanks were abandoned or captured (bottom).

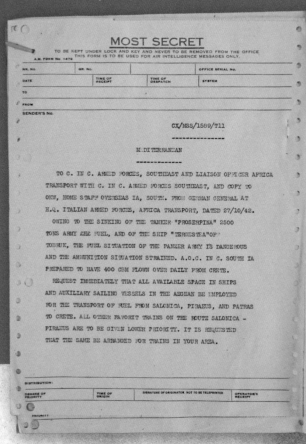

MOST SECRET

TO BE KEPT UNDER LOCK AND KEY AND NEVER TO BE REMOVED FROM THE OFFICE
THIS FORM IS TO BE USED FOR AIR INTELLIGENCE MESSAGES ONLY.

A.M. FORM No. 1478

NR. No.		GR. No.			OFFICE SERIAL No.
DATE		TIME OF RECEIPT	TIME OF DESPATCH	SYSTEM	
TO					
FROM					
SENDER'S No.					

CX/MSS/1589/T11

MEDITERRANEAN

TO C. IN C. ARMED FORCES, SOUTHEAST AND LIAISON OFFICER AFRICA
TRANSPORT WITH C. IN C. ARMED FORCES SOUTHEAST, AND COPY TO
OKW, HOME STAFF OVERSEAS IA, SOUTH. FROM GERMAN GENERAL AT
H.Q. ITALIAN ARMED FORCES, AFRICA TRANSPORT, DATED 27/10/42.
OWING TO THE SINKING OF THE TANKER "PROSERPINA" 2500
TONS ARMY AND FUEL, AND OF THE SHIP "TERGESTEA" OFF
TOBRUK, THE FUEL SITUATION OF THE PANZER ARMY IS DANGEROUS
AND THE AMMUNITION SITUATION STRAINED. A.O.C. IN C. SOUTH IA
PREPARED TO HAVE 400 CBM FLOWN OVER DAILY FROM CRETE.
REQUEST IMMEDIATELY THAT ALL AVAILABLE SPACE IN SHIPS
AND AUXILIARY SAILING VESSELS IN THE AEGEAN BE EMPLOYED
FOR THE TRANSPORT OF FUEL FROM SALONICA, PIRAEUS, AND PATRAS
TO CRETE. ALL OTHER FAVORIT TRAINS ON THE ROUTE SALONICA –
PIRAEUS ARE TO BE GIVEN LOWER PRIORITY. IT IS REQUESTED
THAT THE SAME BE ARRANGED FOR TRAINS IN YOUR AREA.

DISTRIBUTION:			
DEGREE OF PRIORITY	TIME OF ORIGIN	SIGNATURE OF ORIGINATOR. NOT TO BE TELEPRINTED	OPERATOR'S RECEIPT
PRIORITY			

BB/AM/ADY   KKK

CX/MSS/1591/T19

MEDITERRANEAN.
===============

A.O.C. IN C. SOUTH IA TO FLIEGERKORPS X ON 28/10:
OPERATIONAL ORDER FOR NIGHT OF 28-29/10: WIM OPERATION
FOR TANKER LUISIANA CONVOY, PROTECTED BY 3 T BOATS AND
LEAVING NAVARINO AT 1600 HRS, SPEED 7.5 KNOTS, RECOGNITION
LETTER I.
POSITION   0001/29/10 – 23 EAST 0765
           0400   – 23 EAST 0621
           0800   – 23 EAST 0653
           1600   – 23 EAST 9542(+)
           0001/30/10 – 23 EAST 9429(+)
           0900   – 23 EAEAH
                 /////BXEAST 9343(+)
           ARRIVING BENGHAZI 1600/30/10.
SS ETIOPIA WILL LEAVE ON THE SAME COURSE AT 1600 HRS, SPEED
6 KNOTS. IN ADDITION 1 BOMBER OF FLIEGERKORPS (ROMAN) II WILL
BE/~~CONSTANTLY~~ CONSTANTLY WITH THE CONVOY. OPERATIONAL ORDER
FOR 29/10 FOLLOWS.
===============

NOTE: (+) ALTHOUGH 9 WAS CLEARLY WRITTEN IN EACH CASE, IT MUST
      HAVE BEEN AN ERROR FOR O. COMPARE ZTPI/20081 (1590/3).

BB/AM/ADY   WHD/DAC/R   2105/28/10/42

PASSED AT 1947/28/10/42 GMT AS:
QT/4588 AL/3016 MA/3142 .

B/A   HDD/CBT/XD   2019/C/28/10/42.
RM BB

| DISTRIBUTION: | | | |
| DEGREE OF PRIORITY | TIME OF ORIGIN | SIGNATURE OF ORIGINATOR. NOT TO BE TELEPRINTED | OPERATOR'S RECEIPT |

firepower but also in brainpower and computing power, which continued to unlock Axis codes and ciphers and divulge enemy plans.

VICTORY AT SEA

On October 30, 1942, while fighting was raging at El Alamein, an event of some consequence for the long-running Battle of the Atlantic occurred in the eastern Mediterranean off Port Said, Egypt. An RAF reconnaissance aircraft spotted a German submarine, *U-559,* lurking in waters often traveled by Allied convoys. British warships converged on the U-boat, which submerged but was badly damaged by depth charges and forced to the surface, where it came under fire. A boarding party from the destroyer H.M.S. *Petard* entered the crippled sub, which had been abandoned by its surviving crewmembers and was taking on water. They succeeded in removing Enigma documents before *U-559* sank, taking down with it two brave men in the party, Lt. Anthony Fasson and Able Seaman Colin Grazier. Among the documents they salvaged at the cost of their lives were code tables for German naval weather reports. Encoding those reports before they were enciphered on Enigmas was an essential precaution because they were often repetitive, providing cryptanalysts with good cribs that could be used to attack the challenging four-rotor Enigma installed in U-boats and decipher its output.

LOST IN ACTION Lt. Anthony Fasson (right) and Able Seaman Colin Grazier (left) from the destroyer H.M.S. *Petard* perished on October 30, 1942, when *U-559,* a disabled German sub from which they were retrieving codebooks and equipment, sank with them aboard. Among the items they salvaged with the help of the *Petard's* young canteen assistant, Tommy Brown—who barely escaped with his life—was a manual for encoding weather reports, similar to the one below. That manual helped cryptanalysts at Bletchley Park solve the four-rotor naval Enigma on which coded weather reports were enciphered.

The trove from *U-559* was a godsend for those at Bletchley Park. By early December, the head of Hut 10, which worked on decoding weather reports in conjunction with the naval Enigma experts in Hut 8, predicted that they would be able to "read the submarine traffic again shortly through the weather messages." Sure enough, Bletchley began producing Ultra that revealed the location of U-boats in the Atlantic by year's end. The decrypts were often timely enough to allow Allied warships or bombers to target those German subs, which were also being tracked with the aid of new high-frequency radio direction finders, designated HF/DF or "Huff Duff."

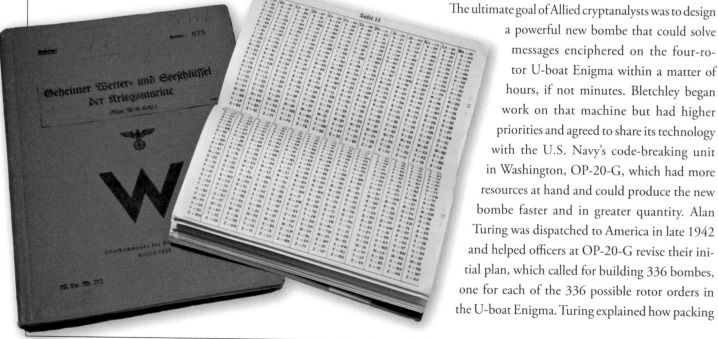

The ultimate goal of Allied cryptanalysts was to design a powerful new bombe that could solve messages enciphered on the four-rotor U-boat Enigma within a matter of hours, if not minutes. Bletchley began work on that machine but had higher priorities and agreed to share its technology with the U.S. Navy's code-breaking unit in Washington, OP-20-G, which had more resources at hand and could produce the new bombe faster and in greater quantity. Alan Turing was dispatched to America in late 1942 and helped officers at OP-20-G revise their initial plan, which called for building 336 bombes, one for each of the 336 possible rotor orders in the U-boat Enigma. Turing explained how packing the rotors of multiple Enigmas into one machine, as he and Welchman did, would allow for quicker and more adaptable processing, and OP-20-G altered its approach accordingly. In June 1943, the first of those American bombes went into service. By then, Adm. Karl Dönitz had withdrawn his U-boat fleet from the North Atlantic after losing 34 subs in May alone. He would later resume sporadic attacks on convoys, but the new bombes helped

ensure that U-boats would never again pose a critical threat to Allied supply lines. As Dönitz later conceded, "We had lost the Battle of the Atlantic." Millions of American troops could now cross that ocean in relative safety to bolster the forces who would soon land on Italian soil or prepare for the momentous Allied invasion of occupied France in 1944.

The Enigma was not the only cipher machine employed by the Germans during the war. In 1941, they introduced a formidable new device for high-level communications between commanders, including the Reich's commander in chief, Adolf Hitler. Dubbed Tunny by the British, the machine had 12 rotors that enciphered text in binary code (0 and 1) and used teletype technology to transmit the scrambled message by radio to a receiver linked to a matching Tunny, which displayed the deciphered message

SUPER-BOMBE Designed with input from Alan Turing, the powerful American bombe (top) speeded decryption of German naval Enigma messages. By the time it debuted in mid-1943, code breaking and advances in detecting submarines had rendered depth-charge attacks like the one above—photographed in April from the deck of the U.S. Coast Guard cutter *Spencer*—so deadly that the U-boat threat was receding.

JOHN CAIRNCROSS: MOLE AT BLETCHLEY

An accomplished linguist fluent in German, John Cairncross seemed well suited for the task when he arrived at Bletchley Park in 1942 to serve as a translator in Hut 3. There was little reason to consider him a security risk. Like some others at Bletchley, his aversion to fascism had pushed him toward the opposite end of the political spectrum as a student in the 1930s, but he stopped short of joining the Communist Party. Had he done so, he might not have been recruited in 1937 as a Soviet mole. The ideal mole had no formal communist ties and a bright future like Cairncross, who aced the Foreign Service entrance examination after graduating from Cambridge University. Sooner or later, such recruits were often entrusted with state secrets and became active spies.

Cairncross passed some intelligence to the Soviets before 1942, but his espionage began in earnest when he entered Hut 3, where decrypts of most German military

> **"I never considered myself a traitor to Britain, but a patriot in the struggle against Nazism."**
>
> JOHN CAIRNCROSS

messages except naval communications were translated, assessed, and distributed as Ultra. He had little trouble removing secret documents from Bletchley. "There was no problem about obtaining the German decrypts for they were left around on the floor after having been processed," wrote Cairncross, who also made off with copies of his translated decrypts: "I concealed the documents in my trousers in order to pass them out of the grounds,

CODE NAME:	LISZT
SPIED FOR:	SOVIET UNION
SPIED AGAINST:	BRITAIN, GERMANY

where I was never subjected to a check."

Cairncross later took credit for helping the Soviets win the Battle of Kursk in 1943. But the Russians also received some intelligence from Bletchley through authorized channels, including the British Embassy in Moscow, and they had another agent who helped them prevail at Kursk—Rudolf Rössler in Switzerland. Although never charged with espionage, Cairncross was awarded the Order of the Red Banner for his services to Russia, which continued sporadically until 1951. Late in life, accused of being the "fifth man" in a spy ring that included the notorious Kim Philby and three other Soviet moles who had studied at Cambridge in the 1930s, he composed a memoir entitled *The Enigma Spy*, in which he defended his espionage at Bletchley. "I never considered myself a traitor to Britain," he declared, "but a patriot in the struggle against Nazism." ✪

KURSK **When German tanks advanced in the Battle of Kursk (left), they came up against formidable Soviet armor, artillery, minefields, and tank traps, prepared by commanders who were well informed on enemy plans and dispositions by disclosures from Cairncross (pictured above in his later years) and other intelligence sources. The Germans withdrew from Kursk in mid-July 1943 and lost ground to the Soviets thereafter.**

on a teleprinter. Turing and two other brilliant cryptanalysts at Bletchley, John Hiltman and William Tutte, eventually solved Tunny. But Tutte's intricate formula for calculating the rotor order—for which there were millions of combinations—would have taken one person more than a lifetime to perform manually. To speed the process, another wizard at Bletchley, electrical engineer Tommy Flowers, put Turing's theory of a universal computing machine into practice by designing one equipped with vacuum tubes as electrical switches. His invention used binary logic—switches that were open or closed—to process Tunny's binary digits and find the combination that unlocked its vault. One of the first electronic digital computers, Colossus contained 1,500 vacuum tubes, weighed a ton, and dazzled cryptanalysts with its speed when it began crunching numbers at Bletchley in early 1944.

By then, Turing was looking ahead to an era in which the computers he conceptualized—and scientists on both sides of the Atlantic developed during World War II for military purposes—would transform society as a whole. He was one of the few individuals who had a major impact both on the war and on the world that emerged from it. His role in launching the digital revolution would be recognized long before details of his contribution to the Allied victory were declassified. At his untimely death in 1954, little more was known about the secret war he waged than that his "work was hush-hush," as one obituary put it, "not to be divulged even to his mother."

"We had lost the Battle of the Atlantic."

ADM. KARL DÖNITZ AFTER WITHDRAWING HIS U-BOAT FLEET FROM THE NORTH ATLANTIC IN JUNE 1943

COLOSSUS Operated by Wrens of the Women's Royal Navy Service, the pioneering electronic digital computer called Colossus was introduced at Bletchley Park in 1944 to combat Tunny, an intricate German cipher machine with 12 rotors. Colossus lacked a memory and had to be programmed manually for each task. But otherwise, designer Tommy Flowers later remarked, "it embodied all the basic features of a modern computer."

THE REICH'S LONG REACH TO AMERICA

By late 1941, Germany and the United States were unofficially at war in the North Atlantic. In October, a U-boat attack sank the U.S.S. *Reuben James,* an American destroyer escorting merchant ships. Faced with the prospect of adding the Americans to his growing list of enemies, Hitler wanted Japan to enter the conflict, if not against Russia then against the U.S. To that end, Foreign Minister Joachim von Ribbentrop secretly began negotiating a pact that would commit all three Axis powers to hostilities if one of them waged war on America, and would prohibit any of them from making a separate peace. Elated when told of the attack on Pearl Harbor, Hitler sealed the deal by declaring war on the U.S. on December 11. With his armies fully engaged on several fronts and a tiny surface fleet, he could not invade America. But Vice Adm. Karl Dönitz proposed a quick and stealthy advance by U-boats that would extend the Battle of the Atlantic to America's shores.

The U.S. Navy had some experience operating against U-boats in the Atlantic, but its coastal defenses were weak and disorganized. Dönitz intended to launch surprise attacks on vulnerable merchant ships in American coastal waters by deploying 12 long-range Type IX U-boats on a transatlantic mission designated Operation Drumbeat. Pressing commitments elsewhere in the Atlantic and in the Mediterranean forced him to reduce that assault force to five U-boats, which left the submarine base at Lorient, France, in late December 1941, crammed with fuel, food, and torpedoes. Dönitz followed that initial foray with further operations that wreaked havoc from the coast of Maine to the Gulf of Mexico and the Caribbean.

Other clandestine attacks were aimed at American soil by the Abwehr, which in 1942 launched Operation Pastorius—a far-reaching plan to infiltrate saboteurs by submarine who would attack factories, power plants, bridges, and other targets, causing havoc that might "stir up discontent and lower fighting resistance" among Americans. Agents were chosen for their familiarity with American customs and their facility with "American" English. While U-boats rampaged along the coast, those saboteurs would try to sow terror on shore. ◎

RINGLEADER This wanted poster was issued by the FBI in July 1942 for Abwehr Lt. Walter Kappe, who had lived in the U.S. prior to the war before returning to Germany, where he recruited agents for Operation Pastorius. Kappe was expected to join those agents in America but scrapped that plan when they were arrested.

MASTERMIND As commander of the U-boat fleet, Vice Adm. Karl Dönitz directed German submarine operations and planned Operation Drumbeat and subsequent attacks along the American coast.

LONG PATROL Two German U-boats cruise on the turbulent surface of the Atlantic en route to the U.S. coast during Operation Drumbeat. U-boats could make better speed when running on the surface using their powerful diesel engines, and they generally submerged only when threatened with detection.

BEACHED A torpedo fired at the oil tanker S.S. *Rafaela* by the submarine *U-67* during operations in the Caribbean lies beached on the Dutch island of Curaçao in February 1942.

TIMER A U-boat stopwatch used to time torpedoes rests on a German naval quadrant chart of the Caribbean and Gulf of Mexico. U-boat commanders knew from their instruments how long a torpedo should take to reach a target. If the running time exceeded that, the torpedo had missed and they fired again or took evasive action.

HEADQUARTERS FIRST CORPS AREA

SPECIAL REGULATIONS
GOVERNING THE CONTROL
of
SEACOAST LIGHTING
on the
CONNECTICUT SHORE, WEST OF THE SAYBROOK BREAKWATER
JUNE 1, 1942

1. The purpose and intent of these Special Regulations are as stated in Section I of the Regulations Governing the Control of Seacoast Lighting dated May 16, 1942, the provisions of which Section I apply hereto.

2. These Special Regulations apply from one-half hour after sunset to one-half hour before sunrise, to the following:

 a. All amusement resorts and parks and places of similar nature within three miles of the north shore of Long Island Sound.

 b. (1) The city of New Haven.

 (2) All of the area southwest of New Haven lying between the Wilbur Cross and Merritt Parkways and the shore of Long Island Sound, as far as the New York state line.

 c. The locations and communities specified in subparagraphs a. and b. above will be governed by the following rules:

 (1) Extinguish all advertising and display signs and lights.

(2) Reduce all display lighting in shop and store windows to the maximum extent consistent with protection from burglary.

(3) Shield or extinguish all outside lights, excluding street and vehicle lights, and diminish all skylights which throw direct light to skyward.

(4) Shield all street lights from skyward or reduce the wattage of unshielded street lights or extinguish unshielded street lights not absolutely necessary for public safety.

(5) Regulate automotive traffic so as to reduce the speed of vehicles and require the minimum lighting compatible with public safety.

3. These Special Regulations apply to all plants, installations and establishments, whether or not engaged in war production. The authorized agencies of the state of Connecticut will not concern themselves with plants, installations or establishments owned by the Federal Government and operated by Federal officials. Decisions regarding compliance with these Special

Regulations in the case of all other plants, installations and establishments will be made by the authorized agencies of the state of Connecticut, who will exact compliance of war production plants to the maximum extent compatible with the continuance of full production and anti-sabotage protection.

4. Plants, installations and establishments owned by the Federal Government and operated by Federal officials will be given appropriate orders in conformity with these Special Regulations by the respective departments of the Federal Government. These orders will be enforced by the respective departments.

5. Penalties for violation of these Special Regulations are covered in paragraph 4, Public Proclamation No. 1.

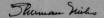

SHERMAN MILES,
Major General, United States Army,
Commanding the First Corps Area.

THE AMERICAN SHOOTING SEASON

On January 11, 1942, after a two-week Atlantic crossing, the lead boat of Operation Drumbeat, *U-123*, struck the first blow, sinking the merchant ship U.S.S. *Cyclops* off Nova Scotia. In the weeks that followed, U-boats operating from the coast of Maine to Cape Hatteras sank an average of one ship a day. During daylight hours, the hunters lurked submerged, surfacing at night to attack vessels unprotected by any convoy system. U-boat captains often found their prey backlit by the lights of American cities, where no blackout orders were given despite the grim spectacle of ships burning off the coast. A single U-boat might claim as many as three kills in one night, while other predators hunted in vain.

Operation Drumbeat concluded in February after sinking 25 ships, but by then a second U-boat assault force was nearing America's Atlantic coast and a third was approaching its hunting grounds off oil ports in the Caribbean and the Gulf of Mexico. The German boats were joined by five long-range Italian Calvi-class

LIGHTS OUT Designed for blackouts, these special bulbs cast a dull, focused beam of light. Military authorities belatedly ordered blackouts in coastal cities, as directed at top.

submarines, assigned to patrol from the Florida Straits to the coast of South America. With all available Type IX boats deployed, Dönitz backed them up with shorter-range Type VII U-boats, dispatched with provisions and munitions packed into every free space. They were refueled at sea by Type XIV supply U-boats, dubbed *Milchkühe* ("milk cows"), which extended their patrol time by four weeks.

Returning U-boat officers referred to Operation Drumbeat as the "American shooting season" or the "Second Happy Time," recalling the first such "Happy Time" in the North Atlantic early in the war. By July 1942, however, defenses against German submarines that were lurking off American shores had been tightened considerably, and the devastating U-boat offensive in American and Caribbean waters was coming to an end (pages 242–43). During that siege, nearly 400 ships totaling more than two million tons were sunk, at a cost of some 5,000 lives. In the process, only seven U-boats were lost. ✪

VICTIMS Pictured above are three tankers torpedoed by U-boats in American waters in 1942—the *Dixie Arrow* (left) and *Byron D. Benson* (center), which were sunk off Cape Hatteras; and the *Pennsylvania Sun*, which was damaged in the Gulf of Mexico, 125 miles from Key West, Florida, but was saved and returned to service. The photograph at left, superimposed on a German naval chart of the upper New England coast, was taken through a U-boat attack periscope and shows a torpedo striking a merchant ship.

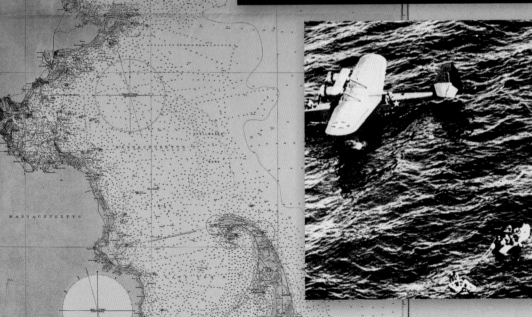

RESCUE MISSION A Douglas Dolphin flying boat operated by the U.S. Coast Guard picks up survivors from a merchant ship torpedoed by a U-boat off the East Coast. The Dolphins also served as patrol aircraft, searching for German submarines along the coast.

NAZI SABOTEURS INFILTRATE AMERICA

Shortly after midnight on June 13, 1942, a team of four men landed on a beach near Amagansett, Long Island, after paddling ashore in a dinghy from the German submarine *U-202*. They carried sufficient explosives, primers, and incendiaries to carry out major sabotage operations. Four days later another four-man team, similarly equipped, landed on Ponte Vedra Beach, near Jacksonville, Florida. The agents were assigned to carry out Operation Pastorius, authorized by Abwehr chief Adm. Wilhelm Canaris, who was under pressure from Hitler to strike a blow at America following the well-publicized arrest of 33 German spies in the U.S. in 1941. Strategic targets for the operation in the U.S. included hydroelectric plants, aluminum factories, locks on the Ohio River, New York's Hell Gate Bridge, and rail yards in Pennsylvania and New Jersey. The scheme was organized by Lt. Walter Kappe of the Abwehr, who had lived in America for some time and selected agents with similar experience who could pass as German Americans. Trained at a sabotage school near Berlin, they were instructed in the manufacture and use of explosives and incendiaries, and were given background "histories" to use when they infiltrated the U.S.

Each team landed with four waterproof crates containing dynamite, coal bombs, fuses, timers, detonators, incendiary devices, and vials of sulfuric acid. They were ordered to bury their munitions near the beach for later recovery and provided with more than $175,000 in U.S. currency to finance their operation. They planned to separate and meet in Cincinnati on July 4 before embarking on a coordinated sabotage campaign. But their risky venture went awry from the start when the four agents who landed on Long Island were discovered by

PRIME TARGET **The arrest of German saboteurs in America in 1942 lent urgency to this recruiting poster for Civilian Defense volunteers, describing New York City as the Nazis' No. 1 target.**

an unarmed Coast Guard patrolman, John Cullen, while in the act of burying their explosives and supplies. Team member Georg Dasch confronted Cullen and claimed that he and his fellows were lost fishermen. He then threatened the suspicious young Coast Guardsman before handing him a bribe and telling him to forget the incident. Cullen took the money and retreated but promptly reported the incident to his superiors. By the time authorities located the explosives cache, the saboteurs had reached New York City by train.

Dasch, who later claimed that he never intended to carry out the operation, soon agreed with fellow agent Ernst Burger to betray the plan and surrender to U.S. authorities. He then traveled to Washington, D.C., contacted the FBI, and not only admitted that he and Burger were involved but also identified the other agents. Armed with Dasch's information, the FBI uncovered the second cache of explosives in Florida and arrested all eight members of the two Pastorius teams by month's end.

The saboteurs were tried in the Justice Department building in Washington, D.C., by a military tribunal appointed by President Roosevelt. All were found guilty and sentenced to death. For their cooperation, President Roosevelt commuted the sentences of Dasch and Burger to prison terms, and they were later deported to postwar Germany. On August 8, 1942, the other six agents were executed. Their abortive operation, intended to shock Americans and weaken their resolve, instead served as a timely warning that Nazi Germany posed a threat to American territory as well as American waters and had to be defeated. As Roosevelt remarked, the saboteurs "were waging battle within our country," and that gave Americans extra incentive to wage war on their country. ✪

SPY HUNTERS At right, FBI agents sort through an explosives cache buried by German saboteurs at Ponte Vedra Beach, Florida, in mid-June 1942. By July, all the agents involved in Operation Pastorius were in custody and on trial, one of whom concealed his face from a photographer outside a Washington, D.C., courtroom (above). The U-boats that inserted the two sabotage teams used German naval quadrant charts like the one here, showing the U.S. Atlantic coast.

INVESTIGATION The encounter of Coast Guard patrolman John Cullen (center) with German saboteurs on Long Island led to a massive manhunt and investigation. The contents of a chest buried by the saboteurs, including explosives, detonators, time delay devices, and vials of acid, were photographed by the FBI (right) and analyzed in its crime laboratories (above left).

TRIBUNAL Among those pictured above at the military tribunal for the accused saboteurs are Maj. Gen. Myron Cramer, judge advocate general and assistant prosecutor (1); Attorney General Francis Biddle, chief prosecutor (2); FBI Director J. Edgar Hoover (3); and Col. Carl Ristine, Georg Dasch's defense attorney (4). At left, an open vehicle containing armed guards leads the way as the saboteurs emerge from their trial at the Justice Department building in a dark van on their way back to prison.

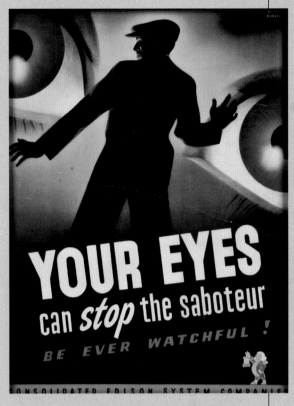

KEEPING WATCH This war poster designed by Weimer Pursell for use in the offices of Consolidated Edison warns employees of the power company to be on the lookout for potential saboteurs.

UNDER ARREST Shown in FBI mug shots from left to right are saboteurs Ernst Burger, Georg Dasch, Werner Thiel, Edward Kerling, Richard Quirin, Heinrich Heinck, Herbert Haupt, and Hermann Neubauer. Because they had entered the country to commit hostile acts while not in uniform, President Roosevelt had them tried by military tribunal as unlawful combatants, subject to the death penalty.

U-BOAT HUNTERS

At first, little could be done to counter the U-boat peril along American shores. With its destroyers deployed in the Pacific and the North Atlantic, the U.S. Navy was hard-pressed to combat German submarines lurking in coastal waters in early 1942. That situation began to improve in the spring, when a force of Royal Navy antisubmarine trawlers and corvettes arrived on loan to help defend the East Coast along with cutters and patrol boats of the U.S. Coast Guard and Navy, some of them equipped with advanced sonar and radar to track U-boats and improved weaponry to attack them. Air support to spot and target those subs was provided by a patrol squadron of the First Army Air Force, which was placed under Navy command in March, as well as pilots of the Civil Air Patrol (above) and an RAF Coastal Command squadron that arrived to cover approaches to New York Harbor in July. By then, blackouts had been ordered in towns and cities along the Atlantic, and coastal convoys had been organized, which by combining air cover with

SPOTTERS **These binoculars were made for use on U-boats by the expert German optical firms of Zeiss and Emil Busch A.G. While U-boat captains scanned for merchant ships along the coast, their own vessels were at risk of being spotted by pilots like those with the Civil Air Patrol at top, standing beside a Stinson L-5 Sentinel patrol plane.**

naval escorts produced an immediate reduction in shipping losses off the East Coast.

Convoys were protected by planes flying from coastal airfields, including long-range Army Air Force bombers and reconnaissance aircraft and Navy blimps, which were well suited for aerial surveillance. When a U-boat was detected, escort vessels attacked with depth charges, forcing their targets to dive deep to escape destruction while the convoy escaped. By August 1942, U-boat attacks in American waters had been reduced from their peak by as much as 80 percent. Dönitz concluded that for all the damage done to coastal shipping, the campaign had not significantly diminished the flow of supplies to Britain and Russia. He withdrew his U-boats from the American coast to bolster his assault on convoys in the North Atlantic, but that onslaught would fail to sever the Allies' vital transatlantic supply lines, shielded by decisive advances in code breaking and antisubmarine warfare. ◉

WRECKED AND RESCUED
At left, smoke shrouds the bow of a Coast Guard patrol boat as it fires a depth charge from its forward K-gun. The K-gun, introduced in 1942, could fire up to 10 depth charges in a row as the escort passed over a target. U-boatmen who escaped from a sunken boat could survive using a Dräger apparatus (above center)—a life jacket containing a rebreather like that used by divers to filter out the carbon dioxide in their exhaled breath and provide fresh oxygen. A survivor of the sunken *U-175* (above left) wears an inflated Dräger as he climbs a cargo net to board the Coast Guard cutter *William J. Duane*. Another *U-175* survivor (above right) is assisted along the cutter's deck.

A WATERY GRAVE The wreckage of the Type IX U-boat *U-166* lies at the bottom of the Gulf of Mexico some 45 miles south of the mouth of the Mississippi River. Reported missing in 1942, its fate was unknown until a survey vessel discovered the wreck in 2001. The photographs here include an extended view of the *U-166*'s crumbling foredeck and close-ups of its 37-mm antiaircraft gun (right) and its conning tower (opposite bottom). In July 1942, *U-166* sank the freighter *Robert E. Lee* and was depth-charged by the Lee's escort, the Navy patrol craft *PC-566*. Marine archaeologists later confirmed that *U-166*'s hull had been shattered by depth charges.

ENDGAME EUROPE

INVASION Allied supplies and reinforcements land a Normandy on June 8, 194 days after D-Day. Ingeniou elaborate deception camp diverted German forces an helped the Allied invasion occupied France succeed.

A WEB OF LIES AND DECEPTION

Officially, Lt. Cmdr. George Earle went to Istanbul in January 1943 to serve as naval attaché at the American Embassy. Unofficially, he was Franklin Roosevelt's not-so-secret agent in Turkey, a neutral country riddled with Allied and Axis spies. "I was responsible to the President," he wrote, "and reported to him alone." Earle's movements were monitored by the Abwehr, the German military intelligence service, whose officers knew of his close ties to Roosevelt and his disdain for Nazis. Shortly before he stepped down as ambassador to Bulgaria in 1941, Earle had brawled in a nightclub with Germans who drew that nation into an alliance with Hitler. Soon after arriving in Istanbul, however, this ardent American foe of the Reich was visited by Hitler's top spymaster. "One morning, a week after I had checked into the luxurious Park Hotel, there was a soft knock on the door of my suite," Earle recalled. "Into the room stepped a short, white-haired man in his fifties. He had bright, inquisitive eyes and wore a heavy overcoat over his civilian clothes. He closed the door behind him and turned the key." After checking to make sure that the windows were shut and locked, the mysterious visitor bowed courteously and introduced himself as "Admiral Wilhelm Canaris, chief of the Abwehr."

DECOY British troops lift a dummy Sherman tank, one of many inflatable rubber decoys placed near the Strait of Dover in early 1944 to give German reconnaissance pilots the false impression that Allied forces would cross there and land near Calais. That crucial deception was reinforced by misinformation sent from double agents under British control to German military intelligence officers of the Abwehr, led by Adm. Wilhelm Canaris (opposite), whose secret opposition to Hitler eventually came to light.

TRAPPED The dazed expression of a German machine-gunner tells of the bitter struggle at Stalingrad, from which Hitler refused to withdraw his doomed forces.

Canaris did not seem like someone engaged in the cutthroat business of wartime espionage. He was "a strange little man who played the flute and loved dogs," Earle noted. "He traveled with several dachshunds and reserved hotel rooms with twin beds, one for them and one for him." But this unassuming figure, described by an acquaintance as "pale and inscrutable," was playing a daring and dangerous game, one that pitted him against his Führer and ultimately exposed him to charges of treason. Without Hitler's knowledge or consent, Canaris went to Istanbul to see if Earle could persuade Roosevelt to abandon his recent insistence on unconditional surrender and offer terms that would allow Germany to avoid utter defeat and subjugation by the Allies. German forces were losing the pivotal Battle of Stalingrad, and Canaris and other secret foes of Hitler's flagging war effort hoped to make a separate peace with the Americans and British before Soviet troops regained their lost ground and wreaked vengeance on the Reich. The plotters saw themselves not as traitors but as patriots, who wove a deceptive web in which they hoped to trap Hitler before he brought their nation to ruin.

Left unsaid by Canaris when he spoke with Earle was that Hitler would have to be removed from power by those Germans who sought peace, for the Allies would never come to terms with the Nazi dictator. Cunning and circumspect, Canaris took care not to make explicit threats against Hitler and left such matters to other conspirators like Baron Kurt von Lersner, who met with Earle in Istanbul not long after Canaris did. Lersner proposed a scheme whereby German officers opposed to the regime in Berlin would seize Hitler, Himmler, and other top Nazis and hand them over to the Americans and British, who could enter the Reich unopposed on condition that they help prevent the Russians from occupying German territory. When Earle asked about the fate of those Nazi leaders, Lersner shrugged and replied: "Hang them, if you like. We do not care . . . We will place the entire German war machine at your disposal to keep the Russians out."

Earle, an anticommunist who considered Stalin as menacing a figure as Hitler, passed this unlikely proposal along to Roosevelt and thought it was worth pursuing. "The Nazis would be crushed," he wrote later. "The Russians, who at heart were no better, would be checked. There would be an end to suffering and bloodshed." But Roosevelt had good reason for rejecting a separate peace that would set the Americans and British against the Soviets, who were bearing the brunt of the war against Germany and emerging as a formidable military power. Even Churchill, who had a greater aversion to Stalin than Roosevelt did, viewed the Soviet leader and his Red Army as indispensable allies, who could not be defied without risking disaster.

British and American leaders also doubted whether Hitler's German foes had the capacity to overthrow him and could be trusted to concede defeat and disarm if they somehow succeeded in toppling his regime. Canaris and other officers who now secretly opposed Hitler had actively supported his prewar efforts to restore German military might, annex Austria, and intervene in the Spanish Civil War on behalf of dictator Francisco Franco. Not until Hitler's aggression risked plunging the Reich into another disastrous conflict like the one that left Germany devastated in 1918 did they begin to conspire against him. Canaris had qualms about the venomous racial policies of the Nazi regime and the involvement of German armed forces in murderous assaults on civilians. "The Wehrmacht would in the final reckoning be held responsible for these atrocities carried out under their very noses," he warned. But his fundamental objection to Hitler was that he was leading Germany to destruction. Canaris and other conspirators hoped by seeking a separate peace to preserve their nation as it was before Hitler took power—an outcome Roosevelt and Churchill rejected because they feared that unless the Reich was thoroughly defeated, occupied, and reconstructed as a peaceful country, German militarism might revive as it did after the First World War.

Some of Hitler's German foes were intent on eliminating him even without Allied assurances that their nation would be spared retribution for the attacks and atrocities he instigated. For Maj. Gen. Henning von Tresckow, who took part in the ill-fated German invasion of Russia, killing Hitler was a moral imperative because the Führer ordered his commanders to conduct a criminal "war of extermination" in the Soviet Union. If those orders were carried out, Tresckow told a fellow officer before that savage campaign unfolded, "then Germany will have finally

CAPTURED Besieged by Soviet troops amid the rubble of Stalingrad (below), German forces surrendered and were led away in captivity (bottom). The debacle at Stalingrad was viewed by some Germans as "the beginning of the end," a confidential SS report stated. Those plotting against Hitler stepped up efforts to eliminate him before he reduced Germany to defeat and degradation.

A CONSCIENTIOUS CONSPIRATOR

Dietrich Bonhoeffer, pictured here in 1939, was one of the war's most unlikely conspirators—a devout Lutheran theologian, pastor, and pacifist who believed he had a sacred duty to help overthrow Hitler. In his late 20s when Hitler came to power, Bonhoeffer protested when Lutherans of Jewish ancestry were barred from serving as pastors. Jews were "brothers of Christians," he said in 1938 shortly before Nazis he called "godless men" attacked Jewish homes, shops, and synagogues on November 9, known as Kristallnacht ("the Night of Broken Glass"). He left for America not long afterward, but he felt obligated to return to Germany as war approached.

Prohibited in 1940 from speaking publicly, Bonhoeffer joined his brother-in-law, Hans von Dohnanyi, as a member of a secret cell of anti-Nazis within the Abwehr and used his influence abroad to seek an Allied truce with Germany if conspirators succeeded in toppling Hitler. In 1942, he met covertly in Sweden with Anglican Bishop George Bell and handed him a list of prominent Germans who hoped to eliminate the Führer and come to terms with the Allies. Bell shared the list with top British officials, but they offered no encouragement to Bonhoeffer or his confederates. He and Dohnanyi also used their influence and Abwehr funds to help Jews escape to Switzerland, which led Gestapo agents to investigate and arrest the two men on suspicion of plotting against Hitler. They held up under interrogation, and not until early 1945 did authorities acquire firm evidence of the conspiracy within the Abwehr. Condemned to death, Bonhoeffer went to the gallows knowing that he had remained true to his faith by opposing the Nazi regime. He was "brave and composed," recalled a doctor present at the execution, who added, "I have hardly ever seen a man die so entirely submissive to the will of God." ✪

lost her honor. The effects will be felt for centuries, and not only Hitler will bear the guilt. Everyone will be guilty, you and me, your wife and my wife, your children and my children." Tresckow believed that assassinating Hitler would help expiate the guilt he and other Germans bore for serving their malevolent Führer. On March 13, 1943, after Hitler visited the headquarters of Army Group Center in occupied Russia, Tresckow and a fellow officer planted a bomb in his plane, timed to explode after it took off. The bomb failed to detonate, and the plot went undetected. Tresckow continued to conspire against Hitler with other dissident officers.

Among those who aided and abetted Tresckow and other would-be assassins was Maj. Gen. Hans Oster, Canaris's chief of staff. Oster led a shadowy group of anti-Nazis within the Abwehr who used the agency as cover for efforts to end the regime and seek an armistice. Although Canaris avoided direct involvement in attempts to kill Hitler, he knew what Oster was up to and tacitly approved ousting the Führer as a means of drawing the reluctant Americans and British into peace talks. By April 1943, however, his overture to Roosevelt through Earle in Istanbul had come to naught and his hopes for a separate peace were fading. Meanwhile, Gestapo agents were closing in on Oster, following the arrest of an Abwehr operative who informed on him and several of his confederates. The Gestapo raided Abwehr headquarters and found evidence that Oster's group had made unauthorized peace overtures to the British through the Vatican and a prominent German Protestant clergyman, Dietrich Bonhoeffer, who was both a public critic of Hitler and a secret conspirator against him. Bonhoeffer and his brother-in-law, Abwehr officer Hans von Dohnanyi, were imprisoned in April and grilled repeatedly. They denied plotting Hitler's downfall, but Oster was placed under house arrest as the investigation proceeded.

Canaris remained free because Gestapo agents did not yet have proof of his guilt and were told not to press the case against him by none other than SS chief Himmler. "Kindly leave Canaris alone!" Himmler insisted—a mystifying order from a man who had long sought to discredit Canaris and hoped to absorb the Abwehr, bringing all German intelligence operations within the SS. Himmler may have kept Canaris afloat with the idea of using his links to the British and Americans to send peace feelers to the West if, as feared, the Soviets pressed German troops back to their border and threatened to invade the Reich. Or he may have calculated that the best way to break Canaris's grip on the Abwehr was to leave him in charge until Hitler lost all faith in the admiral and dispensed with him. By the time Oster came under suspicion, Canaris was tarnished by notable intelligence breakdowns, including the arrest of numerous Abwehr spies and saboteurs in the United States and the agency's failure to anticipate the Allied invasion of Morocco and Algeria in November 1942. "Once again," complained Maj. Gen. Alfred Jodl, chief of the Wehrmacht under Hitler, "Canaris's imprudence and inconsistency has landed us in the soup." His reputation as a spymaster would be further damaged in July 1943 when Allied forces crossed from North Africa to Sicily and broke Benito Mussolini's stranglehold on Italy—an advance aided by ruses that left the Abwehr and Wehrmacht guessing as to where the blow would fall until shortly before those landings occurred. That in turn would set the stage for an ever greater deception, staged to divert Hitler's attention from the massive D-Day onslaught that doomed his Reich.

THE ART OF DECEPTION

The invasion of Sicily, code-named Operation Husky, was the largest amphibious operation yet attempted by any armed force. It would be surpassed only by the Allied landings at Normandy a year later. A huge invasion fleet assembled along the coast of Tunisia, within 150 miles of Sicily. Most of the Axis troops defending that island were Italians, many of whom were ill equipped and demoralized by Benito Mussolini's military fiascoes in the Balkans and North Africa. But they would be backed by two tough German divisions, and if Hitler recognized Sicily as the target and sent ample reinforcements, prospects for the invasion would be grim. General Eisenhower, who served as Supreme Allied Commander, and his chiefs—including British Gen. Harold Alexander, who would have operational command in Sicily— warned that "if substantial German ground troops should be placed in the region prior to the attack, the chances for success become practically nil and the project should be abandoned."

The difficult task of diverting enemy attention and forces away from nearby Sicily toward other possible targets in the Mediterranean was assigned to Col. Dudley Clarke, the British Army's master of deception, who had survived a scandalous incident that could have wrecked the career of a less accomplished officer. In late 1941, Clarke had been arrested by Spanish police in Madrid while dressed as a woman. Police photos of him in drag raised eyebrows among his baffled superiors, including Prime Minister Churchill. His arrest could have been disastrous if Spanish authorities, who cooperated with the Abwehr and Gestapo, had handed him over to the Germans for interrogation. Among the strategic secrets he harbored was that many British units that Axis commanders thought existed in North Africa were figments of his fertile imagination. Clarke had initiated the Allied ploy of inventing notional brigades, divisions, and armies and making them seem credible to the enemy with false reports from double agents, contrived radio signals, and dummy tanks, trucks, and aircraft that looked convincing when viewed from reconnaissance aircraft. Kim Philby, one of several British intelligence officers who spied for the Soviets during and after World War II, reported to

DISGUISE ARTIST A master of strategic deception, Col. Dudley Clarke (top) was arrested in Madrid in 1941 in women's clothing (above) on what may have been a covert mission that went awry. Perhaps, wrote Guy Liddell of MI5, he saw himself as a "super secret service agent."

THE SECRET WORLD OF FORTRESS GIBRALTAR

A strategic British bastion at Spain's southern tip, overlooking the narrow entrance to the Mediterranean, Gibraltar was a frequent source of conflict, intrigue, and subterfuge during the war. The towering Rock of Gibraltar bristled with big guns and contained over 30 miles of tunnels, sheltering some 15,000 troops from bombardment and air raids. More than just a military fortress, it was a vital intelligence center in a region dominated by the Axis until Spanish dictator Francisco Franco began distancing himself from Hitler and Vichy French North Africa fell to Allied forces in late 1942. Before invading the Soviet Union, Hitler planned to send German troops into Spain and seize Gibraltar. But Franco would not allow that, influenced in part by Admiral Canaris, who had helped Franco win the Spanish Civil War and informed him that Hitler no longer intended to invade Britain, which might prove a formidable opponent for Spain if Franco yielded to Hitler and German forces became mired in Russia. Canaris may have been acting simply as a friend of Franco—or as an opponent of Hitler's reckless aggression who hoped to preserve for Germany the option of coming to terms with Britain.

Churchill, meanwhile, had taken out a hefty insurance policy for Gibraltar by secretly depositing 10 million dollars in the New York branch of a Swiss bank for the use of Franco's top commanders, one of whom promised that Spaniards would fight the Germans if they came in. The British could not be sure of that, so Adm. John Godfrey, director of naval intelligence, authorized Operation Tracer, which called for six sentinels to remain sealed in a cave within the Rock of Gibraltar if the bastion had to be evacuated. Slits would allow them to view the sea and report by radio on enemy ships, but there would be no way in or out of the cave, whose occupants would subsist on stored rations and generate electricity by pedaling a bicycle. Known as the Stay Behind Cave, it was excavated but never occupied because the Allies maintained their grip on Gibraltar, which served as a signals intelligence post for the interception and decryption of German, Italian, and Spanish radio messages. Gibraltar's defenders remained subject to Axis air raids and naval forays as well as sabotage by Spaniards who felt that the Rock rightfully belonged to them. British intelligence officer David Scherr neutralized that Spanish threat in 1943 by turning several agents at odds with Franco into double agents who spied on the saboteurs, enabling Scherr to thwart their plans. ✪

BRITISH ROCK At left, the Rock of Gibraltar looms above a British and Allied airfield that often came under attack during the war, as did the naval base there. Defenders could hold out in tunnels deep within the Rock (above), but a sustained German assault overland by way of Spain would almost certainly have doomed the bastion.

Moscow after Clarke was released from jail that he had "under his command three dummy infantry divisions, one dummy tank brigade and several squadrons of dummy aircraft. His position is therefore of great importance from the intelligence viewpoint."

Why Clarke assumed a disguise so conspicuous that Spanish police arrested him for indecency was unclear. British authorities concluded that "he undertook a foolhardy and misjudged action with a definite purpose, for which he had rehearsed his part beforehand . . . we can reasonably expect that this escapade and its consequences will have given him a sufficient shock to make him more prudent in the immediate future." Clarke rewarded his superiors for giving him a second chance by continuing to direct A Force, his deception agency in North Africa, with a skilled hand. In the spring of 1943, he drew up plans to screen the upcoming Sicily campaign by simulating preparations for two assaults on other targets in the Mediterranean. One was supposedly directed against German-occupied Crete and Greece by the notional British Twelfth Army based in Egypt, and the other was aimed at Sardinia, an island farther from Tunisia than Sicily but close enough to be a possible objective for the invasion fleet, whose buildup could not be disguised from the enemy.

Clarke's preference when practicing deception was to feed the opposition numerous false clues, which might seem insignificant individually but when added up gave Axis intelligence officers the satisfaction of solving a complex puzzle, when in fact they were being led to the wrong conclusion. He knew that spymasters grew wary when offered glaring evidence of enemy intentions, and he distrusted overambitious ruses that might invite suspicion. So Clarke was initially skeptical when asked to approve one of the most audacious and imaginative deception schemes ever contrived, code-named Operation Mincemeat.

Mincemeat was inspired by an accident in late September 1942 when an RAF Catalina flying boat crashed in a storm off the south coast of Spain. All seven crewmen and three passengers perished, and their bodies were recovered at sea by Spanish authorities. One of the passengers was a Royal Navy staff officer carrying a letter revealing plans for Operation Torch—the assault on French North Africa that began six weeks later—and another was an officer under Charles de Gaulle whose briefcase contained documents identifying Free French agents in North Africa. If German agents in Spain got hold of such intelligence, the results could be disastrous. The naval officer's remains were soon returned to the British, who determined that the crucial letter had not been removed from his coat and opened—a conclusion confirmed by Ultra decrypts from Bletchley Park, where code breakers were deciphering messages sent by Abwehr officers in Spain to their superiors. But Ultra also revealed that Spanish authorities had shared the contents of the French officer's briefcase with the Abwehr. When RAF Flight Lt. Charles Cholmondeley learned of that fact, it occurred to him that if a corpse dressed as a British courier washed ashore in Spain with official documents designed to divert attention from the assault on Sicily, Spanish officials might well share those papers with the Germans.

Cholmondeley was familiar with deception, serving as he did on John Masterman's Twenty Committee, which oversaw MI5's ambitious Double Cross operation and determined what accurate details double agents could feed to the Germans to give their misleading reports credibility. When Cholmondeley broached his idea to the committee, it was taken up enthusiastically by another member, Lt. Cmdr. Ewen Montagu of Naval

DESIGNER **Flight Lt. Charles Cholmondeley of the RAF came up with the idea of planting documents on a corpse to deceive the Germans, as done in Operation Mincemeat.**

DEVELOPER **Lt. Cmdr. Ewen Montagu of naval intelligence refined Mincemeat with Cholmondeley and helped the risky operation win approval at high levels.**

"It would be a mistake to play for high deception stakes."

COL. DUDLEY CLARKE'S INITIAL RESPONSE TO OPERATION MINCEMEAT

Intelligence. Montagu was higher in rank than Cholmondeley and a persuasive lawyer by training, which proved vital as they sought approval for Mincemeat first from Col. John Bevan—head of the London Controlling Section, which supervised all British strategic deception operations—and then from Dudley Clarke. The plan presented to Clarke called for including among the dead courier's documents a letter from one prominent British commander to another that would attract the attention of Hitler and his chiefs and point them toward targets other than Sicily. That approach was too daring and direct to suit Clarke, who told Bevan that "it would be a mistake to play for high deception stakes." Montagu and Bevan pressed their case, however, and Clarke came around. Downplaying such an obvious objective as Sicily, he concluded, required a bold scheme that was aimed at the "inmost circles of the German war machine" and would exploit Hitler's fears, including the threat of an Allied attack on the Balkan Peninsula, where German forces were already under assault by partisans.

Given the go-ahead, Montagu and Bevan drafted a letter from Lt. Gen. Archibald Nye, vice chief of the Imperial General Staff in London, to General Alexander in Tunisia. Nye himself then put the finishing touches on the note. "We have had recent information that the Bosche have been reinforcing and strengthening their defenses in Greece and Crete," his letter stated. In response, he added, the general staff had decided to commit additional forces to the forthcoming Allied assault there—a fiction designed to keep German forces tied down in the eastern Mediterranean while Operation Husky unfolded. The letter also claimed that the Allies would launch a "heavy air bombardment" of Sicily, as in fact they would before troops went ashore there, to mask an assault on another target in the western Mediterranean. "We stand a very good chance of making him [the enemy] think we will go for Sicily," Nye wrote Alexander; "it is an obvious objective and one about which he must be nervous."

Nye's letter did not mention the target that would supposedly be attacked instead of Sicily, but Montagu dropped a broad hint in a cover letter he drafted from Lord Louis Mountbatten, chief of Combined Operations, to Adm. Andrew Cunningham, the naval commander for Husky. That note introduced the bogus courier who would carry the Mincemeat documents as Maj. William Martin of the Royal Marines and asked Cunningham to arrange "for the onward transmission of the letter he has with him for General Alexander." Mountbatten signed the note to Cunningham, which concluded with a request that Martin be sent back to headquarters in London "as soon as the assault is over. He might bring some sardines with him—they are 'on points' here!" Montagu trusted that "sardines" (on ration points in Britain) would be interpreted as a reference to the supposed assault on Sardinia and thought the Germans would enjoy the joke.

"He might bring some sardines with him—they are 'on points' here!"

LT. CMDR. EWEN MONTAGU IN A LETTER SIGNED BY LORD LOUIS MOUNTBATTEN, HINTING AT SARDINIA AS AN ALLIED INVASION TARGET

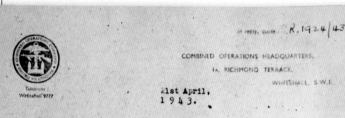

DEAD MAN'S BLUFF Typed on official stationery at Mountbatten's headquarters, this letter identified the dead body employed in Operation Mincemeat as that of the fictitious Maj. William Martin, carrying documents meant to suggest to the Germans that Allied forces who were preparing to invade Sicily might land elsewhere.

Meanwhile, a local coroner had helped the deception team in London obtain a corpse to serve as Major Martin. The body was that of Glyndwr Michael, a 34-year-old Welshman who had fallen on hard times and lost touch with his next of kin, who made no claim to his remains after he committed suicide by ingesting rat poison. A leading pathologist concluded that if Spanish authorities conducted an autopsy after recovering his body at sea, there was little chance that the cause of death would be regarded as anything other than drowning. Michael's corpse was frozen to prevent decomposition while Cholmondeley and others set about contriving an identity card, uniform, and personal effects for Major Martin, including love letters from a fiancée named Pam. Victoire "Paddy" Ridsdale—an assistant to Montagu's colleague in Naval Intelligence, Ian Fleming, who may have modeled James Bond's secretary, Miss Moneypenny, after her—later claimed credit for composing those poignant letters, one of which concluded: "Bill darling, do let me know as soon as you get fixed & can make some more plans, & don't please let them send you off into the blue the horrible way they do nowadays—now that we've found each other out of the whole world, don't think I could bear it."

Unlike Pam's letters and other personal items, which were placed in the notional major's coat and pockets when he was clothed, the crucial deception letters were locked in a briefcase chained to his body. That would prevent them from possibly being washed away after the body was released from a submarine off the coast of Spain and would help bring them to the attention of Spanish authorities. The accident in 1942 that inspired Mincemeat had shown that documents on the body of the deceased might not necessarily be removed and examined, which involved handling a corpse in a state of decay, whereas the contents of a briefcase were likely to be inspected and shared with German agents. Final approval for the operation came in mid-April from Prime Minister Churchill—who reveled in deception and shrugged off the risk that the enemy might see through the elaborate scheme—and from General Eisenhower. Cholmondeley and Montagu helped dress the corpse, a grim process that involved thawing the frozen feet of the deceased with an electric heater until they were flexible enough for the major's boots to be put on. The body was then packed in dry ice and shipped aboard the submarine H.M.S. *Seraph* to within sight of the Spanish port of Huelva, where it was fitted with an inflated

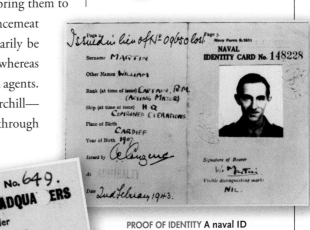

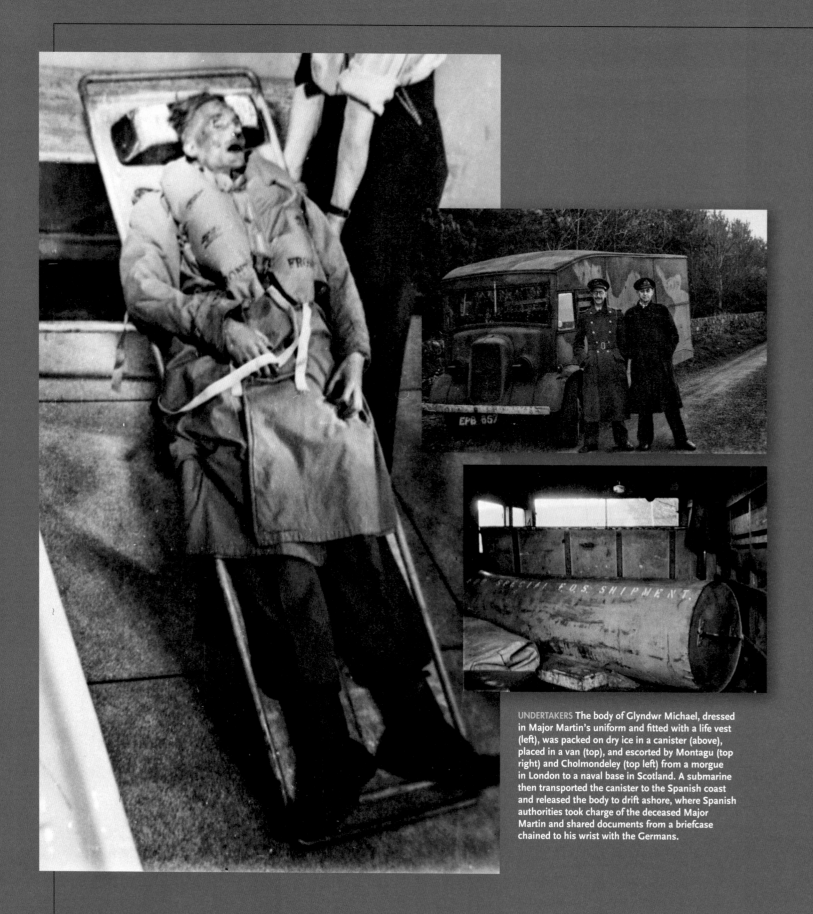

UNDERTAKERS The body of Glyndwr Michael, dressed in Major Martin's uniform and fitted with a life vest (left), was packed on dry ice in a canister (above), placed in a van (top), and escorted by Montagu (top right) and Cholmondeley (top left) from a morgue in London to a naval base in Scotland. A submarine then transported the canister to the Spanish coast and released the body to drift ashore, where Spanish authorities took charge of the deceased Major Martin and shared documents from a briefcase chained to his wrist with the Germans.

life vest to keep it afloat and suggest that Martin had survived a plane crash before drowning. Shortly before dawn on April 30, the body was committed to the sea as the sub's commander read a suitable psalm: "I will keep my mouth as it were with a bridle while the ungodly is in my sight. / I held my tongue, and spake nothing."

The body was spotted floating off Huelva by a fisherman that same day and was taken into custody by the Spanish Navy, an outcome that the planners had hoped to avoid because Spanish naval officers tended to be sympathetic to the British and might not share what they found with the Germans. The scheme was nearly foiled when a naval officer politely offered the deceased major's briefcase to Francis Haselden, the British vice consul in Huelva, soon after it was found attached to the corpse. Haselden, who had been briefed on Mincemeat, thanked the Spaniard for his kind offer but advised him to hold on to the briefcase until he checked with his superiors, who might blame him for releasing Martin's effects without authorization. That did the trick. Not until after the contents of the briefcase had passed up the Spanish chain of command to Francisco Franco, who ordered photographic copies of the documents given to the Abwehr, were they restored to the British. On May 14, an Ultra decrypt of a message to German commanders in the Mediterranean provided details of the supposed assault on Greece as contained in the letter from Nye to Alexander and stated that they came from "a source which may be considered absolutely reliable." Churchill, who was conferring with Roosevelt in Washington, received a cable that delighted him: "Mincemeat swallowed rod, line and sinker by right people and from best information they look like acting on it."

One leading Nazi who was not inclined to swallow Mincemeat whole was Propaganda Minister Joseph Goebbels, a man well versed in lies and deceit. He asked Admiral Canaris if the "very revealing" letter from Nye to Alexander might "only be a deception." Canaris vouched for its authenticity, and Hitler was taken in as well. Mussolini fretted about a possible invasion of Sicily, but the official record of a meeting Hitler held in mid-May stated that the "Führer does not agree with the Duce that the most likely invasion point is Sicily." Hitler concluded from the documents found in Major Martin's possession "that the planned attacks will be directed mainly against Sardinia and the Peloponnesus," at the southern tip of Greece. With that in mind, he ordered the 1st Panzer Division redeployed from France to Greece. Had he instead sent that armored division to Sicily, it would have given Eisenhower pause and clouded prospects for the invasion.

By late June, the evidence pointing to an invasion of Sicily was overwhelming, but it was too late for Hitler to make major redeployments. The two German divisions on the island were insufficient to prevent Italian

THE HUMAN TORPEDO

In early January 1943, six months before Allied troops invaded Sicily, British frogmen steering submersible torpedoes called Chariots (below) launched a covert attack on Italian ships in the Sicilian port of Palermo. Their Chariots were developed in response to a secret weapon devised by the Italian Navy called the *Maiale,* meaning "pig," a fitting name for a human torpedo that was hard to ride and guide. Beginning in 1941, two-man Italian teams perched on the Maiale, and wearing underwater breathing gear carried out attacks on British ships docked at Gibraltar, Alexandria, and other Mediterranean harbors by approaching at night on the surface and submerging as they neared their target. They then detached from the torpedo a limpet mine, which clung to the ship's iron hull magnetically and was timed to allow the team to escape before it exploded. The British Chariot was similar in design, using flotation tanks like those in submarines that submerged the vessel when filled with water. Five two-man teams took part in the daring Palermo raid, which sank an Italian cruiser and badly damaged a troop ship. One frogman perished when his Chariot capsized, and seven others were captured. Despite the risks associated with human torpedoes, other models were developed and deployed by the Germans as well as the Japanese, whose Kaiten torpedo was a suicide weapon, which exploded on impact when the operator drove it into the hull of a ship. ✪

NAVAL CHARIOT **This two-man craft, launched from a submarine, had a detachable limpet mine used to torpedo ships.**

forces from giving way when the assault began there on July 10, and those Axis troops who were not killed or captured soon withdrew from Sicily to the Italian mainland. Disgraced by the debacle, Mussolini was ousted, and his successor entered into secret peace talks with the Allies. The vaunted Pact of Steel between Nazi Germany and Fascist Italy had been shattered with the help of Major Martin, a man who never was, and the wizards who invented him.

THE OSS AT WAR

Among the officers who landed in Sicily soon after the first troops came ashore was 60-year-old William Donovan, chief of the OSS. Donovan, who now held the rank of brigadier general, always wanted to be in on the action. While a captain was escorting him inland in a jeep, he spotted an Italian patrol, grabbed a submachine gun, and opened fire. "He shot up the Italians single-handed," the captain recalled. "He was happy as a clam." The thrill soon faded, however, for Donovan had been denied permission to infiltrate OSS agents into Sicily before Allied troops landed, so as to avoid alerting the enemy to the invasion. The first OSS team in Sicily—consisting of Sicilian Americans led by one of their own, Maj. Biagio Max Corvo—did not arrive until three days after the invasion began, too late to do much more than interview Italian prisoners of war.

When American and British forces prepared to advance from Sicily to the Italian mainland in September 1943, Donovan was again barred from sending agents in ahead of the troops. But Corvo and other OSS officers were soon deeply involved in secret operations on Italian soil, including the island of Sardinia, where German troops were greatly outnumbered by Italian forces. Most of those Italians lost any incentive to fight when Mussolini's successor, Field Marshal Pietro Badoglio, surrendered to the Allies on September 8, one day before Allied troops landed at Salerno, Italy. But some Italian troops were dedicated members of the Fascist Party and reluctant to abandon the Axis cause. Donovan asked 52-year-old Lt. Col. Serge Obolensky, a Russian aristocrat who had fled the Bolshevik takeover of his homeland and emigrated to the U.S., to parachute into Sardinia and persuade the Italian commander there to turn against the Germans. "General, I don't speak Italian," Obolensky objected. "I know you can do it," replied Donovan, who had a knack for encouraging subordinates to take on tough assignments.

On the night of September 13, Obolensky landed in Sardinia as head of a four-man operational group—an OSS unit whose members functioned as commandos in U.S. military uniforms. With him were Lt. Michael Formichelli, an Italian American who served as his interpreter, and two radio operators who remained in hiding while Obolensky and Formichelli walked 15 miles to Cagliari, the capital of Sardinia, and asked startled police officers there to take them to the island's commander, Lt. Gen. Antonio Basso. As Obolensky related, "I told the general that the Allied headquarters expected him to press

> "All men operating against German troops in so-called Commando raids in Europe . . . are to be annihilated to the last man."
>
> HITLER'S COMMANDO ORDER, WHICH CAUSED SOME OSS RECRUITS OPERATING IN UNIFORM TO BE EXECUTED

INVADING SICILY **British soldiers form a chain to unload supplies from a landing craft soon after the first Allied troops came ashore in Sicily on July 10, 1943. The invasion of Sicily marked the beginning of OSS military operations in Europe.**

Frank Monteleone
OSS

Lt Richard Kelly
OSS

Major Archie
Colquhoun GSI (CL)

Captain William Bliden
OSS

Major Jean Caneri
PPA

Captain Thiele
OSS

Captain Maitland
27 Lancers

Lt Vic Hallett
PPA

Lt Sartiano
OSS

Col Villanova
Nucleo "I"

the Germans relentlessly and in every way try and destroy them during the process of their evacuation. I also told him that we had some special units that we could send to him for that purpose." Basso replied that he would do all he could "to push the Germans out of Sardinia" but did not want Allied commandos sent in because Italian troops sympathetic to the Germans might clash with them. "Except for one or two skirmishes with the Germans," Obolensky observed, "the Italian troops never really fought them but just moved up when the Germans had evacuated a place." He could not induce Basso to wage war on his former Axis partners, but he put enough pressure on the general to ensure that he nudged the Germans out and surrendered Sardinia to the Allies.

OSS teams also helped resistance fighters liberate the French island of Corsica, north of Sardinia, and used that as a base from which to launch raids into mainland Italy, which Hitler ordered his forces to occupy after Badoglio surrendered. All OSS agents who infiltrated German-occupied territory risked being treated as spies and executed if captured, even if in uniform. In October 1942, Hitler had ordered that henceforth, "all men operating against German troops in so-called Commando raids in Europe or in Africa, are to be annihilated to the last man. This is to be carried out whether they be soldiers in uniform,

ALLIED INFILTRATORS Pictured here at Allied headquarters in Caserta, Italy, are some of those who operated behind German lines in northern Italy, including Lt. Richard Kelly of the OSS Maritime Unit, which infiltrated Axis territory by sea, OSS officers attached to the Eighth Army in Italy, and members of the British General Service Intelligence (GSI) and Popski's Private Army (PPA), a British special forces unit organized in North Africa by Vladimir Peniakoff, alias Popski. With them at far right is an Italian officer who switched to their side.

COMMANDEERING IL DUCE Austrian-born Otto Skorzeny (right) acquired a conspicuous dueling scar on his left cheek as a student in Vienna before joining the Waffen-SS and earning an Iron Cross in combat in Russia. He took charge of German commandos in 1943 and was sent by Hitler that September to Italy to extract the captive Mussolini (below), shown approaching the plane in which Skorzeny spirited him away to Germany. Skorzeny went on to conduct other covert missions for the Führer, while Mussolini returned to northern Italy as Hitler's puppet and was ultimately seized by Italian partisans and executed in April 1945.

ᛋᛋ-Sturmbannführer SKORZENY

or saboteurs, with or without arms; and whether fighting or seeking to escape." He justified that order by claiming that Allied commandos were behaving in a "particularly brutal and underhand manner" and were killing "unarmed captives who they think might prove an encumbrance to them."

In fact, the number of prisoners killed by Allied commandos was negligible compared with the numerous Allied captives who were slain by Axis troops or died of neglect in prison camps. Despite his professed disdain for enemy commandos, Hitler envied their exploits and assigned several secret operations to his own ruthless commando chief, Capt. Otto Skorzeny of the Waffen-SS. Soon after Mussolini was ousted and placed under arrest by Italian authorities, Hitler dispatched Skorzeny to extract him from a remote hotel on a mountainside in central Italy where he was detained. On September 12, Skorzeny's special forces crash-landed in gliders near the hotel and routed those guarding the deposed dictator. "The Führer sent me to free you!" Skorzeny told the startled Mussolini, who replied: "I knew my friend Adolf wouldn't desert me." Crammed into a small plane, Mussolini and Skorzeny—who was promoted to major for this exploit—flew to Berlin, where Hitler embraced his old ally and sent him back to German-occupied northern Italy as a Fascist figurehead.

As Allied forces advanced slowly and painfully northward from the boot of Italy toward Rome against fierce German opposition, Donovan secured permission to deploy OSS agents as spies and saboteurs in advance of the troops. In late March 1944, an OSS operational group consisting of 15 Italian Americans led by Lt. Vincent Russo landed in dinghies along the northwest coast of Italy with 650 pounds of explosives, which they planned to use to wreck a railroad tunnel through which supplies and reinforcements were funneled to German forces in and around Rome. Russo's men hid out in a barn while plotting their

"I knew my friend Adolf wouldn't desert me."
MUSSOLINI WHEN HE WAS RESCUED BY SKORZENY

EXECUTION Condemned to death by an American military tribunal for executing 15 OSS prisoners of war who were seized while operating in uniform behind German lines in March 1944, Gen. Anton Dostler is tied to a stake before facing a firing squad on December 1, 1945. The tribunal rejected Dostler's plea that he was following orders from superiors, including Hitler's directive that all those captured while conducting commando raids in or out of uniform should be put to death.

FRENCH RESISTANCE
HELPS THROTTLE THE BOCHE

attack but were spotted by local Fascists who summoned German troops. After a firefight in which Russo and several others were wounded, the OSS commandos surrendered. On March 26, all 15 men were executed at the insistence of Gen. Anton Dostler, who dismissed objections from subordinates opposed to killing the prisoners. Dostler's defense that he was following orders from Hitler and Field Marshal Albert Kesselring, the supreme German commander in Italy, did not spare him from later being convicted as a war criminal by an Allied military tribunal, which sentenced him to the same fate as the commandos he condemned—death by firing squad.

Other Italian American OSS units succeeded in severing enemy supply lines and funneling weapons to partisans at war with the Germans, who withdrew toward the Alps after abandoning Rome in early June 1944. A team led by Lieutenant Formichelli, who had helped secure Sardinia, armed partisans around the northern Italian city of Parma and trained them in sabotage and guerrilla warfare. Within a span of five months, Formichelli reported, the guerrillas he aided destroyed two trainloads of munitions and 13 bridges, and killed, wounded, or captured nearly 3,000 German troops. Mussolini himself fell victim to Italian partisans as the war drew to a close and German resistance in Italy crumbled.

The OSS infiltrated several other German-occupied countries in Europe, including Greece and Yugoslavia, but its agents were most active in France, which they first pene-

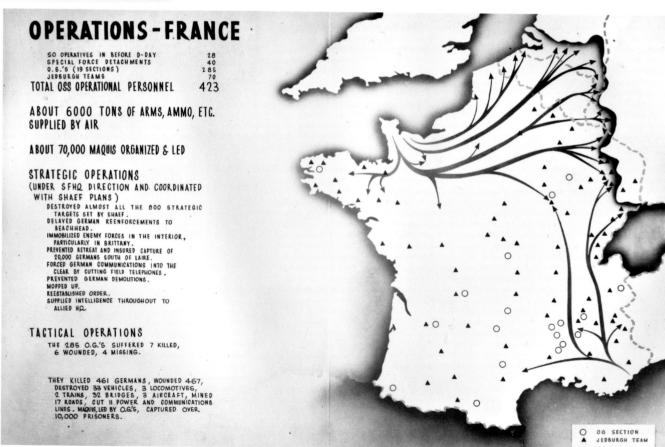

PATHS OF LIBERATION An OSS chart lists the agency's contributions to the liberation of France, including operations launched before and after D-Day and the Allied landings in southern France in August 1944. Many OSS operations were conducted with the Maquis and others in France who resisted German occupiers and were honored in the poster at top, published in London in 1944, which evokes the "flame of French resistance" that Charles de Gaulle said must never be put out.

trated in mid-1943 as Allied commanders began planning for a momentous invasion there in 1944. Henry Hyde, a 28-year-old American lawyer who was born in Paris and joined the OSS in Algiers, recruited French exiles in North Africa and sent them back to their homeland to spy on German forces. Hyde had no aircraft at his disposal but launched his operation, code-named Penny Farthing, by arranging for two of his French recruits, Jacques de Roquefort and Mario Marret, to be flown by the SOE to France, where they landed by parachute in July 1943 in the vicinity of Lyon, a hotbed of resistance. That airlift marked the start of a fruitful collaboration in France between the OSS and SOE, which had been infiltrating its own agents there since 1940 but had lost many of them in German crackdowns that shattered some SOE networks.

Roquefort and Marret were aided by a diverse group of resisters and informants in Lyon, ranging from a Catholic priest to prostitutes in a local brothel, who extracted intelligence from German soldiers by chatting with them or waiting until when they were undressed and preoccupied to examine their *soldbuch* ("pay book"), which resembled a passport and identified the soldiers and the present and past units to which they belonged. By 1944, Hyde had planted more than a dozen two-man teams in southern France whose reports, submitted in code by radio, revealed German military strength and movements in the region and aided Allied officers preparing for the second stage of the invasion of France—an amphibious assault along the Mediterranean coast that would follow the massive D-Day landings in Normandy. Meanwhile, other OSS agents in France were organizing and equipping resistance groups for attacks that would precede D-Day and an armed uprising against the Germans that would begin then. Donovan's agency now had support from the U.S. Army Air Force's 801st Bombardment Group, whose pilots, known as Carpetbaggers, flew B-24s that were designed for low-level antisubmarine warfare and adapted to deliver weapons and operatives to occupied France. For such missions, the ball turret at the belly of the B-24 was replaced by a hatch known as a "Joe hole" for the "Joes" who dropped through it and parachuted into enemy territory.

The OSS had both Joes and Janes—female agents who worked undercover. None took greater risks in defiance of the Nazis than Virginia Hall, who was born in Maryland in 1906 and educated in Europe, where she mastered French and other languages. Unwilling to wait for the U.S. to enter the war, she approached the SOE in London in May 1941 and persuaded Maurice Buckmaster, head of the agency's French section, to train her for covert operations in occupied France. Because he was not yet authorized to send women there, she worked initially as a freelancer, traveling under her own name as a foreign correspondent for the *New York Post*. She soon linked up with anti-Nazis around Lyon, nurtured resistance networks, and helped fugitives evade German authorities and escape France. By late 1942, she herself was being pursued by the Gestapo and fled the German occupation of southern France by crossing the Pyrenees to Spain on foot, no small accomplishment for a woman who had suffered a prewar hunting accident that left her with a wooden leg.

Hall remained with the SOE—whose officers thought she would be a marked woman in France and employed her instead in Spain—until early 1944, when she transferred to the OSS and offered to resume work with French partisans in advance of the invasion. The odds

(continued on page 268)

PORTRAIT OF AN AGENT This sketch of 37-year-old OSS agent Virginia Hall, code-named Diane Heckler, was made by fellow agent Peter Harratt, code-named Aramis, who infiltrated occupied France with her by boat in March 1944. It shows her shortly before she dyed her hair gray and assumed the guise of an elderly French peasant woman, which enabled her to elude the Gestapo while she helped arm the Maquis.

"The woman who limps is one of the most dangerous Allied agents in France."
A GESTAPO OFFICER DESCRIBING OSS AGENT VIRGINIA HALL

RESCUING DOWNED AIRMEN IN YUGOSLAVIA

Allied covert operations in German-occupied Yugoslavia were complicated by a fierce rivalry between two resistance groups there—Communists led by Josip Broz, a Croatian better known as Tito, and Chetniks led by Draza Mihailovic, a Serbian monarchist. Churchill concluded that Tito's forces were far more effective in combating the Germans and got Roosevelt to agree at the Tehran Conference that the Allies should support Tito rather than Mihailovic. But William Donovan wanted his OSS agents to continue working with the Chetniks as well as the Communists in order to evacuate downed Allied airmen that both factions were harboring. Many were Americans who flew from bases in Italy against Romanian oil refineries vital to the German war effort and took hits that forced them to bail out over Yugoslavia on the way back. "Screw the British," Donovan reportedly told Roosevelt, "Let's get our boys out." FDR swayed the British, who went along with an OSS rescue effort dubbed Operation Halyard, aimed at airmen sheltered by the Chetniks, on condition that Americans not aid that group.

On August 2, 1944, Lt. George Musulin, a Serbian American who had initiated OSS ties with the Chetniks, returned to Yugoslavia to

GUIDANCE **The pilot of the first C-47 to land on the airstrip at Pranjani in August 1944 guides another pilot in by radio to evacuate downed airmen.**

direct Operation Halyard, landing by parachute with Sgt. Mike Rajacich and radio operator Arthur Jibilian. They were conducted to Chetnik headquarters at Pranjani, where over 250 airmen were sheltered. "It was a tremendous thrill to see them coming in," recalled one American pilot, "because we knew that things were underway to get us out of there." Chetnik troops and Serbian civilians cleared an airstrip to accommodate C-47s of the 15th American Army Air Force, which began evacuating airmen to Italy just one week after the OSS team arrived. Musulin could not resist offering some aid to the beleaguered Chetniks, who were under mounting pressure from Tito's advancing forces, and was recalled for doing so. He was replaced by OSS Lt. Nick Lalich, who carried on the operation.

By December, when Halyard came to a close, some 500 airmen had been safely evacuated from Chetnik territory. That brought the total number rescued in Yugoslavia during the war to nearly 2,000 and vindicated Donovan's decision to continue working with two feuding factions that could not work with each other. ✪

RESCUED **Above, Lt. Nick Lalich (left) prepares a message to be sent by radio operator Arthur Jibilian (right) during Operation Halyard. Among those rescued were the three airmen at center in the photograph at left, flanked by Chetniks in dark uniforms and about to board the plane behind them. Jibilian recalled that some grateful airmen gave their shoes to needy Serbs who had sheltered them.**

MEDICAL AID Capt. J. H. Mitrani (second from right), a surgeon with the 15th Army Air Force, treats a wounded Chetnik at Pranjani. The prohibition against American aid for Chetniks did not prevent Mitrani from helping those who were sick or injured.

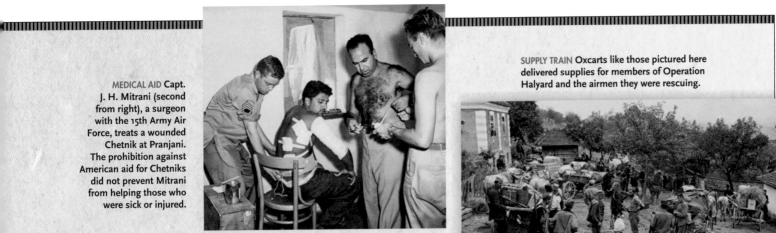

SUPPLY TRAIN Oxcarts like those pictured here delivered supplies for members of Operation Halyard and the airmen they were rescuing.

TRANSPORTS Rescued airmen prepare to depart Yugoslavia aboard C-47s provided by the 15th Army Air Force, which also furnished fighter cover for the transports.

RESTLESS NIGHT Sleeping close together on hay-strewn floors, OSS men often had to contend with fleas. "Within five minutes everyone was up scratchin' to beat hell," one of them noted.

HEADING HOME Wearing life jackets as a precaution, airmen embark in a C-47 on a flight across the Adriatic to an American base in Italy.

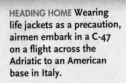

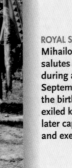

ROYAL SALUTE Gen. Draza Mihailovic (foreground) salutes his Chetnik troops during a ceremony on September 6, 1944, honoring the birthday of Yugoslavia's exiled king. Mihailovic was later captured by Tito's forces and executed in 1946.

against her appeared steep when she landed by boat on the coast of Brittany in March 1944. "The woman who limps is one of the most dangerous Allied agents in France," a Gestapo officer declared. "We must find and destroy her." But she evaded arrest by dyeing her hair gray and posing as a hobbled old peasant woman. She worked with elusive French guerrillas known as the Maquis and arranged drop zones by radio for weapons they required. Like other OSS agents in France, Hall continued to fuel the fires of resistance after D-Day—an assault that was long anticipated by the Germans but that still caught them by surprise, thanks to the most elaborate and effective campaign of military secrecy, subterfuge, and misdirection conducted in modern times.

OVERLORD AND BODYGUARD

The Allied plan to invade Normandy, code-named Operation Overlord, was approved at the highest level when Roosevelt, Churchill, and Stalin met for confidential talks at the Iranian capital of Tehran in late 1943. Stalin had long been pressing for an Anglo-American assault on occupied France to relieve pressure on Soviet troops who were slowly advancing against German forces in Eastern Europe at great cost. Churchill, who feared disaster if the enemy anticipated the invasion and concentrated their forces in Normandy, stressed the need to deceive the Germans and divert their attention to other possible landing sites. "In wartime," he remarked, "truth is so precious that she should always be attended by a bodyguard of lies." Stalin, who often hid the truth from his fellow Soviets, needed no prodding from Churchill to deceive the enemy. "This is what we call military cunning," he told the prime minister.

The elaborate D-Day deceptions that ensued were orchestrated largely by British officers who had honed their skills earlier in the war by turning German agents against their masters and misleading Axis commanders with false leads, phony signals, and fictitious forces. In a sly nod to Churchill, the deception campaign as a whole was code-named Bodyguard. At its core was a crucial scheme labeled Fortitude South, designed to reinforce Hitler's assumption that Allied troops would take the shortest path to Germany by crossing the narrow Strait of Dover (Pas de Calais) and landing around Calais, not far from the strategic Belgian port of Antwerp, which could be used to support the invasion. Allied commanders decided against that option because it meant assaulting the strongest sector of the Atlantic Wall—a long chain of German coastal fortifications, which were less formidable in Normandy. Even after American and British troops landed there on D-Day, tentatively scheduled for June 1, 1944, their assault would be portrayed as a prelude to a larger invasion at Calais to keep German forces defending that sector from being redeployed to Normandy. That was the biggest of many lies purveyed by the masterminds of Operation Bodyguard to disguise the true nature of Overlord.

Their ambitious deception plan could backfire ruinously if the enemy saw through it and

BIG THREE Stalin, Roosevelt, and Churchill present a united front at the Tehran Conference that convened in the Iranian capital in late November 1943. Although the Big Three settled on plans for an Anglo-American invasion of occupied France in 1944 and a campaign to deceive the Germans as to where the landings would take place, tensions arose over the fate of Poland and other lands that Soviet troops would occupy as they advanced toward Berlin.

recognized the real objective. But Allied officers were able to assess that risk and reduce it because they had broken Axis codes and were reading the enemy's thoughts. When American cryptanalysts solved Japan's Purple machine in 1940 and began deciphering that nation's diplomatic messages, they acquired crucial intelligence on the Axis as whole, provided by envoys such as Lt. Gen. Hiroshi Oshima, who served as Japanese ambassador to Germany from early 1941 until the end of the war. Oshima became a trusted confidant of Hitler and spied unwittingly on his regime by sending detailed reports from Berlin to Tokyo that were scrambled on Purple, transmitted by radio, and intercepted, deciphered, and distributed to Allied leaders, including President Roosevelt and U.S. Army Chief George Marshall, who called Oshima "our main basis of information regarding Hitler's intentions in Europe." In October 1943, Oshima toured the Atlantic Wall and reported to Tokyo at length on the deep German defenses at Calais and the less imposing fortifications in Normandy. That encouraged Churchill to back Overlord and confirmed that Hitler anticipated an Allied invasion at Calais—an expectation that deception planners reinforced and continued to monitor through intercepts of messages from Oshima and others close to the Führer as D-Day loomed.

Equally important to efforts to screen the Normandy invasion were Ultra decrypts from Bletchley Park, including Abwehr reports indicating which double agents on MI5's roster were most highly regarded in Berlin and could best be used for D-Day deceptions. Two who loomed large in those efforts were Juan Pujol of Spain (code-named Garbo) and Dusko Popov of Yugoslavia (code-named Tricycle). Popov had regained the trust of the Abwehr after returning in 1942 from America, where his extravagant lifestyle and publicized affair with an actress brought him under suspicion both by J. Edgar Hoover and by his German controller in Spain, who was reassured when Popov returned to Britain and resumed sending tantalizing reports that mixed genuine nuggets of intelligence approved for disclosure by the Twenty Committee with fool's gold. Pujol, meanwhile, had enhanced his reputation in Berlin by warning the Abwehr of the Allied invasion of French North Africa in a letter that was conveniently delayed in transit by British authorities and arrived just after those

(continued on page 272)

THE ATLANTIC WALL AND ALLIED INVASION OF NORMANDY
June 6, 1944

PIERCING THE WALL The long chain of German fortifications called the Atlantic Wall was strongest along the Strait of Dover (Pas de Calais), which offered the shortest path from the English coast to the German border. Planners of Operation Overlord chose a longer invasion path by way of less heavily fortified Normandy and depended on the various deception campaigns of Operation Bodyguard to keep German forces pinned down elsewhere, defending against a possible invasion from Norway to the Mediterranean.

THE ATLANTIC WALL

When Japan's ambassador to Germany, Lt. Gen. Hiroshi Oshima, toured fortifications of the Atlantic Wall in late 1943 (below), no one suspected that he was spying unwittingly for the Allies. Oshima fervently hoped that German forces would repulse an Allied invasion, expected somewhere along the Atlantic coast of occupied Europe. But his detailed reports to Tokyo on German preparations were intercepted and deciphered by American cryptanalysts, who shared their Magic with the planners of Operation Overlord. Oshima's initial report on the Atlantic Wall in November (right) summed up the German defensive plan, which was to crush any attempted invasion "as close to the water edge as possible." Oshima added that Allied invaders might not be "stopped everywhere along the line; but even if some men did succeed in getting ashore, it would not be easy for them to smash the powerful counterattack of the German Reserves, who can rally with lightning speed."

Oshima's assessment supported the conclusion of those planning Operation Bodyguard—the deception campaign undertaken to shield Overlord—that victory depended not just on misleading the enemy as to where Allied forces would land but on keeping all available German reserves from rushing there after the invasion occurred. Oshima's subsequent reports confirmed that the area around Calais was more strongly fortified than Normandy and backed by powerful reserves—and that Hitler was susceptible to deceptions designed to keep those forces in place, defending against an expected invasion at Calais after the supposedly diversionary landings occurred at Normandy. With help from such intelligence acquired through code breaking, the Allied deception campaign proved so effective that when the Atlantic Wall was breached at Normandy in June 1944, the German response was not as swift or powerful as Oshima predicted and failed to stem the tide. ✪

INFORMANT Wearing his military uniform, Oshima (right) inspects an observation post on the Atlantic Wall. Shown here are the first two pages of a Magic decrypt of Oshima's report on his tour, transmitted to Tokyo on November 10, 1943.

From: Berlin (OSHIMA)
To: Tokyo
10 November 1943

#1349 (6-part message complete)

Reference my #1347ª.

My impressions and views on this inspection tour are as follows:

1.) All the German fortifications on the French coast are very close to the shore and it is quite clear that the Germans plan to smash any enemy attempt to land as close to the water edge as possible. Nevertheless, on the other hand, the forts centering around Naval bases are defending the frontal coasts by using excellent and effective posts and even within the scope of the smallest forts they are invested with the freedom of action which will permit them to hold out independently for a very long time. They are prepared with large Reserve Units which can be moved to the central theatre. From the Heeresgruppe (army groups) above to the regiments below, who are directly in charge of defending the coasts, it is the same. Were the enemy successful in a partial landing, lateral shell fire from the neighboring defense posts and the appearance of mobile forces would annihilate them. This may be called Germany's conception of defense in the West. Furthermore, in order to avoid futile losses in the fortifications, in men and materiel by the shelling and bombing of the enemy and to attain the maximum effect from a minimum number of soldiers performing defense

Japanese   #101709

                            Page #1

---

work, even individual machine gun nests are, without stint, strengthened with ferro-concrete. However, at the same time they have the facility of advancing directly to a counter-attack whenever the enemy should try an invasion. This is the same idea that was evident at the West Wall but in these fortifications the quality is ever so much better.

2.) The whole coast fortified by the Germans is very vast and now particularly when we cannot but realize the high quality of the aerial forces (sic), should the enemy gather together a powerful fleet and regardless of sacrifices, attempt to land, naturally it cannot necessarily be expected that they could be stopped everywhere along the line; but even if some men did succeed in getting ashore, it would not be easy for them to smash the counter-attack of the powerful German Reserves, who can rally with lightning speed. If you want my opinion, I say that we may well calculate that even though the American and British forces, for a short time, establish a bridge-head, under the present circumstances, it would be utterly impossible for them to form any new second front in France. I will tell you why I think so; in spite of the fact that the areas which I have just inspected are areas regarded as --G-- the way they are so efficiently prepared deepens this feeling in me. Moreover, they are actively expanding the engineering work. When we realize what a good job has been done, together with what they are still going to do, we can see what a hard time the enemy would have.

3.) What pleased me most on this tour was the morale and military spirit of the soldiers.

Japanese   #101709

                            Page #2

GUARDING THE WALL In this color-enhanced photographic image, a German sentinel stands beside a fearsome Krupp 380-mm artillery gun protruding from a concrete battery on the French coast. Such massive fortifications were built around Calais, but the Atlantic Wall was less formidable in Normandy.

OBSTACLES Field Marshal Erwin Rommel (front row, third from left) and other top German officers inspect a beach near Calais in April 1944, where obstructions have been placed to snag landing craft and amphibious tanks. Rommel took charge of coastal defenses along the Atlantic Wall in France and Belgium in late 1943 and fortified the beaches.

landings occurred in November 1942. He then scolded the Abwehr for not providing him with a radio to send such warnings instantaneously. MI5 soon equipped Pujol with a transmitter, which he claimed was provided by one of many accomplices in his fictional network of subagents scattered around Britain. Their reports supposedly formed the basis for more than 500 messages he sent by radio in the five months preceding D-Day to his case officer in Madrid, Maj. Karl-Erich Kühlenthal, who relayed that skewed intelligence to Berlin. Meanwhile, Pujol continued to send personal letters penned in invisible ink to his Abwehr superiors that portrayed him as a dedicated agent, who had left his beloved homeland and risked execution as a spy in Britain to help Hitler crush communism. In one note to Kühlenthal, he wrote that if not for his esteem for that officer and their shared determination to eradicate the Red "plague" in Europe, "I must tell you in all sincerity, and as a friend, that I would have returned to Spain long ago."

Pujol, Popov, and other double agents figured prominently in Fortitude South—the core effort to portray Calais as the main invasion target—and also contributed to peripheral deceptions designed to heighten German fears of attacks on occupied countries far from France, including Norway and Greece, and keep enemy forces tied down there. The supposed threat to Norway, where 12 German divisions were stationed, was code-named Fortitude North and involved simulating the presence of the fictitious British Fourth Army in Scotland, from which its imaginary troops would embark across the North Sea. A team of a few dozen wireless operators worked frantically to mimic the radio traffic of an entire army for eavesdroppers at distant German listening posts. Dummy warplanes made of plywood and canvas appeared overnight at bogus airfields that would look real enough to any Luftwaffe reconnaissance aircraft that evaded RAF defenses on a clear day. To lend substance to the illusion, genuine British warships and transports began assembling in the Firth of Forth on Scotland's east coast in late April to pose as an invasion fleet. Juan Pujol reported to Kühlenthal that one of his subagents observed troops in Scotland training for an amphibious assault. Meanwhile, British diplomats pressured neutral Sweden to allow Allied reconnaissance flights over its territory and hinted privately in Stockholm that an invasion of Norway was imminent, knowing that Swedish informants in league with the Germans would share that secret with them. By late May, Hitler was so alarmed that he sent more troops to Norway.

Deceptions were also staged in the Mediterranean, where Dudley Clarke used his own roster of double agents to warn German spymasters of a forthcoming British assault on Greece that never materialized. That scheme proved more effective than the ploy carried out by M. E. Clifton James, a British actor who bore an uncanny resemblance to Gen. Bernard Montgomery, assigned to command the Normandy invasion forces. After meticulous rehearsals in which he learned to mimic Monty's gait and gestures, James was sent to Gibraltar and North Africa in late May to impersonate the famous general and give the impression that he was planning something momentous in that theater rather than in France. While touring as the abstemious Montgomery, James was forbidden to smoke or

BOMBING RUN On June 5, 1944, an American B-17 bombs German coastal defenses near Boulogne, France, located southwest of Calais along the Strait of Dover. Such bombing runs intensified as D-Day approached to reinforce the impression that the Allied invasion forces would make their big push in this area rather than on the Normandy coast.

SHADOW WAR At left, two photos pasted into a confidential British report on visual concealment and deception show how a three-dimensional dummy Spitfire cast a more convincing shadow than did a flat model of the same fighter. Because such details might be noticed by German reconnaissance pilots or photo-reconnaissance analysts, British deception artists went to the trouble of producing fully formed dummy aircraft.

THREE DIMENSIONAL SPITFIRE.
In this case built on old "Moth" undercarriage.

FLAT SPITFIRE.

THREE DIMENSIONAL DUMMY BOSTON

THREE DIMENSIONAL DUMMY BOSTON
SHOWING CONSTRUCTION

BOGUS BOMBER At right, a dummy RAF Boston light bomber—a British version of the Douglas A-20 Havoc—is pictured under construction (bottom) and in finished form (top), with a paint job that made the dummy's hollow wooden shell look deceptively fit for combat.

MONTY'S DOUBLE Actor M. E. Clifton James (top) mimicked Gen. Bernard Montgomery (above) in variety shows before he was called on to impersonate him officially. James posed as the renowned Allied commander on a trip to Gibraltar and North Africa in May 1944 to make German observers suspect that Monty, who was busy preparing for the invasion of occupied France, was instead planning an offensive in the Mediterranean.

drink, but he kept a flask under wraps and became so intoxicated on an overnight flight that aides were barely able to sober him up for his next appearance. His performances fooled some onlookers but failed to sway their intended audience—German intelligence officers, who had little doubt by the time James began posing as Monty that the next big Allied blow would fall somewhere along the Atlantic Wall. Indeed, reports from agents they trusted in England, including the highly regarded Juan Pujol, indicated that the formidable First U.S. Army Group (FUSAG) would soon land at Calais under a commander whose reputation in Germany rivaled Monty's, Maj. Gen. George S. Patton.

In fact, Patton was playing a role that was far more delicate and devious than the one James was assigned. An exponent of hard-charging armored assaults of the sort that enabled German forces to conquer France within a matter of weeks in 1940, Patton helped secure North Africa and Sicily for the Allies in 1943 and appeared destined for a leading role in the campaign to liberate France until Eisenhower rebuked him for rashly accusing two hospitalized American soldiers of shirking their duty and slapping them. That notorious incident did little to diminish Patton's stature in the eyes of German generals, who viewed him as one of their toughest foes. They were not surprised by reports that he had regained Ike's trust and been placed in charge in FUSAG. What they did not know was that Patton's command was purely ceremonial and that FUSAG was a hoax, consisting of some real units that were destined for other assignments and many fictional divisions. Patton was itching to lead troops in battle in France and would eventually do so as commander of the U.S. Third Army, but his imposing presence and theatrical flair suited him for this deceptive role. Newspaper accounts of his public appearances near the supposed FUSAG staging area along the Strait of Dover helped confirm German intelligence officers in their assessment that what they called Armeegruppe Patton posed an imminent threat to Calais.

The FUSAG bluff was a major production, whose special effects included hundreds of dummy tanks, airplanes, and landing craft, produced with the help of motion picture technicians adept at fabricating convincing props. They were proof against aerial reconnaissance but would not stand up to close inspection, so British officials imposed a 10-mile exclusion zone on the coast, guarded by checkpoints, to shield the phony buildup along the Strait of Dover and the massive concentration of real troops and munitions at Southampton and other ports along the English Channel, across from Normandy.

The greatest challenge facing the planners of Fortitude South was to sustain the bogus FUSAG threat after D-Day and prevent a rapid redeployment of German forces from Calais to Normandy. That task was assigned to MI5's most accomplished double agents, who inflated the Allied order of battle in Britain by adding FUSAG's fictional units to those in General Montgomery's 21st Army Group, which would do the actual fighting. Intelligence chiefs in Berlin concluded from reports submitted by Dusko Popov and other spies under MI5's control that there were over 90 Allied divisions in Britain, nearly twice the actual number and more than enough to launch a second invasion across the strait after Monty's troops landed at Normandy.

One development that worried John Masterman, head of the Twenty Committee, and others overseeing the Double Cross system in London was the ouster of Admiral Canaris, who lost control of the Abwehr in February 1944 when Hitler ordered the creation of a "unified German secret intelligence service" under the command of Reichsführer-SS Himmler. Hitler did not yet consider Canaris a traitor, but he sacked the admiral and placed him under house arrest for the same reason that MI5 hoped he would remain in office—mounting evidence that Abwehr officers serving under him were incompetent, corrupt, and in some cases disloyal to the Nazi regime. Masterman feared that with the Abwehr under SS control, "new brooms would sweep away much that we had tried to preserve," including the cozy relationship between Popov and his controller in Spain, Maj. Ludovico von Karsthoff, who profited by vouching for his star agent and skimming off funds authorized to support Popov and his supposed spy ring. Karsthoff was ousted soon after the SS took charge of the Abwehr. Another officer involved in financial irregularities, Johann Jebsen—who had recruited Popov for the Abwehr—was seized in Madrid in late April and hauled off to Berlin, where he was grilled by the Gestapo.

Jebsen's arrest posed a dire threat to the Double Cross operation and the D-Day deceptions because he too had been turned by MI5 and knew that Popov's reports on FUSAG were meant to fool Hitler and his chiefs. He was also aware that Juan Pujol was a double agent working for MI5. With Jebsen in custody and under interrogation, wrote Col. Roger Hesketh, who implemented the FUSAG hoax, the Germans might realize that some if not all of their spies in England "were under Allied control. They would then conclude that the messages they were receiving were the opposite of the truth." That would negate efforts to portray Calais as the main target and point the Germans to the obvious alternative—an all-out assault on Normandy. Masterman recognized that risk, but he and the Twenty Committee decided to stay the course and hope that the case against Jebsen in Berlin was limited to his "personal delinquencies" in financial matters. Gestapo agents may have suspected him of being a double agent and tried to beat the truth out of him, but if so they failed. Jebsen ended up in a concentration camp and probably died there. Unaware of his fate, MI5 decided to shut down his closest link within the agency, Popov, but Pujol and other double agents remained in business.

Another crisis faced by deception planners in London as the invasion approached involved Russian-born journalist Nathalie "Lily" Sergueiew, who had been recruited as an Abwehr spy in Paris by Maj. Emile Kliemann and offered to spy for him in England, where she had relatives. She arrived there by way of Spain in 1943, after making contact with a British intelligence officer in Madrid, and became a double agent for MI5 under the code name Treasure. Described by Masterman as "exceptionally temperamental and troublesome," she was plagued by a kidney ailment and depressed by the loss of her pet dog, which was quarantined in Spain as required by the British and died. Yet she proved quite valuable to MI5. The reports she mailed Kliemann were so highly regarded that he supplied her with a radio when she met with him in neutral Portugal in early 1944. Returning to London, she helped promote the FUSAG threat by signaling Kliemann that she had a lover in that

(continued on page 278)

PATTON'S PLOY Lt. Gen. George Patton inspects some genuine troops in his largely fictional First U.S. Army Group (FUSAG), portrayed as a massive force that was preparing to cross the Strait of Dover and land near Calais. Taking part in this deception, intended to keep German forces in place around Calais while the invasion unfolded at Normandy, came easily to Patton, who called himself a "goddamn natural-born ham."

"When they have established bridgeheads in Normandy and Brittany—they will then come forward with an all-out Second Front across the Straits of Dover."

HITLER TO JAPANESE AMBASSADOR HIROSHI OSHIMA, PREDICTING ALLIED INVASION PLANS

MAPPING THE INVASION

No military operation conducted during World War II was more dependent on accurate intelligence and strict secrecy than Overlord, the massive invasion aimed at Omaha Beach—charted in the top secret map at right—and nearby landing sites on the coast of Normandy. Allied Supreme Commander Dwight Eisenhower received a grim preview of what might happen if the enemy learned of the invasion plans when he staged a major training exercise for Overlord on the English coast in late April 1944, involving nearly 30,000 troops. Alerted by heavy radio traffic from units participating in the drill, German torpedo boats moved in at night and targeted LSTs (landing ship tanks), claiming the lives of 749 men. Survivors were forbidden to speak of the disaster.

Mapping landing sites for Overlord was risky if it suggested to the Germans that Normandy was the target but essential if the complex operation was to succeed. Preliminary intelligence for the mapmakers came from French laborers who were conscripted to build the Atlantic Wall and reported on coastal fortifications through French resistance groups and Allied agents in contact with them. Frogmen made furtive approaches at night to pinpoint the locations of obstructions, pillboxes, and batteries. Aerial reconnaissance was performed openly along the Normandy coast without betraying invasion plans because similar flights were conducted around Calais and other possible landing sites. Pilots swooped down to take close-ups like the one below, risking all to help cartographers produce exquisitely detailed charts that saved lives on D-Day. ✪

CLOSE CALL Workers scurry away as an Allied reconnaissance plane zooms in to photograph French beach obstructions. Aerial reconnaissance was crucial to producing maps like the one at right, marked "Top Secret—Bigot" like other documents detailing the invasion. It was carried into battle by Ensign Joseph Vaghi, who landed at the Easy Red sector of Omaha Beach on D-Day to direct men and equipment as a beachmaster.

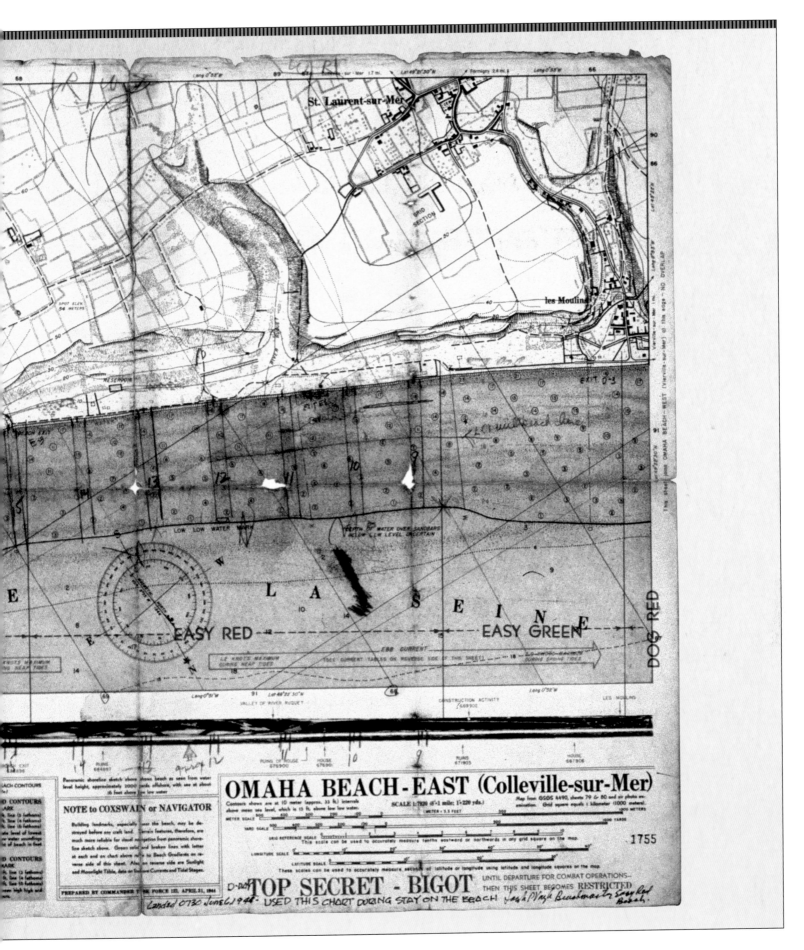

OMAHA BEACH - EAST (Colleville-sur-Mer)

SCALE 1:7920 (6"=1 mile; 1"=220 yds.)

NOTE to COXSWAIN or NAVIGATOR

TOP SECRET - BIGOT

A GALLERY OF DOUBLE AGENTS

An international cast of characters, the double agents pictured here—all of whom served Britain's MI5 while pretending to spy for Germany—came from five different European countries and varied widely in temperament, ranging from the supremely confident Dusko Popov to the moody, mercurial Lily Sergueiew. What they had in common was a genius for duplicity or the ability to appear to be what they were not—faithful servants of Hitler's Reich, risking their lives to help Germany triumph. ✪

CODE NAME: TRICYCLE

SPIED FOR: GREAT BRITAIN

SPIED AGAINST: GERMANY

DUSKO POPOV Under suspicion by the Germans after he failed to acquire any useful intelligence for them during his journey to America in 1941–42—when he was actually working for the Allies—Yugoslav playboy Popov exonerated himself by blaming his Abwehr handlers: "You send me there with no help whatsoever, no contacts, a few miserable dollars, and you expect me to produce results in no time." Cowed by his prize agent, Popov's German case officer agreed with him that it was all "Berlin's fault."

CODE NAME: GARBO

SPIED FOR: GREAT BRITAIN

SPIED AGAINST: GERMANY

JUAN PUJOL An inventive Spaniard, Pujol was constantly adding to the roster of fictional subagents who supposedly provided him with the misleading information he relayed to German intelligence officers. They included a covert band of pro-Nazi Welsh nationalists known as Brothers in the Aryan World Order and a secretary at the War Office whom he claimed to be involved with and described as "delightfully indiscreet," providing him with confidential details on Allied plans as D-Day approached.

force, which was supposedly gathering strength along the Strait of Dover. In May, however, she shocked her handler, Mary Sherer, by confiding that she and Kliemann had arranged for a coded signal to be inserted in her messages if she was forced to send him false information—and was tempted to use it because she resented her British overseers and blamed them for the loss of her dog. MI5's Tar Robertson feared that she had already alerted Kliemann to the FUSAG deception or might yet do so, despite her confession to Sherer. He had later messages from her composed by others and sent by a trusted radio operator. She eventually revealed the signal to Sherer, who reviewed her messages and confirmed that she had not betrayed the Allies by using it.

Another agent whose loyalty to the British was initially questioned performed admirably for MI5 in the buildup to D-Day. Roman Garby-Czerniawski was an officer in the Polish Air Force who had fled to France in 1939 and remained there after the Germans occupied Paris, where he organized a spy network called Interallié to supply the Allies with intelligence on German defenses and military movements. He was captured in 1941 by Sgt. Hugo Bleicher, a cunning Abwehr officer who allowed him to escape from prison and sent him to spy for the Reich in England. Instead, he confessed to an officer of the Polish government-in-exile there and said he wanted to work for the British. After interrogating him at length, Tar Robertson and staff concluded that his devotion to Poland was such that he could be trusted not to betray its British allies. Enlisted as a double agent under the code name Brutus, he proved crucial to the Fortitude deceptions because Bleicher still believed in him and he could be attached to fictional Allied military forces, as other Polish exiles were to real British units. In mid-May 1944, he reported by radio that he had been posted as a liaison officer to FUSAG headquarters. He provided the SS-controlled Abwehr with a thorough order of battle for Armeegruppe Patton and won rave reviews from German officers, one of whom wrote that his "outstanding reports greatly contributed to the clarification of the enemy picture."

In fact, that picture had been thoroughly muddled by false leads that left Hitler expecting diversionary assaults at Normandy and elsewhere before Patton's fabled army group delivered the big blow. In late May, the Führer met with Ambassador Oshima, who summed up their conversation in a report to Tokyo that was intercepted and deciphered, providing Allied planners with proof that the true nature of Overlord had been successfully obscured by the artful lies of Operation Bodyguard. Hitler told Oshima that he expected "diversionary attacks" in several places, including Norway, Normandy, and Brittany in southwest France—a threat puffed up by another double agent on MI5's roster, Elvira Chaudoir, the seductive daughter of a Peruvian diplomat who sent the Abwehr secrets she supposedly wheedled from men in high places in London. Once the Allies had established "bridgeheads in Normandy and Brittany," Hitler assured Oshima, "they will then come forward with an all-out Second Front across the Straits of Dover."

DOUBLE-CROSSED AND DEFEATED

The invasion of Normandy, postponed until June 6 because of foul weather, was so massive that it could not easily be portrayed as a diversion once it began. But MI5 managed to sustain that illusion with a stellar performance from double agent Juan Pujol, who lived up to his code name Garbo by delivering an ingenious script he coauthored with his handler, Tommy Harris, and others at the agency. To help ensure that the Germans would not lose faith in Pujol after D-Day because his previous reports had diverted their attention from Normandy, MI5 got permission from Eisenhower for him to warn his controller in Madrid by radio of the invasion several hours before the first troops came ashore there on the sixth. That warning would then be relayed to Berlin and was meant to arrive there just as the invasion was getting under way. As it turned out, Pujol's report did not get through until later that morning because the Abwehr radio operator in Madrid skipped his night shift and did not receive the message until day had dawned. Pujol then blamed his controller, Kühlenthal, for the foul-up: "This makes me question your seriousness and your sense of responsibility . . . Were it not for my ideals and my faith I would abandon this work." Appalled by the thought of losing his prize agent, Kühlenthal told him that he was cherished by the Abwehr and begged him to remain "with us in the supreme and decisive hours of the struggle for the future of Europe."

Assured that he was still in good standing with his German overseers, Pujol followed up with a lengthy radio report on June 9 that described the operations in Normandy—where nearly 200,000 Allied troops had already landed and more than a million would come ashore by month's end—as "a diversionary maneuver designed to draw off enemy reserves in order then to make a decisive attack in another place." Citing the inflated estimates of troop strength in Britain that other double agents had spooned out and intelligence officers in Berlin had swallowed, Pujol reckoned that the Allies were "left with some fifty divisions with which to attempt a second blow." Most were stationed in southeast England, he claimed, and would

CODE NAME: ARTIST

SPIED FOR: GREAT BRITAIN

SPIED AGAINST: GERMANY

JOHANN JEBSEN Fearing he might soon be arrested for financial fraud as an Abwehr officer in Spain, Jebsen concocted a story to escape to England without alerting superiors that both he and his confidant Popov were working for the British. Jebsen claimed that his father had once saved the life of the banker Lord Rothschild, who owed "a debt of gratitude" to Jebsen and was pulling strings to have him admitted to Britain, where he could then spy for Germany. That scheme was foiled when the Gestapo seized him.

CODE NAME: TREASURE

SPIED FOR: GREAT BRITAIN

SPIED AGAINST: GERMANY

NATHALIE "LILY" SERGUEIEW Born in Russia and raised in Paris, Sergueiew often got along better with her Abwehr handler, Maj. Emile Kliemann, than she did with her British controllers. "He has always treated me very well," she told them, "and it makes me feel very badly to have to lie to him and cheat him." Yet she continued to feed him false leads. "For three years I have been acting a part," she noted in her diary. "If I survive the war, will I be able to readapt? Will I be able to become *normal* again?"

CODE NAME: BRUTUS

SPIED FOR: GREAT BRITAIN

SPIED AGAINST: GERMANY

ROMAN GARBY-CZERNIAWSKI Like Juan Pujol, this Polish patriot continued to mislead the Germans after D-Day, indicating that Patton's fictitious FUSAG would soon launch a massive invasion across the Strait of Dover. Garby-Czerniawski apologized for not giving Berlin warning of the Normandy landings, explaining that he was totally caught up in his duties at FUSAG headquarters, which was in a "state of alert." Patton's army group, he added, was ready to attack "at any moment."

JEDBURGH TEAM Sgt. A. E. Holdham, a British radio operator, stands at right in liberated Paris with another member of his three-man Jedburgh team, which parachuted into France on August 14, 1944. A joint effort by the SOE, OSS, and Charles de Gaulle's government-in-exile to help French resistance groups fight German occupation forces, Jedburgh teams each had one radio operator and one or more French members.

KEEPSAKES One Jedburgh team member prepared for close combat by carrying the knuckle-duster above when he infiltrated France. Some British recruits on Jedburgh missions proudly wore their special forces wings (far left).

NIGHT DROP Fitted with parachutes, life vests, and other gear, Jedburgh team members prepare to embark on a mission from Harrington Airfield in England on the B-24 in the background, which would drop them into France before the night ended. In June and July of 1944, "Carpetbaggers" of the U.S. Army Air Force's 801st Bombardment Group flew 1,300 such sorties to France in modified B-24s, equipped with "Joe holes" through which parachutists descended.

have ample air support if, as appeared likely, they crossed the Strait of Dover and took the shortest route to their "final objective," Berlin. His considered opinion based on reports from his subagents was that the landings in Normandy were a trap set by the Allies "to make us move all our reserves in a hurried strategical disposition which we would later regret."

The gist of Pujol's message reached Hitler that same evening, along with a note from Col. Friedrich Krummacher, who served as liaison between the SS-controlled intelligence service and the German high command, stating that the report "underlines the opinion already formed by us that a further attack is to be expected in another place (Belgium?)." Reinforced in his belief that the Allies still planned to land along the Pas de Calais near the French border with Belgium, Hitler left the German 15th Army in place there for six weeks while Allied troops broke out of their bridgehead in Normandy. Eisenhower's intelligence chief, Maj. Gen. Kenneth Strong, wrote later that had the Germans "moved their divisions from the Pas de Calais to Normandy in the early days when bad weather hampered the buildup and air support, the Allied invasion would have been in great jeopardy."

Some German divisions were redeployed promptly to Normandy from elsewhere in France, but they were tracked by Allied commanders using Ultra, slowed by air raids that blasted French railways and highways, and harried by French partisans, who launched widespread attacks against German occupation forces on cue from the BBC, which broadcast a seemingly innocuous line of French poetry on the evening of June 5 as a signal for the uprising to begin. An Abwehr counterintelligence officer had learned of that signal months in advance and warned superiors that it would precede an invasion. But the only listeners who picked up the broadcast and realized its significance were with the 15th Army, and their alert did not reach German forces defending Normandy.

Fearing murderous reprisals by German troops, Eisenhower had reluctantly approved plans to support the uprising in France by arming and training partisans there. Beginning on the night of June 5, the SOE and OSS combined to implement Operation Jedburgh, carried out by small commando teams who dropped by parachute behind German lines, first in France and later in Belgium and the Netherlands as the Allied offensive in Western Europe expanded. Jedburgh teams in France included members of de Gaulle's Free French forces, who directed covert operations there in conjunction with the Maquis and other resistance fighters.

Partisan assaults on German forces proved costly for civilians, particularly those in the path of the 2nd SS Panzer Division ("Das Reich"), which was redeployed from southern France to Normandy and brutally retaliated for attacks intended to stall its advance. One woman in the town of Tulle returned home from shopping on June 9 to find her husband and son hanging from the balcony of her house. "They were just two of a hundred men seized at random and killed in cold blood by the SS," she testified. "The children and wives were forced to watch while they strung them up to the lamp-posts and balconies outside their own homes." On June 10, SS troops of Das Reich entered the village of Oradour-sur-Glane and slaughtered virtually the entire population, including more than 400 women and children who were locked inside a church, which was then set afire. That was a terrible price to pay, but partisan attacks and the Allied bombing

"These operations [in Normandy] are a diversionary maneuver designed to draw off enemy reserves in order then to make a decisive attack in another place."

JUAN PUJOL IN A POST-D-DAY REPORT TO INTELLIGENCE OFFICERS IN BERLIN

DECEPTIVE CHAFF A British war worker turns out chaff—strips of aluminum used to confuse enemy radar. On D-Day, Allied planes sought to divert German attention from Normandy by dropping large bundles of chaff over the Strait of Dover to simulate the radar reflections produced by an invasion fleet approaching Calais.

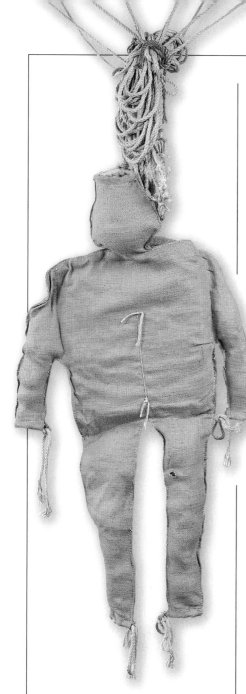

D-DAY DUMMY Hundreds of these dummies, dubbed "Ruperts," were dropped by parachute before dawn on D-Day in areas far from the actual landing zones of real Allied paratroopers to distract and confuse German defenders. Fireworks triggered when they hit the ground added to the illusion that those dummies—which looked lifelike when glimpsed in the dark from a distance—meant business.

campaign—which also claimed civilian lives—delayed that SS division and other German units dispatched to Normandy and contributed to the liberation of France.

The D-Day deceptions were seemingly exposed when the phantom FUSAG threat failed to materialize and its alleged commander, Patton, ended up bolstering the invasion of Normandy with his U.S. Third Army. Yet Juan Pujol retained the trust of German spymasters by claiming that the Allies were shifting FUSAG forces to Normandy to overcome stiff German opposition there, a redeployment that supposedly led Patton to protest so vehemently to Eisenhower that he cut the FUSAG chief down a notch and subordinated him to General Montgomery in France. Far from being suspected of misleading the Abwehr, Pujol was notified by his controller in July that "the Führer has awarded the Iron Cross to you for your extraordinary merits." Pujol modestly replied that "this prize has been won not only by me but also by the other comrades, who, through their advice and directives, have made possible my work here." That was an apparent reference to his fictional subagents in Britain, but it was also a veiled tribute to his real comrades at MI5, who managed his case and others so skillfully that some Germans on the receiving end did not realize they had been double-crossed until long after they were defeated.

THE VALKYRIE PLOT

The successful Allied landings at Normandy came as a bitter blow not only to German officers who were loyal to Hitler but also to one of his most determined foes within the Wehrmacht, 36-year-old Col. Claus von Stauffenberg, chief of staff of the German Reserve Army. Like others who were secretly conspiring against their Führer, he had clung to the faint hope that the U.S. and Britain might reach a separate peace with Germany if Hitler was assassinated. But the invasion of France signaled that the Americans and British were no less determined to defeat and occupy the Reich than were their Soviet allies approaching Germany from the east. If the conspirators succeeded in killing Hitler and ending the Nazi regime, they would then have to choose between prolonging a war that would surely end in a crushing defeat for Germany or surrendering unconditionally to the Allies, who would carve up the Reich into occupation zones.

Surrendering might spare hundreds of thousands of Germans from being sacrificed for a lost cause, but it would not be an easy concession for Stauffenberg, an aristocrat whose ancestors had long led Germans into battle. He was a proud nationalist who had supported the Führer's efforts to forge a Greater German Reich and served under him without qualms until the disastrous invasion of Russia, when he concluded that Hitler was as great a menace to his own army and nation as he was to the Jews his SS task forces slaughtered with the complicity of German commanders, covering the Wehrmacht in shame. Stauffenberg was glad when he was transferred from Russia to North Africa, but his combat role ended when his car was strafed and bombed in Tunisia in April 1943. Although he lost an eye, his right forearm, and two fingers on his left hand, he emerged convinced that he had received new lease on life for the purpose of taking Hitler's life. He had second thoughts after D-Day when he realized that toppling the regime in Berlin would not save Germany from defeat, but he was reassured by a fellow conspirator, General Tresckow, who had tried to kill

Hitler a year earlier. "The assassination must be attempted, at any cost," Tresckow insisted. "Even should that fail, the attempt to seize power in the capital must be undertaken. We must prove to the world and to future generations that the men of the German resistance movement dared to take the decisive step and to hazard their lives upon it."

Stauffenberg's prominent position with the Reserve Army in Berlin placed him at the heart of a conspiracy designed to exploit an existing plan called Operation Valkyrie, which Hitler had approved. It involved using forces not on combat duty—including reservists under the command of Stauffenberg's superior, Gen. Friedrich Fromm—to suppress civil unrest in Germany, including a possible uprising by conscripted foreign laborers, who toiled for the Reich in conditions little better than that of slave laborers in German concentration camps. Aided and encouraged by Gen. Friedrich Olbricht, Stauffenberg secretly altered the plan to enable officers conspiring with them to take charge of Valkyrie troops and suppress SS forces and other Nazi loyalists following Hitler's assassination. It was a precarious scheme that involved inducing the wavering General Fromm to set Valkyrie in motion. Fromm made no firm commitment to the conspirators, but he knew what they were plotting and hinted that he would back them once Hitler was eliminated. They hoped to form a new government led by prominent figures long opposed to the Führer such as Gen. Ludwig Beck, Field Marshal Erwin von Witzleben, and Carl Friedrich Goerdeler, former mayor of Leipzig, who had sought British support against Hitler before the war and would serve as chancellor if the coup succeeded, using his ties to the Allies to try to spare Germany harsh treatment in defeat.

"The assassination must be attempted, at any cost."

GEN. HENNING VON TRESCKOW TO COL. CLAUS VON STAUFFENBERG, WHO WORRIED AFTER D-DAY THAT KILLING HITLER MIGHT NOT SAVE GERMANY

BEGINNING OF THE END An American soldier lays low under fire on Omaha Beach in this famous D-Day picture by war photographer Robert Capa. Despite heavy losses here on June 6, the Allies established a bridgehead and poured in so many troops that German commanders grew increasingly pessimistic. Rommel wrote Hitler on July 14 that "the unequal struggle is nearing an end," and offered tacit approval to officers who hoped to spare Germany from ruin by eliminating Hitler.

After D-Day, Stauffenberg was summoned on several occasions to brief Hitler on the readiness of the Reserve Army, which might be needed in combat. He had proposed conducting a suicide mission in which he would blow himself up along with Hitler, but other conspirators considered him too valuable and wanted him in Berlin after the assassination to spur Fromm into action and ensure the success of Valkyrie. So Stauffenberg planned to carry a time bomb in a briefcase, place it as close as possible to Hitler during a conference, and excuse himself before it detonated. He hoped to do so when Reichsführer-SS Himmler and Reichsmarschall Hermann Göring were present and might be killed as well, but no such occasion arose. By mid-July, he could wait no longer without risking exposure of the wide-ranging conspiracy. When he was called to a meeting on July 20 with Hitler and other officers at the Wolf's Lair, the Führer's fortified command center in East Prussia, Stauffenberg knew the time had come. As he told one of his confederates, "We have crossed the Rubicon."

MISSED CHANCE Colonel Stauffenberg stands at attention at left as Hitler greets another officer at his Wolf's Lair headquarters on July 15, 1944. Stauffenberg was unable to target Hitler on this occasion but resolved to carry out the deed the next time he was summoned to headquarters.

Stauffenberg and his aide, Lt. Werner von Haeften, flew from Berlin to the Wolf's Lair that morning, with two concealed bombs that Stauffenberg planned to carry into the 12:30 meeting in his briefcase. It was a hot day, and he asked for a room where he could change his sweat-soaked shirt with Haeften's help. That gave Stauffenberg cover as he began priming the first of the two bombs by using pliers to break a vial containing acid, which would silently eat away at a detonator wire and trigger the device. He had practiced the procedure but only managed to prime one bomb before he was summoned to the meeting. Acid-activated fuses were imprecise, and he could not be sure if the bomb would explode in as little as 10 or 15 minutes or take twice as long to go off. Among those present was Gen. Walter Warlimont, who later marveled at Stauffenberg's composure as he entered the conference room, "one eye covered by a black patch, a maimed arm in an empty uniform sleeve, standing tall and upright, looking directly at Hitler." He took his place three seats to the right of Hitler around 12:35, with the briefcase at his feet.

Asked if he wished to hear from Stauffenberg, Hitler replied that his report could wait until later. Stauffenberg then slipped out, explaining that he had to confer with a colleague in Berlin by phone and would soon return. In his absence, the officer seated to his right, Col. Heinz Brandt, knocked over Stauffenberg's briefcase, then picked it up and placed it behind one of the table's heavy wooden legs, farther away from Hitler. At 12:42, the bomb detonated with such force that some at the Wolf's Lair thought an air raid was under way. Stauffenberg and Haeften had left the building and were approaching their car when the explosion occurred. Assuming that Hitler was dead, they exited the compound amid the confusion and flew back to Berlin. Soon after the blast, however, Hitler stumbled from the wreckage, his hair singed and his eardrums punctured but in no danger of dying. Brandt, two other officers, and a stenographer seated near the briefcase lost their lives, but it would have taken both bombs to kill the more distant Hitler.

Word that he had survived the attempt on his life soon reached General Fromm in Berlin, who refused to activate Operation Valkyrie. When Stauffenberg returned that afternoon, he and other conspirators locked up Fromm, insisted that Hitler was dead, and ordered officers to take action against the Nazi regime. In Paris, more than a thousand Gestapo agents and other SS men were rounded up and placed under armed guard that evening. But by 10 p.m., the coup in Berlin had collapsed. Troops loyal to Hitler stormed Reserve Army headquarters and freed Fromm, who tried to conceal his prior knowledge of the plot—for which he would later be executed—by ordering ringleaders who had gathered at his headquarters eliminated. General Beck, former chief of the German general staff, was allowed to shoot himself, but Stauffenberg, Haeften, Olbricht, and several others died before a firing squad shortly after midnight.

Their fate was preferable to that of other conspirators who were later arrested, convicted, and hanged from meat hooks in such a way that they died slowly by strangulation—agonizing executions that were recorded on film and watched eagerly by Hitler. Ultimately, several thousand Germans came under suspicion and paid with their lives, among them prominent figures such as Field Marshal Erwin Rommel who had neither plotted to kill Hitler nor alerted him to the threat when asked by conspirators to join them. Rommel took his own life rather than be condemned and executed—as did General Tresckow, who was wholly committed to killing the Nazi dictator. With his last words, Tresckow spoke for many who perished in Valkyrie's bitter aftermath: "I am convinced, now as much as ever, that we have done the right thing. I believe that Hitler is the arch-enemy, not only of Germany, but of the entire world."

HITLER'S LAST GASP

Failure of the Valkyrie plot left Germany in the hands of a dictator who would sooner see his nation reduced to rubble than yield to his foes. Hitler had long vowed never to surrender, however desperate Germany's plight might be. "We may be destroyed," he declared, "but if we are, we shall drag a world with us—a world in flames." By late 1944, large sectors of Berlin and other German cities had been bombed and incinerated. Allied armies were approaching from both the west and the east, where an invasion by Russians intent on avenging Hitler's horrific assault on their homeland posed a dire threat to the German populace. Soviet forces had entered Nazi-occupied Poland in July and advanced to within striking distance of Warsaw, where resistance fighters of the Polish Home Army tried to liberate their capital before it fell to the Russians and were crushed by SS troops. Polish resisters who survived that tragic uprising would later be arrested by the NKVD—the dreaded Soviet security force that supplanted the SS as the Red Army forced the Wehrmacht out of Poland and other Eastern European countries. Victims of that takeover included not only those seized as political prisoners by Soviet authorities but also civilians in nations allied with Germany such as Hungary who were attacked, pillaged, or raped by Russian troops—a grim preview of the fate awaiting millions of people when the Red Army invaded the Reich.

"We have crossed the Rubicon."

COL. CLAUS VON STAUFFENBERG AFTER BEING CALLED TO ATTEND ANOTHER CONFERENCE WITH HITLER AT THE WOLF'S LAIR ON JULY 20, 1944

WRECKAGE Hitler's conference room sustained the damage shown here after a bomb planted by Stauffenberg detonated under the collapsed table at center. The explosion was so loud that Stauffenberg, who left the room shortly before the bomb went off on July 20, thought that Hitler had been killed, only to discover after returning to Berlin that the Führer was alive and the plot to seize power was collapsing.

SAFE TO EAT Whether dining in style or eating unceremoniously with German officers (left), Hitler habitually had his food tasted beforehand to make sure he was not being poisoned. Among those who served him as a food taster was Maria Wölk (above), who was in her mid-20s when she was forced into Hitler's service and lived to tell of her experiences seven decades later.

THE BITTER ORDEAL OF HITLER'S LAST SURVIVING FOOD TASTER

Maria Wölk, the young wife of a German soldier who was off fighting in Russia, thought she had found refuge from the horrors of war when she left her parents' bombed-out home in Berlin and went to live with her mother-in-law in a quiet village in East Prussia. But Hitler's wartime headquarters, the Wolf's Lair, was only a few miles away. One day in 1942, SS men came to the door and forced her to join a group of 15 young women who served as Hitler's food tasters while he was at headquarters. Like despised monarchs of old who lived in constant fear of being poisoned, he had all the food that would be served to him tasted an hour before he consumed it.

Lacking volunteers for that task, the SS forced women like Wölk to serve as Hitler's guinea pigs. They sat together around a table, tasting different items in a morbid ritual that was repeated daily and often left the tasters in tears. "There was never meat because Hitler was a vegetarian," Wölk recalled. "The food was good—very good. But we couldn't enjoy it."

Wölk was at the Wolf's Lair when the bomb planted by Stauffenberg detonated. She was jarred by the explosion and heard someone yell that Hitler was dead, which would have released her from her grim task. But he survived and her plight grew worse. Security was tightened at the Wolf's Lair, and she and others who had been living at home were instead penned up at headquarters "like caged animals," she said. One night, an SS man climbed a ladder, crawled through her window, and raped her.

In late 1944, as Soviet troops approached East Prussia, the Wolf's Lair was evacuated. The other food tasters were left behind there to face the wrath of the Russians, but an officer took pity on Wölk and found her a place on one of the last trains to Berlin. She was later told that those other women were shot by the Soviets. When the Russians reached Berlin, Wölk had no defense against them and was raped repeatedly. "It was hell on earth. The nightmare never goes away," she said of those assaults, which left her unable to bear children. Unlike many German women who were widowed by the war, however, she was reunited in 1946 with her husband, whom she had given up for dead. He was barely recognizable, having almost starved to death in a POW camp, but he recuperated in her care. Wölk tried to put her ordeal behind her, but it haunted her dreams. Not until her 95th birthday, nearly 70 years after the conflict ended, did Hitler's last surviving food taster speak publicly of her bitter wartime experiences. "I never saw Hitler," she remarked, "but I had to risk my life for him every day." ✪

German officers recognized that the Soviets to their east would be far more dangerous conquerors than the Allies to their west. Many who had plotted against Hitler hoped to come to terms with those western Allies or, if that was not possible and defeat was unavoidable, favored allowing them to occupy the Reich while holding off the Russians as long as possible. But surrender on either front was out of the question while Hitler remained in power. Commanders who survived the purge that followed the assassination attempt in July were powerless to prevent him from pursuing a strategy many regarded as futile if not suicidal for Germany—committing what resources the Reich held in reserve, including secret weapons that were years in the making, to a desperate effort to repulse the western Allies before the Soviets broke through in the east. Hitler envisioned another German blitzkrieg like the one that sliced through enemy defenses to Dunkirk in 1940, only this time the target would be Antwerp, the crucial supply base for Allied troops in France and Belgium. But the Wehrmacht was no longer capable of such lightning strikes. Short of fuel and backed by ill-trained reserves ranging in age from 16 to 60, the forces Hitler committed to that offensive in December 1944 made quick gains initially but were trapped in the salient they forged and defeated in the grueling Battle of the Bulge. Hitler ended up losing nearly 100,000 men and 600 tanks in that debacle as the Soviets renewed their offensive in January 1945 and closed in on Germany. Gen. Heinz Guderian, the

DOOMED UPRISING **At left, partisans of the Polish Home Army fight in the rubble against German forces during the 1944 Warsaw Uprising, which was crushed in August by SS forces who conducted murderous reprisals. Some resistance fighters were executed by firing squad (below), while other people who took no part in the fighting perished in tenements that were set afire while SS troops waited outside with machine guns to shoot those who fled. "The front entrance was full of the bodies of those who had tried to escape from the flames," recalled one survivor. "No one came out alive unless by miracle."**

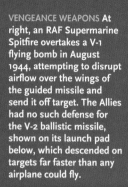

VENGEANCE WEAPONS **At right, an RAF Supermarine Spitfire overtakes a V-1 flying bomb in August 1944, attempting to disrupt airflow over the wings of the guided missile and send it off target. The Allies had no such defense for the V-2 ballistic missile, shown on its launch pad below, which descended on targets far faster than any airplane could fly.**

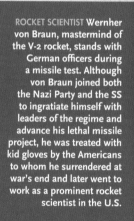

ROCKET SCIENTIST **Wernher von Braun, mastermind of the V-2 rocket, stands with German officers during a missile test. Although von Braun joined both the Nazi Party and the SS to ingratiate himself with leaders of the regime and advance his lethal missile project, he was treated with kid gloves by the Americans to whom he surrendered at war's end and later went to work as a prominent rocket scientist in the U.S.**

ILLUSTRATED MANUAL **To provide this deadly serious German booklet on the V-2 (diagrammed on the left-hand page) with comic relief, the manual's artist sketched a German soldier and his sweetheart on the right-hand page.**

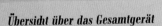

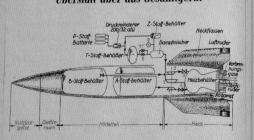

Wehrmacht's chief of staff, urged Hitler to abandon the fight in the west and throw all remaining forces against the Russians. But Hitler would not hear of it and dispensed with Guderian by sending him on sick leave.

Hitler's dream of staving off defeat with secret weapons proved as hopeless as his doomed western offensive. Since early in the war, much effort and expense had been devoted to developing two so-called Vergeltung ("Vengeance") weapons—a cruise missile designated V-1 and a ballistic missile labeled V-2. Because of technical difficulties and production delays, neither was ready for deployment until the last year of the conflict when Germany's fate was all but sealed. The V-1 went into action one week after D-Day, when 10 of those rockets were fired at London. The new weapon was terrifying, but it had a range of only about 150 miles and a top speed of 375 miles an hour, which left it vulnerable to attack by fighter planes and antiaircraft batteries. Furthermore, its development was no secret to Allied intelligence chiefs, including Reginald Jones of the British Air Ministry, who by the time the first V-1s fell on London had been thoroughly briefed on the missile's design and characteristics by spies and informants. Jones worked with the Twenty Committee and MI5's double agents to conceal from the Germans the fact that many V-1s were falling short of their target in central London, where they would inflict the heaviest casualties and do most to disrupt the government and its war effort. In all, more than 20,000 V-1s were launched, initially at London and later at Antwerp and other places liberated by Allied forces after D-Day. Over 50,000 people were killed or wounded in those attacks, but the toll was small compared with that inflicted on the Reich by Allied bombing raids, which caused more than a million German casualties.

The first V-2s were unleashed against London in September 1944 and descended from the stratosphere at more than 2,000 miles an hour, making them impossible to defend against. Yet the V-2's explosive payload was not much larger than that of the V-1 and its range was not much greater. It could not reach strategic targets in Russia or Russian-occupied territory and was used exclusively against England and Allied-occupied Belgium and France. Meanwhile, vengeful Soviet forces bore down on Germany unimpeded by Hitler's vengeance weapons. Designed by Wernher von Braun, a gifted and ruthlessly ambitious rocket scientist who joined the Nazi Party to advance his career, the V-2 was produced at enormous cost, including the lives of some 20,000 concentration camp inmates who labored in wretched conditions in a bombproof subterranean factory and succumbed to disease, starvation, or abuse by their guards. The death toll among those slave laborers far exceeded the number killed or wounded in V-2 attacks, which inflicted about 12,500 casualties and had a negligible impact on the war.

In the end, all that remained for Hitler and his Nazi loyalists as utter defeat loomed in 1945 was to eliminate those they branded enemies of the state before the Reich collapsed. Unlike Hitler, who resolved to take his own life rather than be captured and tried as a war

(continued on page 292)

"We may be destroyed, but if we are, we shall drag a world with us—a world in flames."

HITLER'S VOW NEVER TO SURRENDER

BLASTED A V-2 rocket struck a market here in London with devastating impact in March 1945, killing over 100 people and injuring many more. Such vengeance attacks did nothing to alter the fact that Nazi Germany was now doomed to defeat.

THE NIGHTMARE OF SUBTERRANEAN SLAVE LABOR

The V-1 and V-2 were among the war's most sophisticated weapons, but many of them were produced in the most primitive and degrading conditions by tens of thousands of slave laborers. In late 1943, following a heavy Allied bombing raid on the German rocket complex at Peenemünde, production was shifted to a deep mine in the Harz Mountains, which was expanded to accommodate a factory called Mittelwerk (Central Works) and a concentration camp designated Dora for the workers confined there. Their SS overseer, Hans Kammler, cared little whether they lived or died, because they could always be replaced. "Pay no attention to the human cost," he instructed his underlings. "The work must go ahead, and in the shortest possible time." Quarters for the laborers were cold, dark, and unsanitary, equipped with toilets that consisted of planks atop oil drums into which guards sometimes pushed the laborers while they were seated. One prisoner described how the men in his shift, after working 15 hours, were so exhausted that many collapsed on the floor of their cavernous dormitory without reaching their beds, stacked four bunks high: "Soon over a thousand despairing men, at the limit of their existence and racked with thirst, lie there hoping for sleep which never comes; for the shouts of the guards, the noise of the machines, the explosions and the ringing of the bell reach them even there."

Casualty rates at Mittelwerk-Dora were appalling. Laborers succumbed in droves to dysentery and other diseases or collapsed from malnutrition and mistreatment. By war's end, a staggering 20,000 of the 60,000 men forced to toil at Mittelwerk-Dora had perished there—far more than died in all the V-2 rocket attacks put together. ⊙

FORCED LABOR Inmates work on components for V-rockets at Mittelwerk-Dora, situated deep within a hillside (top) where old mines were converted into a vast underground workplace and concentration camp. Those excavations were performed at great effort and risk by the first prisoners who arrived there in late 1943. All the laborers lived in wretched subterranean caverns until mid-1944, when quarters for prisoners were completed outside the entrance.

SURVIVOR A dazed inmate sits amid the bodies of dead laborers at Mittelwerk-Dora after Allied forces arrived there in April 1945. By then, most of the able-bodied prisoners had been evacuated by their German overseers, leaving behind those who were too sick to move.

DEATH CAMP Allied troops came upon this emaciated survivor (left) at a camp in the town of Nordhausen where inmates too weak to work any longer at nearby Mittelwerk-Dora were left to die of starvation and buried in a shallow grave (right).

COSTLY OUTPUT On average, about two laborers died for every German missile produced underground, including several thousand V-1s like the one in the foreground and 6,000 V-2s.

criminal, Heinrich Himmler hoped in vain to escape retribution by destroying evidence of the monumental crimes committed by his SS. He shut down the gas chambers and ordered Auschwitz and other concentration camps that lay in the path of advancing Soviet forces in Poland razed. That did not mean sparing the inmates. They too were damning evidence of Nazi atrocities and were sent on forced marches to distant camps. Many perished in transit, and those who survived were crammed in with other prisoners and left to starve. Virulent anti-Semitism governed the Nazi regime from its inception to its destruction, as expressed in the last testament of Hitler, who stated that the "real people to blame for this murderous struggle" were the Jews, whom he libeled and reviled to his dying day.

Not long before Hitler committed suicide in his Berlin bunker on April 30, 1945, Adm. Wilhelm Canaris, Gen. Hans Oster, and others accused of conspiring against their Führer while serving in the Abwehr were summarily tried and condemned to death. Canaris's recently uncovered diary convinced Hitler that plots against him by Oster and others within the intelligence agency had been aided and abetted by the admiral in charge. After initially denying involvement, Canaris was confronted with testimony from Oster that he had shielded and supported the conspirators, and he admitted doing so. Before he was hanged on April 9 for defying the leader who brought the Reich to ruin, Canaris tapped out his own epitaph in code to another prisoner in his cell block: "My time is up," he signaled. "Was not a traitor. Did my duty as a German."

VANQUISHED Hitler committed suicide in the Berlin bunker shown below on April 30, 1945, rather than be captured by Soviet forces, who raised their flag over the German capital two days later (bottom).

THE STARS AND STRIPES

EXTRA | EXTRA

Daily Newspaper of U.S. Armed Forces — in the European Theater of Operations

Vol. 1—No. 279 ★ 1 Fr. 1 Fr. Wednesday, May 2, 1945

German Radio Reports:

HITLER DEAD

The German radio announced last night that Adolf Hitler had died yesterday afternoon, and that Adm. Doenitz, former commander-in-chief of the German Navy, had succeeded him as ruler of the Reich.

Doenitz, speaking later over the German radio, Reuter said, declared that "Hitler has fallen at his command post."

"My first task," Doenitz said, "is to save the German people from destruction by Bolshevism. If only for this task, the struggle will continue."

The announcement preceding the proclamation by Doenitz said: "It is reported from the Fuehrer's headquarters that our Fuehrer, Adolf Hitler, has fallen this afternoon at his command post in the Reich Chancellery, fighting to the last breath against Bolshevism and for his country. On April 30, the Fuehrer appointed Grand Adm. Doenitz as his successor. The new Fuehrer will speak to the German people."

The talk by Doenitz then followed, Reuter said. Doenitz said: "German men and women, soldiers of the German Wehrmacht, our Fuehrer, Adolf Hitler, has fallen. German people are in deepest mourning and veneration."

"Adolf Hitler recognized beforehand the terrible danger of Bolshevism," Doenitz said, "and devoted his life to fighting it. At the end of this, his battle, and of his unswerving straight path of life, stands his death as a hero in the capital of the Reich.

"All his life meant service to the German people. His battle against the Bolshevik flood benefited not only Europe but the whole world. The Fuehrer has

(Continued on Page 8)

Churchill Hints Peace Is at Hand

Winston Churchill indicated in a brief address to Commons yesterday that peace in Europe might come before Saturday.

Although he declined to give any statement on the reported surrender negotiations, the Prime Minister acknowledged that an important announcement was possible before the House adjourned Friday night. The admission was regarded as confirmation that the negotiations are well under way.

In Stockholm, meanwhile, Count Folke Bernadotte, head of the Swedish Red Cross, gave virtual denial at a press conference that he was acting as go-between in peace negotiations between the Allies and the German government.

"I have not seen Himmler during my last visit to Germany and Denmark, and I have not forwarded any message from Himmler or

(Continued on Page 8)

Pope Prepares Speech

ROME, May 1 (UP).—Reliable Vatican quarters said today that the Papal apartment has been prepared for an imminent worldwide broadcast by the Pope. The subject of the address is expected to be in connection with the end of the European war.

BLACK PROPAGANDA:
THE SECRET WAR OF WORDS

n March 1945, as Germany faced defeat, Propaganda Minister Joseph Goebbels urged Hitler to address the nation by radio and call for continued defiance of the Allies, as he did in January when he told Germans that "however grave the crisis may be at the moment, it will, despite everything, finally be mastered by our unalterable will." But Hitler knew better than to try again to rouse the public with a voice that now "sounded shrill with despair," as one listener put it. He and Goebbels were no longer masters of the airwaves. Radio, once the means by which they enthralled followers and intimidated foes, was being used effectively by the Allies to spread demoralizing rumors in broadcasts that appeared to originate within the Reich. Such black propaganda, one Nazi official wrote, was exhausting "the fighting spirit of the Army and the endurance of the people."

In effect, the Allies were treating the faltering Nazi regime to a noxious dose of its own medicine. In 1939, the Propaganda Ministry run by Goebbels had joined with the Foreign Ministry to establish a department called Büro Concordia, which produced black propaganda broadcasts that seemingly emanated from France, Britain, and other nations at odds with Germany. Radio Berlin, the Reich's official propaganda

INSTIGATOR Joseph Goebbels fired the first shots in the black propaganda war, but the Allies proved better at undermining German morale in the long run.

station, also broadcast to people in those countries in their own language but did not conceal where its programs originated. William Joyce, a British fascist who defected to Germany in 1939, began his broadcasts for Radio Berlin with the words "Germany calling." Known as Lord Haw-Haw to British listeners, many of whom were more amused than bothered by his diatribes, he lost popularity in the spring of 1940 when the "Phoney War" with Germany became a real struggle with dire consequences.

Joyce continued to broadcast white propaganda, whose origins were transparent, while scripting black propaganda for Büro

Concordia, which operated five English-language stations aimed at Britain. Those programs were not very subtle, and few listeners were swayed by them. But it was unnerving for those being bombed by Germany in 1940 to hear announcers who claimed to be on their side denouncing the British war effort. "Don't wait until hunger and starvation cripple you," said a spokesman for the "black" station Workers' Challenge who urged listeners to rebel against capitalist warmongers. "Get peace now. Strike while the iron is hot, for a workers' state is worth fighting for."

The British struck back in that war of words by enlisting the services of a gifted journalist turned propagandist, Sefton Delmer, raised in Germany by Australian parents. As a German-language announcer for the BBC, Delmer peppered his white propaganda with harsh words for Nazis and warnings of the hot reception awaiting Germans if they invaded England. He reinforced a rumor instigated by a covert propaganda committee in London and spread by agents abroad that the British were coating their coastal waters with a highly flammable substance that would incinerate invaders. "I burn... you burn... he burns," recited Delmer in a broadcast aimed at German soldiers before it became clear that Hitler would not risk an invasion. In 1941, Delmer shifted to "black" programs as mastermind of the German-language radio station GS1 (Gustav Siegfried Eins), featuring a shadowy figure called Der Chef ("the Chief") who railed against perverted Nazis who were ruining the Reich. Those lurid broadcasts made GS1 one of the war's most successful black propaganda shows until it went off the air in 1943 amid a simulated burst of Gestapo gunfire that silenced the Chief. Delmer also directed black propaganda in print for the Political Warfare Executive, an agency that used words and images as weapons to demoralize the enemy and inspired similar efforts by the OSS. ✪

DEFIANT WORDS Sefton Delmer debuted as a German-language announcer for the BBC in July 1940 by rejecting Hitler's peace offer, which amounted to an ultimatum. "We hurl it right back at you," he said, "right in your evil smelling teeth." Delmer later issued the warning at right as an English lesson for Germans who might invade Britain.

"Now, I will give you a verb
   that should come in useful.
   Again please repeat after me:
"*Ich brenne* . . . I burn;
"*Du brennst* . . . you burn;
"*Er brennt* . . . he burns;
"*Wir brennen* . . . we burn;
"*Ihr brennt* . . . you are burning.
"*Sie brennen* . . . they burn.
"*Der SS-Sturmführer brennt auch
   ganz schön* . . . The SS Captain is
   also burning quite nicely."

SEFTON DELMER, EARLY 1941

PEOPLE'S RECEIVER In 1938, Germans obtain free radios to mark Goebbels's birthday on October 29. Labeled *Volksempfänger* ("people's receiver"), the cheap radio produced for distribution in Nazi Germany had limited reception and came with a printed warning: "Listening to foreign broadcasts is a crime against the national security of our people."

THIS IS NOT BIG-HEARTED ARTHUR, NOR IS IT OLD STINKER---OH, NO! IT'S THE DONKEY THAT'S BRAYING FROM HAMBURG,
LORD HAW-HAW,
HEE-HAW,- HAW, HEE-HAW!

GERMANY CALLING German propaganda aimed at the British included broadcasts by Lord Haw-Haw, satirized above, and a fake London *Evening Standard* dated February 17, 1940, claiming heavy losses by the RAF, which had barely begun to fight.

X Ha № 611116 ✻

Zweite
Reichskleiderkarte

für Herrn _____

Wohnort _____

Wohnung _____

(Mit Tinte auszufüllen)

Die Karte gilt bis 31. August 1941; sie ist nicht übertragbar. Die Karte darf nur zur Befriedigung des Bedarfs des Karteninhabers benutzt werden. Mißbräuchliche Benutzung wird bestraft. Aus dem Zusammenhang der Karte gelöste Kartenteile und Abschnitte sind ungültig.

Auf die Karte können die umstehend genannten Waren bezogen werden. Bei jeder Ware ist angegeben, wieviel Abschnitte von dem Verkäufer vor Aushändigung der Ware von der Karte abgetrennt werden. Beim Bezug von Socken und Strümpfen trennt der Verkäufer außerdem den entsprechenden Bezugsnachweis ab. Der Bezug von Socken und Strümpfen ist auf 6 Paare beschränkt. Davon sind 4 Paare gegen Entwertung der vorgesehenen Abschnitte erhältlich. Zwei weitere Paar Socken oder Strümpfe können nur gegen die 1½fache Anzahl von Abschnitten bezogen werden. Die Abschnitte I—VII sind für den Bezug von Waren vorgesehen, die gegebenenfalls besonders bekanntgemacht werden.

Für bestimmte Stoffe und Fertigwaren sind Sonderregelungen ergangen. Sie können in den Geschäften erfragt werden.

FOOD STAMPS The ration book above and stamps at left, good for 50 grams of bread, were forged by the PWE to disrupt wartime food allotments to an increasingly hungry German populace. The forged "Führer's Gift" ration coupons at right were for soldiers on leave.

BRITISH MASTERS OF THE BLACK ART

Much of the black propaganda directed at German soldiers and civilians was printed rather than broadcast and produced covertly by the Political Warfare Executive (PWE) under the expert direction of Sefton Delmer and designer Ellic Howe. Equipped with an encyclopedic knowledge of printing history and techniques, including those in use in wartime Germany, Howe came to Delmer's attention after applying in 1941 to the Directorate of Military Intelligence for a position that suited his expertise. "In time of war," he wrote, "the printing press allied with the typewriter and the technique of calligraphic forgery or deception is a powerful weapon. Documents can reach persons or places that are outside the reach of our armoured divisions or agents."

Howe was soon collaborating with Delmer on graphic projects as dark and devious as they were ingenious, including a demoralizing leaflet warning German *Hausfrauen* ("housewives") in bombed-out areas to boil water tainted by dead bodies (opposite). Unlike the SOE, which sometimes freed forgers from prison to counterfeit enemy documents, Howe's PWE print unit had no ex-convicts. "My staff was entirely respectable," he remarked. Lacking criminal experience,

they honed their skills at producing fakes or forgeries through trial and error. A bogus stamp they designed to portray Heinrich Himmler as Germany's would-be Führer (page 298) was initially criticized because it made the SS chief look like he had a skin disease. "I expect these blemishes will be removed from the stamps in their final form," the critic wrote, as they in fact were, resulting in what one SOE agent called "beautiful forgeries" that found their way into Nazi Germany as well as President Roosevelt's personal stamp collection.

Black propaganda printed by the PWE and other agencies was disseminated by various means. Some was sent by mail or delivered by agents to resistance groups in occupied Europe, who left leaflets in places where German troops congregated that fed their fears and encouraged them to malinger or desert. Distribution within Germany was achieved mostly by airdrops from planes or balloons, which rode west winds from Allied territory and released bundles of subversive literature over the Reich. German propagandists tried to fight back and Americans tried to keep up, but no Axis or Allied nation could match the graphic output of Howe, Delmer, and other British masters of the black art in quality or quantity. ❂

DELIVERY SYSTEM Members of M unit, formed by the RAF early in the war, fill balloons with hydrogen to deliver propaganda to Germany for the PWE. The balloons had automatic valves that kept them at a constant altitude and fuses timed to release packets of printed material over targeted areas based on the wind speed.

100.000 Mark Belohnung!

Nächtlicher Frauenmord!

Jede Nacht werden 56 Frauen ermordet.

Der Mörder heißt Fritz Sauckel, Gauleiter und Reichsstatthalter von Thüringen, Generalbevollmächtigter für den Arbeitseinsatz.

Sauckel mordet, indem er deutsche Frauen und Mädchen zur Nachtarbeit zwingt und sie so schindet, daß sie vor Erschöpfung Betriebsunfällen zum Opfer fallen.

Im Monat Juli 1943 gab es laut Reichsunfallstatistik 236.700 Betriebsunfälle von Arbeiterinnen, davon 187.360 zwischen 6 Uhr abends und 6 Uhr morgens. Von diesen 187.360 bei Nachtarbeit verunglückten Frauen verloren 1736 ihr Leben. Das heißt 56 Frauen in jeder Nacht.

Jede Nacht werden 56 Frauen von Sauckel ermordet.

Der Frauenmörder Sauckel muß unschädlich gemacht werden!

Europa–Festung ohne Dach

SOLDAT!
WAS HAST DU SCHON DAVON?

Drei grosse Gefahren für die Innere Front:

1. *Die Bombenangriffe*

Dadurch werden Flecktyphus, Diphteritis, Scharlach usw. mit erschreckender Schnelligkeit verbreitet.

Und schliesslich — wenn die Frauen mal murren und meckern — jede Frau meckert —, dann greift die Gestapo ein.

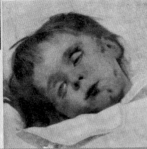

2. *Die ausländischen Arbeiter*

Heute gibt es schon über zehn Millionen lüsterner, geiler Ausländer in allen Teilen des Reiches. Und—

Eure Frauen fühlen sich einsam!

FEEDING FEARS A PWE leaflet aimed at German occupation forces in Belgium shows three threats to their loved ones on the home front—Allied air raids (above), foreign workers who might consort with their lonely wives or sweethearts (far left), and the evacuation of children from threatened cities to rural camps, portrayed as breeding grounds for disease (left).

HAUSFRAUEN!
Kocht nach Luftangriffen das Trinkwasser ab!

Immer wieder wird in deutschen Städten die Erfahrung gemacht, daß auf die feigen Luftangriffe des Feindes Seuchen wie Ruhr und Typhus folgen.

Diese Seuchen werden durch die Verunreinigung von Trinkwasser verursacht als Folge der Beschädigung des Trinkwasser-und Abwässernetzes durch Luftangriffe. Verschiedentlich kam es sogar vor, wie z. B. in Karlsruhe, daß Leichen in die Wassersammelbecken geschwemmt wurden und das Wasser verpesteten. Erst bei der Leerung der Sammelbecken wurden die Leichen (siehe Abbildung) gefunden, sodaß das Übel abgestellt werden konnte.

Um den Gefahren vorzubeugen, die sich aus der Wasserverseuchung ergeben, muß Trinkwasser nach einem Luftangriff grundsätzlich vor dem Genuß abgekocht werden.

HAUSFRAUEN! ACHTET DARAUF!
Nach Luftangriffen mindestens 60 Stunden kein Genuss von unabgekochtem Trinkwasser!

Hauptamt für Volkswohlfahrt, Berlin, Maibach-Ufer 48-51

Druck: Paul Schmidt, Berlin N. 54, Zehdenicker Str. 5

BLACK BULLETINS Howe's versatile print unit used a modern font of the sort favored by Nazi authorities for the grim notice above, warning that bombing victims were contaminating drinking water, and the traditional German Fraktur typeface for the wanted poster at top, offering a hefty reward for Nazi official Fritz Sauckel, who ran deadly slave labor facilities.

WASTE PAPER Produced by Ellic Howe and dropped over Germany, this note mimicked real currency issued to troops but had scathing messages on the back, including one stating: "I am Hitler's asswipe [toilet paper]."

HEIL HIMMLER Portrayed at left on fake stamps as a Nazi leader who might replace Hitler, Himmler demands funds at gunpoint for the charity Winter Help (top). Another forged stamp for that cause (above) portrays a horribly maimed soldier.

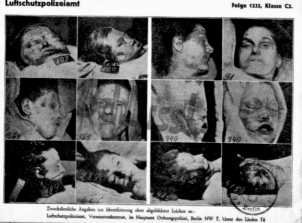

VICTIMS Bearing the seal of the Luftschutzpolizei (Air Defense Police) in Berlin, this black propaganda poster seeks the identity of the air raid victims pictured. Many such PWE forgeries were stamped *"Schluss!"* ("End it!"), the supposed slogan of a German resistance movement.

PROPHECIES Howe's PWE unit printed this lightweight, miniature German edition of supposed Nostradamus prophecies, forecasting ruin for the Reich, to counter similar German propaganda that predicted defeat for the Allies.

BOMBING RUN American airmen pack propaganda leaflets into large bombshells (near right) that will then be loaded in a heavy bomber (far right) and dropped over Germany. Such propaganda bombs were designed to burst open more than a mile above the ground, showering a wide area with their contents.

MALINGERING PAPERS One of many schemes conceived by Delmer and produced by Howe, this brand-name packet for cigarette papers (right) contained instructions for 10 ways to avoid military duty (below right) and could be dropped surreptitiously into a soldier's coat pocket.

DAMAGE REPORT Based on RAF intelligence flights, this PWE leaflet lists streets in German cities that sustained severe bomb damage and bears the mark of the Red Circle, a fictitious German resistance group. Such reports alarmed Germans troops, some of whom deserted or sought leave to care for their families.

BOMBS AWAY Photographed from the plane that released them over Germany, these propaganda bombs resembling large firecrackers had fuses set to trigger a small explosion at an altitude of 6,000 feet that broke open the container without harming the contents.

AFTERSHOCK Attributed to a Nazi doctor, this PWE pamphlet was designed to instill fear of "Bomb Shock," a nervous disorder that supposedly plagued air raid survivors. Sufferers should be isolated, it urged, and sent to rest homes.

OSS EUROPEAN OPERATIONS

Latecomers to the war, Americans took cues from the British when devising black propaganda, conducted by a branch of the OSS called Morale Operations (MO), which followed in the path of the PWE. The radio station Soldatensender West, for example, which posed as a German channel for German troops but was broadcast from England, was a collaborative effort between the OSS and the PWE. Sefton Delmer originated such broadcasts aimed at German troops, which combined "cover" in the form of popular music with "dirt"—propaganda meant to turn soldiers against Hitler's faltering war effort. Soldatensender West spread dirt by linking many high-ranking Germans to the July 1944 attempt to kill Hitler, some of whom were not involved in that plot.

Beginning in 1944, OSS MO agents in Italy devised ingenious black propaganda schemes, which included publishing a bogus anti-Nazi newspaper, *Das Neue Deutschland* (right). That was a tall order, but a team led by former reporters Richard Lee and Eugene Warner received help from German POWs in Italy who were fed up with the Nazis and gladly wrote copy for the paper. Graphic flair and humor was provided by artist Saul Steinberg, an MO recruit whose drawings for the *New Yorker* later won him renown. It took several weeks for the team to obtain print keys for umlauts—the two dots placed over some German vowels like the "ü" in Führer—but they brought out their first issue in late June 1944 with a print run of 75,000 copies. The paper was aimed initially at troops in German-occupied territory and distributed by agents or resistance groups. But later editions reached the Reich, including thousands of copies infiltrated into the German postal system using forged Hitler stamps in Operation Cornflakes.

Another MO black propaganda project, Operation Sauerkraut, involved sending anti-Nazi Germans recruited in POW camps behind enemy lines in Wehrmacht uniforms to incite dissent and desertion with rumors and propaganda leaflets. Messages from the fictional League of Lonely War Women urged soldiers to return home and embrace those women before foreigners working in Germany did. That league was devised by OSS Cpl. Barbara Lauwers (opposite, top), who was raised in Czechoslovakia and also produced MO broadcasts and leaflets that induced hundreds of Czech and Slovak soldiers serving under German command in Italy to desert to the Allies. ◎

TARGETING HITLER The top headline on this September 1944 issue of the black propaganda newspaper *Das Neue Deutschland* states that Hitler will not make peace and shows the Führer, who had survived numerous assassination attempts, holding a gun to his head in a drawing labeled "The Last Attempt." Copies of the newspaper ended up in the hands of German troops (left) as well as civilians.

LONELY HEARTS Barbara Lauwers (left) composed an appeal to German soldiers (right) from the League of Lonely War Women. "We are waiting for you," the leaflet states, promising men who return home and display the league's emblem (at lower left on the leaflet) that the "longings of your lonely nights will be fulfilled."

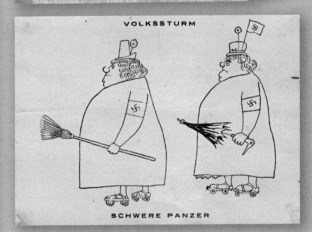

Sommer 1944.

Lieber Frontsoldat!
Wann kommst Du wieder auf Urlaub?

Wann wirst Du Deine harten Soldatenpflichten wieder einmal vergessen können, wenigstens für ein paar Tage voll Freude, Glück und Liebe? Wir in der Heimat wissen von Deinem heldenhaften Kampf, wir verstehen aber, dass auch der Tapferste einmal müde wird und ein sanftes Kissen, Zärtlichkeit und gesundes Vergnügen braucht.

WIR WARTEN AUF DICH:
auf Dich, der in einer fremden Stadt allein seinen Urlaub verbringen muss; auf Dich, dem der Krieg sein Heim genommen hat; auf Dich, der ohne Frau, Braut oder Flirt in der Welt steht.

WIR WARTEN AUF DICH:
schneide unser Abzeichen aus diesem Briefe aus. In jedem Kaffee, in jeder Bar in der Nähe eines Bahnhofs, lehne es sichtbar an Dein Glas; gar bald wird sich ein Mitglied unseres V.E.K. Deiner annehmen, und Deine Frontträume und die Sehnsucht einsamer Nächte werden Erfüllung finden... Wir wollen Dich, nicht Dein Geld, darum lass Dir stets unsere Mitgliedskarte vorher zeigen. Mitglieder gibt es überall, da wir deutsche Frauen unsere Pflichten zur Heimat und ihren Verteidigern verstanden haben.

Natürlich sind wir auch selbstsüchtig — jahrelang von unseren Männern getrennt, mit all den Fremden um uns herum, möchten wir wieder einmal einen richtigen deutschen Jungen an's Herz drücken. Nur keine Hemmungen: Deine Frau, Schwester oder Geliebte ist auch eine der unseren.

Wir denken an Dich und auch an Deutschlands Zukunft. Was rastet — rostet...

VEREIN EINSAMER KRIEGERFRAUEN

HEAVY ARMOR Illustrated by Saul Steinberg for distribution to German troops in Operation Sauerkraut, this postcard mocks the Volkssturm—a people's militia authorized by Hitler in late 1944 to compensate for heavy German losses in battle—by showing two ladies on roller skates above the caption *Schwere Panzer* ("Heavy Armor").

DEADLY SIGNS Many images meant to chill Germans and encourage desertion raised the specter of death, including the soldier crucified on a swastika above and the stickers at right showing a sentry's skeletal shadow, Hitler's skull and bones, a ghostly figure captioned "Strength Through Fear," and a morbid Hitler labeled "The Culprit."

TIGHTENING THE NOOSE

The grim fate awaiting Germany at war's end was forecast by a map in a September 1944 issue of an Allied black propaganda newspaper aimed at German troops (right), showing Germany's borders about to be pierced. Hitler tried to avert that disaster with a desperate counterattack in Belgium, but his forces were repulsed in the Battle of the Bulge at year's end. In early 1945, the Allied onslaught intensified, and Germans faced a reckoning even worse than envisioned in the black propaganda directed at them. The "Bomb Shock" described earlier in a PWE pamphlet was mild compared with the blistering impact of incendiaries dropped on Dresden in February, which fueled a firestorm that killed 35,000 people and left survivors traumatized. Warnings that German women might fall into foreign hands were realized in brutal fashion as vengeful Russians advanced on Berlin, raping and pillaging with impunity.

One scenario proposed by Allied propagandists that never materialized was a German uprising against the Nazis. Following the July 1944 attempt on Hitler's life, thousands of real or suspected foes of his regime were executed, leaving few potential leaders for an insurrection. But that did not stop the SOE and PWE from simulating a German underground movement against the regime in Operation Periwig, which included infiltrating German POWs into the Reich as resistance agents to lend credibility to the plot. Howe's print unit produced over 2,000 postcards like the one opposite, which bore the mark of a militant group called the Red Horse and warned Nazi leaders to hang themselves or face an excruciating death when they were tracked down.

As the regime crumbled, suicide was in fact the last recourse for a number of its leaders, including the Führer and his appointed successor, Goebbels, who survived Hitler for less than a day before he and his wife poisoned themselves and their six children. Once masters of the big lie, Hitler and Goebbels had no answer in the end for Allied propaganda campaigns filled with distortions but based on a fundamental truth—that Nazi leaders were driving Germany to ruin. ⊙

1. Januar 1945

An den Fronten **4 780 000** gefallene Soldaten

In der Heimat **11 660 000** Bombengeschädigte

Schluss!

ALTERNATIVE NEWS Black propaganda publications such as *Nachrichten für die Truppe (News for the Troops)*, produced jointly by the PWE and OSS, appealed to Germans distrustful of Nazi news reports. The PWE sticker at left with the resistance slogan *Schluss!* exploited that skepticism by offering alarmingly high casualty figures for German civilians (bottom figure) in relation to German war deaths (top figure).

DISPROPORTIONATE LOSSES
Another PWE German casualty sticker dated January 1, 1945, seeks to drive a wedge between the populace and the ruling party responsible for the war by stating that losses by percentage were 15 times higher for German soldiers (left figure) than for Nazi officials (right figure).

So sieht die Blutbilanz aus!

Von Kriegsbeginn bis 1. Januar 1945:

Von **18 672 334** Soldaten sind gefallen, vermißt oder gefangen: **7 068 509** Mann.

Das kämpfende Volk verlor: **37.8%**

Von **1 551 709** politischen Leitern sind gefallen, vermißt oder gefangen: **38 102** Mann.

Die Parteileitung verlor: **2½%**

Die Verluste der gewöhnlichen Volksgenossen im wehrfähigen Alter sind prozentual 15 mal so groß wie die der politischen Leiter der NSDAP.

Achtung, Pferd!

Ein primitives Tierbild aus ein paar einfachen Strichen, das aussieht wie ein Pferd, sieht man jetzt in der Reichshauptstadt

und zahlreichen anderen Städten des Reichs mit Kreide oder Rötel auf zahlreichen Häuserwänden in Treppenhäusern, Luftschutzbunkern und auf Wohnungstüren aufgezeichnet.

Auch eine Anzahl von Parteibeamten hat Drohbriefe mit dem Pferdezeichen anstelle einer Unterschrift erhalten.

MENACING GRAFFITI This notice, which appeared in *Nachrichten für die Truppe* in February 1945, states that mysterious drawings of a horse like one shown here were appearing on walls in Berlin and other German cities and on threatening notes sent to Nazi officials. Those supposedly responsible for the drawings were labeled the Red Horse group.

DEATH THREAT This postcard with its Red Horse emblem was one of many printed for Operation Periwig that instructed recipients how to hang themselves so as to "spare yourself unnecessary pains." A suspicious card like this would likely be intercepted by German postal officials before reaching its destination, but the operation was intended to alarm authorities and make them waste effort pursuing a phantom resistance group.

CHAPTER 6

ZERO HOUR IN THE PACIFIC

ISLAND FIGHTING U.S. Marines land in a tracked vehicle on Tinian, secured from Japanese forces in August 1944. A year later, B-29s taking off from Tinian dropped the war's ultimate secret weapons on Japan—atomic bombs.

GUARDING THE WAR'S BIGGEST SECRET

When physicist J. Robert Oppenheimer arrived in New Mexico in April 1943 to take charge of a new government laboratory under construction at Los Alamos, a remote site in the mountains northwest of Santa Fe, he became crucial to the Manhattan Project, a massive effort to build an atomic bomb capable of altering, if not ending, the war in short order. The project was the greatest secret weapons program ever undertaken, and few people were more important to America's national security than the 39-year-old Oppenheimer. But he did not yet have a security clearance and was suspected by the FBI and G-2, the U.S. Army's intelligence agency, of being linked to a spy ring run not by Germany or Japan but by America's Soviet allies. One G-2 officer stationed at Los Alamos accused Oppenheimer in writing of "playing a key part in the attempts of the Soviet Union to secure, by espionage, highly secret information which is vital to the security of the United States."

The charges against Oppenheimer stemmed from the fact that several people close to him, including his younger brother Frank and his wife Kitty, were past or present members of the Communist Party. Oppenheimer denied ever joining that party, but while teaching at

OFF LIMITS The sign at the gate to Los Alamos gives no hint as to the nature of the project conducted at that closely guarded facility in New Mexico, where some of the world's top scientists began designing an atomic bomb in 1943. Physicist J. Robert Oppenheimer (opposite), the project's director, was investigated at length before he was granted a security clearance.

NAME: J. ROBERT OPPENHEIMER
OCCUPATION: PHYSICIST
ASSIGNMENT: UNLEASH ATOMIC ENERGY

JANUARY 1942 President Roosevelt authorizes the top secret Manhattan Project to produce atomic bombs.

APRIL 1942 William Donovan activates Detachment 101, which will conduct covert operations for the OSS against Japanese forces in the China-Burma-India Theater.

APRIL 1943 Scientific work on nuclear weapons begins at Los Alamos in New Mexico.

MARCH–APRIL 1944 Adm. Mineichi Koga, Yamamoto's successor as commander of Japan's Combined Fleet, dies in a plane crash off the Philippine island of Cebu, and his secret Plan Z for repulsing the U.S. Pacific Fleet falls into American hands.

JULY–AUGUST 1944 U.S. forces capture Saipan and Tinian in the western Pacific, bringing Japan within range of strategic bombers based on airfields constructed there.

JULY 1945 An atomic bomb developed at Los Alamos is tested successfully at the Trinity Site in New Mexico.

AUGUST 1945 Japan surrenders unconditionally after nuclear weapons devastate Hiroshima and Nagasaki.

AUGUST 1949 The Soviet Union successfully tests an atomic bomb developed with the aid of nuclear espionage, intensifying the Cold War.

"Los Alamos' amazing success grew out of the brilliance, enthusiasm and charisma with which Oppenheimer led it."

EDWARD TELLER,
PHYSICIST AT LOS ALAMOS

the University of California in the late 1930s, he had supported causes that brought him into frequent contact with Communists or communist sympathizers, including members of the Abraham Lincoln Brigade, who defied U.S. Neutrality Acts by fighting in Spain against dictator Francisco Franco, backed by Hitler and Mussolini. Oppenheimer shared with those fighters a hatred for fascism in all its forms. "I had a continuing, smouldering fury about the treatment of Jews in Germany," he remarked, and he helped Jewish relatives and fellow Jewish scientists there flee the Nazi regime and settle in the United States.

In 1940, while attending a benefit in Berkeley for refugees of the Spanish Civil War, Oppenheimer met a Communist named Steve Nelson, a veteran of the Abraham Lincoln Brigade. They found that they had more in common than opposition to Franco and Hitler, for Nelson was a close friend and comrade of Kitty Oppenheimer's ex-husband Joe Dallett, who died fighting in Spain. Nelson was not only chairman of the local branch of the Communist Party but also a secret Soviet agent, who reported to Peter Ivanov, an intelligence officer at the Soviet consulate in San Francisco. The FBI suspected Nelson of spying and tapped his phone, obtaining evidence that linked him to Oppenheimer and several of his associates at the university, including graduate students he had mentored who worked at the Radiation Laboratory in Berkeley, where research vital to the Manhattan Project was conducted. In one phone call monitored by the FBI around the time Oppenheimer was chosen to head the nuclear weapons effort at Los Alamos, Nelson referred to him as a scientist who was once considered a "Red" but was now "too jittery" to aid Communists because he worked for the government and hoped to "escape his past."

Such statements heightened concerns about Oppenheimer at the FBI, whose agents shared their suspicions with Lt. Col. Boris Pash, G-2's counterintelligence chief on the West Coast. A Russian American born in San Francisco who fought against the Red Army in the civil war that convulsed Russia following the Bolshevik Revolution in 1917, Pash was a fervent anticommunist intent on tracking down Soviet agents. He interrogated Oppenheimer on several occasions and pressed him for details about an alarming incident that occurred at his home in Berkeley in early 1943, shortly before he left for Los Alamos. On that occasion, another professor at the university told him that a British chemist in the area named George Eltenton—who like Nelson was in touch with Ivanov at the Soviet consulate—was prepared to pass "technical information to Soviet scientists." Fearing that the professor was about to ask him to betray nuclear secrets, Oppenheimer cut him off and said that what Eltenton proposed was treasonous. When questioned by Pash, Oppenheimer declined to name that professor or identify other scientists he said were approached with requests for information of interest to the Russians. Pash took his refusal to provide names and his evasive answers to other questions as evidence that he could not be trusted and should be denied a security clearance and ousted as director at Los Alamos.

Oppenheimer's job was saved by a superior officer for whom security at Los Alamos was of utmost concern—Brig. Gen. Leslie Groves, director of the Manhattan Project. Groves chose Oppenheimer to lead the Los Alamos effort and believed he alone was capable of overcoming the theoretical and technical challenges of building an atomic bomb by coordinating the efforts of other brilliant scientists, whose huge egos were easily bruised. One of those temperamental scientists, Edward Teller, who later fell out with Oppenheimer, explained why he was uniquely qualified for the historic task he took on: "Throughout the war years, Oppie knew in detail what was going on in every part of the Laboratory. He was incredibly quick and perceptive in analyzing human as well as technical problems . . . He knew how to organize, cajole, humor, soothe feelings—how to lead powerfully without seeming to do so . . . Los Alamos' amazing success grew out of the brilliance, enthusiasm and charisma with which Oppenheimer led it."

General Groves recognized those rare qualities in Oppenheimer that made him indispensable to the Manhattan Project and trusted in the judgment of his own security officer at Los Alamos, Capt. John Lansdale, who concluded that Oppenheimer was not and never had been a communist, which Lansdale defined as someone loyal to the Soviet Union rather than the United States. Indeed, Oppenheimer loved America and its liberties, including freedom of expression, which made him reluctant to reveal to investigators the names of friends and associates who espoused political views that some considered un-American. He ultimately identified the professor who spoke to him in Berkeley about sharing "technical information" with the Soviets as a French scholar and avowed Communist named Haakon Chevalier. But he made that disclosure only at the insistence of Groves, after the general overruled Boris Pash and ordered that Oppenheimer be granted a security clearance.

SPLITTING THE ATOM

Reprieved by Groves, Oppenheimer was free to carry out a monumental scientific task—unleashing atomic energy, a feat made possible by the discovery of a nuclear particle that he did not know existed when he studied physics in college in the 1920s. At that time, the atom was thought to consist of a nucleus of positively charged protons around which smaller, negatively charged electrons orbited like infinitesimal planets. Ernest Rutherford, a pioneering nuclear physicist who proposed that model, speculated that there might be an additional particle that added mass to the nucleus. It remained to his assistant at Oxford University's Cavendish Laboratory, James Chadwick, a future participant in the Manhattan Project, to confirm the existence of the neutron, roughly equal in weight to the proton. Chadwick's announcement in 1932 raised the possibility of splitting atoms by bombarding them with neutrons, which had no electrical charge and would not be repelled by protons in the nucleus. Hungarian-born physicist Leo

R. Oppenheimer

SECURITY AT LOS ALAMOS

As far as the public was concerned, Los Alamos did not exist. It appeared on no map, and those who lived there had no address other than a post office box. An outer fence surrounded the facility, and an inner fence separated the residential area from the offices and labs where atomic bombs were conceived. All who entered that inner sanctum wore badges that displayed their photo and were color-coded to indicate how much access they had. Those with white badges had the most access to the project and its classified information, but Brig. Gen. Leslie Groves and Robert Oppenheimer—shown here on their badges—differed as to how broad that access should be. Groves wanted to compartmentalize projects so that only a select few knew everything that was going on and could be kept under close surveillance like Oppenheimer, whose phone was bugged. Oppenheimer insisted that communication between top scientists on various projects was essential and won that argument.

Security at Los Alamos was tight but not foolproof. If all those who ever associated with Communists had been barred from employment there, the project would have lost the services of Oppenheimer and other brilliant physicists. As a result, a few scientists who posed real security risks were admitted, including Theodore Hall, a 19-year-old prodigy who began betraying nuclear secrets to Soviet agents soon after he arrived at Los Alamos and received his white badge in 1944. Some sensitive information was also divulged in print, notably a March 1944 column in a Cleveland newspaper referring to Los Alamos as a "mystery city" where secret weapons research was performed under Oppenheimer, described as a "second Einstein." Groves was furious and wanted to have the columnist drafted and sent to fight in the Pacific until he discovered that the author was 60 years old. ✪

NUCLEAR WARNING Physicist Leo Szilard (above) sought the help of his celebrated colleague Albert Einstein (top) in drafting the letter at right, addressed to President Roosevelt in August 1939. Signed by Einstein, it warned the president that it might soon be possible to produce an atomic bomb using uranium as fuel and urged him to take steps to promote nuclear research in the U.S., and to obtain a supply of high-grade uranium, as Germany had recently done by occupying Czechoslovakia. Although the letter states that atomic bombs "might very well prove to be too heavy for transportation by air," B-29 Superfortress bombers introduced in 1944 were capable of delivering the first nuclear weapons produced at Los Alamos.

Albert Einstein
Old Grove Rd.
Nassau Point
Peconic, Long Island

August 2nd, 1939

F.D. Roosevelt,
President of the United States,
White House
Washington, D.C.

Sir:

Some recent work by E.Fermi and L. Szilard, which has been communicated to me in manuscript, leads me to expect that the element uranium may be turned into a new and important source of energy in the immediate future. Certain aspects of the situation which has arisen seem to call for watchfulness and, if necessary, quick action on the part of the Administration. I believe therefore that it is my duty to bring to your attention the following facts and recommendations:

In the course of the last four months it has been made probable - through the work of Joliot in France as well as Fermi and Szilard in America - that it may become possible to set up a nuclear chain reaction in a large mass of uranium,by which vast amounts of power and large quantities of new radium-like elements would be generated. Now it appears almost certain that this could be achieved in the immediate future.

This new phenomenon would also lead to the construction of bombs, and it is conceivable - though much less certain - that extremely powerful bombs of a new type may thus be constructed. A single bomb of this type, carried by boat and exploded in a port, might very well destroy the whole port together with some of the surrounding territory. However, such bombs might very well prove to be too heavy for transportation by air.

-2-

The United States has only very poor ores of uranium in moderate quantities. There is some good ore in Canada and the former Czechoslovakia, while the most important source of uranium is Belgian Congo.

In view of this situation you may think it desirable to have some permanent contact maintained between the Administration and the group of physicists working on chain reactions in America. One possible way of achieving this might be for you to entrust with this task a person who has your confidence and who could perhaps serve in an inofficial capacity. His task might comprise the following:

a) to approach Government Departments, keep them informed of the further development, and put forward recommendations for Government action, giving particular attention to the problem of securing a supply of uranium ore for the United States;

b) to speed up the experimental work,which is at present being carried on within the limits of the budgets of University laboratories, by providing funds, if such funds be required, through his contacts with private persons who are willing to make contributions for this cause, and perhaps also by obtaining the co-operation of industrial laboratories which have the necessary equipment.

I understand that Germany has actually stopped the sale of uranium from the Czechoslovakian mines which she has taken over. That she should have taken such early action might perhaps be understood on the ground that the son of the German Under-Secretary of State, von Weizsäcker, is attached to the Kaiser-Wilhelm-Institut in Berlin where some of the American work on uranium is now being repeated.

Yours very truly,

A. Einstein

(Albert Einstein)

Szilard was among the first to recognize that this might lead to a powerful new weapon. Not long after Chadwick's discovery, Szilard recalled, he realized that "if we could find an element which is split by neutrons and which would emit *two* neutrons when it absorbs *one* neutron," the result might be a nuclear chain reaction that would release huge amounts of energy with shattering impact. Before Hitler took power, Szilard had studied in Germany with Albert Einstein, whose famous equation $E=mc^2$ (energy equals mass times the speed of light squared) indicated that a single bomb undergoing nuclear fission (the splitting of atoms) could unleash enough energy to devastate a vast area.

Italian physicist Enrico Fermi followed up on Chadwick's discovery by generating neutron emissions and exposing various elements to them. When Fermi bombarded uranium with neutrons, he observed a "very intense effect" that far exceeded the radioactivity emitted naturally by uranium as it slowly decays. He and his team at the University of Rome were at the forefront of nuclear physics in 1938 when Mussolini drew closer to Hitler and issued

a manifesto declaring that "Jews do not belong to the Italian race." Fermi, whose wife was Jewish, left Italy later that year to receive the Nobel Prize in physics in Stockholm and was granted asylum with his family in the U.S., where he continued his research. He was one of several elite physicists, including Einstein, Szilard, and Edward Teller, who found refuge in America from the menacing anti-Semitic policies of the Axis dictators and their collaborators.

Despite driving away such luminaries, Nazi Germany retained gifted scientists, including Otto Hahn and Fritz Strassmann, who announced in early 1939 that they had achieved fission by splitting the uranium nucleus, using techniques similar to those Fermi employed. Confirmation of their breakthrough came from analysis of their findings by two former colleagues who had fled the Reich, Lise Meitner and her nephew, Otto Frisch. (Frisch later contributed to the Manhattan Project, but Meitner declined to take part, saying that she would have "nothing to do with a bomb.") Word that fission had been achieved in Germany alarmed Szilard, who was experimenting on uranium with Fermi and other scientists at Columbia University in Manhattan and feared dire consequences if Hitler obtained an atomic bomb. Szilard appealed to Einstein, who signed a letter to President Roosevelt that reflected their shared concerns. Delivered to the White House by Alexander Sachs, a prominent economist who had served under Roosevelt, the letter stated that it might soon "become possible to set up a nuclear chain reaction in a large mass of uranium,"

MASTERMINDS Pictured above are three top physicists in the Manhattan Project. Edward Teller (top), shown on his Hungarian passport, worked with Oppenheimer and conceived the hydrogen bomb. Enrico Fermi (center) produced the first controlled nuclear chain reaction. Ernest Lawrence (bottom) invented the cyclotron and used it to enrich uranium.

leading to the construction of a bomb powerful enough to destroy a city. Germany had recently seized control of uranium mines in Czechoslovakia, warned Einstein, who urged executive action to secure a plentiful supply of high-grade uranium ore for the U.S. and to support American nuclear research and development. Sachs offered a lengthy statement of his own to reinforce the letter, but Roosevelt needed no convincing and cut to the heart of the matter. "Alex," he said, "what you are after is to see that the Nazis don't blow us up."

What began as a modest effort by the administration to promote nuclear research using

LIFE AT TENNESSEE'S SECRET CITY

One of General Groves's first official acts as boss of the Manhattan Project in 1942 was to acquire 59,000 sparsely populated acres along the Clinch River in eastern Tennessee. Families living within the boundaries of that new government reservation were removed, and a massive construction project was set in motion for the Clinton Engineer Works, where uranium would be processed using centrifuges called calutrons and other methods to produce the isotope U-235 as fuel for atomic bombs. The plan called for 13,000 workers and their family members to be housed there in a town called Oak Ridge. But by 1945, Oak Ridge was Tennessee's seventh largest city with a population of 75,000 and top secret facilities that consumed nearly 15 percent of all the electricity generated in the U.S.

Few people at Oak Ridge knew precisely what was being produced there during the war. "Do you know what they make here?" one visitor asked a young boy in town. "Molasses," he replied. Trainees were told only that they were involved

WIRED Lie detector tests like this one were administered for security purposes at Oak Ridge.

in war work. Those whose jobs might give them some inkling of what the project was about were closely monitored. One woman who worked as a secretary for the manager of a plant where U-235 was extracted was required to undergo several polygraph tests. None of them was more revealing than a simple question from her boss, who asked her late in the war if she knew what they were working on. "I think we're making a bomb," she replied, "but I don't know what kind." He walked away without saying a word.

Ed Westcott was the only photographer authorized to take pictures at Oak Ridge during the war. Sampled here, they show what was in some ways an ordinary community involved in an extraordinary effort, one so complex that it took nearly two years from the time construction began in 1943 to produce enough U-235 for the first atomic bomb, dropped on Hiroshima. Not until then did many at Oak Ridge realize that their secret efforts had fueled a weapon that would end the war and change the world. ⊙

MINDING THEIR BUSINESS
Like maintenance workers at the secret city (near right), who knew only that they were keeping intricate machines running, the women below operated calutrons (far right) without realizing that those particle accelerators were producing fuel for an atomic bomb.

MINUTES COUNT Billboards similar to the one below, erected at Oak Ridge in early 1944, appeared in many places to encourage American war workers to be more efficient. But nowhere did time matter more than at facilities of the Manhattan Project, intended to shorten the war.

WHOSE SON WILL DIE IN THE LAST MINUTE OF THE WAR?

MINUTES COUNT!

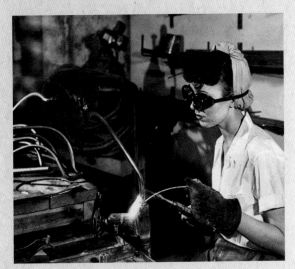

WELDER Women like this welder made up the majority of the wartime workforce at Oak Ridge.

SPRAWL Prefabricated homes for workers and their families proliferated as the secret city swelled.

COMIC RELIEF The population boom at Oak Ridge furnished customers for this boy selling comic books.

uranium became an all-out effort to produce an atomic bomb once the U.S. entered the war. Authorized by Roosevelt in January 1942, the Manhattan Project was managed by the U.S. Army Corps of Engineers, and one of its most accomplished officers—the hard-driving General Groves, described by his aide, Lt. Col. Kenneth Nichols, as "the biggest sonofabitch I've ever met in my life, but also one of the most capable individuals . . . He had absolute confidence in his decisions and he was absolutely ruthless in how he approached a problem to get it done." By the time Groves took charge of the project, scientists had determined that only a small component of uranium—the isotope U-235—was highly fissionable, capable of sustaining an explosive chain reaction when its nucleus split. Several methods were pursued for separating U-235 from the main component of uranium, U-238. (Those numbers indicate their atomic mass, or the sum of protons and neutrons in the nucleus.) The separation technique in which Groves made the biggest investment was devised by Ernest Lawrence, the director of the Radiation Laboratory at Berkeley and designer of the cyclotron, using electromagnets to accelerate and energize nuclear particles. Lawrence developed a similar accelerator called the calutron in which electromagnets propelled the heavier U-238 to a higher speed, leaving small amounts of the lighter U-235 behind to be collected. Hundreds of calutrons were built at Oak Ridge, Tennessee, a sprawling compound devoted to the Manhattan Project where secrecy was so strict that few of the 13,000 people who worked there during the war knew they were producing fuel for nuclear weapons.

Meanwhile, Fermi and his associates had joined the Manhattan Project and moved to the Metallurgical Laboratory at the University of Chicago, where they devised a small experimental reactor, which in late 1942 produced the first controlled nuclear chain reaction, generated within a critical mass of uranium—enough to sustain such a reaction. "The Italian navigator has landed in the New World," reported the lab's proud director, Arthur Compton. Controlling the chain reaction meant that such reactors might one day generate nuclear power for peaceful purposes, but they could also be used to transform uranium into plutonium, a new man-made element whose isotope Pu-239 was even more fissionable than U-235. Producing that plutonium isotope would be hazardous because large reactors generated intense heat during fission and could melt down and spew out deadly radioactive particles unless they were cooled. Groves settled on a remote site at Hanford, Washington, where the nearby Columbia

"The Italian navigator has landed in the New World,"

ARTHUR COMPTON,
DIRECTOR OF THE METALLURGICAL LABORATORY AT THE UNIVERSITY OF CHICAGO, ANNOUNCING ENRICO FERMI'S CONTROLLED NUCLEAR CHAIN REACTION

River provided water to cool the reactors as well as hydroelectric power to control them. Residents of Hanford and White Bluffs, a small town nearby, were given 30 days' notice to evacuate the area and were told only that the land was required for unspecified war work.

At Los Alamos, where Oppenheimer assembled the greatest concentration of scientific talent ever brought together for one purpose, work proceeded on the design of two bombs, one fueled by uranium-235 and the other by plutonium-239. Oppenheimer and his wizards faced huge technical challenges and feared that German scientists might produce a nuclear weapon before they did. One such warning came from physicist Niels Bohr, who fled to England from German-occupied Denmark in 1943 as the Gestapo prepared to round up Jews there. Bohr informed British authorities that his former pupil, Werner Heisenberg, now in charge of Germany's atomic weapons program, was seeking to develop a nuclear reactor that would use heavy water as a moderator—a substance that slows neutrons so they can be captured by the gravitational field of the heavy uranium nucleus and cause a chain reaction. Fermi had employed graphite as a moderator, but heavy water, a compound that does not occur naturally, was potentially even better for use in a nuclear reactor, which could produce fuel for an atomic bomb. When the Germans occupied Norway, they gained access to the first plant to manufacture heavy water on a large scale, located in the town of Vemork. In February 1943, the British dispatched six Norwegian refugees on a daring commando raid that disabled the plant for several months. A year later, after production resumed at Vemork, another commando team sank a ferry loaded with drums of heavy water destined for Germany.

That sabotage further hampered Heisenberg's pursuit of an atomic bomb, at which he never came close to succeeding. By 1944, Germany was subject to devastating strategic bombing and had too few elite scientists, skilled laborers, and industrial resources to spare for a secret weapons program like the Manhattan Project, which employed over 130,000 people at its peak and cost more than two billion dollars. In fact, the project was so complex and demanding that it was possible the U.S. might not have atomic bombs at its disposal before Germany was invaded and defeated. Japan, on the other hand, was an island nation that would not be occupied without a terrific struggle and might still be defiant when the first nuclear weapons were ready for deployment. That raised a moral dilemma for those who considered their work on the Manhattan Project justifiable if the fearsome weapons they produced were used to end Hitler's reign of terror. Some would question whether dropping those bombs to compel Japan's unconditional surrender was warranted and feared that doing so would set an ominous precedent as a new struggle for global supremacy loomed between the U.S. and U.S.S.R., whose spies persisted in efforts to steal American nuclear secrets. Were the atomic weapons under development at Los Alamos a gift that would bring a welcome conclusion to this war and discourage future wars? Or were they a scourge that might destroy civilization in the

URGENT NOTICE

1. **Fighting men and materials are being shifted for final phases of the war with Japan.**

2. **The enemy is using desperate measures to obtain all information which will help him delay his complete defeat.**
   Such information is reaching Japan.

3. **The small bit of information you discuss may help the Jap determine where, when, and with how much we strike.**

4. **Don't discuss:**

   (a) Location or movements of men, ships and materials within, to or from Asiatic-Pacific areas.

   (b) New weapons.

   (c) Military information gained in confidence.

Clayton Bissell, Major General, GSC
Assistant Chief of Staff, G-2

Hewlett Thebaud, Rear Admiral, U. S. Navy
Director of Naval Intelligence

J. Edgar Hoover, Director
Federal Bureau of Investigation

KEEPING MUM A poster issued in 1945, bearing the signatures of FBI Director J. Edgar Hoover and commanders responsible for U.S. Army Intelligence (G-2) and Naval Intelligence, warns war workers and military personnel against discussing new weapons or other sensitive military information as the war against Japan enters its "final phases."

next great conflict? Oppenheimer would long be troubled by that question and dogged by lingering suspicions as to his loyalty, which were seemingly laid to rest during World War II, only to resurface during the contentious Cold War that followed.

COVERT OPERATIONS IN ASIA

While scientists at Los Alamos used advanced technology to inaugurate a revolutionary new era in warfare, Allied troops were engaged in a rudimentary struggle against Japanese forces in which modern rules of war often gave way to the ancient law of the jungle. Science and secret intelligence breakthroughs had earlier loomed large in the Pacific War when cryptanalysts cracked Japanese codes and helped American forces recover from the calamitous attack on Pearl Harbor by prevailing at Midway and killing Admiral Yamamoto. But ousting Japanese soldiers from the many Pacific islands and Asian countries they occupied was often a matter of brute force. Covert operations figured in the fighting, but those conducting them had to be prepared to steep their boots in mud and their hands in blood. Nowhere was the combat more brutal or basic than in Burma, occupied in 1942 by the Japanese, who clung tenaciously to that country, wedged between British-ruled India and China, where an American commander, Lt. Gen. Joseph Stilwell, was aiding Chinese Nationalist forces led by Chiang Kai-shek in their fight against Japanese invaders. The focus of the contest was Myitkyina in northern Burma, site of a strategic airfield and rail depot controlled by Japanese forces, who fiercely opposed Allied efforts to reclaim the area and restore the Burma Road to China as a supply line for the Nationalists.

Northern Burma was so remote and its jungle so dense that modern weaponry in the form of warplanes, tanks, and artillery played little part in the struggle. Foot soldiers mired there faced numerous hazards besides being shot, knifed, or bayoneted by the enemy, including encounters with bloodthirsty leeches, man-eating tigers, poisonous snakes, and swarms of mosquitoes that spread malaria and other plagues. Laced with narrow trails bordered by thickets, it was an ideal setting for booby traps, ambushes, and other forms of guerrilla warfare. William Donovan saw an opportunity there to inject his OSS operatives into the Asian war and handed the assignment to Capt. Carl Eifler, whose outfit was designated Detachment 101. A bruising, 250-pound bear of a man, Eifler had served under Stilwell and prevailed on "Vinegar Joe," who was skeptical of covert operations, to allow the detachment to conduct sabotage behind enemy lines in Burma. "All I want to hear is booms from the jungle," Stilwell told him.

Eifler set up camp at Nazira, India, with some two dozen OSS agents drawn from the U.S. armed forces for this hazardous venture. "Men were expected to volunteer blindly," he recalled. "They were advised they would likely be signing their own death warrant." Eifler

> ## "All I want to hear is booms from the jungle."
> LT. GEN. JOSEPH STILWELL TO CAPT. CARL EIFLER, WHO LED THE OSS DETACHMENT 101 BEHIND ENEMY LINES IN BURMA

SNAKE CHARMER As shown here handling a poisonous snake, Carl Eifler was something of a daredevil. But as commander of Detachment 101, he rejected any volunteer who appeared to be "a hell-raiser or a glory-seeker." Following an accident during a covert mission in Burma that left him dazed and deaf in one ear, Donovan replaced him as commander in late 1943 with Col. William Peers.

BURMA
1939–1945

BHUTAN
Ledo
Nazira
INDIA
Kohima
Imphal
Brahmaputra
Ledo
Road
Myitkyina
Sumprabum
CHINA
Burma Road
To
Kunming
Chindwin
Lashio
Mandalay
BURMA
Irrawaddy
Salween
Mekong
FRENCH
INDOCHINA
Magwe
(Magway)
Prome
(Pyay)
Toungoo
(Taungoo)
BAY OF
BENGAL
Pegu
(Bago)
Rangoon
(Yangon)
THAILAND
Thanbyuzayat
Thai–Burma
Railway
Bangkok
(Krung
Thep)
Ban
Pong

Burma Road
Ledo Road
Railway
Kachin
Territory

ANDAMAN
SEA

0 mi   100
0 km   100
1939 boundaries are shown.

OUTREACH OSS Lt. Vincent Curl, standing here beside a Kachin tribesman, recruited and armed hundreds of Kachin to fight the Japanese in northern Burma, wedged between India and China (see map at top). Bolstered by those recruits, Detachment 101 helped Allied troops capture Myitkyina in 1944 and secure the Burma and Ledo Roads as supply lines for Chinese Nationalist troops.

bolstered the detachment with Burmese refugees in India who sympathized with the British and their American allies. But his keenest recruits were Kachin tribesmen who lived in northern Burma and defied Japanese occupiers and allied warriors of the Shan tribe, age-old rivals of the Kachin. In 1943, Eifler dispatched Capt. Vincent Curl to establish a base among Kachins near Myitkyina, gather intelligence on Japanese forces in the vicinity, sabotage roads and bridges they used, and help rescue downed Allied airmen. "Vince Curl could charm a snake," a fellow officer recalled. "I've never known him to go into a Kachin village without instantly attracting a retinue of Kachin kids, all crowding around him, all talking and laughing . . . Vince Curl was America's secret weapon in Burma."

Soon after setting up his base, Curl learned of a Kachin chief named Zhing Htaw Naw who was launching hit-and-run attacks on the Japanese from a distant mountain stronghold. Curl set out to meet with him, only to be informed at the end of a long, grueling journey that Zhing was gravely ill and must not be disturbed. "I can cure him," Curl declared, without knowing what Zhing was suffering from or whether the medicine he carried would prevent the chief from dying, for which Curl might then be blamed. He was relieved to discover that Zhing had contracted malaria, which Curl treated with quinine. When the chief's fever abated, he agreed to make common cause against the Japanese with the OSS, which supplied arms to nearly 1,000 Kachin warriors over the next few months. Their traditional weapons were spears and blowguns, but they proved handy with firearms, including old muzzle-loading shotguns, which Eifler obtained for them so that they could use "the nuts and bolts from wrecked vehicles for ammunition."

The struggle between Japanese troops and Kachin warriors was ferocious. "Most of the Kachins lived on inaccessible mountain ridges," wrote Richard Dunlop, a veteran of Detachment 101, "but on the valley floor there were several villages that were vulnerable to Japanese attack." According to Dunlop, rival Shan tribesmen advised officers of the Kempeitai—the dreaded Japanese security force responsible for maintaining security in occupied territories—that they could "terrorize the Kachin mountain warriors into making peace by carrying out ferocious attacks on the lowland villages. Fire, rape, and the mutilation of young boys would intimidate the Kachins into surrender." Instead, those brutal assaults, conducted by regular troops as ordered by the Kempeitai, enraged Kachin warriors, who often tortured and killed Japanese soldiers who fell into their hands. OSS recruits could do little to prevent such acts of vengeance, and some Americans in Burma shared the feeling that the enemy deserved no mercy. "Hostility against Japanese military units was understandably high among some of our guerrilla teams," recalled Richard Morse, who served under Eifler's OSS successor, Col. William Peers. "In one case this went to an extreme. Word reached us by radio from the field that an enlisted man had tied dynamite to a prisoner and blown him up." When Peers learned of the incident, he had the culprit

These photos and those on the next page offer an intimate look at Detachment 101 and its Kachin recruits operating against the Japanese in Burma in conjunction with American airmen and British troops. Pictured here are a cameraman amid curious villagers, elephants hauling supplies, a man with a pet monkey, a mixed force of OSS and Kachin commandos in transit, medical aid for a young villager, and hunters hauling a tiger they killed back to camp.

JUNGLE WARFARE **These views of combat operations by Detachment 101 and their tribal allies include a machine gunner posing in a plane, an Allied patrol filing through the jungle, weapons instruction for Kachins gathered around a table, a furtive snapshot of Japanese soldiers standing amid the wreckage of a downed aircraft, a Kachin warrior kneeling beside a fallen foe, and a caged Japanese captive.**

court-martialed and sent a message "to all field units spelling out the rules of war on prisoners, and warning that anyone violating those rules would meet immediate punishment." Such was Peers's reputation for upholding the rules of war that he was chosen many years later to head the commission investigating the My Lai Massacre in Vietnam.

In all, some 10,000 Kachins waged guerrilla warfare against the Japanese in Burma. Together with Detachment 101, they cleared Japanese forces from nearly 10,000 square miles of Burmese territory and set the stage for Stilwell's forces to invade Burma and capture Myitkyina in August 1944. Meanwhile, an OSS Morale Operations (MO) branch in New Delhi, India, was doing its best to deceive and demoralize Japanese troops in Burma and their family members back home. This was the first assignment for Elizabeth "Betty" McIntosh, a 29-year-old journalist born in Hawaii who studied Japanese there and was recruited by the OSS in 1943 to help devise and disseminate black propaganda in Asia—information that appeared to come from Japanese sources but was contrived to confound the enemy. She and her MO colleagues in New Delhi, including Japanese Americans she had known in Hawaii, began by altering a large bundle of postcards that Japanese soldiers had written home before a recent battle, during which they were defeated and their correspondence fell into Allied hands. The OSS team erased the messages without leaving a trace and substituted words of gloom and doom that countered official Japanese claims that the troops were holding up well under pressure and were sure to prevail. McIntosh then asked Colonel Peers to have Kachins furtively slip the bundle into a Japanese postal van. "Mission accomplished," Peers notified her a few days later. "Every reason to believe material will reach objective."

McIntosh went on to implement a more ambitious deception after Gen. Hideki Tojo resigned as Japan's prime minister in July 1944 amid ominous setbacks for imperial forces in Asia and the Pacific. It occurred to her that embattled Japanese officers in Burma might wonder if the new regime in Tokyo would continue to insist that soldiers in desperate straits fight to the death. "While Tojo was in control," she noted, "Japanese troops were indoctrinated with the fanatical belief that surrender was dishonorable . . . If recaptured after surrender, a Japanese soldier was subjected to penalties ranging from death by firing squad to banishment from Japan." McIntosh and her team forged an order from Tokyo to the Japanese headquarters in Rangoon, Burma, stating that when troops were out of ammunition or "hopelessly outnumbered in battle," it was permissible for them to surrender so as to "preserve Japanese manhood" for the postwar era. Once again, Detachment 101 lent a hand by assigning a Kachin warrior to kill an enemy courier and slip the forged document into his pouch, where it was later retrieved by Japanese troops. To ensure wider circulation for the phony order, it was copied and dropped from aircraft as a leaflet by the thousands over Japanese-occupied territory. The impact of such black propaganda was hard to measure, but officers with Detachment 101 later told

(continued on page 322)

OSS MAP Close surveillance of Japanese movements produced this map of a contested area near Myitkyina, prepared by Detachment 101. A note at upper right near a "very important suspension bridge" states that "during raids Japs hide in bushes." Maps like this one were used to plan operations in Burma, and copies were submitted to OSS headquarters.

THE SECRET WORLD OF BETTY McINTOSH

When the forces of imperial Japan struck Pearl Harbor on the morning of December 7, 1941, Elizabeth "Betty" McIntosh was a well-established 26-year-old journalist in her native Hawaii. Having studied Japanese, her ambition had long been to live and work in Japan, a dream that evaporated in the smoke of a devastated American fleet. Although issued press credentials as a war correspondent covering Adm. Chester Nimitz's Pacific Theater, she was soon transferred to Washington. D.C., where she wrote a "home front" column on women's issues and was granted frequent interviews with First Lady Eleanor Roosevelt. McIntosh still hoped to become an overseas correspondent, but her opportunity to serve abroad came instead from the OSS, which recruited her in 1943 for its newly formed Morale Operations (MO) branch. She had been trained as a reporter to deal in truth and transparency, but her new duties required that she learn to deceive, demoralize, and confuse the enemy through black propaganda. In her case, that meant producing deceptive letters, pamphlets, and radio broadcasts that purported to originate in Japan or Japanese territory but came from OSS stations elsewhere in Asia.

Betty McIntosh was first assigned to New Delhi, where she was tasked with getting a new MO shop up and running. That was no small challenge, considering she started out with no printing press, ink, or paper. She solved these problems by befriending her British counterparts and trading her cigarette rations for the use of their materials. Soon MO Delhi was producing pamphlets fomenting rumors that Russian forces were poised to pour across the border into Japanese-occupied Manchuria, radio scripts describing bleak conditions on the home islands, and a variety of other schemes designed to demoralize the increasingly isolated, famished, and frightened Japanese soldiers who were retreating through the jungles of Burma in 1944. By the spring of 1945, when she was ordered to fly "over the hump" of the Himalayas to Kunming, China, she had been put in charge of Morale Operations for the entire China-Burma-India Theater. She spent the rest of the war practicing her craft in Kunming, and ultimately played a role in OSS Mercy Missions, which rescued Allied POWs from Japanese prison camps as hostilities came to a close. ✪

MO TEAM Betty McIntosh poses at war's end with two of her colleagues at the door of their OSS Morale Operations print shop in Kunming, China, which was inundated by a flood that occurred soon after the destruction of Hiroshima and Nagasaki.

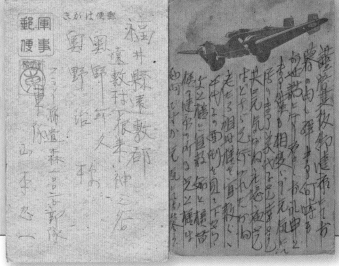

FALSE NOTES McIntosh's team in New Delhi forged certificates issued to tribal headmen who collaborated with the Japanese (left) and splattered the documents with blood to warn collaborators that their blood would be spilled too. The postcard below was one of many on which the team replaced notes written home by Japanese soldiers with messages describing a demoralized army in Burma.

MATCHBOX MESSAGE The note at right, written on thin paper for insertion in a matchbox with a fake Japanese cover (above), warned those on Formosa that Japan could not defend the island against American attacks.

Bombing of Japan

PURPOSE: Picture folders similar to these were designed to shake morale among Japanese soldiers in Burma.

DESCRIPTION: Photos are faked and are inscribed on reverse side in Japanese script, as if written by someone who recently left Japan and brought the pictures with him. Translations are beneath each picture.

They left our city in flames

This was a factory worker

He was strafed near his sampan

Aoki's house caved in

Killed on her way to a shelter

Bodies were burned in factories

Bomb concussion wrecked

BOMB DAMAGE Captioned in English, the photographs here were faked and had notes on the back in Japanese referring to the devastation in bomb-ravaged Japan. The purpose was to convince anxious soldiers that their government was hiding the truth about the dire situation facing their families back home as American bombers targeted Japanese cities.

NOTE: The Chinese text is written in a jingle form which there is no attempt to approximate in the English translation.

1. If you laugh....
2. The Japs will yank your gold teeth....
3. So never smile!
4. If you work hard...
5. The Japs will break your back working for them.....
6. So loaf and have a gay time!
7. If the Japs see your women....
8. Even the ugliest will be taken for prostitution...
9. So hide them or send them away!

SUBVERSIVE CARTOON Designed to counter claims by the Japanese that they were liberating occupied populations and freeing Asians from colonial oppression, this cartoon suggests that a much darker future awaits those living under Japanese authority—enslavement.

PROMISES AND THREATS Leaflets aimed at hungry Japanese troops promise that they will be well fed if they surrender to Americans (above) and warn that Burmese guerrillas will kill them (left) and leave their bodies to rot in the jungle.

THE NIGHTMARE OF "COMFORT WOMEN"

During the war, Japanese military authorities maintained hundreds of so-called comfort stations for troops in occupied territory where women and girls were forced to serve as prostitutes. The commander who established the first comfort stations in China said that he did so to stop Japanese troops from raping Chinese women. But many comfort women were abducted and raped before they were thrown into the brothels. Others were lured away from home on false pretenses. Comfort stations were supposed to prevent the spread of venereal disease, but women were often infected or impregnated by soldiers who took no precautions. One woman recalled that she and others at her station "had to serve 20 to 30 soldiers a day" and ended up "half dead."

Tens of thousands of women from Korea and other occupied countries were reduced to servitude in those brothels, and the total may have exceeded 100,000. Not until long after the conflict ended did women who had been forced into prostitution by the Japanese begin to speak publicly of their ordeal and shed light on one of the war's last dark secrets. "Why haven't I been able to lead a normal life, free from shame, like other people?" one of them asked. "I feel I could tear apart, limb by limb, those who took away my innocence and made me as I am." ◗

RESCUED A pregnant woman rests with three other Koreans after they escaped from a Japanese comfort station in China in 1944 with the help of the Chinese soldier beside them.

McIntosh "they believed the forgery had a direct impact on Japanese soldiers' will to resist, particularly toward the end of the Burma campaign."

She was later sent to China and flew "over the Hump" of the Himalayas with other OSS women, including Julia McWilliams, who handled classified documents for the agency and later wed her OSS colleague, Paul Child, to become the famous cook Julia Child. During the harrowing flight, McIntosh recalled, Julia "calmly read a book while all the rest of us were preparing to die." McIntosh's final wartime assignment in 1945 involved writing scripts for MO radio broadcasts to Japan. She and her associates concocted grim prophecies for the Japanese populace that they attributed to a Chinese visionary called the Hermit. One of those predictions turned out by chance to be eerily accurate. Broadcast in 1945 as the Manhattan Project neared its explosive conclusion, it stated that "a disaster of catastrophic proportions will take place in a Japanese city sometime during the first week in August."

The Japanese also produced propaganda radio broadcasts, including a show called *Zero Hour,* which was aimed at Allied forces and featured popular music interspersed with seductive appeals in English from women who sounded sympathetic but read scripts designed to demoralize the soldiers. Those announcers sounded much alike to American forces in the Pacific, who lumped them together under the title "Tokyo Rose." One of them—Iva Toguri, a Japanese American who went to visit relatives and became stranded in Japan when the war broke out—was later convicted of treason in the U.S., but ultimately received a presidential pardon. She and others were pressured into broadcasting propaganda, in some cases by the Kempeitai, which was authorized to seize, torture, and execute spies, defiant prisoners of war, or suspect foreigners in Japan and its occupied territories. The Kempeitai also compelled women from Korea, Taiwan, and other occupied Asian countries to serve as prostitutes in brothels for Japanese troops. Those "comfort women" worked at "comfort stations" established to prevent soldiers from visiting unauthorized brothels, where they might contract venereal disease or reveal military secrets to prostitutes serving as spies. Kempeitai agents regularly visited the stations to ensure that comfort women or Japanese troops who visited them were not engaged in espionage.

Despite Kempeitai surveillance of POW camps, some Allied inmates formed secret networks and forged links with the outside world. Capt. Lionel Matthews of the Australian Army Signal Corps and others confined at the notorious Sandakan POW camp on Borneo were forced to labor on a military road and airfield for the Japanese. That was a violation of international law but helped them make surreptitious contact with sympathetic civilians outside the compound, who provided them with medicine, radio components, and small weapons that they cached. They hoped to stage an uprising in concert with local resistance fighters, but the Kempeitai seized one of their collaborators and forced him to talk, leading to the arrest of Matthews and several members of his network. Under torture, he refused to reveal the names of other POWs or civilians involved in the operation, and was executed in March 1944 by firing squad—a rare concession to military convention by the Kempeitai, who often beheaded their victims with swords. Conditions worsened at Sandakan thereafter. As Allied forces approached Borneo in late 1944, some 2,000 emaciated POWs were evacuated from the camp and conducted to the interior of the island on a death march, during which many collapsed and expired and others who could not keep up were killed by their guards. Only six Australian escapees survived the ordeal.

SNATCHING JAPAN'S PLAN Z

Resistance to Japanese occupation was widespread in the Philippines, where guerrillas had long opposed foreign domination, fighting first against Spanish colonizers and later against American troops who seized the islands from Spain in 1898. By the time Japanese troops arrived in December 1941, Filipinos had been promised independence within five years and were more inclined to trust in Americans who made that pledge than in Japanese who posed as liberators but acted like yet another intrusive colonial power, imposing their will by force of arms. While most American and Filipino soldiers retreated to the Bataan Peninsula with General MacArthur and eventually surrendered to the Japanese, some fled to remote areas on Luzon, Mindanao, Leyte, or smaller Philippine islands and resisted the occupiers. Attacks on Japanese troops and installations brought fierce reprisals. MacArthur, who had been evacuated to Australia, communicated by radio with officers holding out on the islands and urged them to concentrate on gathering intelligence on Japanese military strength and movements until his forces returned to the Philippines, which would trigger an uprising by resistance fighters. In the spring of 1944, as MacArthur prepared to return as promised, members of the Filipino-American resistance network pulled off the most dramatic intelligence coup in the Pacific theater since the downing of Admiral Yamamoto's plane a year earlier by snatching the strategic plan of his successor, Adm. Mineichi Koga, commander of Japan's Combined Fleet.

By March 1944, Koga's battered fleet was hard-pressed by the fast-expanding U.S. Pacific Fleet. Japanese forces in the Pacific were left holding a defensive line extending from Koga's base at Palau, some 500 miles east of the Philippines, northward to the Marianas Islands and the more distant Volcano Islands, including Iwo Jima, due south of Japan's home islands. Koga was prepared to risk all on a desperate naval battle that he hoped would turn the tide and save what remained of the Japanese Empire. Winning such a decisive battle had long been the supreme ambition of Japanese admirals, including Yamamoto, who had sought that triumph at Midway and instead suffered a devastating setback. Koga now hoped to alter the course of the war with a fleet that faced much longer odds than Yamamoto's did. He laid out his prospectus for victory, known as Plan Z, in a secret order issued on March 8 from his flagship *Musashi,* anchored at Palau. It was not a specific battle plan because it

CLINGING TO HOPE Adm. Mineichi Koga, who became commander in chief of Japan's Combined Fleet following the death of Isoroku Yamamoto in April 1943, drew up Plan Z, a proposal for luring the U.S. Pacific Fleet into an exposed position where it might be defeated in a decisive battle. Japanese commanders clung to that hope until late in the war, despite the massive buildup of American naval power in the Pacific.

"What man can say that there is no chance for our fleet to turn the tide of war in a decisive battle?"

VICE ADM. TAKEO KURITA, OCTOBER 1944

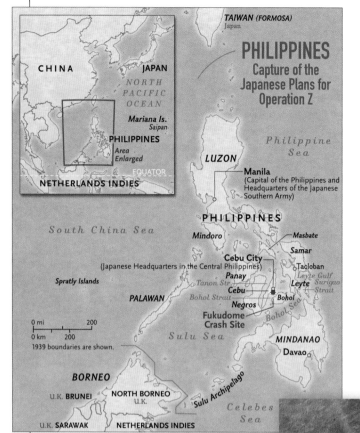

PHILIPPINES
Capture of the
Japanese Plans for
Operation Z

CAPTURED Seated here with family, Rear Adm. Shigeru Fukudome was flying separately and survived the storm in which Admiral Koga died when his plane went down on the night of March 31, 1944. But Fukudome was captured by pro-American Filipinos after his flying boat, similar to the one at upper right, made a crash landing off Cebu in the Philippines. Amid the wreckage was Plan Z, which washed ashore in a box near the crash site (see map at top) and was delivered to American intelligence officers.

involved reacting to the next big push by the Pacific Fleet, which could come at various points along his defensive line. When that advance occurred, he proposed luring American aircraft carriers into a pursuit that would bring them within range of land-based Japanese warplanes, which would then combine with carriers and other warships of the Combined Fleet in an all-out attack intended to repel the Pacific Fleet and secure Japan's "last line of defense."

In late March, bombers from an American carrier task force attacked Palau. It was not the big push that Koga anticipated, but the heavy air raid damaged his superbattleship *Musashi,* sank more than a dozen other vessels, and destroyed 150 aircraft. On March 31, he and his staff took off for Davao in the Philippines, which was less exposed to attack and would serve as their new base. Much as Yamamoto did before his fatal flight a year earlier, Koga arranged for several of his top officers to fly separately—among them his chief of staff, Rear Adm. Shigeru Fukudome—to reduce the risk that all would be lost in a crash. This time, it was not enemy fire but hostile elements that brought down the commander of the Combined Fleet. Koga's plane encountered a severe tropical storm and disappeared without a trace. Fukudome's plane skirted the worst of that storm but ran low on fuel and crashed into the sea while attempting an emergency landing at night on the Philippine island of Cebu. Fukudome swam from the wreckage and nearly drowned before fishermen rescued him and 10 other survivors. To his horror, guerrillas then took them as prisoners, a bitter fate for any Japanese soldier but particularly shameful for a high-ranking officer. He assumed that secret documents entrusted to him—including the Z Plan and an order indicating where Japanese warships and naval aircraft should be deployed in advance of the operation—had been lost in the crash and would not fall into enemy hands. But they survived because the leather pouch holding them was stored in a wooden box that floated ashore, where a resistance member found and hid the documents to prevent Japanese soldiers from recovering them.

The guerrillas took their prisoners to a remote camp on Cebu commanded by Lt. Col. James Cushing, an American mining engineer who had enlisted in the U.S. Army when the Japanese invaded the Philippines. Cushing's wife was Filipino, and he had close ties to local officials and villagers, many of whom joined forces with him. After a doctor at the base treated Fukudome for wounds sustained in the crash, Cushing questioned the admiral, who spoke English. He could not conceal the fact that he was a senior officer to whom other prisoners deferred but gave a false name and rank to throw Cushing off. Meanwhile, Japanese forces were searching frantically for survivors of the plane crash and for the secret documents, which were conveyed to Cushing soon after the prisoners reached his camp. Kempeitai officers seized and interrogated suspects on Cebu, some of whom were executed, and troops took hostages and torched the homes of people who refused to cooperate. To avoid further reprisals against the populace, Cushing released the captives to the enemy commander on Cebu. "Jap prisoners too hot for us to hold," he notified MacArthur's Australian headquarters by radio. "I made terms that civilians are not to be molested in future, in exchange for the prisoners." Cushing held on to the documents—which only he and those reporting to him knew for sure had survived the crash—and smuggled them to a superior officer on the island of Negros, Lt. Col. Edwin Andrews, who was under less pressure from Japanese troops.

On May 11, the submarine U.S.S. *Crevalle* surfaced off Negros and picked up 40 American refugees destined for Australia and a small packet whose contents astounded MacArthur's intelligence officers when it reached them. The prize item was "Secret Combined Fleet Order No. 73," whose red cover was inscribed with the letter Z. In it, the fleet's late commander, Admiral Koga, pledged to "maintain our hold on vital areas" by bringing to bear "the combined maximum strength of all our forces to meet and destroy the enemy." When copies of that order and other documents salvaged from the plane crash off Cebu reached Edwin Layton, Admiral Nimitz's intelligence chief in Honolulu, he alerted his boss as to their significance. Despite severe losses at Midway and elsewhere in the Pacific over the past two years, the Imperial Japanese Navy was adhering to the doctrine of a decisive battle, in which it would risk its remaining assets to repulse the American onslaught. Layton had little doubt that under Koga's successor, Adm. Soemu Toyoda, the Japanese would respond to "our next advance into their island defense system" by hurling "everything they had against us."

Nimitz shared that intelligence with Vice Adm. Raymond Spruance, whose powerful U.S. Fifth Fleet was approaching the Marianas to support a massive amphibious assault on Saipan, which began on June 14. Anticipating a stiff challenge from Toyoda, Spruance sent a carrier task force commanded by Rear Adm. Marc Mitscher west of the Marianas to guard against Japanese aircraft carriers approaching from the Philippines. He warned Mitscher not to be lured into a headlong pursuit of the enemy, a chase that might expose him to attack by land-based Japanese warplanes, as envisioned in Plan Z. Confident in his airmen, who were now better trained and equipped than their Japanese counterparts, Mitscher went out on a limb and prevailed in battle against the task force dispatched by

SECRET

12 APRIL, 1944

TO : GENERAL MACARTHUR

FROM : CUSHING (VIA WAT)

NR 12   9 APRIL

JAP PRISONERS TOO HOT FOR US TO HOLD. DUE TO NUMBER OF CIVILIANS BEING KILLED, I MADE TERMS THAT CIVILIANS ARE NOT TO BE MOLESTED IN FUTURE, IN EXCHANGE FOR THE PRISONERS. ALTHOUGH THE ENEMY DID NOT KNOW IT, WE HAD ONLY 25 SOLDIERS BETWEEN THE ATTACKING FORCE OF APPROXIMATELY FIVE HUNDRED AND OUR POSITION. ALSO, WE WERE UNABLE TO MANEUVER OUT OF OUR POSITION. ENEMY NOW WITHDRAWING TOWARDS CITY. IN SOUTHERN CEBU, JAPS WERE REPORTED TWO THOUSAND STRONG, LOOKING FOR THE PRISONERS.

NOTE: THE FIRST REPORT OF THE CAPTURE OF THE PRISONERS REACHED GHQ ON THE DAY THIS MESSAGE WAS SENT, OR AFTER THE PRISONERS HAD BEEN RETURNED TO THE ENEMY.

CONFIDENTIAL CARDED
SECRET   LOGGED 12

TOO HOT TO HANDLE Lt. Col. James Cushing of the U.S. Army, in hiding with Filipino guerrillas on Cebu, took charge of Admiral Fukudome and other prisoners before releasing them under pressure from Japanese forces who were retaliating against civilians, as stated here in Cushing's radio message to General MacArthur's headquarters. Intelligence officers there regretted missing the chance to interrogate Fukudome but were delighted when Cushing relayed Plan Z to them.

> ## "Would it not be a shame to have the fleet intact while our nation perishes?"
>
> VICE ADM. TAKEO KURITA
> BEFORE THE BATTLE OF LEYTE GULF

Toyoda, whose fleet was too widely dispersed to be concentrated off the Marianas, as he had hoped. Far from being the decisive victory he sought, the Battle of the Philippine Sea was another punishing setback for the Combined Fleet, which lost three carriers and nearly 300 aircraft in fighting that jubilant Americans dubbed the "Great Marianas Turkey Shoot." Spruance was criticized for not going all out to do even more harm to the enemy. But the intelligence he received counseled caution, and his overriding task was to shield the invasion of Saipan, which succeeded and provided the U.S. Army Air Force with a base from which to bomb Japan.

Following that Japanese debacle, the decisive-battle doctrine affirmed by Plan Z was reduced to a last-ditch effort by Admiral Toyoda and his commanders to uphold their honor by sacrificing the fleet in action, if necessary. As Vice Adm. Takeo Kurita remarked, they were possessed by a "suicide spirit," not unlike that of the kamikaze pilots who sought a glorious death by crashing their planes into enemy warships. In October 1944, Kurita was assigned the forbidding task of threading perilous straits near the Philippine island of Leyte, where MacArthur's forces were about to land, and attacking the U.S. Third and Seventh Fleets, which were shielding the invasion. Kurita knew that the much diminished Combined Fleet was no match for such opposition but believed that its forces must fight for Japan to the bitter end. "Would it not be a shame to have the fleet intact while our nation perishes?" he asked his officers. Lest they lose hope, he repeated the mantra that helped them keep fighting as their plight worsened: "What man can say that there is no chance for our fleet to turn the tide of war in a decisive battle?"

The Battle of Leyte Gulf was close-fought, but when it ended little was left of the Combined Fleet. Toyoda was powerless to prevent his foes from retaking the Philippines and closing in on Japan's home islands. Special operations contributed to those Allied advances, including daring forays by OSS frogmen, who reconnoitered some Japanese-occupied islands before they were attacked and used explosives to clear paths for landing craft through coral reefs. Captured Japanese maps and U.S. submarine surveillance missions helped chart enemy territory for troops who came ashore, and Navajo code talkers provided units in action with radio communications that were indecipherable by the Japanese. No stratagems or subterfuge, however, spared American forces from facing horrific combat and suffering heavy casualties when they stormed fiercely defended Iwo Jima in February 1945 and invaded Okinawa two months later. Judging by those costly victories, it was estimated that as many as one million Americans might be killed or wounded if Japan held out and had to be invaded, which appeared likely. Not even the firebombing of Tokyo and other Japanese cities, which killed hundreds of thousands of civilians, impelled Emperor Hirohito and his ministers to accept the bitter necessity of surrendering. U.S. Marines and soldiers who survived earlier bloodbaths in the Pacific prayed that somehow victory could be achieved without an invasion, unaware that a secret weapon of unimaginable power was about to be tested in New Mexico.

TOP SECRET

GUIDING PLAN OF "Z" OPERATIONS

Page 22

8 Mar 44
Combined Fleet HQ   8/10

Page 23

1. Estimate of concentrated forces

A. Air strength of bases.

Area		Estimated strength 10 Mar		Estimated strength End of Mar		Estimated strength End of Apr
Central PACIFIC	MARIANNAS	fighters A (*1)	120	fighters	140	Same as preceding + fighters B (*3) 36 and some others
		bombers	35	bombers	35	
		land based attack planes	50	land based attack planes	60	
		(1 Air Fleet) fighters C (*2)	10	land based bombers	80	
				(1 Air Fleet) fighters C	15	
	Eastern CAROLINES	fighters	130	fighters	150	Some additional
		attack planes	30	attack planes	30	
		land based attack planes	60	land based attack planes	30	
		(22 Air Wing)(sf) (25 Air Wing)		fighters C	10	
	Western CAROLINES	fighters	20	fighters A	75	(battle strength gradually increasing) some additional
		land based attack planes	10	bombers	30	
		bombers	20	land based attack planes	20	
		(26 Air Wing)				
	IWO Island (TN Volcano Is)	bombers (22 Air Wing)	38	bombers	38	
	North-Eastern Area	(51 Air Wing) fighters	30	fighters	60	
		bombers	30	bombers	36	
		attack planes	3	attack planes	18	
		land based attack planes	20	land based attack planes	27	
				flying boats	10	
					151 planes	

(Continued on following page)

(*1) etc:-

(1) 甲   (3) 乙

(2) 丙

TOP SECRET
-11-

AIR STRENGTH Capturing Plan Z provided American naval commanders not just with insights into Japanese strategic thinking but with these details on air strength at enemy bases in the Pacific.

CHINA

Okinawa
Ryukyu Islands J A P A N
TAIWAN (FORMOSA)
Japan

South China Sea

LUZON

PHILIPPINES

PHILIPPINE ISLANDS

Palawan

N. BORNEO
U.K.

Sulu Sea

MINDANAO

Celebes Sea

BORNEO

NETHERLANDS INDIES

EQUATOR

0 mi 400
0 km 400

Philippine Sea

Task Force 58 (Mitscher)

1st Mobile Fleet (Ozawa)
June 15

June 15

June 19

Yap Islands

Palau

Caroline Islands

Ulithi Atoll

Bonin Is.

Iwo Jima

Mariana Islands

Pagan

Saipan
Tinian
Rota
Guam

June 19

June 12

BATTLE OF THE PHILIPPINE SEA
June 19 – 20, 1944

SHOT DOWN **A stricken fighter plummets during the Battle of the Philippine Sea in June 1944 (map at top). Rear Adm. Marc Mitscher (above), commander of Task Force 58, was shielding American troops as they landed on Saipan and was guarding against attack as urged by Vice Adm. Raymond Spruance, who knew of Plan Z. On June 19, Mitscher's carrier-based fighters met warplanes from Japan's 1st Mobile Fleet, 300 of which went down in the Great Marianas Turkey Shoot.**

NATIVE AMERICAN CODE TALKERS

In the heat of battle during World War II, radio messages were often sent in plain language by combatants who did not have the time or means to use cipher machines or codebooks. That exposed their messages to enemy listeners who knew their language and led to the deployment of signalmen who spoke little-known languages. For that purpose, the U.S. Army and Marine Corps recruited hundreds of Native Americans from such tribes as the Navajo, Hopi, Comanche, and Choctaw. They sometimes communicated in their tribal language, but for extra security they developed codes to foil any foes who knew their language—a possibility that could not be ruled out because German and Japanese scholars had studied American Indian languages before the war. Comanche code talkers landed in Normandy on D-Day to provide troops with secure radio communications.

More than 350 Navajo code talkers served with the Marines in the Pacific, using a system they devised that included code words for each letter in the alphabet. "C" was encoded as the Navajo word for cat, for example, and "D" by their word for dog. In addition, they had code words for common military terms such as "tank," which they encoded as the Navajo word for turtle. They mastered that code readily and communicated rapidly because their rich oral tradition gave them quick tongues and sharp memories. "For us, everything is memory," remarked Navajo code talker Carl Gorman. "Our songs, our prayers, our stories, they're all handed down from grandfather to father to children." They also drew on tribal traditions of bravery to hold steady under fire on fiercely contested Pacific islands such as Saipan and Iwo Jima, where their services were essential. Without them, their signal officer said, "the Marines would never have taken Iwo Jima." ✪

AWARD Code talkers received this combat service medal for their hazardous duty overseas.

SIGNALMEN A Navajo code talker with a portable radio like the Navy TBY at right in his backpack communicates with another member of his unit while a signalman at his side transcribes a message received in code.

A BLINDING NUCLEAR DAWN

By the time Germany was defeated in May 1945, scientists working under Oppenheimer's direction at Los Alamos had received enough fuel from the Oak Ridge and Hanford facilities to produce atomic bombs of two types, one containing uranium-235 and the other plutonium-239. The uranium bomb, dubbed "Little Boy," would be detonated by a gun that shot a plug of U-235 into a larger amount of that isotope, producing an explosive, supercritical mass. That method would not work for the plutonium bomb, because the isotope Pu-239 underwent spontaneous fission at such a high rate that no gun could bring it to a supercritical mass fast enough to prevent the bomb from fizzling. Scientists solved that problem—the greatest technical challenge faced at Los Alamos—by producing "Fat Man," a round bomb with Pu-239 at its core, surrounded by explosives rigged to implode and compress the fuel to a supercritical mass instantaneously. That implosion technique would be tested by detonating the bomb at a proving ground designated the Trinity Site, in the southern New Mexico desert.

With no immediate end to the war in sight, scientists and officials debated privately whether atomic bombs should be used against Japan—and if so, where. The work at Los Alamos had been so demanding and intensive that few of those involved in producing the first nuclear weapons had spent much time considering the consequences of their actions.

(continued on page 332)

"What do they know about Japanese psychology? How can they judge the way to end the war?"

J. ROBERT OPPENHEIMER ON SCIENTISTS WHO OPPOSED MILITARY PLANS TO USE NUCLEAR WEAPONS AGAINST JAPAN

IWO JIMA U.S. Marines hunker down on Iwo Jima during the American onslaught that continued for a month after Marines raised their flag atop Mount Suribachi in the background on February 23, 1945. Steep casualties here and elsewhere as U.S. forces approached Japan reinforced the military argument for dropping atomic bombs.

OPERATION DOWNFALL: THE SECRET PLAN TO INVADE THE JAPANESE HOMELAND

When plans were drawn up confidentially in early 1945 for Operation Downfall, the proposed invasion of Japan, many of those involved in the planning were unaware of another operation of great consequence for the war against Japan that was even more tightly veiled in secrecy—the Manhattan Project. Some top commanders knew that American scientists were working on a bomb that might prove enormously powerful, but no one yet knew if it would work or when it would be ready. The underlying assumption behind Operation Downfall was that an invasion was the only sure way to defeat Japan. Some commanders argued for delaying the invasion to see if Japan would be reduced to submission by continued strategic bombing raids like the one that ignited a terrible firestorm in Tokyo in early March 1945 and killed over 80,000 people. But the Joint Chiefs of Staff decided in May to push ahead with plans for Operation Downfall, which would involve two massive amphibious

SEEKING SURRENDER An American propaganda leaflet designed to be dropped from the air over Japan in 1945 portrays President Truman and includes a message from him in Japanese stating that unconditional surrender did not mean "obliteration of the Japanese people or bondage."

assaults. The first, designated Operation Olympic and scheduled for late 1945, would involve using Okinawa—seized by American forces in June at great cost—as the staging base for an invasion of Kyushu, the southernmost of Japan's home islands (see map opposite). Kyushu, in turn, would serve as the staging area for Operation Coronet, an invasion of Japan's main island, Honshu, and Tokyo in the spring of 1946.

Those invasions would surpass even Operation Overlord in scope. Compared with the 12 divisions that landed initially at Normandy, 14 divisions would land with the first wave on Kyushu and 25 divisions would storm Honshu. Japan was preparing to meet that onslaught with extreme measures, which included committing nearly all remaining Japanese military aircraft—more than 10,000 in all—to kamikaze attacks, aimed primarily at sinking U.S. troop transports before they reached shore. A bombproof subterranean headquarters was prepared for Emperor Hirohito and the Imperial General Staff, and civilians were organized into home defense forces consisting of all men from 15 to 60 who were not already in uniform, and all women from 17 to 40, armed with rudimentary weapons ranging from old firearms to bamboo spears. Casualty estimates for Operation

Downfall varied widely, but some projected figures for the number of Americans killed or wounded surpassed a million, with Japanese casualties estimated at several million if civilians entered battle.

The final decision on Downfall rested with America's new commander in chief, Harry Truman, thrust into office by Roosevelt's death in April. On June 18, Truman and some of his advisers met in the White House with the Joint Chiefs to consider the operation. Most of the chiefs endorsed the planned invasion, but Adm. William Leahy, in charge of the Navy, objected that it was not worth incurring massive losses to obtain the unconditional surrender of Japan, a demand that would "only result in making the Japanese more desperate and thereby increase our casualty lists." Truman was not prepared to abandon the demand for unconditional surrender, but he was inclined to agree when Assistant Secretary of War John McCloy said that "we ought to have our heads examined if we don't explore some other method by which we can terminate this war than just by another conventional attack and landing." McCoy proposed a message that would offer Japanese leaders some assurances if they surrendered, and threaten them if they refused with the new weapon that the U.S. was about to obtain through the Manhattan Project. Truman agreed to include in that declaration a pledge that if Japan yielded, American occupation forces would leave that country as soon as a "peacefully inclined and responsible government" was established there. But he rejected language that would have allowed Emperor Hirohito, whom many Americans blamed for the war, to remain in power as head of a "constitutional monarchy."

The Potsdam Declaration, issued by Allied leaders in occupied Germany on July 26, closed with a stern warning that did not mention the fearsome new bombs at America's disposal: "We call upon the government of Japan to proclaim now the unconditional surrender of all Japanese armed forces . . . The alternative for Japan is prompt and utter destruction." When Japan refused to yield, Truman felt he had no choice but to authorize the use of atomic bombs, which might end the war without resort to Operation Downfall—an invasion that would be horrendous for American troops and calamitous for Japan. ○

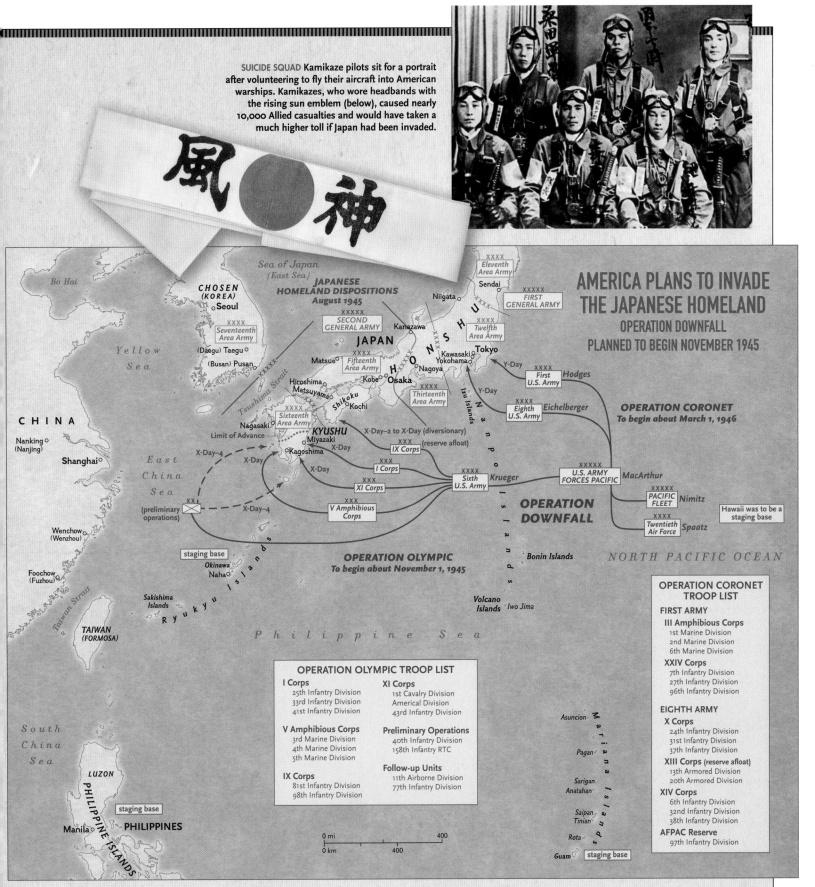

SUICIDE SQUAD Kamikaze pilots sit for a portrait after volunteering to fly their aircraft into American warships. Kamikazes, who wore headbands with the rising sun emblem (below), caused nearly 10,000 Allied casualties and would have taken a much higher toll if Japan had been invaded.

風 ● 神

AMERICA PLANS TO INVADE THE JAPANESE HOMELAND
OPERATION DOWNFALL
PLANNED TO BEGIN NOVEMBER 1945

JAPANESE HOMELAND DISPOSITIONS August 1945

Bo Hai

CHOSEN (KOREA) — Seoul

XXXX — Seventeenth Area Army

(Daegu) Taegu
(Busan) Pusan

Yellow Sea

Tsushima Strait

SECOND GENERAL ARMY

JAPAN

Matsue — XXXX Fifteenth Area Army
Kobe — Osaka
Hiroshima
Matsuyama — Shikoku — Kochi
HONSHU
Kanazawa — XXXX Twelfth Area Army
Nagoya
Niigata — Sendai — XXXX Eleventh Area Army
XXXXX FIRST GENERAL ARMY
Kawasaki — Yokohama — Tokyo
Y-Day — First U.S. Army — Hodges
Y-Day — Eighth U.S. Army — Eichelberger
XXXX Thirteenth Area Army

OPERATION CORONET
To begin about March 1, 1946

CHINA
Nanking (Nanjing)
Shanghai

East China Sea

Nagasaki — XXXX Sixteenth Area Army — KYUSHU
Limit of Advance — Miyazaki
X-Day-4 — Kagoshima — X-Day
X-Day — X-Day
XI Corps
V Amphibious Corps
I Corps
IX Corps
X-Day-2 to X-Day (diversionary)
(reserve afloat)
XXXX Sixth U.S. Army — Krueger

OPERATION DOWNFALL

XXXXX U.S. ARMY FORCES PACIFIC — MacArthur
XXXXX PACIFIC FLEET — Nimitz
XXXX Twentieth Air Force — Spaatz

Hawaii was to be a staging base

Wenchow (Wenzhou)

(preliminary operations) — X-Day-4

Foochow (Fuzhou)

staging base

Okinawa
Naha

Sakishima Islands

Ryukyu Islands

OPERATION OLYMPIC
To begin about November 1, 1945

Bonin Islands

Volcano Islands — Iwo Jima

NORTH PACIFIC OCEAN

TAIWAN (FORMOSA)

Taiwan Strait

Philippine Sea

South China Sea

LUZON

PHILIPPINE ISLANDS

staging base

Manila — PHILIPPINES

0 mi 400
0 km 400

OPERATION OLYMPIC TROOP LIST

I Corps
25th Infantry Division
33rd Infantry Division
41st Infantry Division

V Amphibious Corps
3rd Marine Division
4th Marine Division
5th Marine Division

IX Corps
81st Infantry Division
98th Infantry Division

XI Corps
1st Cavalry Division
Americal Division
43rd Infantry Division

Preliminary Operations
40th Infantry Division
158th Infantry RTC

Follow-up Units
11th Airborne Division
77th Infantry Division

Asuncion
Pagan
Sarigan
Anatahan
Saipan
Tinian
Rota
Guam — staging base

Mariana Islands

OPERATION CORONET TROOP LIST

FIRST ARMY

III Amphibious Corps
1st Marine Division
2nd Marine Division
6th Marine Division

XXIV Corps
7th Infantry Division
27th Infantry Division
96th Infantry Division

EIGHTH ARMY

X Corps
24th Infantry Division
31st Infantry Division
37th Infantry Division

XIII Corps (reserve afloat)
13th Armored Division
20th Armored Division

XIV Corps
6th Infantry Division
32nd Infantry Division
38th Infantry Division

AFPAC Reserve
97th Infantry Division

INVASION PLAN This map charts the two phases of Operation Downfall, the first aimed at Kyushu and the second at Honshu, encompassing Tokyo and other major Japanese cities. Several million U.S. Marines, sailors, soldiers, and airmen were expected to take part under Gen. Douglas MacArthur and Adm. Chester Nimitz.

FAT MAN AND LITTLE BOY Pictured here after assembly are the two atomic bombs that were dropped on Japan in August 1945—"Little Boy" (below), fueled with uranium-235 produced at Oak Ridge, Tennessee, and "Fat Man" (bottom), fueled with plutonium-239 generated at Hanford, Washington. The implosion method for detonating a plutonium bomb was tested at the Trinity Site in New Mexico on July 16 before Fat Man was assembled at Tinian, where the photo here was taken showing the bomb in its carriage.

One of the first scientists to ponder what unleashing nuclear energy for destructive purposes might mean for the world was Niels Bohr, who did not join the Manhattan Project but visited Los Alamos and shared with Oppenheimer and others his view that the new weapons under development could be a curse for humanity or a blessing, depending on whether the world's major powers recognized that a nuclear war was unwinnable and chose to cooperate rather than compete for supremacy. Bohr considered the secrecy surrounding the Manhattan Project futile and counterproductive as far as the Soviets were concerned. "It was perfectly absurd to believe that the Russians cannot do what others can," he said later. Among scientists, he added, there "never was any secret about nuclear energy."

Bohr met with Prime Minister Churchill in 1944 and urged that the Americans and British, who contributed substantially to the success of the Manhattan Project, inform their Soviet allies about the atomic bombs under development and work with the Russians to control those weapons and avoid an arms race. Churchill, however, had no intention of sharing nuclear secrets with Stalin and thought proposing to do so bordered on treason. "Bohr should be confined," Churchill remarked afterward, "or at any rate made to see that he is very near the edge of mortal crimes." Bohr later met with President Roosevelt, who was more sympathetic but sided with Churchill on the need to keep the Manhattan Project under wraps until the new weapons were ready for deployment. So tight was the secrecy that Vice President Harry S. Truman knew nothing of the atomic bomb when he took the oath as commander in chief following Roosevelt's death on April 12, 1945. Truman, who had served as a company commander with the American Expeditionary Force in France during World War I, viewed the new weapon much as General Groves and other officers privy to the Manhattan Project did—as a great military asset that should be denied as long as possible to the Soviets and other potential postwar rivals and used to compel Japan to surrender, saving the lives of American troops.

Not all those in high positions in Washington were as sure as Truman that dropping the bomb was dictated by military necessity. Secretary of War Henry Stimson, who had taken a hard line toward Japan as war loomed in 1941, was appalled by the firebombing of Tokyo and other Japanese cities and worried that compounding the carnage by using a dreadful new weapon might harm America's reputation for "fair play and humanitarianism" and make it harder for the U.S. to keep the peace when the war ended. Yet all Stimson was able to accomplish was to strike one Japanese city off the short list of potential targets for nuclear annihilation—Kyoto, the nation's historical and cultural center. Sparing Kyoto shifted another city that remained intact to the top of that list, Hiroshima. As stated by the top secret Target Committee on which Stimson and Oppenheimer served, Hiroshima was of "such a size that a large part of the city could be extensively damaged. There are adjacent hills which are likely to produce a focusing effect which would considerably increase the blast damage."

Some who helped produce the first atomic bombs did not want them dropped on any Japanese target. Leo Szilard circulated a petition among scientists involved in the Manhattan Project, asking them to state "their opposition on moral grounds to the use of these bombs in the present phase of the war . . . The fact that the people in the United States are unaware of the choice which faces us increases our responsibility in this matter." Szilard also organized a scientific committee that issued a confidential report urging that the bomb be tested before international witnesses to demonstrate its destructive power and give the Japanese a chance to surrender before being targeted. Oppenheimer did not back that appeal, which the government rejected. He doubted that a demonstration would induce the Japanese to yield and thought that officers engaged in the conflict were better qualified to decide how to use the weapons than the scientists who designed them. "What do they know about Japanese psychology?" he asked. "How can they judge the way to end the war?" Oppenheimer favored informing the Russians in advance that the bomb would be used against the Japanese, but he knew that would not forestall an arms race, which was already under way, as evidenced by determined Soviet efforts to steal nuclear secrets.

Truman was preparing to meet with Stalin and Churchill at Potsdam in occupied Germany when scientists from Los Alamos gathered at the Trinity Site before dawn on July 16 to observe the test of the plutonium bomb from afar. "Suddenly, there was an enormous flash of light," wrote physicist Isidor I. Rabi, "the brightest light I have ever seen or that I think anyone has ever seen. It blasted; it pounced; it bored right through you." The initial reaction of Oppenheimer and others on hand was astonishment at what they had achieved, followed in some cases by a sense of foreboding. "Some people claim to have wondered at the time about the future of mankind," recalled Norris Bradbury, Oppenheimer's eventual

"Suddenly, there was an enormous flash of light, the brightest light I have ever seen or that I think anyone has ever seen. It blasted; it pounced; it bored right through you."

PHYSICIST ISIDOR I. RABI, WHO GATHERED WITH OTHER SCIENTISTS FROM LOS ALAMOS AT THE TRINITY SITE BEFORE DAWN ON JULY 16 TO OBSERVE THE TEST OF THE PLUTONIUM BOMB

UNEASY ALLIANCE Churchill, Truman, and Stalin join hands for photographers at the tense Potsdam Conference in July 1945, which foreshadowed the Cold War. As the conference was getting under way, Truman learned of the successful predawn atomic test at the Trinity Site that produced the blinding explosion below. He then informed Stalin of the new weapon, but a nuclear rivalry between the U.S. and U.S.S.R. was already under way and would intensify in years to come.

successor as director of Los Alamos. "I didn't. We were at war and the damned thing worked." Truman learned of the successful test when a coded cable reached him at Potsdam: "Operated on this morning. Diagnosis not yet complete but results seem satisfactory and already exceed expectations . . . Dr. Groves pleased." Truman then informed the Soviet leader of America's new strategic asset. "I casually mentioned to Stalin that we had a new weapon of unusual destructive force," Truman related. "The Russian Premier showed no special interest. All he said was that he was glad to hear it and hoped we would make 'good use of it against the Japanese.'" In fact, Stalin already knew of the Manhattan Project and had a Soviet nuclear weapons program under way, aided by disclosures from spies at Los Alamos who eluded detection until after the conflict ended.

The stage was set for the war's shattering conclusion on July 26 when the Potsdam Declaration was issued, calling on Japan to surrender unconditionally or face "prompt and utter destruction." Unwilling to yield if Emperor Hirohito was not allowed to remain the country's supreme leader, a condition Truman had rejected, Prime Minister Kantaro Suzuki dismissed the declaration. Two blinding atomic blasts finally impelled Hirohito to surrender—the first unleashed on August 6 by a uranium bomb that devastated Hiroshima and the second triggered three days later by a plutonium bomb that shattered Nagasaki. More than 150,000 people were killed in the attacks, and tens of thousands more were contaminated by radioactive fallout and died later as a result. Scientists had not anticipated

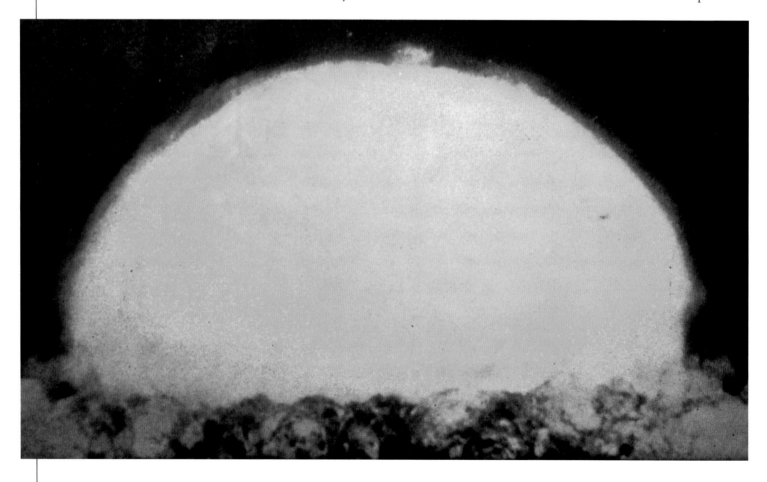

that dreadful aftermath, and Groves and other officers dismissed initial accounts of radiation sickness among survivors as Japanese propaganda. Now that the war was over, however, authorities responsible for keeping secrets or concealing calamities were challenged by those intent on revealing the truth, among them journalist John Hersey, who exposed the horrific impact of nuclear warfare on the people of Hiroshima. Hersey's disturbing account belied assurances like those offered by General Groves, who when radiation sickness could no longer be denied testified before a Senate Committee that doctors told him it was "a very pleasant way to die."

AN ENDURING SECRET WAR

The bombing of Hiroshima and Nagasaki in August 1945 brought the costliest war ever waged to a sobering conclusion. People celebrated in the streets, but the jubilation was short-lived. As commentator Edward R. Murrow remarked, "Seldom, if ever, has a war ended with such a sense of uncertainty and fear, with such a realization that the future is obscure and that survival is not assured." Nowhere was concern for the future greater than at Los Alamos, where scientists knew that nuclear weapons of far greater power than those deployed against Japan might soon be developed. Edward Teller was hard at work on the so-called "super" bomb—a thermonuclear device that would use the intense heat generated by nuclear fission to produce nuclear fusion, welding hydrogen atoms together to form helium and releasing massive amounts of energy in the process. Such H-bombs had the potential to trigger explosions ranging in intensity up to a staggering 100 million tons of TNT, compared with 12,500 tons for the bomb that blasted Hiroshima.

Even physicists like Ernest Lawrence who had strongly supported the wartime use of atomic bombs and efforts to keep the Manhattan Project under wraps now favored international efforts to control the spread of nuclear weapons, including cooperation with the secretive Soviets. "There is no doubt in my mind," Lawrence wrote, "that the best channel of information about what is going on in Russia would be developed by encouraging free interchange of science and scientists." Oppenheimer went to Washington to urge President Truman and his advisers to secure the nation against attack not by engaging in a nuclear arms race but by seeking agreements with Russia and other potential nuclear powers to prevent wars of annihilation. But the Russians were no longer America's allies, and few in the administration were willing to trust in Stalin, who had promised free elections in Soviet-occupied Eastern Europe but was transforming Poland and other countries into Soviet satellites, where officeholders did Moscow's bidding. A report from an attaché at the U.S. Embassy in Moscow in December 1945 confirmed what many in Washington already suspected, that "the U.S.S.R. is out to get the atomic bomb" and would spare no effort to do so. Far from encouraging American officials to negotiate with the Soviet

(continued on page 338)

TANDEM AT TRINITY **Robert Oppenheimer and Leslie Groves stand amid the debris following the test at the Trinity Site. "The war is over," declared an officer who observed the explosion there, to which General Groves replied, "Yes, after we drop two bombs on Japan."**

"Operated on this morning. Diagnosis not yet complete but results seem satisfactory and already exceed expectations . . . Dr. Groves pleased."

A CODED CABLE SENT TO TRUMAN AT POTSDAM ABOUT THE SUCCESSFUL BOMB TEST

TARGETING HIROSHIMA

In May 1945, an elite unit known as the 509th Composite Group, including B-29 pilots, aircrews, ground crews, ordnance specialists, and other personnel, completed training exercises at a secret air base in Utah and flew to Tinian, chosen because its long airstrip allowed takeoffs by B-29s carrying extra-heavy loads. Only the group's commander, Col. Paul Tibbets, and Maj. Charles Sweeney, second in command, knew that their mission was to drop atomic bombs on Japan. They occupied a windowless, air-conditioned compound at Tinian behind a fence patrolled by armed guards. "We had brand-new planes and were getting the best of treatment," one of them recalled. To other airmen on Tinian, he added, "it didn't seem we were doing anything to end the war."

On August 6, 1945, Tibbets guided the *Enola Gay*—a B-29 named for his mother with the 9,000-pound Little Boy in its bomb bay—down the airstrip and lifted off just as he reached the end of pavement at 2:45 a.m. The crew had been briefed a few hours earlier that they were delivering the most destructive weapon ever built, which was armed after takeoff to avoid a disaster if the plane crashed on Tinian. Several hours into the flight, a weather plane informed Tibbets that skies were clear over Hiroshima, their primary target. The bomb was released from an altitude of 31,000 feet at 8:15 a.m. Hiroshima time and exploded 49 seconds later, some 2,000 feet above the city to maximize the damage. Tibbets executed a sharp, diving turn to accelerate away from Hiroshima and escape the worst of the shock waves, but the plane was still rocked. Looking back toward the city, he saw only a monstrous cloud, "boiling up, mushrooming, terrible and incredibly tall." If any of doubt remained as to what they had done, Tibbets dispelled it. "Fellows," he told the crew, "you have just dropped the first atomic bomb." ✪

COUNTDOWN Below, Col. Paul Tibbets stands at center with members of his aircrew beside the *Enola Gay*, the B-29 he piloted to Hiroshima on August 6. The secret itinerary at far left lists times for briefings and religious services on the evening of August 5, and the names of pilots who flew weather planes and the B-29s that accompanied the *Enola Gay* to record the event and conduct scientific tests. The aerial photo at near left shows the aiming point at Hiroshima for the bomb.

ZERO HOUR The clock at left was stopped by the atomic blast that occurred at 8:16 a.m., leveling almost all the buildings in the heart of Hiroshima (bottom) and producing a towering mushroom cloud (far left). Many who survived the blast suffered burns like the woman below or died later of radiation sickness.

Union, that intelligence made them more determined to stay ahead of the Russians and maintain strict nuclear secrecy. Oppenheimer's personal appeal to Truman to seek international control of atomic weapons that might prove far deadlier than those that fell on Hiroshima and Nagasaki went for naught. "Mr. President," he said of those attacks, "I feel I have blood on my hands." Truman replied sternly that the blood was "on my hands . . . let me worry about that."

Efforts by Oppenheimer and other scientists to dispel the secrecy surrounding nuclear weapons and encourage talks were thwarted because the secret war did not end when Germany and Japan were defeated, and instead became more deeply entrenched as global alliances shifted. That undercover war had been waged not just between the Allied and Axis powers but between the Anglo-Americans and the Soviets, who were united only in opposition to Hitler and deeply distrusted each other. The struggle that became known as the Cold War began in earnest long before World War II ended with Soviet efforts to obtain through espionage state secrets that leaders in Washington and London refused to share with Stalin's regime in Moscow. Few things did more to exacerbate the Cold War and the anticommunist convulsion in America known as the Red Scare than the revelation that Soviet agents had penetrated the Manhattan Project and extracted intelligence that helped the Russians produce an atomic bomb, which they successfully tested in August 1949. By then, U.S. Army counterintelligence officers with G-2 had learned of that nuclear espionage with the help of cryptanalysts at the Signals Intelligence Service, who broke the code used in cables sent to Moscow from Soviet agents in the U.S. Instigated in 1943 under the code name Venona, that program produced its first decrypts three years later and revealed the existence of more than 300 Americans who spied for the Soviets. Many were in sensitive government positions, and several had access to Los Alamos while the first nuclear weapons were being developed there.

DISCLOSURE The veil of secrecy that shrouded the Manhattan Project for years was lifted right after Hiroshima was blasted by an atomic bomb, linked in this August 6 edition of a Knoxville newspaper to nearby Oak Ridge and the Clinton Engineer Works (CEW), where the bomb's fuel was produced. As proclaimed in one headline here, the "War's Big Secret" was now out.

One of those Los Alamos spies—physicist Theodore Hall, who became the youngest scientist working on atomic bombs when he arrived there in 1944 at the age of 19—never faced charges because the government could not prosecute him without introducing top secret Venona decrypts as evidence. In another spy case, however, the FBI shared Venona intelligence confidentially with British authorities, who then arrested physicist Klaus Fuchs in February 1950. Fuchs had joined the Communist Party in Germany before fleeing the Nazi regime and settling in England, where he engaged in nuclear research and was later assigned to the Manhattan Project at Los Alamos. No one furnished the Soviets with more significant disclosures on nuclear weapons than he did by providing details on the design of both the plutonium and the hydrogen bombs. Yet the stiffest sentence went not to Fuchs, who served only nine years in prison, or to his courier in America, Harry Gold, or to David Greenglass, an engineer at Los Alamos whose espionage was exposed by Gold, but to two accused agents in New York who were convicted and executed after Greenglass testified against them—his sister Ethel Rosenberg and her husband Julius Rosenberg. Her conviction would long be controversial, but evidence presented in court, as well as Venona transcripts declassified several decades later, indicated that Julius Rosenberg was guilty of passing secrets obtained from Greenglass and other spies to Soviet intelligence officers. Many Americans viewed the trial and execution of the Rosenbergs as proof that the Red Scare was well founded. But some saw the proceedings as a "witch hunt," driven by the need to assign blame for the frightening spread of nuclear weapons, which scientists had long doubted could be kept secret and monopolized by the U.S.

The Cold War was an extension of the Second World War not just in espionage but in covert operations, carried out extensively by the CIA—established in 1947 as the successor to the OSS—and by its Soviet counterpart, the KGB, which succeeded the NKVD. Prominent OSS veterans such as Allen Dulles and William Casey served as directors of the CIA during the Cold War and followed in the path of OSS chief William Donovan by combining the collection and analysis of intelligence with aggressive campaigns to demoralize, disrupt, and subvert the enemy, broadly defined as any foreign party or government that espoused communism or might aid the Soviet Union or the People's Republic of China, founded in 1949 after Mao Zedong's Red Army defeated Chiang Kai-shek's Nationalists. In that same year, the CIA backed efforts by Britain's MI6 to overthrow the communist government in Albania, an operation thwarted by Kim Philby, who became counterintelligence chief for MI6 while secretly serving the KGB. Philby and three other accomplished Soviet spies who had been friends at Cambridge University—Donald Maclean, Guy Burgess, and Anthony Blunt—betrayed numerous Anglo-American secrets and covert operations to Moscow with results that were sometimes fatal for the agents involved.

As World War II gave way to the Cold War, the U.S. enlisted the services of numerous German scientists and spies, some of them ardent Nazis who had committed war crimes but were spared prosecution. President Truman's order authorizing Project Paperclip—code name for the recruitment of German scientists—excluded from the program anyone who had been "a member of the Nazi Party and more than a nominal participant in its activities, or an active supporter of Nazi militarism." If enforced strictly, that would have ruled out many of those who ended up

NUCLEAR SPIES A former member of the German Communist Party who became a British citizen, physicist Klaus Fuchs—pictured at top on his Los Alamos badge—was arrested in early 1950 for betraying nuclear secrets to the Soviets. That led to the arrest of David Greenglass in June 1950, on charges of spying for the Soviets while working as a mechanic at Los Alamos. Greenglass then incriminated his sister Ethel Rosenberg and her husband Julius Rosenberg (left), who were convicted and executed in 1953.

SOVIET MOLES INSIDE BRITISH SECRET SERVICES

When Kim Philby was sent to serve as British intelligence chief in Washington in 1949, he gained access to America's top secrets. The posting was a coup not just for Philby but also for the KGB, for whom he had worked secretly while acting as a spymaster at MI6 and betraying to Moscow a number of agents who lost their lives. Philby and several other Soviet moles had been friends since their days as elite young scholars at Cambridge University. The group included Anthony Blunt, a wartime counterespionage officer with MI5, and two members of the Foreign Office with

access to state secrets—Donald Maclean, back in London now after serving in Washington, and Guy Burgess (inset), who was living in a basement apartment at Philby's home. Their interwoven schemes began to unravel when Philby obtained Venona decrypts referring to Maclean under a code name as a Soviet agent who betrayed American nuclear secrets before he left Washington in 1948. Philby sent Burgess to warn Maclean, who defected with Burgess to Moscow in 1951. Philby then came under suspicion for his ties to the defectors and resigned from MI6. In 1963, he too fled to Moscow. Blunt confessed a year later after being granted immunity. For all the damage they did, none of those Cambridge spies was ever prosecuted. They remained privileged members of the British ruling class even as they violated its code. ✪

CODE NAME:	HICKS
SPIED FOR:	RUSSIA
SPIED AGAINST:	GREAT BRITAIN, UNITED STATES

THIRD MAN Kim Philby faces the press in London in 1955 after word of his ties to defectors Guy Burgess and Donald Maclean leaked out, leading to charges that he was the third man in the spy ring. He was exonerated that year, but revelations from a Soviet defector later forced him to seek refuge in Moscow. Philby and Burgess—pictured above lounging by the Black Sea after he fled to the Soviet Union in 1951—were reckless in their personal lives. Both were heavy drinkers who had numerous affairs, Philby with other women and Burgess with other men.

CODE NAME:	STANLEY
SPIED FOR:	RUSSIA
SPIED AGAINST:	GREAT BRITAIN, UNITED STATES

SCHOLAR AND SPY **Spared prosecution, Anthony Blunt remained a leading art historian and was not exposed until 1979, when Prime Minister Margaret Thatcher identified him as the fourth man in the spy ring.**

WEAK LINK **Donald Maclean was the first in the ring to be suspected when decrypts revealed that agent Homer (his KGB code name) had divulged secrets to which Maclean had access as a diplomat in Washington.**

working for the U.S., including Wernher von Braun, who had joined the Nazi Party and the SS, which sustained his V-2 ballistic missile program with brutal forced labor by concentration camp inmates. The director of Project Paperclip argued that there was no point in "beating a dead Nazi horse" by barring Germans like von Braun who had strategic skills that the Soviets would likely employ if the Americans did not. References to the Nazi past of German scientists were expunged from their records or toned down so that they could immigrate to the U.S. One flagrant case involved Arthur Rudolph, who oversaw V-2 missile production by concentration camp inmates at Mittelwerk-Dora and was assessed by an American military interrogator at war's end as "100% NAZI, dangerous type, security threat . . . *suggest internment."* Yet he was later ruled eligible for Project Paperclip because there was supposedly "nothing in his records indicating that he was a war criminal, an ardent Nazi or otherwise objectionable." Von Braun, Rudolph, and other German scientists admitted to the U.S. figured prominently in the "space race" against the Soviet Union—which also employed former Nazi scientists— by designing rockets that could boost manned spacecraft or spy satellites into orbit and by developing intercontinental ballistic missiles armed with nuclear warheads.

> **"Seldom, if ever, has a war ended with such a sense of uncertainty and fear, with such a realization that the future is obscure and that survival is not assured."**
>
> COMMENTATOR EDWARD R. MURROW

Other former Nazis ended up working for the CIA or the U.S. Army's Counter Intelligence Corps (CIC), which was assigned to operate abroad to avoid overlapping with G-2's domestic counterintelligence efforts. In 1947, the CIC enlisted the services of former Gestapo officer Klaus Barbie, the notorious "Butcher of Lyon," responsible for the death of French resistance leader Jean Moulin and many others targeted by the SS. Barbie provided the CIC with information on Gestapo informants and communist cells in France. In return, he was shielded from prosecution for his war crimes and given safe passage to South America when French authorities began to close in on him. (Not until the 1980s was he brought to justice in France, where he died in prison in 1991.) Although the CIA had no direct connection with Barbie, many former SS officers joined the CIA-sponsored Gehlen Organization, operated by Reinhard Gehlen, a German intelligence chief during World War II who offered his vast store of knowledge on Soviet military and security operations to Allen Dulles after the conflict ended. Gehlen's spies dueled in bitterly divided postwar Germany with Soviet agents, whose ranks

> ## "Wisdom cannot flourish, nor even truth be determined, without debate and criticism."
>
> J. ROBERT OPPENHEIMER, ON WHY MAJOR DECISIONS SUCH AS DEVELOPING NEW WEAPONS OF MASS DESTRUCTION SHOULD NOT BE MADE ON THE BASIS OF FACTS HELD SECRET

SWITCHING SIDES Wernher von Braun, with his left arm in a cast following a car accident, surrenders with other German rocket scientists to American occupation forces on May 2, 1945. The directors of Project Paperclip were not supposed to recruit German scientists who had been active Nazis or militarists to work in the U.S., but they made an exception for von Braun and others who might help America prevail in the Cold War.

also included former Nazis. Some of them infiltrated the Gehlen Organization, which later became the official intelligence service of West Germany, where tensions along the border with communist East Germany threatened to bring the Cold War to a boil.

While some former enemies were enlisted as allies and aided America in its struggle against communism, others who had been honored as heroes during World War II came under dark clouds of suspicion during the Cold War. After stepping down as director at Los Alamos, Oppenheimer became chairman of the General Advisory Committee to the Atomic Energy Commission (AEC). In 1949, that committee recommended against a crash program to develop the hydrogen bomb, described in a report signed by Oppenheimer and several other nuclear scientists as a "weapon of genocide." At a time when revelations about genocide by the Nazi regime were still fresh and deeply disturbing, they could not endorse a weapons program that would increase exponentially the destructive power of the nation's nuclear arsenal and commit the U.S. to a strategic "policy of exterminating civilian populations."

The committee's recommendation alarmed Edward Teller and those who supported his efforts to develop the H-bomb, including Lewis Strauss, an influential member of the AEC who later became its chairman. Strauss urged the president not to renounce "any weapon which an enemy can reasonably be expected to possess." In early 1950, Truman revealed the existence of Teller's previously secret project and gave it the go-ahead by directing the AEC to continue work "on all forms of atomic weapons, including the so-called hydrogen

or super bomb." Oppenheimer was dismayed and resigned from the committee in 1952 under mounting pressure from Strauss, Teller, and others for opposing a weapon they considered essential to the nation's security.

When Strauss took charge of the AEC in 1953, he resolved to oust Oppenheimer, who still served as a consultant to the commission, from any involvement in nuclear policy. Strauss could have waited for Oppenheimer's security clearance to expire in June 1954, but instead suspended that clearance and placed him under surveillance, setting the stage for a hearing to determine if the man hailed as the "father of the atomic bomb" was a security risk. That hearing revealed little that had not been dredged up in 1943 when Oppenheimer was originally investigated and sifted through again in 1947 when his security clearance was renewed. But times had changed, and some who had once been ardent admirers of him now cast doubt on whether he could be trusted to keep the nation's secrets. Teller testified that he "assumed" Oppenheimer was loyal to the U.S., but would feel more secure if "the vital interests of this country" were no longer in his hands. In May 1954, he was declared a security risk by the verdict of two of the three officials who presided over the hearing. The third dissented, pointing out that all were in agreement as to Oppenheimer's loyalty and that to deny him clearance for what he had earlier been cleared seemed "hardly the procedure to be adopted in a free country."

Unlike the momentous war against Germany and Japan that united America as never before, the Cold War divided the nation and fostered bitter disputes like that between Oppenheimer and his foes. He knew as well as they did that secrecy was often necessary to protect national security, as it did during World War II. But he warned against an endless secret war in which matters bearing on the nation's future and the world's welfare were determined behind closed doors. There was "grave danger," he remarked, when decisions such as developing new weapons of mass destruction were made "on the basis of facts held secret. That is not because the men who must contribute to the decisions, or must make them, are lacking in wisdom; it is because wisdom cannot flourish, nor even truth be determined, without debate and criticism." The outcome of Oppenheimer's hearing generated considerable debate and criticism, but he was never restored to a position of trust within the government. Few people could have imagined when World War II ended that Wernher von Braun whose rockets rained terror on London and Antwerp would later be awarded a medal for his contributions to American science—or that Robert Oppenheimer, who did as much as any civilian to secure victory over Japan, would one day be barred from serving his country.

BACK IN FAVOR A major figure in America's drive to win the "space race" against Russia, Wernher von Braun (center) conducts President John F. Kennedy (left) and Vice President Lyndon B. Johnson (right) on a 1962 tour of the Marshall Space Flight Center in Huntsville, Alabama, where von Braun developed the Saturn C-1 booster rocket in the background. His wartime role as designer of the V-2 vengeance rocket for Hitler was overshadowed by his contribution to the American space program, for which he received the National Medal of Science in 1977.

ABBREVIATION KEY:

Getty Images (GI), Library of Congress Prints and Photographs Division (LOC), U.S. National Archives and Records Administration (NARA)

Front cover, Roger-Viollet/GI; back cover, front row (L-R) Erich Lessing/Art Resource; The National Archives of the UK, Image Library; Kenneth W. Rendell, Museum of World War II, Boston. Back row (L-R), Kenneth W. Rendell, Museum of World War II, Boston; CIA Museum; akg-images; U.S. National Archives.; spine, Photobank gallery/Shutterstock; back flap (UP), Lisa Kagan; back flap (LO), Dee Cohn.

1, Kenneth W. Rendell, Museum of World War II, Boston; 2, Erich Lessing/Art Resource, NY; 4-5, akg-images/picture-alliance; 6, John Florea/The LIFE Picture Collection/GI; 8-15, Kenneth W. Rendell, Museum of World War II, Boston; 16-7, AP Photo/File; 18, Wikimedia Commons/Public Domain; 19, AP Photo; 20 (LE), Agnes Smedley Photographs, University Archives, Arizona State University Libraries; 20 (CTR), Uliana Bazar; 20 (RT), Sueddeutsche Zeitung Photo/Alamy Stock Photo; 21, Cartoon from Mucha weekly, Warsaw, September 8, 1939/Public Domain; 22, akg-images/ullstein bild; 23 (BOTH), Kenneth W. Rendell, Museum of World War II, Boston; 24, Bundesarchiv, Bild 102-14393/Photo: Georg Pahl; 25 (BOTH), ullstein bild/GI; 26-7 (ALL), The Institute of National Remembrance, Warsaw; 28 (UP), Gamma-Keystone/GI; 28 (LE), Uliana Bazar; 28 (CTR LE), Laski Collection/GI; 28 (CTR RT), Hanns Hubmann/ullstein bild via GI; 28 (RT), Bundesarchiv; 29, Laski Collection/GI; 30, Bettmann/GI; 31 (UP), Sidney Beadell/The Times/News Syndication; 31 (LO LE), Kenneth W. Rendell, Museum of World War II, Boston; 31 (LO RT), Kenneth W. Rendell, Museum of World War II, Boston; 32, ullstein bild/GI; 33 (UP LE), Sueddeutsche Zeitung Photo/Alamy Stock Photo; 33 (UP RT), Berlin, Sammlung Archiv für Kunst und Geschichte/akg-images; 33 (LO), SZ Photo/Scherl/The Image Works; 34, NARA; 35 (ALL), The National Archives of the UK; 36 (UP), The National Archives of the UK; 36 (CTR), Imperial War Museum; 36 (LO LE), The National Archives of the UK; 36 (LO CTR), The National Archives of the UK; 36 (LO RT), The National Archives of the UK; 37 (UP), The National Archives of the UK; 37 (CTR LE), Imperial War Museum; 37 (CTR RT), Erich Lessing/Art Resource, NY; 37 (LO LE), Imperial War Museum; 37 (LO RT), Erich Lessing/Art Resource, NY; 38, The National Archives of the UK; 39 (UP), Mary Evans/Higginbotham Collection/The Image Works; 39 (CTR), Public Domain, reproduction courtesy Madoc Roberts; 39 (LO), Imperial War Museum; 40 (UP), from Spy, Counterspy (Grosset & Dunlap, 1974); 40 (LO), Walter Stoneman/National Portrait Gallery, London; 41 (BOTH), The National Archives of the UK; 42 (LO), Roger-Viollet/The Image Works; 42 (UP LE), courtesy Gerry Czerniawski; 42 (UP CTR), from Colonel Henri's Story (William Kimber & Company, 1954); 42 (UP RT), The National Archives of the UK; 43, Bettmann/GI; 44 (UP), from Englandspiel (Van Holkema & Warendorf, 1978); 44 (CTR), courtesy of Adri Wines/ www.englandspiel.eu; 44 (LO), NIOD, Institute for War, Holocaust and Genocide Studies; 46 (BOTH), AP Photo; 47, Kenneth W. Rendell, Museum of World War II, Boston; 48 (LE), Fox Photos/Hulton Archive/GI; 48 (RT), Franklin D. Roosevelt Presidential Library and Museum; 49, Kenneth W. Rendell, Museum of World War II, Boston; 50 (UP), Erich Lessing/ Art Resource, NY; 50 (LO), The National Archives of the UK; 51, The National Archives of the UK; 52-3 (ALL), UC San Diego Library; 54, Bettmann/GI; 55, LOC; 56-8 (ALL), Kenneth W. Rendell, Museum of World War II, Boston; 59, AP Photo; 60 (LE), Polo Museale Veneziano; 60 (RT), Wikimedia Commons at https://commons.wikimedia.org/wiki/File: _!_1941.jpg. License at https://creativecommons.org/licenses/by-sa/4.0/legalcode; 61, bpk, Berlin/Art Resource, NY; 62 (UP LE), Swim Ink 2, LLC/Corbis; 62 (UP RT), Kenneth W. Rendell, Museum of World War II, Boston; 62 (LO LE), Kenneth W. Rendell, Museum of World War II, Boston; 62 (LO RT), Kenneth W. Rendell, Museum of World War II, Boston; 63, Kenneth W. Rendell, Museum of World War II, Boston; 64 (UP LE), NARA; 64 (UP RT), Kenneth W. Rendell, Museum of World War II, Boston; 64 (LO LE), Kenneth W. Rendell, Museum of World War II, Boston; 64 (LO RT), Kenneth W. Rendell, Museum of World War II, Boston; 65-7 (ALL), Kenneth W. Rendell, Museum of World War II, Boston; 68-9, Naval History and Heritage Command; 70, Kenneth W. Rendell, Museum of World War II; 71, Universal History Archive/GI; 72, Gamma-Keystone/GI; 73, from Reports of General MacArthur, vol. II, part 1 (Department of the Army, 1966), p. 69; 74, ©TopFoto/ The Image Works; 75, Bettmann/Corbis; 76 (UP), Fotosearch/GI; 76 (LO), Rebecca Hale/ National Geographic Staff (photo), National Cryptologic Museum (artifact); 77 (UP), Fotosearch/GI; 77 (LO), Rebecca Hale/National Geographic Staff (photo), National Cryptologic Museum (artifact); 78, from At Dawn We Slept: The Untold Story of Pearl Harbor, by Gordon W. Prange, (Penguin Books Inc., 1981), courtesy Donald M. Goldstein; 79 (LE), NARA; 79 (CTR), National Archives at Kansas City; 79 (RT), NARA; 80 (BOTH), Naval History and Heritage Command; 81 (UP), Naval History and Heritage Command; 81 (LO), from Reports of General MacArthur, vol. II, part 1 (Department of the Army, 1966), p. 69; 82, Naval History and Heritage Command; 83 (UP), NARA; 83 (CTR), Naval History and Heritage Command; 83 (LO), Kenneth W. Rendell, Museum of World War II, Boston; 84 (UP), Bettmann/Corbis; 84 (CTR), Naval History and Heritage Command; 84 (LO), Naval

History and Heritage Command; 85 (UP LE), Naval History and Heritage Command; 85 (UP RT), Naval History and Heritage Command; 85 (LO), Naval History and Heritage Command; 86, Kenneth W. Rendell, Museum of World War II, Boston; 87, The Mainichi Newspapers/AFLO; 89 (UP), Naval History and Heritage Command; 89 (CTR), National Cryptologic Museum; 89 (LO), National Cryptologic Museum; 90 (BOTH), from the estate of William Harten, Jr. and Jeane L. Harten, Valerie Harten Briggs, Personal Representative; 91 (LO), Naval History and Heritage Command; 92 (UP LE), The LIFE Picture Collection/ GI; 92 (UP RT), Kenneth W. Rendell, Museum of World War II, Boston; 92 (LO), Bettmann/ GI; 93 (UP), Naval History and Heritage Command; 93 (CTR), NARA; 93 (LO), Universal History Archive/GI; 94 (UP), Kenneth W. Rendell, Museum of World War II, Boston; 94 (CTR), used with permission of The Oakland Tribune, copyright © 2016. All rights reserved; 94 (LO), Planet News Archive/SSPL/GI; 95 (UP), Kenneth W. Rendell, Museum of World War II, Boston; 95 (LO), LOC; 96, Naval History and Heritage Command; 97, NARA; 98 (BOTH), Naval History and Heritage Command; 99, ©TopFoto/The Image Works; 101 (UP), Australian War Memorial Museum; 101 (LO), Naval History and Heritage Command; 102-105 , Australian War Memorial Museum; 106, Nationaal Museum van Wereldculturen. Coll. no. TM-10013732; 107 (UP), LOC; 107 (LO), Time Life Pictures/Mansell/The LIFE Picture Collection/GI; 108, Naval History and Heritage Command; 109 (UP), Australian War Memorial Museum; 109 (LO), Naval History and Heritage Command; 111 (UP), NARA; 111 (CTR), NARA; 111 (LO), ullstein bild via GI; 112-13, Kenneth W. Rendell, Museum of World War II, Boston; 114 (UP), CIA Museum; 114 (LO LE), CIA Museum; 114 (LO CTR), Courtesy of the collection of H. Keith Melton at the International Spy Museum; 114 (LO RT), CIA Museum (photo), courtesy Lorna Catling (passport); 115, CIA Museum; 116, NARA; 117 (UP), National Archives/Interim Archives/GI; 117 (LO LE), CIA Museum; 117 (LO RT), CIA Museum; 118 (UP), NARA; 118 (CTR), NARA; 118 (LO LE), CIA Museum; 118 (LO RT), Princeton University Library; 119 (UP) NARA; 119 (LO), CIA Museum; 120 (UP), CIA Museum; 120 (LO LE), CIA Museum; 120 (LO CTR), CIA Museum; 120 (LO RT), Kenneth W. Rendell, Museum of World War II, Boston; 121 (UP LE), CIA Museum; 121 (UP RT), CIA Museum; 121 (CTR), Kenneth W. Rendell, Museum of World War II, Boston; 121 (LO LE), CIA Museum; 121 (LO RT), NARA; 122 (LE), Fred Ramage/GI; 122 (RT), SMG Herb Friedman/Psywarrior.com; 123 , NARA; 124 (UP), NARA; 124 (LO), Keystone/Hulton Archive/GI; 125, courtesy of the Colby family collection; 126-7, Roger-Viollet/GI; 128, Kenneth W. Rendell, Museum of World War II, Boston; 129, Imperial War Museum; 130, Imperial War Museum; 131 (UP), Imperial War Museum; 131 (LO), Haywood Magee/GI; 132 (LE), The National Archives of the UK; 132 (UP RT), Imperial War Museum; 132 (CTR RT), The National Archives of the UK; 132 (LO RT), Australian War Memorial Museum; 133 (ALL), Imperial War Museum; 134, Kenneth W. Rendell, Museum of World War II, Boston; 135 (UP), Kenneth W. Rendell, Museum of World War II, Boston; 135 (LO), RDA/Tallandier/GI; 136 (UP), Imperial War Museum; 136 (LO), Imperial War Museum; 138-9 (ALL), Erich Lessing/Art Resource, NY; 140-43, Kenneth W. Rendell, Museum of World War II, Boston; 144, United States Holocaust Memorial Museum, courtesy of Sharon Paquette; 145, United States Holocaust Memorial Museum, courtesy of Leopold Page Photographic Collection; 146, Military History Institute, Prague; 147 (ALL), The National Archives of the UK; 148 (UP), Imperial War Museum; 148 (LO), CTK Photobank/Multimedia; 149 (UP), Imagno/Votava/The Image Works; 149 (LO), akg-images/The Image Works; 150-51 (ALL), German Resistance Memorial Center; 153 (ALL), Kenneth W. Rendell, Museum of World War II, Boston; 154 (LE), George (Jürgen) Wittenstein/akg-images; 154 (UP RT and LO RT), Kenneth W. Rendell, Museum of World War II, Boston; 155, Keystone/ GI; 156, Bundesarchiv; 157, RIA-Novosti/The Image Works; 158, LOC; 159, Kenneth W. Rendell, Museum of World War II, Boston; 160, AP Images; 161 (UP), Uliana Bazar; 161 (LO), Keystone-France/GI; 162, NARA; 163 (ALL), NARA; 164, Roger-Viollet/GI; 165, LAPI/Roger-Viollet/GI; 166 (UP), United States Holocaust Memorial Museum, courtesy of Jan Karski; 166 (LO), Ministry of Foreign Affairs, Republic of Poland; 167, NARA; 168, Roger-Viollet/GI; 169, Kenneth W. Rendell, Museum of World War II, Boston; 170, Gabriel Hackett/GI; 171, AP Photo/MBR/AFP; 172-3, Robert Doisneau/Gamma-Rapho/GI; 173, Kenneth W. Rendell, Museum of World War II, Boston; 174-5 (ALL), Kenneth W. Rendell, Museum of World War II, Boston; 176 (LE), akg-images; 176 (RT), Kenneth W. Rendell, Museum of World War II, Boston; 177 (UP LE), Uliana Bazar; 177 (UP RT), Imperial War Museum; 177 (CTR), Kenneth W. Rendell, Museum of World War II, Boston; 177 (LO), Kenneth W. Rendell, Museum of World War II, Boston; 178 (LE), Popperfoto/GI; 178 (CTR), Kenneth W. Rendell, Museum of World War II, Boston; 178 (RT), Kenneth W. Rendell, Museum of World War II, Boston; 179 (ALL), Kenneth W. Rendell, Museum of World War II, Boston; 180, Mondadori Portfolio/GI; 181-4 (ALL), Kenneth W. Rendell, Museum of World War II, Boston; 185 (UP), ullstein bild/akg-images; 185 (LO), Kenneth W. Rendell, Museum of World War II, Boston; 186-7 (ALL), Kenneth W. Rendell, Museum of World War II, Boston; 188 (UP), Kenneth W. Rendell, Museum of World War II, Boston; 188 (LO), Apic/GI; 189 (UP), LAPI/Roger-Viollet/GI; 189 (LO), Kenneth W. Rendell, Museum of World War II, Boston; 190 (ALL), Kenneth W. Rendell, Museum of World War II, Boston; 191 (UP), Three Lions/GI; 191 (LO), Kenneth W. Rendell,

Museum of World War II, Boston; 192 (LE), Durham County Record Office; 192 (RT), Kenneth W. Rendell, Museum of World War II, Boston; 193 (LE), Durham County Record Office; 193 (UP RT), Kenneth W. Rendell, Museum of World War II, Boston; 193 (LO RT), Durham County Record Office; 194, Kenneth W. Rendell, Museum of World War II, Boston; 195 (UP LE), courtesy Capt. Nick Lalich/The LIFE Picture Collection/GI; 195 (UP RT), Kenneth W. Rendell, Museum of World War II, Boston; 195 (LO), Kenneth W. Rendell, Museum of World War II, Boston; 196 (ALL), Kenneth W. Rendell, Museum of World War II, Boston; 197 (UP LE), Kenneth W. Rendell, Museum of World War II, Boston; 197 (CTR LE), Durham County Record Office; 197 (LO LE), Durham County Record Office; 197 (CTR), Kenneth W. Rendell, Museum of World War II, Boston; 197 (LO CTR LE), Kenneth W. Rendell, Museum of World War II, Boston; 197 (LO CTR RT), Kenneth W. Rendell, Museum of World War II, Boston; 197 (LO RT), Kenneth W. Rendell, Museum of World War II, Boston; 197 (UP RT), Kenneth W. Rendell, Museum of World War II, Boston; 198 (UP LE), Durham County Record Office; 198 (LO LE), Durham County Record Office; 198 (CTR), Durham County Record Office; 198 (RT), Kenneth W. Rendell, Museum of World War II, Boston; 199 (UP), Kenneth W. Rendell, Museum of World War II, Boston; 199 (LO LE), Durham County Record Office; 199 (LO RT), Wikimedia Commons, PD-1996; 200-1, Hulton-Deutsch Collection/Corbis; 202, Kenneth W. Rendell, Museum of World War II, Boston; 203, National Portrait Gallery, London; 204, Ace Stock Limited/ Alamy Stock Photo; 205-206 (ALL), The National Archives of the UK; 207, Wikimedia Commons/Public Domain (PD-US-patent-no notice); 208, PAP/Archives/Reproduction; 209 (UP), Bundesarchiv; 209 (LO BOTH), from The Enigma War (Charles Scribner's Sons, 1980), p. 40; 210, from Enigma: How the Poles Broke the Nazi Code (Hippocrene Books, 2004), p. 78; 211, Evening Standard/GI; 212, courtesy Rosamond Welchman; 213 (UP), Bletchley Park Trust/GI; 213 (CTR), Bletchley Park Trust/GI; 213 (LO), Brian Harris/Alamy Stock Photo; 214 (LE), Interfoto/Friedrich/akg-images; 214 (RT), Fotosearch/GI; 215 (ALL), Kenneth W. Rendell, Museum of World War II, Boston; 216, National Museum of the U.S. Air Force; 217, courtesy Bletchley Park Research/Kerry Howard, see www.bletchley-parkresearch.co.uk/research-notes/women-codebreakers/; 218 (UP), Bundesarchiv; 218 (LO), ullstein bild/GI; 219 (UP LE), akg-images; 219 (UP RT), Keystone-France/GI; 219 (CTR), ullstein bild/GI; 219 (LO LE), ullstein bild/GI; 219 (LO RT), ullstein bild/GI; 220 (BOTH), Peter Hore; 221 (ALL), The National Archives of the UK; 222 (UP), NARA; 222 (LO), MPI/ GI; 223 (UP), Gilbert Spencer/© 2016 Artists Rights Society (ARS), New York/DACS, London; 223 (LO), courtesy Bletchley Park Trust and Lever family; 224-5 (ALL), The National Archives of the UK; 226 (UP), from Operation Condor: Rommel's Spy (Macdonald and Jane's, 1974), p.126; 226 (LO), from Operation Condor: Rommel's Spy (Macdonald and Jane's, 1974), p.128; 227 (UP), George Rodger/Magnum Photos; 227 (LO), Bob Landry/ The LIFE Picture Collection/GI; 228, The National Archives of the UK; 229 (UP LE), The National Archives of the UK; 229 (UP RT), The National Archives of the UK; 229 (LO), Fotosearch/GI; 230 (UP LE), Trinity Mirror Publishing Ltd.; 230 (UP RT), David Pike; 230 (LO), Rebecca Hale/National Geographic Staff (photo), National Cryptologic Museum (artifact); 231 (UP), Rebecca Hale/National Geographic Staff/original courtesy National Cryptologic Museum; 231 (LO), NARA; 232 (UP), Pascal Parrot/Sygma/Corbis; 232 (LO), Sovfoto/UIG/GI; 233, Bletchley Park Trust/GI; 234, Kenneth W. Rendell, Museum of World War II, Boston; 235 (UP LE), Kenneth W. Rendell, Museum of World War II, Boston; 235 (UP RT), ullstein bild/GI; 235 (CTR RT), AP Images; 235 (LO), Kenneth W. Rendell, Museum of World War II, Boston; 235 (LO RT), Kenneth W. Rendell, Museum of World War II, Boston; 236 (BOTH), Kenneth W. Rendell, Museum of World War II, Boston; 237 (UP LE), NARA/Public Domain; 237 (UP CTR), US Navy/Museum of Science and Industry, Chicago/GI; 237 (UP RT), NARA/Public Domain; 237 (CTR), ullstein bild/GI; 237 (LO LE), Kenneth W. Rendell, Museum of World War II, Boston; 237 (LO RT), Popperfoto/GI; 238, Kenneth W. Rendell, Museum of World War II, Boston; 239 (UP), akg-images; 239 (CTR), Kenneth W. Rendell, Museum of World War II, Boston; 239 (LO), NARA/Pubic Domain; 240 (UP LE), akg-images; 240 (UP CTR), Bettmann/GI; 240 (UP RT), akg-images; 240 (LO 1), MPI/GI; 240 (LO 2 and 4), Bettmann/Corbis; 240 (LO 3 and 5), Bettmann/ Corbis; 241 (UP LE), NARA/Public Domain; 240 (UP RT), Kenneth W. Rendell, Museum of World War II, Boston; 240 (CTR), akg-images; 241 (LO 1), MPI/GI; 241 (LO 2), LOC; 241 (LO 3), LOC; 242 (UP), Office of Civilian Defense/Public Domain (PD-USGov); 242 (LO), Kenneth W. Rendell, Museum of World War II, Boston; 243 (UP LE), Bob Gates/ United States Coast Guard/Public Domain; 243 (UP CTR), Kenneth W. Rendell, Museum of World War II, Boston; 243 (UP RT), Bob Gates/United States Coast Guard/Public Domain; 243 (LO), Corbis; 244-5 (ALL), Ocean Exploration Trust Inc./National Geographic; 246-7, Popperfoto/GI; 248, Roger-Viollet/GI; 249, Tita Binz/ullstein bild/GI; 250, Keystone/GI; 251 (UP), Hulton Archive/GI; 251 (LO), Sovfoto/UIG/GI; 252, Bundesarchiv; 253 (BOTH), The National Archives of the UK; 254 (UP), LorenFFile/GI; 254 (LO), Imperial War Museum; 255 (BOTH), Public Domain; 256-7 (ALL), The National Archives of the UK; 258 (LE), Mary Evans/National Archives, London/The Image Works; 258 (UP RT), Estate of Ewen Montagu; 258 (LO RT), The National Archives of the UK; 259, Corbis; 260, Popperfoto/ GI; 261, Friends of PPA; 262 (UP), Kenneth W. Rendell, Museum of World War II, Boston;

262 (LO), Mondadori Portfolio/GI; 263, by Mads Madsen, available at Colorized-History. com; 264 (UP), Kenneth W. Rendell, Museum of World War II, Boston; 264 (LO), NARA; 265-7 (ALL), NARA; 268, LOC; 270 (LO LE), Keystone/Hulton Archive/GI; 270 (UP), NARA; 270 (LO RT), NARA; 271 (UP), Hermann Harz/PhotoQuest/GI; 271 (LO), Bundesarchiv; 272, Imperial War Museum; 273 (BOTH), NARA; 274 (UP), Express/Hulton Archive/GI; 274 (LO), George Rodger/Time & Life Pictures/GI; 275, PhotoQuest/GI; 276, AP Images; 276-7, Joseph P. Vaghi, Jr.; 278 (UP), Imperial War Museum; 278 (LO), The National Archives of the UK; 279 (UP), The National Archives of the UK; 279 (CTR), The National Archives of the UK; 279 (LO), courtesy Gerry Czerniawski; 280 (UP LE), Imperial War Museum; 280 (UP RT), Imperial War Museum; 280 (CTR), Imperial War Museum; 280 (LO), NARA; 281, Imperial War Museum; 282, Kenneth W. Rendell, Museum of World War II, Boston; 283, Robert Capa/International Center of Photography/Magnum Photos; 284, Bundesarchiv; 285, akg-images; 286 (LE), Berliner Verlag/Archiv/dpa/Corbis; 286 (RT), AP Images/Markus Schreiber; 287 (UP), Sovfoto/UIG/GI; 287 (LO), ullstein bild/GI; 288 (UP), IWM/GI; 288 (LE), Fox Photos/GI; 288 (RT), dpa/Corbis; 288 (LO), Kenneth W. Rendell, Museum of World War II, Boston; 289, Topical Press Agency/GI; 290 (UP), Foundation Buchenwald and Mittelbau-Dora Memorial Foundation; 290 (LO), Walter Frentz/ ullstein bild; 291 (UP), Galerie Bilderwelt/GI; 291 (LE), Galerie Bilderwelt/GI; 291 (LO LE), Foundation Buchenwald and Mittelbau-Dora Memorial Foundation; 291 (LO RT), Hulton Archive/GI; 292 (UP), William Vandivert/The LIFE Picture Collection/GI; 292 (LO), photograph by Evgeni Khaldei, LOC; 293, Kenneth W. Rendell, Museum of World War II, Boston; 294, Bundesarchiv; 295 (UP), Kurt Hutton/Picture Post/Hulton Archive/GI; 295 (CTR LE), Bundesarchiv; 295 (CTR RT), Popperfoto/GI; 295 (LO), The National Archives of the UK; 296 (ALL), Kenneth W. Rendell, Museum of World War II, Boston; 297 (UP LE), Imperial War Museum; 297 (UP RT), Kenneth W. Rendell, Museum of World War II, Boston; 297 (CTR), Kenneth W. Rendell, Museum of World War II, Boston; 297 (LO LE), Kenneth W. Rendell, Museum of World War II, Boston; 297 (LO CTR), Imperial War Museum; 297 (LO RT), Imperial War Museum; 298 (UP LE), Imperial War Museum; 298 (UP RT), Imperial War Museum; 298 (CTR LE), Kenneth W. Rendell, Museum of World War II, Boston; 298 (CTR RT), Kenneth W. Rendell, Museum of World War II, Boston; 298 (LO LE), Imperial War Museum; 298 (LO RT), Imperial War Museum; 299 (UP), Imperial War Museum; 299 (CTR LE), Kenneth W. Rendell, Museum of World War II, Boston; 299 (CTR RT), Imperial War Museum; 299 (LO LE), Imperial War Museum; 299 (LO RT), Imperial War Museum; 300 (UP), SMG Herb Friedman/Psywarrior.com; 300 (LO), NARA; 301 (UP LE), The OSS Society; 301 (UP RT), SMG Herb Friedman/Psywarrior.com; 301 (CTR LE), Imperial War Museum; 301 (CTR RT), SMG Herb Friedman/Psywarrior.com; 301 (LO), Imperial War Museum; 302 (UP), Imperial War Museum; 302 (LO), Kenneth W. Rendell, Museum of World War II, Boston; 303 (UP), Imperial War Museum; 303 (LE), Imperial War Museum; 303 (RT), Imperial War Museum; 304-5, Time Life Pictures/U.S. Coast Guard/The LIFE Picture Collection/GI; 306, Corbis; 307, Alfred Eisenstaedt/Pix Inc./ Time & Life Pictures/GI; 309 (UP), Corbis; 309 (LO), U.S. Department of Energy/Public Domain; 310 (UP LE), Popperfoto/GI; 310 (LO LE), AP Photo/Henry Griffin; 310 (UP RT/ LO RT), courtesy of the Franklin D. Roosevelt Presidential Library and Museum, Hyde Park, New York; 311 (UP), Corbis; 311 (CTR), University of Chicago, courtesy AIP Emilio Segre Visual Archives; 311 (LO), Lawrence Berkeley National Laboratory; 312 (UP), Galerie Bilderwelt/GI; 312 (CTR LE/CTR RT), Ed Westcott/U.S. Department of Energy/Public Domain; 312 (LO LE/LO RT), Galerie Bilderwelt/GI; 313 (ALL), Ed Westcott/U.S. Department of Energy/Public Domain; 314, Kenneth W. Rendell, Museum of World War II, Boston; 315, from Behind Japanese Lines (Rand McNally & Co., 1979), opposite p.123; 316, U.S. Army Military History Institute/Public Domain; 317-21 (ALL), NARA; 322, Pictures From History/The Image Works; 323, Corbis; 324 (LE), Corbis; 324 (RT), NARA; 325-6, NARA; 327 (LE), Corbis; 327 (RT), Kingendai/AFLO//Nippon News/Corbis; 328 (LO LE), Bettmann/Corbis; 328 (LO RT), Kenneth W. Rendell, Museum of World War II, Boston; 328 (UP), Kenneth W. Rendell, Museum of World War II, Boston; 329, Louis R. Lowery/US Marine Corps/Time & Life Pictures/GI; 330, Kenneth W. Rendell, Museum of World War II, Boston; 331 (UP LE), Kenneth W. Rendell, Museum of World War II, Boston; 331 (UP RT), Gamma-Keystone/GI; 332 (UP), Popperfoto/Getty Image; 332 (LO), Universal History Archive/UIG/GI; 334 (UP), Gamma-Keystone/GI; 334 (LO), Universal History Archive/ UIG/GI; 335, Rolls Press/Popperfoto/GI; 336 (LE), Kenneth W. Rendell, Museum of World War II, Boston; 336 (UP), Kenneth W. Rendell, Museum of World War II, Boston; 336 (LO RT), AFP/GI; 337 (UP LE), Universal History Archive/GI; 337 (UP CTR), Brian Brake/ Science Source; 337 (UP RT), Galerie Bilderwelt/GI; 337 (LO), Bettmann/Corbis; 338, Kenneth W. Rendell, Museum of World War II, Boston; 339 (UP), Corbis; 339 (CTR), Gamma-Keystone/GI; 339 (LO), Keystone/GI; 340 (UP), Popperfoto/GI; 340 (LO), Keystone/Hulton Archive/GI; 341 (UP), Express/GI; 341 (LO), Keystone/GI; 342, US Army/ The LIFE Picture Collection/GI; 343, Bob Gomel/The LIFE Images Collection/GI.

Budiansky, Stephen. *Battle of Wits: The Complete Story of Codebreaking in World War II*. New York: Touchstone, 2002.

Center for the Study of Intelligence. *Official OSS Exhibition Catalogue*. Washington, D.C.: Central Intelligence Agency. www.cia.gov/library/publications/intelligence-history/oss-catalogue/index.html.

Coon, Carleton S. *A North Africa Story: The Anthropologist as OSS Agent, 1941–1943*. Ipswich, Mass.: Gambit, 1980.

Crowdy, Terry. *Deceiving Hitler: Double Cross and Deception in World War II*. Oxford, U.K.: Osprey Publishing, 2008.

Davis, Donald A. *Lightning Strike: The Secret Mission to Kill Admiral Yamamoto and Avenge Pearl Harbor*. New York: St. Martin's Press, 2005.

Helm, Sarah. *A Life in Secrets: Vera Atkins and the Missing Agents of WWII*. New York: Nan A. Talese, 2005.

Herken, Gregg. *Brotherhood of the Bomb: The Tangled Lives and Loyalties of Robert Oppenheimer, Ernest Lawrence, and Edward Teller*. New York: Henry Holt, 2002.

Hodges, Andrew. *Alan Turing: The Enigma*. Princeton: Princeton University Press, 2014.

Jones, Nigel. *Countdown to Valkyrie: The July Plot to Assassinate Hitler*. London: Frontline Books, 2008.

Layton, Rear Admiral Edwin T., with Captain Roger Pineau and John Costello. *"And I Was There": Pearl Harbor and Midway—Breaking the Secrets*. Annapolis, Md.: Naval Institute Press, 1985.

Macintyre, Ben. *Double Cross: The True Story of the D-Day Spies*. New York: Broadway Books, 2012.

MacDonald, C. A. *The Killing of SS Obergruppenführer Reinhard Heydrich, 27 May 1942*. New York: Free Press, 1989.

McIntosh, Elizabeth P. *Sisterhood of Spies: The Women of the OSS*. Annapolis, Md.: Naval Institute Press, 1998.

Nelson, Anne. *Red Orchestra: The Story of the Berlin Underground and the Circle of Friends Who Resisted Hitler*. New York: Random House, 2009.

Persico, Joseph. *Roosevelt's Secret War: FDR and World War II Espionage*. New York: Random House, 2002.

Rendell, Kenneth W. *Politics, War, and Personality: Fifty Iconic World War II Documents That Changed the World*. Atlanta: Whitman Publishing, 2013.

_____. *World War II: Saving the Reality: A Collector's Vault*. Atlanta: Whitman Publishing, 2009.

Rhodes, Richard. *The Making of the Atomic Bomb*. New York: Simon and Schuster, 1986.

Richards, Lee. *The Black Art: British Clandestine Psychological Warfare Against the Third Reich*. Peacehaven, U.K., www.psywar.org, 2010.

Russell, Francis. *The Secret War*. Alexandria, Va.: Time-Life Books, 1981.

Smyth, Denis. *Deathly Deception: The Real Story of Operation Mincemeat*. New York: Oxford University Press, 2010.

Snyder, Timothy. *Bloodlands: Europe Between Hitler and Stalin*. New York: Basic Books, 2010.

Time-Life Books, eds. *World War II: War in the Shadows*. Alexandria, Va.: Time-Life Books, 2000.

Waller, Douglas. *Wild Bill Donovan: The Spymaster Who Created the OSS and Modern American Espionage*. New York: Free Press, 2012.

Whymant, Robert. *Stalin's Spy: Richard Sorge and the Tokyo Espionage Ring*. New York: I. B. Tauris, 1996.

ACKNOWLEDGMENTS

Creating a book like *The Secret History of World War II* requires vision and a team of talented people who bring a passion for excellence. Fortunately, Lisa Thomas, National Geographic senior vice president and editorial director, understood the power of the secret war concept from the very beginning and championed it for over five years. I am also grateful for my core creative team, including author Stephen Hyslop, whose brilliant research and writing make this book one of a kind; military historian and writer Harris Andrews, whose wealth of knowledge and storytelling never cease to amaze me; art director Carol Farrar Norton, a true artist at creating timeless illustrated books; and illustration researcher Uliana Bazar, who was responsible for the herculean task of tracking down high-resolution files of the over 700 images that appear in this book.

I also want to thank our board of advisers: Kenneth W. Rendell, founder and executive director of the Museum of World War II, Boston, a great collaborator, who graciously opened his collection to us, allowing us to feature over 240 secret weapons, documents, and devices; Lee Richards, one of the world's foremost experts on psychological warfare and black propaganda; and Ann Todd, an expert on covert activity in the Pacific. In addition, Toni Hiley, CIA Museum director, helped us put together the OSS essay; Rene Stein of the National Cryptologic Museum guided us to some very rare code-breaking material; and Tim Nenninger and Richard Peuser of the National Archives directed us toward top secret decrypts as well as previously unpublished photographs and maps.

At National Geographic Books, Susan Straight, senior editorial project manager, was enormously helpful in guiding the project from beginning to end; Susan Blair, director of photography, along with Meredith Wilcox and Patrick Bagley provided incredible support for all things photographic; and Gregory Ugiansky was responsible for map research and production.

Finally, I want to thank my family, Sharyn, Josh, Lisa, Lewis, and Julius, who gave me support and encouragement throughout this incredible journey.

Neil Kagan,
Editor

Since 1888, the National Geographic Society has funded more than 12,000 research, exploration, and preservation projects around the world. National Geographic Partners distributes a portion of the funds it receives from your purchase to National Geographic Society to support programs including the conservation of animals and their habitats.

National Geographic Partners
1145 17th Street NW
Washington, DC 20036-4688 USA

Become a member of National Geographic and activate your benefits today at natgeo.com/jointoday.

For information about special discounts for bulk purchases, please contact National Geographic Books Special Sales: specialsales@natgeo.com

For rights or permissions inquiries, please contact National Geographic Books Subsidiary Rights: bookrights@natgeo.com

ISBN: 978-1-4262-1701-2
ISBN: 978-1-4262-1821-7 (Deluxe)

Printed in the United States of America

16/QGT-RRDML/1